Mutiny and Aftermath

Mutiny and Aftermath

James Morrison's Account of the Mutiny on the *Bounty* and the Island of Tahiti

Edited by Vanessa Smith
and Nicholas Thomas
with the assistance of Maia Nuku

University of Hawai'i Press
Honolulu

Paperback edition 2021

Printed in the United States of America

26 25 24 23 22 21 6 5 4 3 2 1

Library of Congress Cataloging-in-Publication Data

Morrison, James, 1763 or 4–1807, author.

[Journal of James Morrison]

Mutiny and aftermath : James Morrison's account of the mutiny on the Bounty and the island of Tahiti / edited by Vanessa Smith and Nicholas Thomas ; with the assistance of Maia Nuku.

pages cm

Includes bibliographical references and index.

ISBN 978-0-8248-3676-4 (cloth : alk. paper)

1. Bounty Mutiny, 1789. 2. Tahiti (French Polynesia : Island)—Discovery and exploration—English. 3. Morrison, James, 1763 or 4–1807—Diaries. I. Smith, Vanessa (Vanessa Jane), editor. II. Thomas, Nicholas, editor. III. Title.

DU20.M676 2013

910.9164'8—dc23

2013008415

ISBN 978-0-8248-9281-4 (paperback)

University of Hawai'i Press books are printed on acid-free paper and meet the guidelines for permanence and durability of the Council on Library Resources.

Cover art: "Matavai Bay, Island Otahytey—Sunset," George Tobin, 1792. Reproduced with permission of the Mitchell Library, State Library of NSW.

Cover design by Mardee Melton

Interior design by Josie Herr

Contents

List of Illustrations vii
Preface xiii
Acknowledgments xix

Introduction 1

Part I. The Journal: Mutiny, Mutineers, Islanders
1. The Voyage and the Mutiny 25
2. The Occupation of Tubuai 56
3. Return to Tahiti 88
4. From Tahiti to England 121

Part II. The Account: The Island of Tahiti
5. The Tahitian World 157
6. Tahitian Society, History, and Culture 185
7. Arts, Rites, and Customs 220

Appendix I: Morrison's Polynesian Words and Terms 269
Appendix II: Morrison's People 275
Appendix III: Morrison's Place-names 283
Appendix IV: Morrison's Plants 285
Notes 287
Select Bibliography 321
Index 329

Illustrations

1. Track of the voyage of the *Bounty* xi
2. First page of James Morrison's manuscript xiv
3. "The Breadfruit of Otahytey," George Tobin, 1792 2
4. "Matavai Bay, Island Otahytey—Sunset," George Tobin, 1792 36
5. Map of Tubuai 58
6. Whalebone and ivory necklace, Austral Islands 64
7. Whale ivory ear ornaments, Austral Islands 65
8. *Parae*, Tahiti 71
9. Pearlshell necklace, Tubuai, Austral Islands 78
10. *Tahiri,* flywhisk, Austral Islands 82
11. *Tahiri,* flywhisk (detail), Austral Islands 83
12. "On Matavai River, Island of Otahytey," George Tobin, 1792 90
13. "Morai Point, at Oparrey, Island of Otahytey," George Tobin, 1792 122
14. *Tapa* or barkcloth beater, Tahiti 167
15. *Matau,* fish hooks, and lures, Tahiti 175
16. Map of Tahiti showing political districts, groupings, and key sites. 186
17. *Ti'i,* carved double figure, Tahiti 197
18. "The Morai at Oparrey, Island of Otahytey—Looking towards Matavai," George Tobin, 1792 199
19. *To'o,* god image, Tahiti 201

20. *Taumi,* feather gorget, Tahiti 205
21. Headrest, Tahiti 221
22. "A double Canoe with the Eotooa (God) and provisions on the prow—Island of Otahytey," George Tobin, 1792 224
23. Breadfruit splitter, Tahiti 234
24. *Penu,* pounder, Tahiti 235
25. *Tamau,* braided human hair, Tahiti 245
26. *Pahu,* drum, Tahiti 252
27. "A Toopapow, with the Corpse on it—Island of Otahytey," George Tobin, 1792 259

Mutiny and Aftermath

Figure 1. Map tracking the voyage of the *Bounty*. Courtesy of Nick Keenleyside at Outline Draughting and Graphics Ltd.

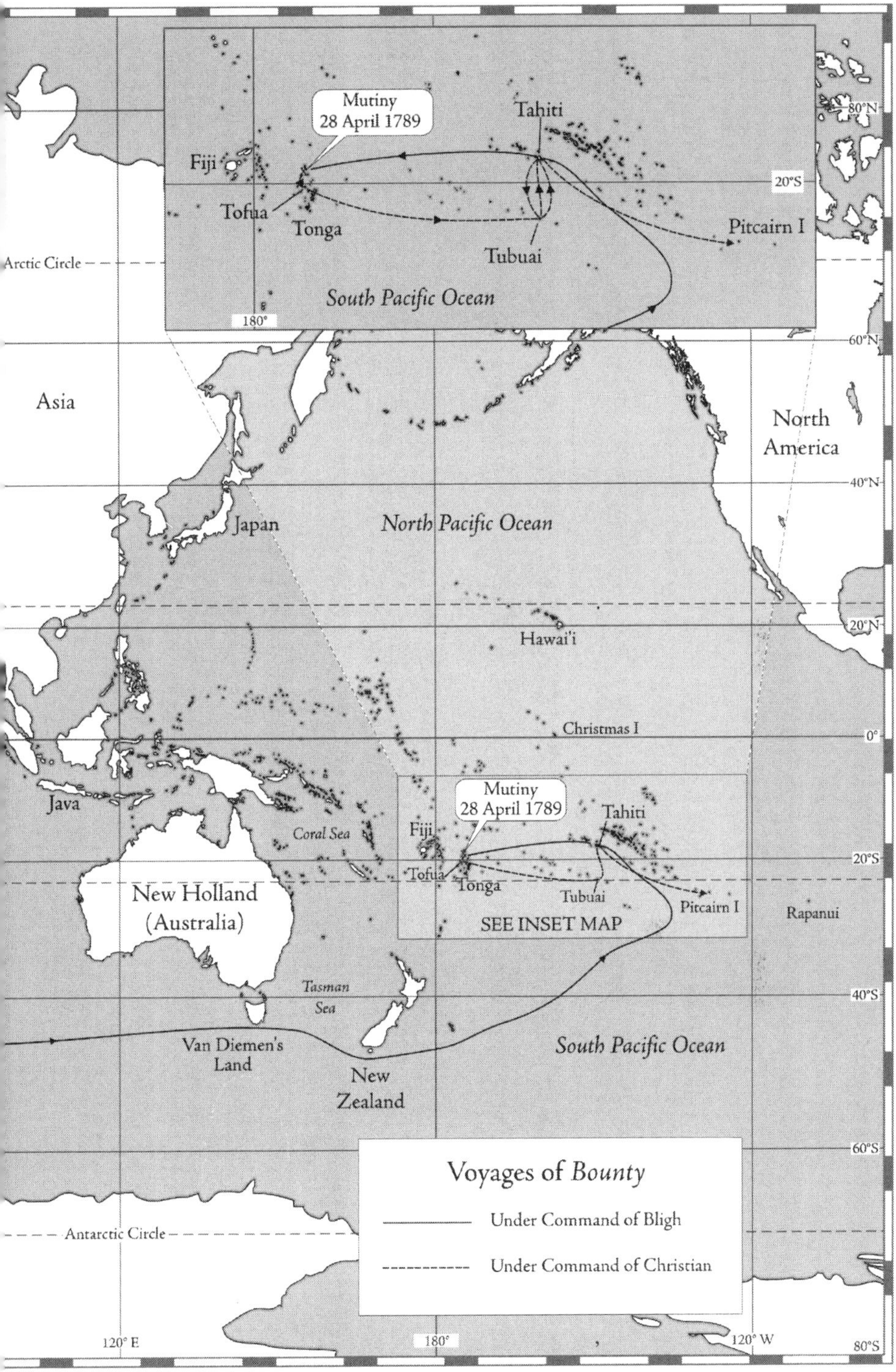
Mutiny
28 April 1789
Tahiti
Fiji
Tofua
Tonga
Tubuai
Pitcairn I
20°S
80°N
Arctic Circle
South Pacific Ocean
180°
60°N
Asia
North
America
40°N
Japan
North Pacific Ocean
20°N
Hawai'i
Christmas I
0°
Java
Coral Sea
Mutiny
28 April 1789
Fiji
Tahiti
20°S
Tofua
Tonga
Tubuai
Pitcairn I
Rapanui
New Holland
(Australia)
SEE INSET MAP
Tasman
Sea
40°S
Van Diemen's
Land
South Pacific Ocean
New
Zealand
60°S
Voyages of Bounty
Under Command of Bligh
Under Command of Christian
Antarctic Circle
120° E
180°
120° W
80°S

Preface

This book publishes a primary historical source of foundational importance for Pacific history. The manuscript that has been commonly referred to among Pacific historians as James Morrison's "Journal" was in fact a retrospective account rather than a diary. It provides a remarkable and wide-ranging description of Tahitian life that was informed by Morrison's observations and experiences over three years that embraced the French revolution of 1789 and almost equally famous events in the Pacific.

The *Bounty* under the captaincy of William Bligh arrived at Tahiti on 25 October 1788 with the purpose of collecting breadfruit cuttings that were to be transported to the West Indies and cultivated there to provide cheap food for slaves. Having obtained the plants, the ship departed on 4 April 1789. After the mutiny, which took place in Tongan waters on 28 April, Fletcher Christian took the ship back to Tahiti, where it arrived on 6 June. He had resolved to settle on the island of Tubuai, which he hoped would be sufficiently remote to preclude the mutineers' capture by any vessel that might be dispatched in pursuit of them. Having to that end obtained a stock of pigs and other provisions, the *Bounty* departed for that island on 16 June.[1]

The effort to colonize Tubuai was resisted and abandoned after three months. The ship returned to Tahiti on 22 September, though Christian and eight other mutineers departed again almost immediately to seek another island home. Only decades later did their settlement of Pitcairn and subsequent history come to light. The sixteen remaining members of the *Bounty*'s crew sought to establish themselves in twos and threes with the Tahitians they knew best and lived on the island until HMS *Pandora* arrived on 23 March 1791. This ship, commanded by Captain Edward Edwards, had been sent in search of the *Bounty* and the mutineers; Morrison was one of those who quickly gave himself up; the rest surrendered or were rounded up within a few days. Morrison and his companions had

1787 ~~On the 9th of Sept. 1787 I entered on board His Majesty's Armed Vessel Bounty Lieut. Wm. Bligh Commander then laying at Deptford~~ — On the 9 13th Oct. 1787 ~~following~~ the Bounty dropd down from Deptford to Longreach & in a few days ~~she sailed~~ for Spithead where she Anchord on the 4 of November. ~~and~~ After several attempts to put to sea in one of which the Fore topsail Yard was carried away, (~~which together with a Cable that was cutt at St. Helens ... returnd at Portsmouth Yard and now once got on the ... Strand~~) She saild on the 23d of December with a fresh Gale Easterly, which Increased to a heavy Gale by the 27th in which the Ships ~~...~~ sweep a Spare Topsail yard & Top Mt. Yard were wash'd from the Quarters (one of the Eyebolts ~~being drawn~~ from the side,) She also shipd a sea, which broke the Boats Chock & tore all the planks from the large Cutters Stern, and Washd some empty Casks overboard ~~which were on the deck~~ another Sea stove in a part of the Stern between the Lights, but did very little other Damage except breaking an Azimuth Compass, & Wetting a few bags of bread in the Cabbin; the breach in the Stern was soon secured, and the Ship hove too, as it became dangerous to Scudd—

When the Weather be moderated ~~...~~ we made sail; the Carpenters repaird the Boat & Chock and the Wet Bread was got up and dried and first used. We Met with no other Accident or any thing Material till the 5th of Jany 1788 when we Made the Island of Tenneriffe and Anchord in the Road of St. Croix on the 6th.

Here ~~we~~ Compleated ~~our~~ our water and took on board some Wine for the Ships use, and several Casks for

therefore had some twenty-three months' exposure to Tahitian life, as well as three months' experience living on Tubuai.

As we explore more fully here, Morrison was virtually the first "participant observer," the first European to inhabit Tahitian society, who went on to compose a rich and extended account of his time there. (Máximo Rodríguez, who lived with Spanish missionaries at Vaitepiha from November 1774 to November 1775, left a diary, an important source in its own right but one that is ethnographically very shallow in comparison to Morrison's). In addition to what it tells us about the Tahitian people, political developments, social relations, and culture, Morrison's text is also highly significant as an account of the *Bounty* voyage and mutiny, events that were bitterly debated in their immediate aftermath and that have remained controversial ever since.

The account was known to nineteenth-century historians of the mutiny, such as Sir John Barrow and Lady Diana Belcher, but became available to a wider audience only after the British soldier, travel writer, and *Bounty* enthusiast Owen Rutter (1889–1944) found out that the manuscript had been bequeathed to the State Library of New South Wales by one A. G. K. L'Estrange, who, it transpired, had been a friend of Lady Belcher and had received it from her. Rutter was associated with a private publishing venture, the Golden Cockerel Press, famous for finely designed handmade limited editions, and it was in this list that Morrison's text first appeared in 1935 as *The Journal of James Morrison, Boatswain's Mate of the* Bounty, *describing the mutiny & subsequent fortunes of the mutineers, together with an account of the Island of Tahiti.* This edition has since been much sought after by bibliophiles. The publication has been of great value to scholars for its relatively accurate transcription of the original, although, as Rutter admitted in his introduction, the final text had been twice transcribed (Rutter himself never viewed the original manuscript), and regular, though minor, inaccuracies can be found throughout the published version.[2] However, the work was not "edited" in the modern sense of the

---

Figure 2. (*Facing page*) First page of manuscript: "James Morrison—journal on HMS *Bounty* and at Tahiti, 9 Sept 1787–1791, written in 1792" [Call no. Safe 1/42 p. 337]. Reproduced with permission of the Mitchell Library, State Library of NSW

word: the endnotes ran to just three pages, and the introduction included little in the way of contextualization or interpretation.

Both of us had been independently interested in Morrison for many years—Vanessa Smith from the perspective of a study of beachcomber writing in the context of broader work on literary culture in the Pacific, and Nicholas Thomas from the angles of early contact history and social and cultural change in Polynesia. We had informal discussions about the desirability of a new edition and began serious work in 2007–2008, which we carried on over a number years in the interstices of other projects and commitments. In our view, so fundamentally important a text as this demanded presentation with fuller commentary, as well as annotation that would give readers some access to broader perspectives on the Tahitian practices, institutions, and political events to which Morrison refers. These lay beyond Rutter's primary interests, but the explanatory notes and comments that we provide here have benefited from two generations of historical and anthropological research that gained momentum only twenty years after his edition appeared. The important work of Douglas L. Oliver has done much to clarify the complex shifts that marked Tahitian politics and history over the course of the eighteenth century; more recent studies by Alfred Gell, Anne Salmond, and Jennifer Newell, among others, have brought fresh perspectives to understandings of cosmology, contact history, and environmental exchanges that we draw upon here.

Our Introduction maps out some of the issues present in Morrison's narrative journal and descriptive account and aims to give readers ways of assessing the text as a more-or-less reliable description of Polynesian society undergoing great change. The annotations comment on points of interest and are intended to make descriptions of events on Tubuai and Tahiti intelligible to those who lack specialist knowledge. It is always difficult to know where to stop with explication and commentary of this nature. We have tried to strike a balance, clarifying important matters that may be obscure and commenting on major points without succumbing to the temptation to write about every issue of interest. A range of studies, many listed in the Bibliography, will enable readers to follow up on particular questions and explore early Polynesian life, and the mutiny, in greater depth.

The main text is an edited transcription of James Morrison's manuscript in the State Library of New South Wales. His manuscript consists of

382 neatly written folio pages, each twenty-six lines long. Sections of the manuscript have been scored through, and substitute phrasing inserted above the line in ink or pencil. A note on the manuscript suggests that the emendations were made by Peter Heywood, who would certainly have had political motivations for toning down the account, and possibly also by Lady Belcher.[3] In all but one area we have adhered closely to Morrison's original, leaving his idiosyncratic spelling, contractions, capitalization, and punctuation (or lack thereof) as they stand. This is in the interest, not of antiquarianism or purism, but of giving readers as direct as possible a sense of the style and level of literacy present in this historic text. In a small number of instances we have rendered abbreviated words in full, or added punctuation, in order to make the sense intelligible.

We have, however, treated Morrison's Polynesian orthography differently. This is in considered response to the changing audiences for books of this kind. Had such an edition been prepared and published in the 1970s, its readers would have been primarily historians and students of European descent in Australia, New Zealand, the United States, and Europe. But now the discipline has changed, and many more people of Islander descent are reading, studying, or writing in the field. To them, and indeed to non-Islander students and scholars, Polynesian names and words are increasingly familiar in their standard modern spellings. It seemed undesirable to diminish the accessibility of this engagingly written text by reproducing unfamiliar and awkward eighteenth-century spellings. In any case, Tahitian politics amounted to a shifting and confusing kaleidoscope. To aid the reader further, Maia Nuku has prepared appendices decoding Morrison's Polynesian words, people, places, and plants that we trust will be valuable in themselves as guides to the language, dramatis personae, geography, and ethnobotany of the period. The division of the manuscript into chapters was done by the editors; with the exception of the significant division between the first and second parts, the breaks are somewhat arbitrary and have been given somewhat arbitrary titles.

In order to give readers a visual sense of the Tahitian environment and of the features of the island's ritual architecture, we have included a number of watercolors by George Tobin (1768–1838), who sailed with William Bligh on the second breadfruit voyage on the *Providence*—there was no artist on the *Bounty* itself. Along with Morrison's account, Tobin's works are now held by the State Library of New South Wales.

Acknowledgments

First and foremost, we are grateful to the State Library of New South Wales for permission to publish Morrison's manuscript and to the University of Hawai'i Press, in particular to our editorial team, Masako Ikeda, Cheri Dunn, and Barbara Folsom, for their interest in and support for our project.

In 2007 we were awarded a University of Sydney Collaborative Short Term Visiting Fellowship to begin work on the project. Research assistance from James Drown, of the Department of History, University of Sydney, who prepared an immaculate typescript from the Mitchell Library manuscript, and other project costs were supported during the early stages by a Leverhulme Major Fellowship awarded to Nicholas Thomas (over 2006–2009). Maia Nuku's help with completing the edition has been facilitated by a project funded by the Economic and Social Research Council, "Artefacts of Encounter: 1765–1840."

For advice and responses to various queries we are grateful to Mark Eddowes, Tara Hiquily of the Musée de Tahiti et ses Îles, Lawrence Miller, Jennifer Newell, Tahiari'i Yoram Pariente, Anne Salmond, and Don Travers.

We also thank Nick Keenleyside at Outline Draughting and Graphics Ltd. for providing us with maps, Elena Govor and Raphael Kabo for their preparation of the index, and Jocelyne Dudding for further photography of artifacts at the Cambridge University Museum of Archaeology and Anthropology.

Introduction

The two central protagonists of the story of the *Bounty*—William Bligh and Fletcher Christian—hold an enduring place in the popular imagination. Both film and scholarship have portrayed one or the other as hero or villain of the mutiny, speculating on the biographical and historical factors that impelled their contest of authority. But a figure equally significant to the historiography of the mutiny remains much less well known.

James Morrison (1761–1807) entered the British Navy in 1779, aged eighteen, and signed on as boatswain's mate of the *Bounty* on 9 September 1787, having previously served as midshipman on the sloop *Termagant.* Berths on the *Bounty* were highly sought after—hence Morrison's willingness to take a demotion to petty officer in order to join the crew—as the ship was known to be voyaging, in the wake of England's most famous navigator, James Cook, to the already mythologized island of Tahiti. Its subsequent destination was to be the Caribbean islands. West Indian planters had petitioned Joseph Banks, the most energetic and powerful scientific entrepreneur of the epoch,[1] to mandate transportation of breadfruit plants from the Pacific to the Caribbean, believing, from descriptions of the fruit's loaf-like qualities, that it might offer a cheap substitute for wheaten bread in the diet of plantation slaves.[2]

The *Bounty*'s passage to Tahiti was not a smooth one: it took the ship almost ten months to arrive at its destination. After battling trade winds at Cape Horn for close to a month, it was eventually forced to turn back from the Cape Horn route and enter the Pacific via the Cape of Good Hope. This in turn resulted in further impediments when the crew members reached Tahiti: they had missed the appropriate season to take breadfruit cuttings and were required to make an extended sojourn of five months on the island before the plants could be established. The cuttings, for which Bligh had negotiated with Tina, the head of the powerful Pomare family, were cultivated in special transport boxes. When the *Bounty* finally left Tahiti on 4 April 1789, these were packed on board at great inconvenience to the

Figure 3. "The Breadfruit of Otahytey," George Tobin, 1792 [Call no. PXA 563 no. 2]. Reproduced with permission of the Mitchell Library, State Library of NSW

crew. The ship was only ninety-one feet long and twenty-three feet wide, and the great cabin and quarterdeck—the sections of the ship reserved for its commander and officers—were almost completely given over to the plants. This meant that different ranks of sailors had to berth together, creating an unusual degree of fraternity between officers and men.

The mutiny occurred on 28 April, not far from Tofua in the Tonga group. Bligh and eighteen crew members were put to sea in the *Bounty*'s launch. Twenty-five men remained on board the *Bounty.* Arguments were later to ensue over how willingly various individuals remained on board or entered the launch with Bligh, the nuances of which were to become life-and-death matters at the mutineers' court martial. The launch made its way to Tofoa, where they encountered local hostility and one crew member, John Norton, sacrificed his life. Bligh decided to navigate to Kupang on the island of Timor rather than risk further violence in unknown territories. He divided the launch's rations, suited to five days at sea, to serve a fifty-day passage. The launch reached Kupang in forty-eight days, with all the crew alive, though weakened (three soon perished at Kupang).

James Morrison was among those who stayed on the *Bounty* and joined Christian in his attempt to establish a settlement on the island of Tubuai. This failed due to local resistance, and the *Bounty* returned to Tahiti on 20 September 1789. Knowing that British efforts to capture the mutineers would inevitably first be directed toward Tahiti, Christian and a party of eight men remained there for only twenty-four hours before departing again in the *Bounty,* accompanied by nineteen women, a female child, and six men—three from Tahiti, two from Tubuai, and one from Ra'iatea. Their destination was unknown to Morrison and the fifteen other crewmen who decided to stay on at Tahiti despite the insecurity their position entailed.[3] They remained there for approximately a year and a half. On 23 March 1791, the ship *Pandora,* sent out by the British Admiralty under the captaincy of Edward Edwards to recapture the mutineers, caught up with them. All were rounded up or turned themselves in and were brutally imprisoned in a cell on the quarterdeck, nicknamed "Pandora's Box," to be taken back to England for trial.

On the evening of 28 August, the *Pandora* struck the Great Barrier Reef at the entrance to Endeavour Straits. Morrison survived the wreck that killed four of the prisoners as well as thirty-one crew members and the ensuing open-boat journey of its survivors to Timor. He thus took his place among ten men who were tried on board HMS *Duke* at Portsmouth Harbour for alleged participation in the mutiny. The others were Peter Heywood, midshipman; Joseph Coleman, armorer; Charles Norman, carpenter's mate; Thomas McIntosh, carpenter's crew; and the seamen Thomas Ellison, Thomas Burkitt, John Millward, William Muspratt, and Michael Byrn.

Bearing Witness

Morrison's text is not only an eyewitness account of the events of the mutiny and life on Tahiti; it is also regarded as having played a direct role in the outcome of the court martial. It was apparently written up in 1792, first as its author awaited trial and then as he recuperated after receiving the king's pardon.[4] Some form of day-to-day notebook probably formed the basis of the final composition. Lady Belcher, in her *Mutineers of the* "Bounty," mentions that Morrison kept notes of "daily occurrences from the period of the departure of the *Bounty* from England to his return as a prisoner."[5] While some scholars have questioned how this primary text could have survived the wreck of the *Pandora* on Morrison's return voyage to London,[6] a couple of explanations suggest themselves. The most obvious is that Morrison carefully secreted away or even memorized the basic text prior to his recapture, fearing that it would be appropriated or destroyed. Another is that this ur-text, even if it was lost, made Morrison's eventual process of writing one of a particular type of recuperation, involving the recollection of a form of words or a set of images rather than the composition of an account. As Owen Rutter pointed out when first publishing Morrison's work, there is internal evidence of both note taking and revision in the final document.[7]

Whatever the relative degrees of on-the-spot and delayed composition, Morrison's text has the impact and authority of an eyewitness report. Moreover, it is the only text with the heft to offer a real counterweight to Bligh's two versions of the mutiny story, the brief *Narrative of the Mutiny, on board his Britannic Majesty's ship* Bounty*: and the subsequent voyage of part of the crew, in the ship's boat, from Tofoa, one of the Friendly Islands, to Timor, a Dutch Settlement in the East-Indies,* published in 1790; and the more extensive *A Voyage to the South Sea, undertaken by command of His Majesty, for the purpose of conveying the bread-fruit tree to the West Indies, in* *his Majesty's ship* Bounty: *commanded by Lieutenant William Bligh. Including an account of the mutiny on board the said ship, and the subsequent voyage of part of the crew, in the ship's boat, from Tofoa, one of the Friendly Islands, to Timor, a Dutch Settlement in the East-Indies,* published in 1792 while Bligh was at sea on his second breadfruit voyage.

Morrison's brief defense at the *Bounty* court martial also took the form of a "Paper Writing to the Court." It was a document that consciously and repeatedly adverted to questions of readability. In addressing his accusers, Morrison drew a distinction between internal zeal and outward conduct, arguing that at times he had indeed played the part of enthusiastic mutineer, but that this was a role he assumed in the hope of regaining the ship for Bligh. He writes, "If there were *No sorrow* mark'd in my Countenance, it was to deceive those whose *Act* I abhorred, that I might be at liberty to *seize* the *first* Opportunity that *might* appear favourable, to the retaking of the Ship."[8] Motives, Morrison argued, are not transparent, and the most complex strategies and performances may be enacted in a virtuous cause. The good reader, his defense implies, must adjudicate between versions of a story by relating them to particular contexts of performance. Morrison's *Journal* and *Account* may in one sense be seen to develop this theme, offering in turn a "story" and a "back story"— a narrative and its context—that require an interreferential mode of reading. But because the text remained unpublished until 1935, the effect it achieved was purely as a draft—as threatened publication and secret document. There is little question, however, that its existence, in whatever partial or rumored form, contributed to Morrison's pardon. The work is thus not merely a record but an artifact of the *Bounty* mutiny: its writing was an event in that history.

At the time James Morrison was standing trial on board the HMS *Duke,* William Bligh was far away, completing the task that the mutiny had so disastrously interrupted. The court martial took place between 12 and 19 September 1792; at that time, Bligh's new ships, the *Providence* and the *Assistant,* were en route from Tahiti. Having steered through the shoals of Torres Strait and along the coast of New Guinea, lost only three hundred and fifty-four of the breadfruit plants they transported, and retained close to a thousand, they made their way to Kupang before heading on to St. Helena, then to St. Vincent and Jamaica in the West Indies. Bligh's "second breadfruit voyage" had been a relatively straightforward one. Soon after arriving in Tahiti, he had felt the need to interrogate Tina as to his degree of involvement with the mutineers, and in particular about his friendship with Fletcher Christian. But he chose to be satisfied with Tina's somewhat flimsy reassurances:

> I asked him how he came to be so friendly to Christian, for that proved to me he was not sincere in what he said. He replied—"I really thought you was living and gone to England untill Christian came back the second time. I was then from home, but all my Friends, as soon as they heard from the Men who came on Shore, on their questioning them, that you was lost, from that time we did not profess any friendship to him, and Christian knew it so well that he only remained a few hours, and went away in such a hurry, that he left a second Anchor behind him. [. . .]" Thus he freed himself from any suspicion on my side, & with his usual good nature and cheerfulness regained my esteem & regard.[9]

The collecting of the breadfruit cuttings had this time been accomplished in just over three months. Bligh's local relationships were consolidated, his observations more confident: his authority seemed assured. Yet there was a novel element of unsettlement in this notoriously fractious commander. He appeared to be afraid of others' writings. Lieutenant Francis Godolphin Bond, first lieutenant of the *Providence,* reported after the voyage, in a letter to his brother, Bligh's paranoia regarding the existence of alternative accounts of the mission:

> Among many circumstances of envy and jealousy he used to deride my keeping a private journal, and would often ironically say he supposed I meant to publish. [. . .] Every officer who has nautical information, a knowledge of natural history, a taste for drawing, or anything to constitute him proper for circumnavigating, becomes odious; for great as he is in his own good opinion, he must have entertained fears some of his ship's company meant to [submit] a spurious Narrative to the judgment and perusal of the publick.

Bond reports that he was admonished by Bligh: "No person can do the duty of a 1st Lieut. who does more than write the day's work of his publick Journal."[10]

To have set out to complete his breadfruit commission, rather than awaiting in person the capture of the mutineers and their trial, bespoke a certain confidence on Bligh's part. It indicated that, although a task had been interrupted, his own role in that turn of events required no personal vindication. Yet Bligh's attitude in print was less sanguine. He had in fact been in some haste to publish his version of the circumstances of the mutiny. His *Narrative of the Mutiny, on board his Britannic Majesty's ship* Bounty was brought out hastily in 1790 and simply gave his account of the events of the mutiny and the open-boat journey to Kupang, his reception there, and his passage to England. In 1792 his second version of the story, *A Voyage to the South Sea,* was published, edited—in some places very freely—by his powerful friends James Burney and Joseph Banks. This second account drew on Bligh's logbook to flesh out the earlier part of the *Bounty* voyage and the five-month stay at Tahiti that preceded the mutiny. It incorporated, with occasional significant emendation, the 1790 narrative of events immediately leading up to and following the mutiny.

Bligh's anxiety to set the story straight before others could give their versions of it preceded Morrison's recapture; it could not, therefore, have been prompted in an immediate way by knowledge of the existence of Morrison's text. But did he have some memory of a note-taking boatswain's mate harboring another account of events? One of the most striking details in Morrison's narrative is its obsessive recording of weights and measures, of the ways in which Bligh appeared to be shortchanging his crew. Was this Morrison's indirect response to Bligh during the *Bounty* voyage—to be seen as recording figures, and the exchanges surrounding them, for some future reckoning?

Bligh no doubt suspected that there were alternative reports to be feared from other members of the crew. One by the ship's master, John Fryer, who had accompanied him in the launch, and with whom he had strained relations from early on in the *Bounty* voyage, seems to have been written shortly after he published the 1790 *Narrative.* Fryer's eldest daughter later claimed that Fryer's text had in fact been penned at Timor in 1789; however, it refers to and takes issue with Bligh's published account and, as Rolf du Reitz has argued, "was written as a kind of commentary to the official version published by Bligh."[11] As well as presenting an unmitigatedly negative portrait of Bligh's command, Fryer's text offers a com-

labour, and where the allurements of dissipation are beyond anything that can be conceived."[14] This explanation draws on stereotypes of the South Sea Islands that had established themselves immediately in the wake of the first European voyages to Tahiti, and whose defining symbol was the breadfruit itself—bread that grew on trees. Whereas the breadfruit mission ironically exploited the symbolism of labor-free sustenance by seeking to feed breadfruit to unpaid laborers, Morrison's own account from the outset, as mentioned earlier, is full of weights and measures and a clear sense of insufficient provision. In it, Bligh, who was purser as well as captain of his ship, is accused of profiting from the men's rations. He is figured as a dodgy shopkeeper, giving short measure or poor substitutes—"pumpions" (pumpkins) in place of loaves, oil and sugar in place of butter and cheese. Though Morrison's computations of day-to-day injustices very quickly take on an evidential tone, this in itself was part of the rhetoric of warrant and petty officers' journals. George Robertson, master of the *Dolphin,* was equally forensic regarding issues of exchange between his ship's crew and Tahitians, grumbling above all about the controlling attitude of First Lieutenant William Clarke, whom he referred to as "Growl" and "Lieut. Knowall."

At Tahiti the battle over rations became a battle over local knowledge. It was Bligh's second visit to the island; he had been there during Cook's third, fatal voyage, on which he had served as master. Prior to arrival he posted a notice that set out a script and stage directions for his crew's interactions on Tahiti. It was closely based on the Admiralty Instructions that were the template for Cook's three voyages, but differed in the degree of specificity proposed regarding projected exchanges and in the level of duplicity he insisted on in dealing with Tahitians:

> Rules to be observed by every Person on Board, or belonging to the "Bounty," for the better establishing a Trade for Supplies or Provisions and good Intercourse with the Natives of the South Sea, wherever the Ship may be at.
>
> 1st. At the Society, or Friendly Islands, no person whatever is to intimate that Captain Cook was killed by Indians; or that he is dead.
>
> 2d. No person is ever to speak, or give the least hint, that we have come on purpose to get the bread-fruit plant, until I have made my plan known to the chiefs.

3d. Every person is to study to gain the good will and esteem of the natives; to treat them with all kindness; and not to take from them by violent means, any thing they may have stolen; and no one is ever to fire, except in defence of his life.

4th. Evry person employed on service is to take care that no arms, or implements of any kind under their charge, are stolen; the value of such thing, being lost shall be charged against their wages.

5th. No man is to embezzle, or offer to sale, directly, or indirectly, any part of the King's stores, of what nature soever.

6th. A proper person or persons will be appointed to regulate trade, and barter with the natives; and no officer or seaman, or other person belonging to the ship, is to trade for any kind of provisions, or curiosities; but if such officer or seaman wishes to purchase any particular thing, he is to apply to the provider to do it for him. By this means a regular market will be carried on, and all disputes, which otherwise may happen with the natives, will be avoided. All boats are to have everything handed out of them at sun-set.

Given under my hand, on board the "Bounty", Otaheite, 25th Oct. 1788.

Wm. BLIGH[15]

Once again, Bligh reveals himself here as a policer of alternative accounts, seeking to restrict in advance terms of interaction that he would later concede eluded his grasp and may have been a cause of the mutiny. The excessiveness of his attempt to preempt and control forms of contact was something even he admitted, writing: "I had given directions to every one on board not to make known to the islanders the purpose of our coming, lest it might enhance the value of the bread-fruit plants, or occasion other difficulties. Perhaps so much caution was not necessary, but at all events I wished to reserve to myself the time and manner of communication."[16]

Morrison gives a number of examples throughout the *Journal* section of his work of ways in which crew members, as they advanced in intimacy with and concomitantly gained knowledge of Tahitians, worked against the script that Bligh had laid down for their interactions. He describes, for instance, how the sailors' Tahitian friends joined in the ongoing fight for food, helping the crew to manipulate Bligh's rationing and undermine his authority:

> The Market for Hogs beginning now to slacken Mr. Bligh seized on all that came to the ship big & small Dead or alive, taking them as his property, and serving them as the Ship's allowance at one pound pr. Man pr. Day. He also seized on those belonging to the Master, & killd them for the ships use, tho He had more then 40 of different sizes on board of his own, and there was then plenty to be purchaced nor was the price much risen since the first, and when the Master spoke to him, telling him the Hogs were his property, he told him that "He Mr. Bligh would convince him that evry thing was *his,* as soon as it was on board, and that He would take nine tenths of any mans property and let him see who dared say any thing to the contrary", those of the seamen were seized without ceremony, and it became a favour for a Man to get a Pound extra of His own hog–
>
> The Natives observing that the Hogs were seized as soon as they Came on board, and not knowing but they would be seized from them, as well as the People, became very shy of bringing a hog in sight of Lieut. Bligh either on board or on shore, and watched all opportunitys when he was on shore to bring provisions to their friends on board but as Mr. Bligh observed this, and saw that His diligence was like to be evaded, he ordered a Book to be kept in the Bittacle wherein the Mate of the Watch was to insert the Number of Hogs or Pigs with the Weight of each that came into the Ship, to remedy this, the Natives took another Method which was Cutting the Pigs up, and wraping them in leaves and covering the Meat with Bread fruit in the Baskets, and sometimes with peeld Cocoa Nuts, by which means, as the Bread was never seized, they were a Match for all his industry; and he never suspected their artifice, by this means provisions were still plenty.

Morrison here asserts the right of crew members as well as captains to accumulate personal rather than just communal property on the basis of individual connections they forged on the beach. He figures the sailors as able to draw on intimacies for sustenance, even while Bligh waved his book of accounts. Despite Bligh's care in managing the breadfruit transactions, false measure is shown here to have been smuggled into loads of breadfruit.

Another, punning example of the value of "local knowledge" is to be found in the codes and practices of sexual exchange that developed between crew members and Tahitians but excluded the abstinent Bligh. Early on, Morrison gives a pointed description of the crew's "easy" friendships with Tahitians: "evry officer & Man in the ship were provided with new friends tho none understood the language, yet we found it very easy to Converse by signs at which these people are adepts, and some of the Weomen who came on board became very Intiligent in a short time and soon brought their quondum husbands into a method of discourse by which evry thing was transacted." The notion of intelligence is crucial here, connoting a kind of experiential knowledge that, as with the smuggling of meat under breadfruit, allowed for transactions that bypassed official orders. Such repeated scenarios make an implicit argument in Morrison's text—namely, that questions of command play themselves out in the ethnographic arena. In this sense, the division of his work into *Journal* and *Account* is arbitrary: both sections are a form of testimony, grounded in the assumption that an embedded local knowledge makes the only valid claim to authority in cross-cultural contexts.

The *Journal* and the *Account* are interrelated in a further sense, the former offering contexts for the purportedly decontextualized knowledge offered in the latter—weaving it back into story—and the account of "customs" equally serving as an extended footnote to various scenarios sketched in the narrative. Take the friendships that figure as significantly imbricated with different forms of trade in both the anecdotes above. The *Account* lays out clearly the specificities of Tahitian ritualized friendship formation.

> When a Man adopts a Friend for his Son the Ceremonie is the same, only placing the Boy in the place of the Woman, the Ceremonie is ratified, and the boy & his friends exchange Names and are ever after lookd as one of the Family the New Friend becoming the adopted son of the Boys Father—this Friendship is most religiously kept, and never disolves till Death, tho they may separate, and make temporary Friends while absent, but when they meet, they always acknowledge each other–

While Morrison draws a comparison between male friendship rituals and heterosexual marriage rituals in Tahiti, friendship appears to be indissoluble in a way that marriage is not, binding the partners in a lifelong commitment to support one another and their families in times of need:

> And should a Brother or one who is an adopted friend become poor or loose his land in War, he has nothing more to do but go to his Brother, or Friend, and live with him partaking of all he posesses as long as he lives & his wife and Family with him if he has any—or if any relation or Friend tho not in immediate want, comes to the House of his Friend, he is always fed while he Stays and is Not only welcome to take away what he pleases but is loaded with presents–

It is only by reading this section of the *Account* that we can understand the way in which retributive justice is operating in the report Morrison provides in the *Journal* of the deaths of Churchill and Thompson in Tahiti. Morrison traces the ways in which local *taio* bonds led to a falling out between the two beachcombers. Thompson and Churchill moved to the district of Taiarapu with John Brown, a violent beachcomber who had been left at Matavai by the *Mercury.* Morrison tells of various allegiances and bitternesses that reconfigured the loyalties of the trio, until finally Thompson "resolved to Shoot Churchill, which He put into execution immediately on his return, for which the Natives had put him to Death." The account is a bald and opaque one until it is read in the light of Morrison's later description of friendship bonds. Both Churchill and Thompson had befriended powerful *ari'i* (district chiefs) at Taiarapu. However, when Vehiatua, Churchill's *taio,* dies, Churchill's status as an embodiment of Vehiatua's identity, which had been instigated by their exchange of names, becomes manifest. This affects the European friends Churchill and Thompson—that is, their former equality as crew members is destabilized by the sanctioned appropriation by one mutineer of the identity of high-ranking chief. The story, like Morrison's text itself, also plays a role within the broader narrative of the mutiny and trial, where Churchill and Thompson are consistently figured as the most reprobate and unequivocal of the accused mutineers. As William Bligh was to put it when reflecting on their careers, "these two Villains affected their own destruction, and avoided the punishment that awaited them."[17] Thus, ironically, they were free to become the focus of blame cast by other men seeking to avoid a different fate.

Material objects, not just human subjects, come into focus *between* the texts of the *Journal* and the *Account.* Morrison's discussions of both "Fruits" and "Manufactures and Traffic" in the *Account,* for instance, enable us to appreciate the ways in which local practices and European models came together in the construction of the boat described in the *Journal.* The process is depicted by Morrison as one of substitution, its main work being the location of local equivalents for familiar metropolitan tools and techniques: "the Purau answerd for the Shells of the Blocks, and the Toa for Shievs & Pins. The Bark of the Purau being Cleand made very good rope. . . ." Once again like Morrison's text itself, the boat has a complex evidential status. He claimed it was built to return the Tahitian party to England, an act that would presuppose their innocence. Captain Edwards, on the other hand, understood it to have been used as a means to avoid recapture and referred to the vessel as "the pirate schooner." Morrison, on his part, claims that the mutineers employed the boat only as a means of temporary escape once the *Pandora* arrived, so that they might retrieve agency by turning themselves in rather than being taken to the ship under arrest. Yet he also informs us that his own desire to use the boat to return to England had to be concealed from the majority of the party at Tahiti: "we resolved to keep the real motive a Secret, and to Say that she was only for the purpose of Pleasuring about the Island." Thus the boat becomes a relic, not just of cross-cultural ingenuity, but of the complex ingenuities of storytelling and witness bearing.

Precisely because the *Journal* and the *Account* work together so tightly, the section of Morrison's *Journal* that covers the two visits made by the mutineers to Tubuai and their attempt to establish a fortified colony there reads as the most undernourished part of the work—and this is reflected in the relatively minor use hitherto made of it in contemporary Pacific scholarship. One of the most significant aspects of this edition is that it offers, in its comprehensive annotations, an "Account of the Island of Tubuai" that aims to give commensurate substance to the Tubuaian experience. Morrison's ethnohistorical observations upon this island are of special importance because there is no further account of it until 1827 (the unpublished journal of the conchologist Cuming); later documentation and discussion are also very sparse, consisting mainly of reports by missionaries belonging to the Congregation of the Sacred Hearts of Jesus and

Mary (the Catholic order active in eastern Polynesia) and Aitken's rather slight 1930 *Ethnology of Tubuai.*

Morrison as Ethnographer and Historian

The "Account" has long been recognized as a foundational source for the culture and society of Tahiti, and of the Society Islands more generally. In the corpus of early sources, drawn upon by ethnohistorians and anthropologists concerned to reconstruct and analyze the indigenous cultures of the place, it falls between the set of voyage accounts from the 1760s and 1770s—of Cook, his immediate predecessors, and his contemporaries—and the archive of the London Missionary Society dating from the establishment of the Tahitian mission in March 1797.

All of these sources provide rich and uneven materials for the study of early Polynesia. None, strictly speaking, documents a "traditional" culture, the Holy Grail of salvage anthropology. True, a good deal can be said about what was happening and what Tahitian social relations were like on the eve of European contact in 1767. But it is clear that considerable change was under way in closely intertwined ritual and political affairs in the Society Islands, and that the situation at that time differed from those ten, or fifty, years earlier. The eve of contact possesses no special authenticity that earlier or later times lack. That said, the early contact period and what can be known of pre-European history remain of particular interest to many Polynesians themselves, as well as to scholars from a variety of disciplines: the records that relate to this period are indeed of unique importance and demand special scrutiny.

For Tahiti the voyage records are rich for two particular reasons. First, and with respect to the Cook voyages specifically, there was an accumulation of experience. Observations made during Samuel Wallis's inaugural British visit in the *Dolphin* (1768) gave Cook and others certain bearings when they arrived in the *Endeavour* in 1769; what was learned during that extended visit was complemented by new information gleaned during the second and third voyages. There was an overlap of personnel—some men had sailed with Wallis and on one or more of Cook's voyages; others participated in two or even all three of his expeditions. Familiarity and linguistic competence grew. If none of the mariners ever acquired a sophisticated fluency in Tahitian, some could certainly converse about a wide range of topics. Second, the parties included natural historians such as Banks, and Johann Reinhold and George Forster (who accompanied Cook's second voyage), who were trained to observe and eager to make the fullest observations they could. Not only did they write extensively, but they set certain standards and encouraged others to describe whatever aspects of Polynesian life they could in a detailed fashion.

The voyage accounts also had their limitations. Most obviously they arose from relatively short visits; the *Endeavour*'s sojourn of three months in order to observe the Transit of Venus was important but exceptional. These periods, as Morrison points out, were, from the Polynesian perspective, highly unusual, both festive and busy. The mariners enjoyed frequent contact with Islanders—though visits were marked also by tension and temporary estrangement—but they never really witnessed the ordinary flow of life. Their observations are sound as far as they go, and surprisingly full in certain areas. Specific practices that attracted European attention, such as tattooing, were described precisely. Some sense of Polynesian political relationships was obtained, and this information remains of tremendous importance; but the cultural rationale, a genuine grasp of the meanings that informed practices and relationships, largely eluded these observers.

The missionaries arrived in Tahiti six years after Morrison left. Some soon abandoned the station, and others withdrew either to Huahine or Sydney during periods of conflict, but there is a continuous record of observation, engagement, and writing over the subsequent decades that in due course informed such systematic works as William Ellis's *Polynesian Researches* (1829) and John Davies's *History of the Tahitian Mission* (unpublished until 1961). These records have strengths and limitations quite different from those of the voyage journals and accounts. Those missionaries who did stay on for extended periods worked hard at learning the language—they needed to do so in order to preach and teach, and to translate scriptures. A few who were genuinely curious made sustained efforts to inquire into customs and beliefs. And J. M. Orsmond recorded many genealogies, chants and myths that were, over a number of decades, put in order by his granddaughter, Teuira Henry, and published thirteen years after her death as *Ancient Tahiti* (1928); the historiographic complexity of this text is reflected in its having no less than five prefaces!

The most commonly cited issue with missionary sources is their prejudice against non-Christian belief, and evangelists did rail against superstition and characterize local rites as irrational and barbaric. The commitment intrinsic to the mission, however, had an uneven impact upon the value of their observations from an ethnohistorical perspective. Some missionaries indeed completely lacked interest or understanding, but others were anthropologically minded and left aside the polemic when they wrote about "manners and customs" for their personal interest or in papers circulated privately. (Later in the nineteenth century, many went on to publish in anthropological journals and to identify themselves as anthropologists.) But all this is less important than the fact that Tahiti changed profoundly over the twenty years between 1790 and 1810. Introduced disease caused a considerable loss of population and customary knowledge. There were major political changes, already mentioned, that are well known, but also a whole range of more particular reorientations of behavior and practice that are difficult to specify. Most of the people the missionaries dealt with in, say, 1800 would not have been born, or were very young, at the time of Wallis's "discovery" of the island. They were of a generation that had grown up with contact and with the new order that contact had both pervasively damaged and energized. Hence, notwithstanding its profound importance—not least as a set of sources for the process of conversion to Christianity itself—the missionary archive is not truly an archive of early Tahitian culture.

Morrison was not the first resident observer. That distinction belongs to the Spanish missionaries established at Vaitepiha by Domingo Boenechea, together with their servant Maxímo Rodríguez, though the mission was a failure and the priests enjoyed only limited rapport with Islanders. Rodríguez did intereact to a greater extent with Tahitians, and his extant account is of interest, but he lacked either the inclination or the ability to write extensively, and unlike some subsequent beachcombers, he was not working with an educated writer who could elicit and articulate, or at least transcribe, his understanding. (The 1818 *Account of the Tongan Islands,* based on William Mariner's communciations, exemplifies the productivity of such partnerships.)[18]

In this respect, James Morrison is exceptional. He prepared an extensive manuscript, evidently without editorial assistance. He was literate, and his writing is in no sense awkward; he had the vocabulary he needed to express what he wanted to say. Yet his writing is workmanlike rather than literary. It is devoid of literary or classical allusion or showy gesture. The details of his social background are unclear, but he was certainly not from an aristocratic family, and his education may be presumed to have been basic, his reading probably primarily of the Bible. This last is important in one respect. There is no internal evidence that Morrison had read much of what had been previously published relating to Pacific peoples. In this respect he differs from many of the voyage writers who came before and after him. In contrast, Cook, the Forsters, and their successors studied compilations of voyages such as those published by Alexander Dalrymple and wrote in terms influenced by them or in opposition to them. It is likely that officers on an exploratory voyage to the Pacific all did a bit of reading, and it is clear that Morrison had at some point read either the official narratives published by Hawkesworth, Cook, and Cook and King for the navigator's first, second, and third voyages respectively, or some collected edition or abridgement of them. That reading, however, seems not to have been fresh in his mind at the time he wrote his own "Account," when very likely he had no access to a library.

This could be seen as one of the text's major strengths. Morrison would seem to match an ideal of an empirical ethnographer: he wrote on the basis of his own observations and experiences; he did not reproduce others' descriptions; nor was he sidetracked by arguments concerning others' mistakes. But this is not to say that he did not bring a good deal of baggage to his description of Tahiti. The exposition is broadly shaped by the conventions of natural history in dealing with topography, plants, animals, and other matters before progressing to questions of government, social relationships, and customs. This was to adhere, however loosely, to conventions of European descriptive writing. These terms implied a set of Western understandings of the relationships between political communities and the natural world—understandings that were profoundly different from and alien to those of Islanders in the period. Yet if this is so at the level of the organization of the "Account," Morrison in fact describes plant life from the perspective of Tahitian life: his botany is an ethnobotany replete with a sense of how plants and trees are used—as foods, as materials out of which artifacts are made, and so on. His writing does not mirror an indigenous understanding (how could it?), but he does foreground an inhabited island world, and the human use of that world.

It is worth flagging another aspect of the relationship between Morrison's text and its predecessors and successors. If we assume that in its writing the author was largely uninfluenced by earlier observations, its long-unpublished status means, conversely, that subsequent writers were uninfluenced by it. Neither Ellis nor Dumont d'Urville, nor Moerenhout nor any other nineteenth-century writer on Tahitian history, it appears, had knowledge or sight of Morrison's "Account." This means that where his remarks agree with those made later, this amounts at best to genuine corroboration, at worst to convergent misinterpretation.

All this is to argue for the strength of the "Account" as an ethnohistorical and anthropological source. Morrison had axes to grind in relation to behavior on board the *Bounty;* he did not have interests in producing any particular image of Polynesian life. He was not trying to argue, as was Cook in Tongatapu, for an implicitly Christian or at least monotheistic set of beliefs; nor like Forster senior was he trying to fashion a particular understanding of a semicivilized society. Much of what he wrote concerns specific events or practices that he witnessed, or that he well understood. His account is largely matter-of-fact and unsensational.

But there are two important domains in which Morrison's renderings of Tahitian life and culture have to be seen as genuinely problematic. The first, and most extreme, is that of religious belief. Notwithstanding the quality and—so far as can be judged—accuracy of the accounts of specific rites and ritual artifacts, the short section in which Morrison deals with Tahitian gods, ideas of spirits, and notions of the afterlife is an awkward amalgam of Christian models and his notions of classical religion. This is the only section of the entire text that would have to be described as genuinely scrambled, as a poor guide to the cosmology it describes.

The second area in which there are issues is that of Tahitian government and social hierarchy. Here the situation is less clear-cut. Morrison uses terms loosely based on European feudal relationships, but he tends to qualify them through use. Any crude application of a European model would certainly be misleading. Polynesian land tenure, for example, was layered, entailing titular sovereignty founded on ritual responsibility as well as use rights. Relationships between chiefs and people were constituted through various forms of reciprocity. Morrison does not fully explicate these contrasts in the manner a modern scholar would be expected to do, but the situated character of his language—that is, its embeddedness in accounts of particular people and events—does a good deal to convey the distinctiveness of the Polynesian order. The issue is further complicated by scope for debate about both the nature of Society Islands relationships—these are not clearly or unambiguously documented in any source, so there is room for much argument about them—and, for that matter, about the nature of European feudal polities. If the latter are subtly analyzed, as Valerio Valeri has done, it may be argued that there are in fact a host of interesting analogies with Polynesian societies. This is only to say that this source is rich and needs to be carefully read. It has limitations, but neither an old-fashioned historical idea of "bias" nor a broad category such as "colonial discourse" is particularly helpful in identifying them.

Perhaps the last of the *Bounty*'s ironies of authorization lies in the fact that our only surviving physical description of Morrison comes from Bligh. When he reached Kupang at the end of his arduous open-boat journey after being put to sea following the mutiny, Bligh had drawn up a list, "made out from the recollection of the persons with me, who were best acquainted with their private marks," to assist with the eventual roundup of the mutineers. Even before he had sought to fix his own version of the mutiny in the public imagination through the publication of his two accounts, Bligh attempted to establish the mutineers forever as characters in his story rather than tellers of their own tales. Among the brief portraits he penned was the following:

> James Morrison, boatswain's mate, aged twenty-eight years, five feet eight inches high, sallow complexion, long black hair, slender made; has lost the use of the upper joint of the forefinger of the right hand; tattooed with a star under his left breast, and a garter round his left leg, with the motto of "Honi soit qui mal y pense"; and has been wounded in one of his arms with a musket-ball.

Marks of injury and tattooing are used to identify most of the mutineers, many of the latter, including Fletcher Christian's, in the Tahitian mode. Morrison's star, garter, and motto, however, are emphatically British. They are emblems of the Order of the Garter, the medieval chivalric order headed by the Prince of Wales, whose members wear a garter with the words "Honi soit qui mal y pense" (Evil to him who evil thinks) emblazoned upon it in gold lettering. Nevertheless, in his description

Bligh enumerates each symbol in dissociated form, refusing to read the tattooed insignia as one unit, thus recognizing its reference to the British Order. Instead, the separate symbols are presented simply as figures of tattooing, that eminently Oceanic practice, not particularly distinguishable from, for instance, arch-mutineers Fletcher Christian's and George Stewart's combination of a star on the left breast and Tahitian-style tattooing "on the backside," or from John Millward's description as "very much tattooed in different parts of the body, and under the pit of the stomach, with a *taoomy* of Otaheite."[19] Yet, like his written defense and his *Journal* and *Account,* Morrison's tattoo seems to resonate in different registers, allowing him to masquerade either as the most loyal of British subjects or as an ironic commentator on British hierarchies. The only thing that is fully clear is his capacity to speak in two ways, using the insights and practices that his experience in crossing the beach had made available to him.

PART I

The Journal

Mutiny, Mutineers, Islanders

1 *The Voyage and the Mutiny*

On the 9th of Sept. 1787 I entered on board His Majestys Armed Vessel Bounty, Lieut. Wm. Bligh Commander, then lying at Deptford—On the 18th Oct following she drop'd down to long reach & in a few days saild for Spithead Where she Anchor'd on the 4th of November and after several attempts in one of which the Fore topsail yard was carried away, (which together with a Cable that was rubb'd at St. Helens were return'd at Portsmouth Yard and new ones got in their stead) she saild on the 23rd, of December with a *fresh* Gale Easterly, which Increased to a *heavy* Gale by the 27th, in which the Ships Oars a spare Topsail yard & Top Gallt. Yard were wash'd from the Quarters, (one of the Eye Bolts being drawn from the side,) She also ship'd a sea, which broke the Boats Chock & tore all the planks from the large Cutters Stem, and Washd some empty Casks overboard which were on the Deck, another Sea stove in a part of the Stern between the Deadlights, but did very little other Damage except breaking an azimuth Compass & Wetting a few bags of bread in the Cabbin; the breach in the stern was soon secured, and the Ship hove to, as it became dangerous to Scudd.[1]

When the weather became Modrate we made sail, the Carpenters repaird the Boat & Chock and the Wet bread was got up and dried and first used we met with no other Accident or any thing Material till the 5th of Jany 1788 when we Made the Island of Tennariffe & anchord in the Road of St. Croix on the 6th.

Here she Compleated her Water and took on board some Wine for the Ships use, two Drip stones were purchased here for refining Water,[2] & a barrel of flour & some Indian Corn for the Stock and several Casks for Gentlemen in England and the West Indies, Four quarters of Miserable Beef a few pumpions[3] & a Goat & Kid (which died soon after) were all the refreshments this Island afforded, the Beef was for the Most part thrown overboard as soon as it was served out by the People[4] who were not yet sufficiently come to their Stomacks to eat what they supposed to be either an Ass or Mule, evry Necessary except Wine was here both scarce & dear, nor Could the loss of the Topsail Yard & Sweeps be here repaird–

The Water being Compleated & the Hold Stowd the boats were got in on the 10th & on the 11th. Weighd and Stood to the SW with a fine breeze and pleasant weather, the Ship's Company were now put in three Watches and Mr. F. Christian appointed to act as Lieutenant by Order of Lieut. Bligh, which was read to the Ships Company—Mr. Bligh then informd them that as the length of the Voyage was uncertain (till He should get into the S. Sea, and that He was not certain whether or no He should be able to get round Cape Horn as the Season was so far spent but at all events was determined to try,) it became Necessary to be Careful of the Provisions (particularly Bread) to Make them Hold out for which reason He ordered the Allowance of Bread to be reduced to two thirds, but let evry thing else remain at full, this was cheerfully received, and the Beer being out Grog[5] was served.

The Weather still Continuing fine a few days after, the Cheese was got up to Air, when on opening the Casks two Cheeses were Missed by Mr. Bligh who declared that they were stolen, the Cooper declared that the Cask had been opend before, while the Ship was in the River by Mr. Samuel's order and the Cheeses sent to Mr. Bligh's house—Mr. Bligh without making any further inquiry into the Matter, ordered the Allowance of Cheese to be stoppd from Officers and Men till the deficiency should be made good, and told the Cooper He would give him a dam'd good flogging If He said any More about it–

These orders were strictly obey'd by Mr. Samuel, who was both Clerk and Steward; and on the next Banyan day[6] butter only was Issued, this the seamen refused, alledging that their acceptance of the Butter without Cheese would be tacitly acknowledging the supposed theft, and Jno. Williams declared that He had Carried the Cheeses to Mr. Blighs house with a Cask of Vinager & some other things which went up in the Boat from Long Reach—as they persisted in their denial of the Butter, it was kept also for two Banyan days and no more notice taken

As the Ship approachd the Equator the Pumpions began to spoil, and being in general too large for the Cabbin Use, they were Issued to the Ships Company in lieu of bread, the People being desirous to know at what rate the exchange was to be, inquired of Mr. Samuel who informd them that they were to have one pound of Pumpion in lieu of two pounds of bread, this they refused, and on Mr. Blighs being informd of it He Came up in a violent passion, and Calld all hands telling Mr. Samuel to Call the first Man of every Mess and let him see Who would dare to refuse it, or any thing else that He should order to be Served, saying "You dam'd Infernal scoundrels, I'll make you eat Grass or any thing you can catch before I have done with you–"

This speech enforced his orders, and evry one took the pumpion as Calld, Officers not excepted, who tho it was in their eyes an imposition said nothing against it, tho it was plain to be seen that they felt it more severely than the Men, who having yet a Good Stock of Potatoes which they had laid in at Spithead did not Immediately feel the effects of such a reduction of their Bread—as the pumpion was always served at one pound pr Man it was frequently thrown together by the seamen and the Cooks of the different Messes drew lots for the Whole, the pumpion was Issued evry other day, till they were all expended, and in all probability the greivance would have ended with them, but private stock began to decreace and the Beef and Pork to appear very light, and there had never yet been any Weighd when Opend, it was supposed that the Casks ran short of their Weight, for which reason the people applyd to the Master, and beggd that he would examine the business and procure them redress–

The Master making this known to Mr. Bligh he order'd all Hands aft and informed them that evry thing relative to the provision was transacted by His Orders[7], and it was therefore Needless to make any Complaint for they would get no redress, as *he* was the fittest Judge of what was right or wrong, he further added, that He would flog the first Man severely who should dare attempt to make any Complaint in future and dismissd them with severe threats–

The seamen seeing that no redress could be had before the end of the Voyage, determined to bear it with patience and Neither Murmur'd or Complaind afterwards, however the Officers were not so easy satisfied and made frequent Murmurings among themselves about the smallness of their Allowance and could not reconcile themselves to such unfair proceedings; but they made no Complaint seeing that the Men had drop'd it, and did not appear either in publick or private to take any notice of it— When a Cask was broached they saw with regret all the prime pieces taken out, for the Cabbin table, while they were forced to take their Chance in Common with the Men, of what remain'd without the satisfaction of knowing whether they had their Weight or Not; being forced to take it as Markd—this Circumstance while it served to increase their distress and to draw forth heavy Curses on the author of it in private helpd to Make the Men reconciled to their part, seeing that it was not level'd at them alone but that all shared alike fate, Nor were they as the Sea phrase expresses it able or calculated "to stand the Wrangle in the Gally" for their Pease, & Oatmeal, which was served in very sparing quantitys—So sparing that there never was any of either left for the Hogs who must have Starved but for bread & the Indian Corn purchased for the Poultry

The Usual allowance of Pease was Seven quarts for the Whole Compliment and of which none faild to partake and of Oatmeal Nine quarts each banyan day, in the Pease was frequently boild four Cakes of Portable beef Broth and some Sourkrout (Salted Cabbage)—The Butter and Cheese being expended Oil and Sugar was served in lieu, in the proportion of half a gill of oil, & one ounce of Sugar pr Man each banyan day–

We Caught very few fish while standing a Cross the trades near the Line we had heavy rain, & filld several Casks of Water both for our selves and stock—& Crossd the Line with the Usual Ceremony.[8]

We Met with No accident or Occurrence worth Mentioning except speaking the British Queen of London since leaving Tennariff, She was bound for the Cape of Good Hope on the Whale Fishery—on board this ship We sent letters for England supposing she would in all probability be the last We should see on this side of Cape Horn—We saw several ships on the Coast of Patagonia, but spoke None of them; and Carried a fair Wind & fair Weather (except at intervals) with us till We made Terra del Fuego which Happend on the 23d. March. The Weather being fine We were all in high Spirits, and hoped soon to get round the Cape but a few days Convinced us that Commodore Anson had not said worse of this Place then it deserved–[9]

One of the Sheep dying this morning Lieut. Bligh order'd it to be Issued in lieu of the Days allowance of Pork & Pease; declaring that it would Make a delisious Meal and that it weighd upwards of Fifty pounds, it was devided and most part of it thrown overboard, and some dried shark supplyd its place for a Sundays dinner, for it was no other then Skin & Bone.

the Day Continued fine, and We stood along the land Crossing the Straight of La Maire; but fair Weather in this Clime is always a fore-runner of Foul, and this we found by experience as soon as we were Clear of Staten Land, but before it set in we got the top Gallt. Masts down & made evry thing ready for it—the Appearance of the Country is rugged & barren—and the Snow on the hills gives it a very Inhospitable look at a Distance what it may be on a Nearer View I do not pretend to say, we saw here Vast quantitys of seals, Pengwins, Shags & other Sea fowles, White & Black Albtrosses—some of which We caught which made an excellent Meal. Some of them Measured upwards of 8 feet from tip to tip of their Wings, the Black ones We Calld Padries, but never Caught any of them. We tried for fish but without success.

The weather becoming very sharp as we stood to the Southward, the people requested that their Rum might be served without water, this was readily agreed to as the water was saved by it, and the allowance of water was now reduced to 3 pints pr day which in such Weather as We had was more than sufficient, having no Method of using it otherwise then as drink, and this indulgence was not lost on the Seamen Whose Spirits seemd to have an additional flow from it, they thought Nothing of Hardship and Notwithstanding fatigue and increasing bad weather they Carried on their duty with alacrity and Cheerfulness; anticipating the Pleasure and profit they hoped to reap by the success of the Voyage.

Wheat & Barly were now boild evry Morning for breakfast, in lieu of the Bargoo,[10] but of this the quantity was so small, that it was no uncommon thing for four Men in a Mess to draw lots for the Breakfast, and to devide their bread by the well known Method of "Who shall have this"; nor was the Officers a hair behind the Men at it

The quantity of Wheat boild was one Gallon for 46 Men, of which they all partook, & of Barley two pounds for the like number—the division of this scanty allowance Caused frequent broils in the Gally, and in the present bad Weather was often like to be attended with bad Consequences and in one of these disputes the Cook Thos. Hall got two of His ribbs broken, & at a Nother time Churchill got his Hand Scalded and it became at last Necessary to have the M.rs Mate of the watch to superintend the division of it–[11]

The Weather Continued to grow Worse evry day, hail rain, sleet & snow or rather large flakes of half formed Ice alternately following each other in heavy squalls, which often reduced us under bare poles & battend Hatches, as the sea made fair breaches over us running in a Manner

Seals on a Rockey Island in the Middle of the Bay Calld by us Seal Island where those Animals resort in great Numbers and lay basking themselves like Swine in the sun, on this Island we found part of a Boat which had been dashed to peices and several Bundles of Seals Skins which were for the most part rotten; as the Island is an entire rock it affords Shelter for No Animals but the Seals, & Sea fowls with which it abounds, and on firing a Musquet they rise up in vast flocks, making a great Noise, and in a Manner forming a Cloud over the Whole Island which is not more than half a Mile in Circumference, the Birds are Gannets, Shags, boobys, Gulls, Cape Hens, Peterels of sorts & Pengwins. We found here a large bird of the Size of a Goose of a Grey Collour which seemd to us unable to fly, several of which we knockd down and from their darting imedeatly at the Eye of those who Came in their reach we Calld them Eye peckers, they were full as heavy as a Goose but their flesh rank & Coarse and indifferent food.

On enquiry Concerning the Boat we found that this place used to Supply the Settlement with oil but that the Boat had been lost in a Gale of Wind & her Crew of Seven hands drownd but the Dutchmen had never been so Curious as to enquire how, the landing being very bad it is possible she might have been dash'd in pieces in attempting to land as part of her was there in our time but as we saw no bones we supposed the Men never reachd the shore—and the Govrnor has never sent a boat there since; this Island lays about 3 leagues Ea.t of Symons Bay

While We remained here the Ship was refitted, the rigging overhauld, and the Sails repaird, the Armour set to work to make new hinges for the Weather boards which had been washd away, the Carpenter & his Mates with two Dutch Caulkers Caulkd the sides & repair'd the Weather Boards, the Hold unstowd to get the Iron Stockd anchor up, & the Sheet put down in lieu, the Water filld, & several long boat loads of stones got in for Ballast, the Bread sifted, & an addition of 9 Cwt. got in for Sea store, and 3 Barrels of Brandy and 2 of Arrack with some flour and Raisins, and the powder taken on shore and aird, to which also was added two Barrels of fine Dutch Powder, from the Fort—Hay and Barly was procured for the stock of Sheep Goats & Poultry–

Evry thing being Compleat by the 1st of July we saild, having on board five live sheep for the Ships Companys use & some Pidgons and we stood to the Eastward with a fine Breeze; as we edged to the Southward the Wind increased to a fresh Gale and Continued with little alteration we passd Close by the Island of St. Paul,[13] but saw no place where a landing might be made with safety, this Island is high & barren affording but a very few trees, & shrubs; but as this was the dead of winter it may have a better appearance in Summer, we Saw no appearance of Water on any Part and a heavy Gale coming on prevented our further examination and We arrived at Adventure bay in N Holland Without any Material accident on the 2nd or 3rd of September where We Wooded & Waterd and Saild about the Middle of the Same Month for Tahiti.[14]

This is a large spacious bay, and the anchoring Good in any Depth from 20 to 5 fathoms white sandy bottom, and any Number of Ships might ride here in safety–

The Country is Mountainous, & Clothed with Wood from the Beach to the tops of the Mountains, the trees are of several kinds and run to a prodigious size; we measured one which had fallen, by being burnt at the root, by the Natives, which was 27 Yards to the first Branch & 9 in Circumference.

The Surf on the Beach makes the labour of Wooding and Watering very severe in the Winter Season, and the water tho plenty, is neither Good nor Convenient

The Soil near the Beach is Sandy, but on the Hills is a strong red loam and in Clear places affords excellent Grass which We Cut & dried for the Sheep & Goats, and on the East part of the Bay planted some Vines Pear trees & Bananas which we brought from Tennariff & the Cape with several kinds of seeds, Marking the adjacent trees with the Ship & Commanders Name & the date of the Year; we saw no quadruped but a dead Opossum, but various kinds of Birds; among which were Black Swans, Ducks, Hawkes, Parroquets, Sea Pyes, & several others which we could not name with numbers of Gannets & other sea fowles.

We hauld the Seine but had no success catching very few fish—we saw several of the Native's huts which consist of nothing more in structure then several pieces of Bark set up against a tree and round them several marks of fire & number of Crab, Muscle & other Shells, and a few days before we saild, some of the Natives Came down on the rocks on the West part of the Bay, where Mr. Bligh, accompanied by Mr. Nelson, went in the Cutter to see them and made them several presents, of which they seemd to take very little notice,[15] as they approachd the Boat, the weomen stayd at some distance, and the Men, in No. 10, thew away their short sticks, and came close down on the rocks, their Collour was nearly black but they appeard to be smutted in several parts with Charcoal, their heads were all Close shorn, so that we could not tell whether they were woolly or not but thought that the short remains lookd more like wool then hair,[16] their Countenances were by no means agreeable, and their teeth black and uneven; they were quite naked, and appeard harmless miserable Creatures. Amongst them was one very much deformd which Mr. Nelson declared to be the same he had seen here on a former Voyage[17]–

Tho' they did not appear in the least Curious to examine any thing given them, they talk'd a good deal which none of us understood, and would frequently Jump up & shout seemingly pleased, When the Boat rose higher then Common on the surf and again When she fell; as we did not land it was not possible to see into their Method of living but from the Number of shells at diffrent places we supposed that Shell fish was their Chief food. We saw no Canoes among them tho they appeard by their lights in the night to be numerous we therefore supposed that they depend on what the sea throws up, and on the whole appear the most miserable creatures on the face of the Earth[18]–

While we were here, the Carpenters sawd some plank while the wooding & watering was going on, bread was served at full allowance, & Water Gruel boild for breakfast, but as soon as we put to Sea we returnd to the former Allowance and here also were sown seeds of eternal discord between Lieut. Bligh and his Officers. He confined the Carpenter, and found fault with the innatention of the rest, to their duty, which produced continual disputes evry one endeavouring to thwart the others in their duty, this made the men exert themselves to divert the storm from falling on them by a strict attention to their duty and in this they found their account and rejoiced in private at their Good success.[19]

Soon after we saild we discovered a Group of small Islands to the Eastward of New Zealand which were Call'd the Bountys Isles,[20] and Jas. Valentine having been let blood his arm festered and turned to a mortification of which he Died. Several of the seamen particularly the oldest began to complain of Pains in their limbs and some simptoms of the Scurvy began to make its appearance and weakness and debility began to be observed throught the Ships Company, for which Essence of Malt was given to those who appeard worst with portable soup & rice from the Surgeons Chest the salt provisions was also stopd & flour given in lieu

During this passage Mr. Bligh and His Mess mates the Master & Surgeon fell out, and separated, each taking his part of the stock, & retiring to live in their own Cabbins, after which they had several disputes & seldom spoke but on duty; and even then with much apperant reserve—previous to making Tahiti, a dispute happend between Mr. Bligh and the Master, relative to signing some books, which the Master had refused to sign, for reasons best known to himself, Upon which all Hands were Calld aft, and the Articles of War read, and some part of the printed Instructions, after Which the Books and papers were produced with a Pen and ink and Mr. Bligh said Now Sir Sign them Books the Master took the Pen and said "I sign in obedience to your Orders, but this may be Cancelled hereafter," the books being signed the People were dismiss'd to return to their duty–

On the 24th of Octr we made the Island of Me'etia (or Osnaburgh Island)[21] and stood Close in with it when Several of the Natives Came down on the Rocks on the North part & waved large pieces of White Cloth,[22] but none attempted to come off and in the afternoon we bore away for Tahiti which we made between 5 and 6 in the N W—at 8 we hove too and at 4 in the Morning of the 25th made sail and anchor'd at 10 in Port Royal (or Matavai) Bay

We were presently surrounded by the Natives in their Canoes, who brought off Hogs, Bread fruit & Cocoa Nuts, in abundance, and a trade for Nails hatchets &ca. was soon Commenced; of the Cocoa Nuts the sick were desired to drink plentifully and these contributed so much to their recovery, that in a few days there was no Appearance of sickness or disorder in the ship, and the Great Plenty of Provisions with the Natives supply'd us soon renewd their Strength–

Imediatly on Anchoring, an order signd by Mr. Bligh was stuck up on the Mizen Mast, Prohibiting the Purchase of *Curiosities* or *any* thing except *Provisions*—There were few or no instances of the order being disobeyd, as no curiosity struck the seamen so forcibly as a roasted pig & some bread fruit, and these Came in abundance evry species of Ships Provision except grog being stop'd.[23]

As soon as the Ship was Moord, a tent was pitched on Point Venus,[24] and Mr. Nelson & his Assistant went on Shore to Collect Plants, the Gunner also went to the Tent to trade for Hogs for the Ships Use; it being found more convenient then trading alongside, as the Canoes came so thick as to put a stop to all Work while she remaind anchourd. Mr.

Figure 4. "Matavai Bay, Island Otahytey—Sunset," George Tobin, 1792 [Call no. PXA 563 no. 33]. Reproduced with permission of the Mitchell Library, State Library of NSW

F. Christian, Mr. Heywood & Mr. Peckover the Gunner & four men were also sent on Shore as a guard in case the natives should behave amiss

A shed was built for the reception of the Plants and the Pots Carried on shore as Mr. Nelson filld them. Mean time the Carpenter and his Mates fitted the Cabbin for their reception. Some hands were employd Cutting Wood & filling Water for present Use, the Forge was set up and the Armourer set to work to make Iron tools for trade and all the Salt in the ship was soon expended in curing pork for sea store and evry thing seemd to go on in a prosperous manner

While the salting time lasted, provisions were in great Plenty, as each Man was allowd two Pounds of the Bones and such parts as were not fit for salting, pr. day, which with what they could get by Purchace themselves was always sufficient to enable them to live well

On the 11th of Decr Departed this life Mr. Thos. Huggan & next day his remains were Inter'd on Point Venus and a board fixd to a tree near his grave with an Inscription on it to his Memory[25]—the sailmaker got the sails on shore to repair

The Market for Hogs beginning now to slacken Mr. Bligh seized on all that came to the ship big & small Dead or alive, taking them as his property, and serving them as the Ship's allowance at one pound pr. Man pr. Day. He also seized on those belonging to the Master, & killd them for the ships use, tho He had more then 40 of different sizes on board of his own, and there was then plenty to be purchaced nor was the price much risen since the first, and when the Master spoke to him, telling him the Hogs were his property, he told him that "He Mr. Bligh would convince him that evry thing was *his,* as soon as it was on board, and that He would take nine tenths of any mans property and let him see who dared say any thing to the contrary", those of the seamen were seized without ceremony, and it became a favour for a Man to get a Pound extra of His own hog–

The Natives observing that the Hogs were seized as soon as they Came on board, and not knowing but they would be seized from them, as well as the People, became very shy of bringing a hog in sight of Lieut. Bligh either on board or on shore, and watched all opportunitys when he was on shore to bring provisions to their friends on board[26] but as Mr. Bligh observed this, and saw that His diligence was like to be evaded, he ordered a Book to be kept in the Bittacle[27] wherein the Mate of the Watch was to insert the Number of Hogs or Pigs with the Weight of each that came into the Ship, to remedy this, the Natives took another Method which was Cutting the Pigs up, and wraping them in leaves and covering the Meat with Bread fruit in the Baskets, and sometimes with peeld Cocoa Nuts, by which means, as the Bread was never seized, they were a Match for all his industry; and he never suspected their artifice, by this means provisions were still plenty.

On the 20th we had heavy rains & a strong Gale of Wind from the N W which brought with it a heavy sea from that Quarter breaking so violently on the Dolphin Bank[28] that the Surge run fairly over the Ship, and the Carpenter who was the evening before Confined to his Cabbin, was now released to secure the Hatches several things were washd overboard & had not the Cables been very good the ship must have gone on shore. Next day the Gale abated, but the surf ran very high on the shore so as to prevent landing either in Canoes or Boats. However several of the Natives found the way off through it, and brought bunches of Cocoa Nuts with them that were full as much as one of us could haul up the side tho they had swam off with them through a tremendous surf.

as the Weather Modrated, the Canoes came off and of them we learnt the situation of the Party on shore who had been in danger of being washd away by the overflowing of the river, and observed them opening a sluice in the Bank which soon assumed the appearance of a large river

As soon as a boat Could land, the sails were got off and Bent, and the Plants got on board, and the Ship unmoord the Master sent to examine Pare Harbour, as this Bay was judged unsafe to remain any longer in, he returned with a favourable account of the Place, and on the Morning of the 25th, the tent was struck & sent down in the launch, at 10 the ship weighd and followed, but standing in, she run on a coral rock which had escaped the Masters sight, the sea Breeze being set in gave us some trouble before we got her off which however we did before night, & moord with one Bower & the Kedge, till Morning; when we Moord with Both bowers: Got the Plants on shore and a house was provided by Tu or Mate,[29] the Chief mentioned by Capt. Cook, in lieu of a Tent for the shore party and a place fenced in for the Plants.

Having got the ship in order, we kept our Christmass on the 28th: each man having double allowance of Grog which was stopd from those who had not Crossd the Equator before this voyage, and on the 1st of Jany 1789 this was repeated, after which the Grog was reduced to half the allowance but as we had plenty of Cocoa Nut Milk, the Grog was not missd and the Natives took care to keep us well supplied with them notwithstanding the frequent seizures made by Mr. Bligh who Drank nothing else in his Grog.

It would be difficult to account for evry transaction that happened while we lay at this Island and I shall only make a few remarks—

On our first Arrival the Ship was visited by numbers of the Inhabitants of all descriptions, among whom were several Chiefs who brought large Presents and were presented in their turn by Mr. Bligh who found some of His old acquaintance as did Mr. Nelson and Coleman who had been here before[30] and evry officer & Man in the ship were provided with new friends tho none understood the language,[31] yet we found it very easy to Converse by signs at which these people are adepts, and some of the Weomen who came on board became very Intiligent in a short time and soon brought their quondum husbands into a method of discourse by which evry thing was transacted and by them we found that the stock left by Capt. Cook was for the most part distroyd, there being but one Sheep in the Island which was killd by the dogs soon after our arrival.[32] I observed that this sheep Contrary to those in most warm Climates had not lost its Wool—the only Horn'd Cattle on the Island were an Old Bull and a Young Cow (the rest being destroyd and Carried away by the Mo'orea People soon after Capt. Cook had left the Island) and these were kept at the Distance of 25 or 30 miles from each other, these Mr. Bligh Purchased & they were brought to Matavai and put under Poeno's Care—Poeno was chief of Matavai[33] & he had the Charge of Captn. Cooks Picture which he brought on board to get repaird and it remaind in the ship till she saild—[34]

We also learnt by them that Ma'i was dead but could not learn by what means he died, but it was thought that he had been killd for the sake of his property, however we were better informd afterwards as shall be shown in its proper place[35]

Tu, the Chief whom we supposed to be King, & 'Itia his Queen often slept on board the ship and frequently entertand Mr. Bligh and the Officers on shore with heiva (or Dances plays, &c.) and such diversions as they thought most pleasing and from which he generally returned with presents of Cloth &ca. They also informed us that the name of O Tu, or Tu was now transfer'd to the son (of the Man whom we knew by that name) who was now e ari'i rahi or king, and that the name of the Father, was now Mate, and that he was only regent during his sons minority—our Imperfect knowledge of the Language prevented us from enquiring into these Misterious Customs, however we learnt that as soon as a Child is born, the honors & titles of the Father immediately become his or hers, and the Father commences Guardian to his Child and honors it as his superior.[36] The Present Tu, King of Tahiti, is a Boy of 9 or 10 Years old but for reasons to be explaind hereafter he never came on board, but Mr. Bligh went once to see him on shore. He frequently paddled round the ship in his Canoe, & received homage from all who saw the canoe. He was generally Carried on the Shoulders of a man who sat on the Bow of the Canoe,[37] it being the Custom of this country to prefer the Bow to the Stern–

When any strange visitors Came they were entertaind by Mr. Bligh, who gratified their curiosity by firing a Gun, at which they appeard much amazed & always stopd their ears & fell down as soon as they saw the Flash, and a Pistol was to all appearance as much dreaded as a four pounder.[38] Mr. Bligh took the opportunity at such times, to shew them the effects of round and Grape Shot, which to them appeard Wonderful, and they always exclaim'd in amaze when they saw the shot fall, scarcely giving credit to what they saw

While we lay in Matavai Bay, the Nun Buoy was Cut from the Best bower Anchor, the Cutters rudder stoln and several Hooks & thimbles Cut from the rigging & several other things missd; on which Mr. Bligh applyd to O Tu or Mate, to have them returned. Some of them were brought back, but the Buoy & Rudder were destroyd, and only some pieces of the wood brought—as these things were readily found it was thought that the Chiefs were accessary to the thefts, the numbers that frequented the ship & tent rendered it impossible to observe all their actions, and as the thefts were not very considerable, and large allowance being made by Mr. Bligh in favour of the Natives, it was thought the best method to prevent thieving was by keeping things as much out of their way as possible, by fixing Wooden Buoys and removing all the loose Iron work into the Store rooms till wanted; and few accidents of the kind happend after–

While we lay at Pare we Cut wood for Sea store, filld our Water and overhauld the Blocks sails & rigging, and here we found the ship began to swarm with Cockroaches to get rid of which evry Method was tried but to no purpose after repeated washing & Carrying evry Chest & box on shore where the Cloaths &ca. were cleard of them they appeard as plenty in two or three days as ever, the Cables appeard alive with them and they seemd to increase instead of deminish tho great quantitys were destroyd evry day. Hot water was now applied twice a Week and the Cables & evry part of the Ship from stem to stern washd with it but to no purpose they flew to the Hold rigging & mast heads & returnd as before, and our attention was now drawn to the Sail room & Store rooms where the Hot water had found its way but had done no other damage then Weting evry thing in them, the Hot water was now disused & the sails & Canvas lines &ca were got on shore & washd with Salt Water dry'd & made up while the Carpenters Caulk'd over the store & sail rooms.

On the 24th of Jany at 4 in the Morning, the Small Cutter was missd from alongside Lieut. Bligh was acquaintd with it, and the Hands being Calld, it was found that Chas. Churchill, Jno Millward & Willm. Musprat were missing, and as Mr. Hayward the Midshipman had been asleep on his watch and a small bag with trade being found on deck, it was readyly supposed that they had taken the boat, especially as it was known that Millward was Centry from 12 till 2, and on examination it was found that with the Boats Arm Chest they had Eight stand of arms compleat, & eight cartouch boxes of ammunition; the large Cutter was hoisted out, & the Master sent in her to Matavai in quest of the Boat and Mr. Hayward ordered in Irons, the Master returned about 8 oClock having met the Cutter with five Natives who were coming to the ship they informd us that the three men before named had brought her to Matavai and left her, taking the Arm Chest on board a Canoe and were saild for Tetiaroa a number of small Island inclosed by a reef 8 Leags North of Pt Venus—on examining Churchills Chest a paper was found Containing his own name & and that of three of the Party on shore, which Churchill had written, on which Lieut. Bligh went on shore to the House and informd Mr. Christian of the Business calling the men and challenging them with being concerned with Churchill and intending to disert. They persisted in their Innocence, and denyd it so firmly, that He was inclined from Circumstances to believe them and said no more to them about it—He then went in quest of Mate who was by this time informd by his men of the affair and was coming to the tent, as soon as Mr. Bligh saw him, he told him the affair & desired him to have the men brought back, which he promised to do, and Several Canoes under the command of Moana an Old Chief, and Ari'ipaea, (Chief of Pare) Mates Brother, were dispatchd after them, with instrctions how to proceed to take them by stratagem, but three weeks elapsed before any account was heard of them when on the 15th of Feby Hitihiti, (the same mentioned by Captain Cook) came on board and informed Mr. Bligh that they were landed at the upper part of Tetaha,[39] about 6 Miles to the westward, on which Mr. Bligh mann'd the Launch and went after them.[40] On coming to the place he learnt from them that they had been oversett within the reef and had lost a Musquet and were near being drown'd, the Night being very bad he did not return to the ship till next morning, when they were put in Irons, and after a months confinement were punished, Churchill with 2 Dozn & the others four dozn each and returned to duty and Mr. Hayward, after receiving a severe rebuke for his neglect of Duty, was also set at liberty and return'd to his duty–

A little time after the small bower Cable was observed to be Cut through two strands at the waters edge but as the Cable hung slack under the bottom it was not observed till a squall from the Westward brought it to bear a head, when we hove it in and spliced it before the wind became sufficiently strong to part it

This gave rise to many opinions, and strict inquiry was made, but no person on board could give any account of it, tho it was the private oppinion of Men as well as Officers that no Native had been so bold as to attempt it tho some supposed they had, as the Buoy was sunk, thinking to be well paid for their trouble in diving after it, as they had been paid for their assistance in Clearing the Cable of the rocks when the ship got on shore coming in at which they were expert and had passd a lead line round a buoy rope before in 17 faths the Buoy having sunk. However tho they are not very guilty of keeping secrets, this remaind a perfound one, and was not found out while the ship remaind here[41]

While we were Watering, the Casks were all got on shore and the Cooper set to work to put them in order at the tent, when after a dark rainy Night a Punchion was miss'd, together with some of the Gunners Bedding out of his Cot and an Azimuth Compass (which was kept at the tent for the Purpose of surveying, Mr. Bligh having made a strict survey of the Harbour & Matavai Bay) broken and part of it Carried away, as soon as Mr Bligh heard of this he went on shore and rebuked the Officers at the tent for neglecting their duty, who alledged that the night was so dark & the rain fell so fast that they could not see or hear each other and that the thief had taken a full Cask tho the Empty ones stood Close by. He then went in a passion to Mate and insisted on having the thief delivered up & in a short time the thief & Cask were both brought to the tent and Mate told Mr. Bligh to shoot him, which he said would make the others afraid to steal. As soon as he was delivered up he was tyed, & brought on board, where he was tyed up and punished with a hundred lashes and put in Irons, Mr Bligh intending to keep him prisoner, till the ship saild; but he found means to get out and make his escape without being perceived by any one but the Centry, who heard him plunge overboard, but never saw any more of Him, the darkness of the Night favouring his escape and we heard no more of Him. It seems he had observed the Yeoman putting the Marlin spikes in by the Fore Mast near which he lay in the Gally, and with one of them He twisted the lock to pieces, without being heard, & going up the fore scuttle Jump'd overboard

Towards the latter end of March, we put the rigging in order and bent the sails and Mr. Nelson having collected upwards of a Thousand fine Bread fruit plants, with many others of value,[42] We got ready for Sea getting them on board by the 1st of April, and the Natives to shew the last token of their Freindship loaded us with presents, & the Ship became lumbered with Hogs Cocoa Nuts & Green Plantains for Sea store—the Plantains were all taken aft, and such hogs as Mr. Bligh thought fit to keep, were pen'd up in the Waist, and the rest either Killd or returned, as the owners thought fit, evry cask being filld & good Store of Fire Wood on board, on the 4th we placed Buoys in the Channel and the Morning being Calm, Weighd, & towd out; when a Breeze sprung up, & we hove to to stow the Boats, and Anchors but on fishing the best bower the stock being much wormeaton broke & fell over board. Captain Cooks picture was now sent on shore by Poeno with the Bountys Name & the intent of Her Voyage put on the Back.

We were followed out by a Number of our friends and Mate & ʻItia, with several others, remaind on board the ship, till three in the afternoon when the small cutter was sent to put them on shore, their parting with the Lieut. and officers was truely a tender scene; the rest being gone in their Canoes, Mr. Bligh gave Mate a Musquet two pistols some powder & Ball flints &c. And a Chest to keep his trade & Amunition in, the Chest being also filld with the Presents Mr. Bligh had made him; the Carpenter also Gave him an American Musquet with all which he seemd highly Pleased, but was quite at a loss how to express himself on the occasion and when they landed loaded the Boat with Cocoa Nuts when she returned & was hoisted in

As the labour of the day had been very great Double Allowance of Grog was Given to all hands and evry thing being secured at 5 in the Evening We bore away and made sail to the W N W, Passing Moʻorea or Eimeo in the Night—evry body seemd in high spirits and began already to talk of Home, affixing the length of the Passage and Count up their Wages and One would readily have Imagined that we had Just left Jamaica instead of Tahiti so far onward did their flattering fancies waft them.[43]

At 10 am we made Huahine and the Hands being Mustered, as Usual most of their Grog was stopd for not being Clean, at Noon we hove too off Fare Harbour to inquire for Maʻi; but could get no other Information but that he was dead some time. The Natives brought off a few Yams & a Hog or two which were purchased for Mr. Bligh, and in the Evening we made sail, leaving Raiatea on the Starbd hand Standing to the SW till Midnight when we altered our Course to the Wd having passd the Islands of Ra'iatea & Taha'a &ca and now took a farwel of the Society Isles

Plantains were now served in lieu of Bread at 6 pr. Man pr. day with one pound of Fresh pork—and when they were expended, the Yams & tarro were Issued at one pound pr. day till we Arrived at Nomuka.

Sunday the 12th we exercised at Backing & filling Making & shortning sail &ca. but the Wind coming to the Westwd & blowing hard gave us an oppotunity of exerting our abilitys in earnest & on the 13th we Discovered an Island which we saild nearly round it appeard to be surrounded by a reef; inside of which was deep water & 5 or 6 small keys, three of the Natives came off in a Canoe. On the 15th the Weather being now Calm & fine they seemd much surprized at evry thing they saw, and as soon as they Came on board they fell down & kissd Mr. Blighs feet giving him the Pearl Shells which they wore on their Breasts, suspended by Collars of Braided hair, in return He gave them each a Knife & some beads of which they seemd very fond tho they knew not the use, he also gave them a Young Boar & Sow as we found by them they had no such animals—their language seemd to differ from that of the Society Isles, tho they knew the Bread fruit Plants by the same name—they were loth to leave the ship and one of them would have staid while the others went on shore for some Cocoa Nuts, but it growing late we could not stay, they Calld the Island Aitutaki, and when they left us they seemd reluctant still looking at the ship as they paddled away, the Canoe differed from those of the Society Isles, being alike at each end and but indifferently built.[44] In the evening a Whirlwind passd us between 7 & 8 o Clock which almost hove the ship about, after which a breeze sprang up and we made sail and on the 16th at 10 at Night passd Savage Island[45]–

On the 19th we made the Islands of Kao and Tofua, two of the Friendly Islands, but Calms & Currents prevented us from reaching Nomuka till the 23rd. This is a low Island one of the Eastern range of the Freindly Isles, (of which there are many) It lies about 16 or 17 Leags to the ESE of Tofua, which is a high lump with a large Volcano on the top, Kao is also a high Peak like a Sugar loaf, and may be seen 15 or 20 leags off in Clear Weather; these two are not more then 3 leags distt from each other—on the 24th a party was sent to wood & Water.

Nomuka or Rotterdam was first discovered by Tasman the Dutch

Navigator who reduced the Natives to good behaviour but their present behaviour seems to be such as the dread of fire arms produces for they were very rude & attempted to take the Casks from the Waterers and the axes from the Wooding party; and if a Musquet was pointed at any of them produced no other affect than a return of the Compliment, by poising their Club or Spear with a menacing look; and as it was Lieut. B.'s orders, that no person should affront them on any occasion, they were emboldened by Meeting no return to their Insolence, and became so troublesom that Mr. Christian, who had the Command of the Watering party, found it difficult to carry on his duty, of this He informd Capt. Bligh, who dam'd him for a Cowardly rascal, asking him if he was afraid of a set of Naked Savages while He had arms; to which Mr. Christian answerd "the Arms are no use while your orders prevent them from being used."[46]

However in the Morning of the 25th Mr. Fryer was sent with the Cutter Armd, to attend the launch but had not long been at a Grapnel before the Natives found means of unbending it from the rope, by stirring up the Mud and thickning the Water, and then diving down as they flockd about the boat, one Man was orderd to hold the rope in his hand, Notwithstanding which they Carried it Clear off before the boat drove, or the Man in the Bow perceivd the rope slack. Mr. Fryer applied to the Chiefs to have it returned, but to no purpose, being obliged at present to put up with the loss and when the Boats returned He informd Lieut. Bligh of what happen'd on which he applyd to some of the chiefs who were then on board, but to no purpose, tho' they made fair promises

During our stay Here the Natives flockd to the Ship in Great Numbers to trafick for Hogs fowles Yams Cocoa Nuts &c all of which they seemd to know the Value of, & would not part with a single plantain without something in return. Several Chiefs & Principal Men were Constantly on board and frequently not less then an hundred Canoes of different sizes about the ship–

Their Canoes will Carry from 2 to 40 Men; they have both double and single Canoes equipt for sailing with well made rope, & large sails which they work in different Methods some being hoisted up by hawlyards, and others the Yard are fixd to Swivel about on the Masthead Having the Weather Yard Arm Confined by a strong tack of 5 or 6 inch Rope, the rope is made of Cocoa Nut Husk platted into sinnet, & then neatly laid & Well twisted in three Strands.[47] The Sails are of a Triangular form with a Yard & boom. They are made of Matting doubled & quilted. Some of those Booms were Longer & Bigger then our Main Yard. Those which hoist & lower their sail Work to Windward in the Same Manner as a Flying Proa of the Ladrones, being both ends alike;[48] but the others are diffrent, and always sail one end first; they are neatly built & well finishd, and sail at an amazing rate in smooth Water but in a rough sea they can never answer–

Their Fish hooks are made of Pearl, Bone and Tortoise Shell of which they have plenty, their Weopons are Clubs of about 3 feet long, of hard wood neatly Carved, & Inlaid with Bone & Pearl, long Spears with barbs of three Inches, fixd at equal distances for three feet in length, Bows of about 6 or 7 feet long of a very elastic wood & Arrows of Reed pointed with the Stings of the Sting Ray, and Slings made of the Husk of the Cocoa Nuts—their Cloathing is in Both sexes alike, and is mostly one piece of Cloth or Matting tyed round the Waist and depending below the Knees, the Matting is chiefly worn at sea, or in Wet Weather and is of several sorts neatly made, their Cloth is made of the Bark of the Cloth tree and they have a Method of Glaizing it to make it keep out Wet; and stain it with Brown & Black which gives it a very handsome appearance.[49]

Both Sexes dress their Hair with lime or Burnt Shells which tho Originally Black, soon turns to Red, Purple & White.

Tho the Countenances of the Men are Open yet they have something in it that gives an unfavourable Idea to strangers; perhaps this might have been heighten'd in our eyes by their Actions which did not correspond with their Name.

We saw here several earthen Vessels well made[50] & many Curious pieces of Workmanship & Ingenuity, and their Canoes appear to be the best made and the neatest Work of any We had Seen, tho not so large as Some, but they are well calculated for their Seas which are mostly Smooth owing to the Number of Islands with reefs round their Eastern side & the shoal water about them–

Both Men and Weomen run of the Common Size, they are of a Copper Collour and are Well Made, the Weomen are Handsome but know how to set a price on their favours, the Men are Tattow'd from the Knee to the Waist which something resembles a pair of Breeches; the Weomen are not tattow'd, but have on their Shoulders several Circles indented with burning hot bamboos of different sizes, and many of Both sexes want a part if not the whole of their little fingers, which we understood was cut off as a tribute to the memory of their deceased friends[51]

Having filld all the Water & Got on board some wood & large Quantitys of Yams some Cocoa Nuts Plantains &c on the 26th we hoisted in the Boats and having but a light air, & the 3 Chiefs who were on board having promised that the Grapnel should be restored if Mr. Bligh would wait till the Canoe returned which they said was gone to another Island after it, we got all ready for weighing and two Hours liberty was given to the people to expend their trade, as this was likely to be the last Island where Iron Currency was the Most valuable, evry one got rid of their trade as fast as they could purchacing Matts, Spears & many Curiositys and a quantity of Yams for Private Store with Cocoa Nuts &c.—and evry thing the Natives had or would dispose of, and what with Yams and Clubs in all Quarters the ship was fairly lumberd that there was scarcely room to stir in any part—about Noon we weighd & stowd the Anchor and the Fore topsail being loose we stood to the Westd with a light air. The Ships Compy were Armd and Drawn up and the Chiefs made prisoners, the Canoes were ordered to Cast off and keep astern. At this the Chiefs seemd much displeased, on which they were ordered down to the Mess room where Mr Bligh followed them and set them to peel Cocoa Nuts for His Dinner.[52] He then came up and dismissd all the Men but two, that were under arms, but not till he had passd the Compliment on officers & Men to tell them that they were a parcel of lubberly rascals and that he would be one of five who would with good sticks would disarm the whole of them, and presenting a Pistol at Wm. McCoy threatend to shoot him for not paying attention

About 4 in the Afternoon We Hove too the Canoes being all Gone, but one double one, on board of which were some weomen who wept bitterly & Cut their faces & shoulders in a terrible Manner, as did the Oldest of the Chiefs who struck himself several violent blows on the face & cut him self on the Cheek bones with his fists.[53] Mr Bligh now Ordered the Canoe alongside seeing no appearance of the Grapnell, and dismissd them with presents which they received and the youngest would have stripd & left his Mat on board if He had been permitted but the others seemd as if they only smotherd their resentment, seeing that they could not revenge the insult, however they went away and stood in for the Island, and it was the oppinion of most on board that if a Weak mand Ship Came in their

Way they would remember this days transactions and make them suffer for it[54]–

The Produce of those Islands is much the same in evry respect the same as the Society Isles but they Cultivate the earth here with much pains and the Yams here are the largest in the World and equally as good as those of the East or West Indies but they are Indifferently waterd the only water at Nomuka being a Stagnate Pool which in a very dry season it is possible may intirely dry up, but this is not much felt by the Natives who use very little water in dressing their food & the Cocoa Nuts supplys them with drink in the Dryest season—their animals are the same as those of the Society Isles but their Hogs are in general small, and the reefs abound with Variety of fine fish–

The Cocoa Nuts Here are very large, but the shells are of a Coarse open Grain, some of them will Hold 5 pints, and serves the Natives to Carry Water in in their Canoes–

Our Stay here being short it was not possible to examine into the Manners & Customs of these People but as Captn Cook has been very Minute in his description of them I must refer the Reader to His Voyage,[55] and return to a more Interesting part of the Business

When the Chiefs were Gone, we made Sail, but the Wind being light & frequently flatning to a Calm we made very little Way, during the Night, as we near'd Tofua[56] we observed Vast Collums of smoke & flame Issuing from the Volcano which appear'd to be a very large one the Weather continuing the same all day, we alter'd our position very little, being within 7 or 8 leagues of the Island all the day and no appearance of a Breeze—In the Afternoon of the 27th Mr. Bligh Came up, and taking a turn about the Quarter Deck when he missed some of the Cocoa Nuts which were piled up between the Guns upon which he said that they were stolen and Could not go without the knowledge of the Officers, who were all Calld and declared that they had not seen a Man toutch them, to which Mr Bligh replied then you must have *taken* them yourselves, and orderd Mr. Elphinstone to go and fetch evry Cocoa nut in the Ship aft, which He obeyd. He then questioned evry Officer in turn concerning the Number they had bought, & Coming to Mr. Christian askd Him, Mr. Christian answered "I do not know Sir, but I hope you dont think me so mean as to be Guilty of Steling yours". Mr Bligh replied "Yes you dam'd Hound I do—You must have stolen them from me or you could give a better account of them—God damn you, you Scoundrels, you are all thieves alike, and combine with the men to rob me—I suppose you'll Steal my Yams next, but I'll sweat you for it, you rascals, I'll make half of you Jump overboard before you get through Endeavour Streights"[57]—He then Calld Mr. Samuel and said "Stop these Villains Grog, and Give them but Half a Pound of Yams tomorrow, and if they steal then, I'll reduce them to a quarter". The Cocoa Nuts were Carried aft, & He Went below, the officers then got together and were heard to murmur much at such treatment, and it was talked among the Men that the Yams would be next seized, as Lieut. Bligh knew that they had purchased large quantitys of them and set about secreting as many as they Could.

The night being Calm we made no way, & in the Morning of the 28th the Boatswain Came to my hammock and waked me telling me to my great surprize that the ship was taken by Mr. Christian. I hurried on deck and found it true, seeing Mr. Bligh in his shirt with his hands tied behind him and Mr. Christian standing by him with a drawn Bayonet in his hand and his Eyes flaming with revenge. Several of the men were under arms, and the Small Cutter hoisted out, and the large one getting ready. I applied to the Boatswain to know how I should proceed, but he was as much at a loss as I, and in a Confused Manner told me to lend a hand in Clearing the Boat and Getting her out, which I did, when she was out the Small one was got in Mr. Christian Calld to Mr. Hayward and Mr. Hallet to get into the Boat and ordered Churchill to See the Master & Clerk into Her. The Lieutenant then began to reason but Mr. Christian replied "Mamoo,[58] Sir, not a word, or deaths your portion". Mr. Hayward & Mr. Hallet begd with tears in their eyes to be sufferd to remain in the ship but Mr. Christian ordered them to be silent. The Boatswain and Carpenter Came aft (the Master & Gunner being Confined below) and beggd for the Launch, which with much hesitation was Granted, and she was ordered out. While I was Clearing her the Master Came up & spoke to Mr. Bligh and afterwards Came to Me, asking me if I had any hand in the Mutiny. I told him I had not, and he then desired me to try what I Could do to raise a party and rescue the Ship, which I promised to do. In consequence of which Jno. Millward who was by me at the time Swore he would stand by me, and went to Musprat, Burket and the Boatswain on that score, but Churchill seeing the Master speaking to me (tho he was Instantly hurried away by Quintrell ordering him down to his Cabbin)

Came and demanded what he had said. I told him that He was asking about the Launch but Alexr. Smith who stood on the other side of the Boat told Churchill to look sharp after me saying "tis a dam'd lye, Chas, for I saw him and Millward shake hands, when the Master spoke to them, and Calld to the others to stand to their Arms, which put them on their Guard". As I saw none near me that seemd inclined to make a push, and the Officers busy getting the boat in order, I was fain to do so too, and the Boat was got out, when evry one ran to get what He could into her and get in themselves as fast as possible. The officers were hurryd in as fast as possible, and when Mr. Bligh found that He must go, He beggd of Mr. Christian to desist, saying "I'll Pawn my Honour, I'll Give My Bond, Mr Christian, never to think of this if you'll desist"; and urged his wife and family, to which Mr. Christian replyd "No, Captain Bligh, if you had any Honor, things had not come to this; and if you Had any regard for your Wife & family, you should Have thought on them before, and not behaved so much like a villain". Lieutenant Bligh attempted again to speak, but was ordered to be silent; the Boatswain also tryd to pacify Him to which He replied tis too late, "I have been in Hell for this Fortnight passd and am determined to bear it no longer, and you know Mr. Cole that I have been used like a Dog all the Voyage". The Master bedg to be permitted to stay, but was ordered into the Boat, and Mr. Christian gave Churchill order to see that no arms went in the Boat. In Getting the things into the Boat a dispute happened between Churchill and the Carpenter about the latters tool Chest which Churchill wanted to keep in the Ship but by Mr. Christians orders it was sufferd to go in the Boat but he told Churchill to keep the Carpenters Mates on board and the Armourer—the Masts & Sails were got in and all the New light Canvas with Nails, Saws (hand Whip & Cross Cut), trade, and the Lieutenants & Masters Cloaths, two Gang Casks of Water, four empty breeves, 3 bags of Bread with Mr. Blighs Case, Some Bottles of Wine and several other things, insomuch that she almost sunk a longside. The Lieut. then Beggd that some of the people would stay, and askd Mr. Christian to let the Master stay with them but he answered, "the men may stay but the Master must go with you". Mr. Bligh then said "Never fear my lads you cant all go with me my lads I'll do you Justice if ever I reach England". He then brought to the Gangway and cast of his hands and he went into the Boat. While the Boatswain was getting his things into the Boat I told him my intention was to stay and take my Chance in the ship, telling him of the Captains Promise and as he saw the situation of the Boat which was scarcely 7 inches free I had no occasion to point out the Danger to Him, he repeated the Lieuts promise saying "God Bless you my boy; were it not for my Wife & family I would stay myself"—after Mr. Bligh was In the Boat he beggd for His Commission and Sextant; the Commission was Instantly Given him with his Pocket Book and private Journal by Mr. Christians order, and He took His own Sextant which Commonly Stood on the Dripstone Case and Handed it into the Boat with a Daily Assistant, saying "there Captn Bligh this is sufficient for evry purpose and you know the Sextant to be a good one"

The Boat was now veerd astern and several things thrown overboard to make room, having on board 19 hands. When the boat was put to rights Mr. Bligh begd for a Musquett But this was refused, and Mr. Christian ordered four Cutlasses to be handed in, and I handed in 25 or 26 four pound pieces of Pork, & two Gourds of water. Several other things were handed in over the stern, and as the ship made little way they got ready for rowing and were Cast off, when they Stood in for the land about 8 or 9 Leagues dist. It was now about 8 oClock in the Morning, the large Cutter was hoisted in and Stowd, and the Arms Collected and put into the Chest when the whole that appeard were 10 Musquets, 2 Pistols and 2 Cutlasses, the Pistols had been taken from the Masters Cabbin and were loaded with powder for the Purpose of firing the Guns

The behaviour of the Officers on this Occasion was dastardly beyond description none of them ever making the least attempt to rescue the ship which would have been effected had any attempt been made by one of them as some of those who were under arms did not know what they were about, and Robt. Lamb who I found Centry at the fore Hatchway when I first came on Deck went away in the Boat & Isaac Martin had laid his arms down & gone into the boat but had been Ordered out again.

Their passive obedience to Mr. Christians orders even surprized himself and he said immediately after the boat was gone that something more than fear had posessd them to suffer themselves to be sent away in such a manner without offering to make resistance.

When the Boat Put off Mr. Stuart and Mr. Heywood who had been Confined in their birth Came up and Mr. Christian related the Cause of this sad affair to the following effect—Finding himself much hurt by the treatment he had received from Mr Bligh, he had determined to quit the ship the preceding evening, and informed the Boatswain, Carpenter, Mr. Stuart and Mr. Hayward of his resolution who supplied Him with some Nails, Beads and part of a roast pig with some other articles which He put into a bag which He got from Mr. Hayward (the bag was produced and I knew it to be the same which I had made for Mr. Hayward some time before), the bag was put into the Clue of Robt. Tinklers hammock, where he found it at Night; but the Matter was then Smothered, & passd off—he also made fast some staves to a stout Plank which lay on the larboard Gangway, with which he intended to make his escape; but finding he could not effect it in the first and Middle Watches, as the people were all a stirring, he went to sleep about half past three in the Morning. When Mr. Stuart calld him to relieve the Watch he had not Slept long, and was much out of order, & Stuart begd him not to attempt swimming away, saying the People are ripe for any thing, this made a forcible impression on his mind & finding that Mr. Hayward the Mate of his Watch (with whom he refused to discourse) soon went to sleep on the Arm Chest which stood between the Guns, and Mr. Hallet not making his appearance, He at once resolved to seize the ship and disclosing his Intention to Quintrell and Martin, they Calld up Churchill, and Thompson who put the business in practice and with Smith, Williams & McCoy He went to Coleman and demanded the Keys of the Arm Chest (which Coleman the Armourer always kept) saying he wanted a Musquet to shoot a shark which happened to Come alongside; and finding Mr. Hallet asleep on the Arm Chest he roused him and sent him on Deck; the keys were Instantly procured and His party armd, as were all the rest who stood in his way, without their knowing for what purpose. In the Mean time Norman had Waked Mr. Hayward to look after the shark, at which He was busy when Mr. Christian Came up the fore Hatchway with his party, he left Thompson to take Care of the Arm Chest, arming Burket and Lamb at the Hatch way and Commanding Mr. Hayward and Mr. Hallet to be silent He proceeded to Secure Lieut. Bligh, whom He brought on Deck placing two Centrys, at the Masters Cabbin door to keep him in, and the Gunner & Mr. Neilson in the Cockpit and proceeded as before described

About 9 oClock a breeze sprang up and sails were trimmd when asking the Oppinion of His party, it was agreed to steer for Tahiti & Stood to ye S.W. When Mr. Christian had related as above I then Recollected seeing him Make the staves fast to the Plank the night before, and hearing the Boatswain say to the Carpenter "It wont do to night", and afterwards seeing Mr. Stuart and Mr Christian several times up and down the Fore Cock pit where the Boatswains and Carpenters Cabbins were, and where Mr. C. seldom or ever went–

At Noon Tofua bore NE 10 Leagues the Boat out of sight under the Land.

Mr. Christian having as beforesaid determined on his Rout Hauld to the Southward in order to proceed to Tahiti toutching at Tubuai[59] in his Way, and Having divided what men that remained on board into *two* watches, he Appointed G. Stuart to the Charge of one, and kept the other himself, and ordered Me to take Charge of the Stores and Act as Boatswain, Thos. McIntosh as Carpenter and Jno. Mills as Gunner, however this is not to be considered as a point of authority and was for no other purpose but that of taking Care of the Stores and that He might have some person to Call on in these departments evry one doing their duty alike and obeying his Orders—and Here it may not be Improper to explain the Affair more Clearly by giving a list of those who went in the Boat as well as what remained

	Those who went in the Boat were			Those who remaind in the Ship were	
1	Wm. Bligh Lieut. & Commander		1	Fletcher Christian	Act. Lieut.
	Jno. Fryer	Master		Geo. Stuart	Mid
	Wm. Elphinstone	Mr's Mte		Edward Young	"
	Wm. Cole	Boatsn		Peter Heywood	"
5	Wm. Purcill	Carpentr	5	Jas. Morrison	Boats Mte
	Wm. Peckover	Gunner		Thos. McIntosh	Carps Mte
	Thos. Hayward	Mid		Jno. Mills	Guns Mte
	Jno. Hallet	Mid		Chas. Norman	Carps Mte
	Jno. Samuel	Clerk		Isaac Martin	Ab
10	Thos. Ledward	Surgns Mte	10	Chas. Churchill	Mastr at Arms
	Robt. Tinkler	Mid		Josh. Coleman	Armourer
	Jno. Norton	Qr. Master		Willm. Muspratt	Capts Steward
	Peter Linkletter	"		Jno. Sumner	Ab
	Geo. Simpson	do. Mt		Jno. Williams	"
15	Lawce. Labogue	Sail Mkr	15	Jno. Millard	"
	Jno. Smith	Capts Cook		Wm. McCoy	"

	Thos. Hall	Ships Cook		Mattw. Thompson	”
	Robt. Lamb	Butcher		Mathw. Quintrell	”
19	David Nelson	Botanist		Alexr. Smith	”
	in all 19		20	Thos. Burkett	2nd Gunner
				Heny. Heidbrandt	Cooper
				Michl. Byrn (blind)	Ab
				Richd. Skinner	Masts Sert
				Thos. Ellison (a boy)	Ab
			26	Wm. Brown	Botants Assistant
				in all Twenty five	

By these Lists it would appear that Mr. Christian had the strongest party, which however was not the Case as Lieut. Bligh himself must, and has already acknowledged, but the Fact was that none seemd Inclined to dispute the superiority, and Mr. Christian at the Head of Eight or Nine Men was permitted to proceed as before desribed, and even after the Boat was gone some of them hardly knew what part they had acted in the Business–

Mr. Christian now finding Himself Master of the Ship ordered the Plants to be thrown overboard to Clear the Cabbin[60] which was finishd by the 1st or 2nd of May and the Effects of the Officers were Collected into it with the Tahiti & Friendly Island Cloth & Curiositys, and Himself took possession of Mr. Blighs Cabbin.

As I had reason to beleive from the Countenance of Affairs that the Ship might yet be recovered if a party could be formd and as I knew that several on board were not at all pleased with their situation, I fixd on a Plan for that purpose and soon gaind several to back my oppinion, when We purposed to take the Opportunity of the Night the ship should anchor at Tahiti when we could easily get rid of those we did not like by putting them on shore, and that in all probability our design might be favoured by an extra allowance of Grog. These matters being settled I had no doubt but that evry one would stand to the test; and to prevent the others from knowing our design affected a shyness towards each other, but I soon found to my unspeakable surprize that Mr. Christian was acquainted with our Intentions, some of his party overhearing some part of the Business—but as he was not positive how many were Conserned he took no further Notice then threatning Coleman that he should be left on shore to Tubuai till the Ship returnd from Tahiti and Got the Arm Chest into the Cabbin taking the Keys from Coleman who had always kept them; they were now given to Churchill who made his bed on the Chest and each of Mr. Christian's party were Armd with a Brace of Pistols, Mr. Christian himself never going without a Pistol in his pocket, the same which Lieut. Bligh formerly used, and a sharp look out was kept by his party one of which took care to make a third when they saw any two in Conversation

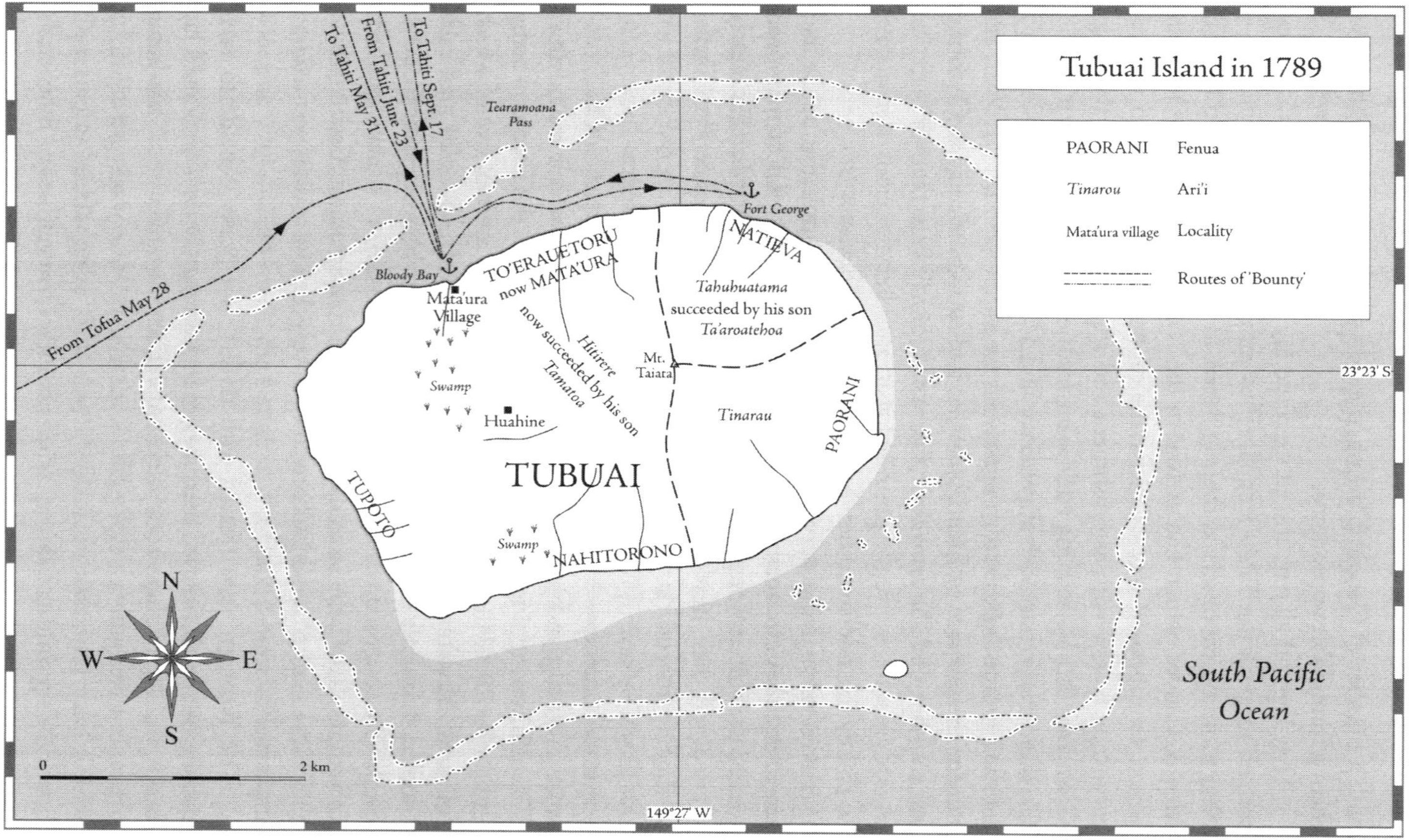
Tubuai Island in 1789
PAORANI Fenua
Tinarou Ari'i
Mata'ura village Locality
Routes of 'Bounty'
To Tahiti May 31
From Tahiti June 23
To Tahiti Sept. 17
Tearamoana Pass
Fort George
Bloody Bay
From Tofua May 28
TO'ERAUETORU now MATA'URA
Mata'ura Village
NATIEVA
Tahuhuatama succeeded by his son Ta'aroatehoa
Hitirere now succeeded by his son Tamatoa
Mt. Taiata
Swamp
Huahine
Tinarau
PAORANI
TUBUAI
TUPOTO
Swamp
NAHITORONO
23°23' S
N
W
E
S
0
2 km
149°27' W
South Pacific Ocean

Mr. Christian gave him two or three smart stripes with a ropes end and sent Him into the Canoe, the others who had not been Idle followed Him as did the Weomen which we did not think prudent to detain, when they put off those in the Canoes began to shew their Weapons which till now they Had kept conceald, brandishing them with many threatning Gestures, and one of them Getting hold of the Buoy cut it away, and was paddling off with it, when he was observed by Mr. Christian who fired a Musket at Him, & a four pounder being fired with Grape, they all paddled to the Shore, the Boats were now mand to follow them, but on Coming to the Beach the landing was vigourously disputed by them plying the Boats smartly with Stones, not seeming to pay any attention to the Musquets till they found some fall, when they took to the Wood and in a few Moments were all out of sight. As they Had left several Canoes on the Beach Mr. Christian ordered them to be towd off, and made fast astern of the Ship, thinking to make them Instrumental in making Peace, but the Wind Coming to the NW, and the Canoes filling, they broke adrift in the night and drove on shore and as the Natives made no further Appearance they were sufferd to remain we found a number of Cords in the Canoes which we supposd were intended for to bind us with,[5] had they succeeded in their plan, and this we afterwards found to be the purpose for which they were brought, this Bay lies on the NW part of the Island abreast of the Opening (the only one in the Reef) described by Capt. Cook, and we Calld it from this time Bloody Bay[6]

on the Morning of the 30th the Natives not Appearing, the Boats were Mand and Arm'd and went round to the East end of the Island Carrying a White flag in the Bow of One and a Union Jack in the other. Mr. Christian landed in Several places leaving presents of hatchets &c. in their Houses, but Saw none of the Natives, tho He made diligent search, and was forced to return without seeing one[7]

Next Morning the 31st some of them came down, and hauld the Canoes up at which they were not disturbed they retired before the Boat Could reach the Shore,—a Boat was sent to land a young Goat & two

Figure 5. Map of Tubuai. Courtesy of Nick Keenleyside at Outline Draughting and Graphics Ltd.

pigs which were sickly and returned without seeing any of ye Natives and the anchors being Weighd We put to Sea Steering to the NNE for Tahiti

Mr. Christian having formd a resolution of settling on this Island, determined to return again as soon as he could procure sufficient stock of Hogs Goats & Poultry of which we Saw None on the Island, tho Bread Cocoa Nuts & Plantains were to appearance Plenty, to this he was the more Inclined as the Island was scarce 18 Miles in Circumference, and he supposed the Inhabitants to be but few, which he had hopes of bringing into friendship either by perswasion, or force;[8] and as the Anchorage for Ships is not enticeing, he Judged that none would make Choise of this Island while they Could reach Tahiti and that He would be permitted to live here in peace, which was all he Now desired knowing that he had taken such steps as had for ever debar'd him from returning to England or any Civilized Place,[9] & dream't of nothing but Settling at Tubuai

However I cannot say that ever I agreed in Oppinion with Mr. Christian with respect to the plan he had formd nor did I ever form a favourable Idea of the Natives of Tubuai whose savage aspect & behaviour could not gain favour in the Eyes of any Man in his senses, but was fully capable of Creating a distate in any one–

On the Passage He Gave orders that no man should tell the name of the Island, or mention It to the Natives and if any person was found to mention the real name he would punish Him severely and declared if any Man diserted he would shoot him as soon he was brought back, which promise evry one knew he had in his power to perform and having appointed his own Party to keep Constant Guard, he distributed the trade amongst all Hands disiring them to make the Best Market they Could, as it was to be the last they would ever have the Opportunity of Making. He also made several distributions of the Cloaths &c which had been left by the Officers & Men who went in the Boat, these were made out in lotts by Churchill & were drawn for by ticketts, but it always happend that Mr. Christian's party Were always better served then these who were thought to be disaffected, however as they had different views No Notice was taken of it at present—

On the 6th of June we anchord in Matavai Bay when the Natives flockd on board in great Numbers; they were glad to see us and Enquired where the rest were, and what had brought us back so soon, where we had left the Plants as they knew our stay had been too Short to have reachd home from the account we had formerly given them of the distance, to all these Questions Mr. Christian answerd them that We had met Captn. Cook who had taken Mr. Bligh and the others with the Plants & the Longboat and had sent us for Hogs Goats &c for a New Settlement which the King had sent him to make which he described to be on New Holland,[10] this being made known to the People none dared to Contradict what he said knowing if they said any thing Contrary it would soon reach his ears, as the Tahitians are not remarkable for Keeping secrets but if this had not been the Case there were few who Could explain the Matter properly as they were not so well versed in the language.

While we lay here the Armourer was set to work to make trade, and Churchill & Myself were sent on Shore to purchace Hogs Goats &c. Meanwhile Mr. Christian intertaind the Chiefs on board plying them with Wine & Arrack of which they became very fond—and evry one on board was busey purchacing Stock & Provisions for them and although the general oppinion when we saild before was that we had impovrishd the Island we were now Convinced that they Had not Missd what we got as we now found the Country full of Hogs and they which before had been kept out of sight and they appeard now better able to supply a Fleet then they seemd before to supply our single Ship and the demand for Iron Work increased so fast, that the Armourer Could not supply them tho Constantly employd and there was a tolerable good stock ready made found in the Ship which had not been expended during our former Stay–

On the 10th Willm. McCoy, being Centinal, fired upon a number of the natives who throngd the Ganway and did not get so fast out of His way as he thought proper, but as no damage was done no notice was taken of it, and on the night of the 14th Churchill observing a Canoe ahead of the Ship haild her but getting no answer he fired at them and they paddled off

It may here be observed that Mr. Christians account of Himself passd very well with the Natives, who had not yet been informd of Captn. Cooks Death, Mr. Bligh having given orders that no person should mention his death, but tell the Natives that He was yet alive in England and that He would probably Come again to Tahiti, and as Mr. Christian informd them that He would Come to Tahiti as soon as he had settled the Country which he Calld Aitutaki,[11] they were perfectly satisfied, and as they were

fresh they went and we saw them no more which however Mr. Christian though no great loss as he never intended to go to Sea any More

On the 8th of July we reachd the place appointed & Moord the Ship with both bowers (head & stem) in 3 fathoms, the Eastermost point of the Island in Sight bearing E S E and the Westermost Key N b E, off shore half a Cables length, unbent the sails and Struck the Top Gallt Yards & Masts–

On the 10th Mr. Christian went on Shore to make Choice of His Ground to build a Fort on, and pitchd on the Spot abreast of the ship and received permission from the Chief Ta'aroatehoa (Who Met him there) to make what use of it he thought proper–

On his return on board he found that Jno. Sumner and Mathew Quintrell were gone on shore without leave and did not return till Next Morning, when he Calld them aft and enquired how they came to go on shore without his leave they answerd "the Ship is Moord and we are now our own Masters, upon which he Clap'd a Pistol to one of their heads (which he always kept in his pocket) and said "I'll let you know who is Master," and ordered them both legs in Irons, this resolute behaviour convinced them that He was not to be playd with, and when they were brought up next day, they beg'd Pardon and promised to behave better for the future on which they were released.

However to prevent the like happening again he gave liberty for two hands to sleep on shore each night and as many as pleased to go on shore evry Sunday. He also made a distribution of red feathers to all hands,[15] but some of them being Missd out of His Cabbin, Thos. Ellison who waited on him and was frequently there, was charged with having taken them, on which he brought to the Ganway stripd and tied up but as he persisted in his Innocence and no person having seen him with any, he was Cast off–

Having ordered that of the Liberty men one boats Crew should go evry Sunday to the Keys, to see the Stock, things were settled for the Present, and the forge got up, the Armourer being set to work to make Iron rammers for the Musquets, the wooden ones being mostly broken, and when these were Compleated He set to work to alterd the Junk Axes and make them fit for Cutting Wood & felling trees

As soon as the Axes were ready, the following regulations were made, W Brown & one Tahitian to Clear a piece of Ground and plant Yams, Josh, Coleman & Willm. McCoy to work at the Forge, Making Spades, hoes & Mattocks, Heny. Heildbrandt to Cook the provisions, Michl. Byrn & Thos. Ellison with some of the Tahiti Boys to take Care of the Boats, and the rest to go on shore Armd to Work, the arms to be left under the Care of a Central in a Convenient place while the others Clear'd the Ground, one boat to return to the Ship and the other to be kept at a Grapnell near the Beach

On the 18th we went on Shore where we were met by the Chief & some of the friends who presented Mr. Christian with two young Plantain trees, and two roots of 'Ava by way of a Peace Offering,[16] & the Ground being Measured out for the Fort posession was taken by turning a Turf and hoisting the Union Jack on a Staff in the Place. On this occasion an extra Allowance of Grog was drank and the Place Calld Fort George,[17] and finding the Place overrun with rats several Cats were brought on shore and let loose among them

While we were Employed in this business we were alarmed by a Great Noise of hedious shrieks & yells which we supposed at first to be a War Cry and took to our Arms sending some of the Tahitians to enquire what it was, who soon returned and informed us that it proceeded from a Funeral Ceremony, it being the Custom in this Island when a Man of any rank dies for all his friends & relations and all who wish him well to attend his funeral, when the Body is put into the Grave, a Priest makes a long Prayer and the bystanders rend the Air with horrid Cries, Cutting their Heads and breasts with Shells, and smearing their body with the Blood;[18] after which the Grave is filld up and they depart leaving the near relations of the deceased to enjoy their Mourning in private—having had this information we returned to our work–

The Ground being Cleared the Fort was laid out in a quaderangular form, Measuring 100 yards on each square outside of the ditch, width of the Ditch 18 feet, depth 20 feet from the top of the Works, thickness of the wall at the base 18 feet, on the top 12, with a Drawbridge on the North side fronting the Beach; on this the Ships ordnance was to be Mounted in the following Manner, one four Pounder on each Corner & on each face two Swivels with two for reserve to be shifted as occasions might require by which means two four Pounders & four Swivels Could be brought to bear in any direction and in Some three four Pounders & Six Swivels

Evry thing being settled, we proceeded the Work tho not a man knew anything Fortification, some Cut stakes others made Battins some Cut

Sods & brought to hand some built, and others Wrought in the ditch, the Carpenters made barrows & Cut timber for the Gates & Drawbridge, & the work began to rise apace. Nor was Mr. Christian an Idle Spectator for He always took a part in the Most laborious part of the Work, and half a Pint of Porter was served twice a day extra–

We Continued at work without any interruption from the Natives who visited us in numbers evry day bringing provisions nor did they now seem so much inclined to thieving as at first, the only thing they fancied was red feathers—and the Cocks with red Heckles became a valuable article being esteemd far superior to the Black or Grey ones, the Natives seeming to view them with particular attention, but Iron Work or our Cloaths they held in no esteem, & although they saw us using our axes, & other Iron tools, they set no value on them and never seemd inclined to have them in their possession, for which we were no way sorry,[19] and as their Cloth is Glazed so as to turn rain they preferd it to ours,[20] and would sooner have a Piece of fine Tahiti Cloth then the Best article of Clothing we had, however our Tahitians were not so ignorant, for they knew which was best, and tho these people preferd their Stone Adzes, to our Axes, they would not tho they never attempted to alter their Oppinion

On the 20th of August Mr. Christian & some others saild round the Island in the large Cutter, he landed on South side and was well received by a Chief Call'd Hitirere and was invited on Shore at several places which the foulness of the Shore prevented him from accepting. When they got off the East end, Tinarau sent a Man off with a peace offering of a Young Plaintain tree & a root of 'Ava, and an invitation to land. He received the offering but the Shore being rocky he could not come within 3/4ths of a Mile of the Beach with the boat, and was forced to decline the invitation and return to the Ship

On the 25th, the Tahiti Men & boys were sent in quest of some Cocoa Nuts, but were set upon by some of the Natives, who drove them off, and nearly Killd one of the Men with a Stone, this News being brought to the Fort by the Boys, Mr. Christian ordered the Party to Arms, and Marchd to the place where a Number of the Natives were in arms—but two Musquets being fired amongst them they fled, and we returned to the Fort—Next day we learnt that one Man was killd but as they had Carried him off we saw nothing of Him

After this We remaind quiet some days, but as the people were fond of sleeping on shore, some of them were decoyd by the Weomen into Tinaraus district where they were Strip'd; and Alexr. Smith was kept prisoner at Tinaraus house, As soon as Mr. Christian was informd of it, he resolved to punnish the Offenders, and Marchd the Party into Tinaraus district, but Tinarau fled at his Approach. When he arrived at Tinaraus house the Woman with whom Smith had been, Conducted him to the Place without any Cloaths but his Shirt, The rest being taken away by Tinaraus Men Mr. Christian then sent several Messingers to Tinarau desiring him to return the things, and make friends both of which He refused, and after waiting some Hours, & sending repeated Messingers, who all returnd with the same answer, He resolved to burn the House which was done accordingly, but before it was set on fire we took out some Clubs and Spears, & two Curious Carved Images of their Household Gods, which were decorated with Pearl Shells, Human Hair teeth & Nails cut in a very Curious Manner, and round them was placed a kind of Grove of red feathers from the tail of the Tropic birds, as Mr. Christian supposed these Images to be of Value to the Owner, he ordered them to be secured;[21] hoping that the return of them might help to make the peace & the House being now in Flames He returned to the Ship The young Woman who had been Smiths Companion came with him on board of Her own Accord saying that Her Country men would use Her ill for her friendship towards him, if She stayed on Shore among them, and when She found some Companions on board, She was perfectly satisfied and pleased.

We returned to Work again and tho it did not seem to go on as well as at first, it still Continued to get forward, & by the 1st of Septr the Gate posts were fixed & 3/4ths of the Walls Completed and on the 2nd Came Tinarau with a great number of attendants, loaded with baskets of Provisions, which he presented to Mr. Christian with a peace offering, begging at the same time that His Household Gods might be restored, which Mr. Christian promised to do on Condition that he restored the things his Men had taken away, and that He would promise, not to use any of His Men ill when they came into his district, all which he readily agreed to, and ordered some 'Ava to be prepared of which he desired Mr. Christian to partake which he refused, upon which He got up in a passion and departed abruptly and was followed by His attendants the reason of which was that he found Mr. Christian aware of His treachery, his party having come Armed till within a small distance of the Works where they hid their Spears, but one of the Tahiti boys having seen them, informed Mr. Christian, who Ordered the party to arms, which Tinarau perceiving thought fit to depart without taking his leave as he saw that Mr. Christian had ordered his Men on the top of the Works Where they were in Good order to receive him—the boy being sent privately off to the Ship with orders to Coleman, as soon as he saw them Appear on the Beach armed, He fired a four Pounder Shotted among them, at which they Fled. The Shot did no other damage then passing through a house where it Cut away a rafter to which a Man was hanging a Gourd of Water, and at which he was so terrified that He left the House, as did all who saw it being alike surprised, the Shot being lost and the House not in sight of the Ship, they Could hardly be perswaded that it came from her, but readily believed it to be something supernatural, and could not be perswaded to return to the house to live Judging it unsafe–

On the 3rd Came Old Tahuhuatama with His Son Ta'aroatehoa Mr. Christians friend, & Daughters, one of which was the young woman who had Come on board at our first anchoring and was Calld 'Aiata,[22] with a number of attendants loaded with provisions which were presented to Mr. Christian and at the request of the Old Man the young weomen performed a dance beating time and singing and went through the performance with much regularity after which the Tahiti Weomen entertaind them with a dance in turn; when they took their leave Mr. Christian invited them to see a Heiva Next day, which they readily accepted and before they arrived in the Morning two of the Weomen were Neatly dressd, and two Men in Pares or the Mourning dress of Tahiti and when the Company were arrived they were entertaind with a Heiva after the Manner of the Society Isles at which they seemd Highly pleased, they were quite taken with the Dress of the Weomen, and appeard astonishd at the Pare's.[23] this was conducted by the Tahitians during which time the party was under arms

Mr. Christian now began to talk of taking the Masts out and dismanteling the Ship when he intended to erect houses and live on shore, and as I had some hopes that I Could reach Tahiti in the large Cutter, I spoke to G. Stuart on the Affair, who told me that He and P. Heywood had formed the same plan; and as I knew that after the Masts were out I could put it out their power to get them in again by destroying the purchace Blocks & fall, and if we reachd Tahiti were in no danger of being pursued I then

Figure 8. *Parae,* Tahiti [Z 28418]. Reproduced with permission of University of Cambridge Museum of Archaeology and Anthropology

advised him to get the Cutter repaired but He said Mr. Christian had said he would not Have the Boats repaird till he was on Shore; and to prevent any suspicion, we had better say nothing about it and was determined to take her as she was; and as We had some Reason too to suppose that others were of the same way of thinking with ourselves we resolved to take the first Opportunity and provided accordingly, but Providence ordered things better and We had no need to make this rash attempt, tho the passage was short and it might perhaps be made with safety in 5 or 6 days, yet had we the Chance to Meet with bad weather our Crazey boat[24] would certainly have made us a Coffin which we did not now foresee

Mr. Christians party finding that the Natives still kept their weomen from amongst us tho they had no objection to their Sleeping with them at their own houses, began to Murmur, and Insisted that Mr. Christian would head them, and bring the Weomen in to live with them by force and refusing to do any work till evry man had a Wife, and as Mr. Christians desire was to perswade rather than force them, He positively refused to have any thing to do with such an absurd demand. Three Days were Spent in debate, and having nothing to employ themselves in, they demanded more Grog This he also refused, when they broke the lock of the Spirit room and took it by force–

Mr. Christian to keep them in temper ordered double allowance to be served evry day, but all to No purpose; and finding all His endeavours in vain he on the 10th Calld all Hands aft to ask their opinion of what was the best plan to proceed on. When it was soon Moved that we should go to Tahiti and there Seperate, where they might get Weomen without force, this proposal at first overruled but was Carried the next day, on a Call for a Shew of Hands, Sixteen appeard for Tahiti; When it was agreed that those went on Shore should have Arms Amunition and part of evry thing on the Ship, the Ship to be left in Charge of Mr. Christian in a proper Condition to go to Sea, with Her sails Tackld & furniture; and evry thing being settled We began to get ready for Sea filling the Water and bending the Sails &ca–

A party were now sent to get Stock sufficient and search for the Cow which we had not seen since she was landed, but they were set upon by the Natives who beat and plundered them, and sent them to tell Mr. Christian that they would serve him the same way—this happened on the 12th when we found that the Tubuai Woman had returned to her friends without giving any previous Notice–

as the Party returned without their errand Mr. Christian ordered 20 Men to be armed on the 13th to go in quest of stock, and to Chastise the Offenders, taking the Nine Tahiti Men and four Boys, one of which always carried the Jack; the party had not proceeded above a mile from the landing before they were surrounded by about 700 of the Natives, who had formd in ambush into which we got before we perceived them. They were all armed with Clubbs Spears & Stones, and fought with more fury then Judgement, otherwise the whole party must have fallen into their hands, However the case was Otherwise and after many Obstinate and furious efforts, they Gave Ground and retired with great loss; and the Stock was Collected without farther trouble–

As we had some reason to think that they would be troublesome, each man was provided accordingly with 24 Rounds of Amunition six of which contained one Musquet and two pistol balls, and Hitihiti being an excellent Shot was Armed with a Musquet, the rest of the Tahitians were unarmed, when we landed at the Fort we were Met by Tahuhuatama, Ta'aroatehoa & Ta'aroamaeva, his younger Brother, with Several others, their friends, who informed Mr. Christian that Tinarau had armed a Number of Men and was determined to dispute his right to the Stock. Mr. Christian then desired his friends to remain at the Fort least any of them should suffer by Mistake, he drew up the party, placing one Tahitian (Who Now Armd themselves with Clubbs from our friends) between two of us and having given the Necessary precautions to all, Marchd in Silence and good order through the Wood to Tinaraus district. We had scarcely got a Mile from the Fort when we Got into a Hollow path beset with thick bushes on each side, and orders were given to keep a good look out, and Burkett, thinking that He heard something stir in the Bush, stepd to look, and receivd a wound in the left side with a Spear, the Tahitian who was next to Burkett instantly leveled the Man, and Seized His Spear; and before Burkett Could either Speak or fire his piece, they started up in a Swarm all round us, rushing on us with great fury & horrid yells, on which we instantly halted and facing different ways, gave a smart fire, which we repeated several times with good effect. Notwithstanding which they kept pouring in from all quarters, seeming not to regard death or Danger. We now found it Necessary to retreat, to a rising ground at a Small distance in our rear, and by this time the Tahitians were all Armed with the Enemies long Spears and behaved Manfully—when we gained the rising ground they follow'd up with redoubled fury dispising us only a handful to them, tho many fell as they approachd, by our Constant fire; however the Bush being thick above us, they plyed us smartly from thence and Several of the Tahitians being wounded and Mr. Christian having in his hurry hurt his hand on his own bayonet we thought it prudent to retreat to a Taro Ground at the distance of about 200 yards which we effected in good order, keeping up a Constant fire to Cover our retreat, retreating and firing alternately till we gaind the Clear ground, and having posted ourselves on the Banks which intersected the Taro Ground at right Angles, we halted to receive them. They followed Close till we were out of the thicket plying us with vollies of stones, but did not like to quit the Bush, however some of the Most daring attempted to rally their Men, and lead them on to renew the attack, one in particular (appearing to be a Chief) came out inviting his Men to follow, and making many menacing gestures he was singled out and Shot tho at a Good distance, as were several others who attempted to follow him, this proved a Check on the others who observed that all who Came in Sight were either killd or wounded and they gave ground and retreated to some distance—in the Mean time Burket growing faint, & Skinner having disabled his Musquet by putting the Cartridge in Whole, was ordered to take Burketts and Convoy him to the Boat.

We staid some time on the Ground but finding that they were not inclined to try us again, we gave them three Cheers, on which they fled and left us Masters of the Field, leaving their dead at our disposal when our Tahitians loaded themselves with such spoils as they thought proper, Chiefly their Clubs & Spears, of which they were very fond–

And here it may not be improper to observe that before we quitted the Field one of the Tahiti boys desired leave to Cut out the Jaw bones of the killd to hand round the quarters of the Ship as Trophies, which he said would strike others with Terrour, and was much displeased when his request was denied;[25] and it was only the fear of being put to death that prevented him from setting about it, begging at least that he might be suffered to take one for himself.

None of the Others seemd inclined that way as they were perhaps better pleased with the plunder and saw that it was Contrary to our inclination

When we returned to the Fort we were Met by the Old Chief and his freinds who expressd much Joy at our Success; and here also Skinner Joind us, having sent Burkett on board—a Party were now sent to Gether in What Stock we wanted, and the Cow was brought to the Fort without Opposisition–

When we Came on board we found that Burkett had got his wound dressd which was in a fair way of doing well, the Spear having struck against one of his ribbs but wanted force to break it and in a short time it got heald—however this affair gave us a very mean oppinion of our bayonets tho Several had fallen by them who always broke the Neck of the Bayonet & left us the Socket on our Musquet while the Blade remaind in their Bodys—our Amunition being all we had to depend on, without which they would have been an Over match for us Man for Man their

Spears being so long that our bayonets could be of little or no use,—we observed that tho their Onset was furious and without order, yet evry party of 18 or 20 men had a leading man who appeard to have some authority and to whose orders they paid some regard–

On the 14th we killd the Cow which proved excellent Meat—This Evening Came on board the young Chief Ta'aroamaeva and two of His Friends, who informd us that 60 Men had been killd; & 6 Weomen, who were supplying them with Spears & Stones, and a great Number Wounded among the killd, were several of Note, and Tinaraus brother, who had been killd by Mr. Christian himself—he said he had been so much Mr. Christian's friend that if He staid on shore, he should be killd. Mr. Christian told him that He was going to Tahiti at which he seemd rejoiced, and askd if he would let him and his two Friends go with Him, to which Mr. Christian agreed and they expressd Much Satisfation, and having filld sufficient fresh water we weighd our anchors on the 17th and dropt down to the Opening without much trouble the Ship being much lighter than before, and having got clear of the Reef we lay by & filld Saltwater to keep her on her legs and at noon made sail, leaving Tubuai well Stockd with Hogs Goats Fowles Dogs & Cats, the Former of which were increased to Four times the Number we landed, but before I take my leave of the Island it may be proper to give some account of it and its Inhabitants.

Tubuai lies between 22° and 23° South and about 209° East Longd, is about 6 Miles in length from East to West, and about 22 miles in Circumference, being surrounded by a reef, a full mile from the Shore, and on the East part near 3 miles, having but one break or entrance on the N W part where the passage is but indifferent; tho in some places there is 4 or 5 fathoms—Within the Reef are six small keys Cover'd with Wood, Chiefly the Toa, a hard Wood, of which, the Natives make their Clubs & Spears—Four of these Islands or keys are on the NE Part and the others on the SE–

The Island is Mountainous with a border of Flat land running almost quite round of a Mile or a Mile and a half wide, great part of which is Covered with trees and underwood, which makes it difficult to pass by any other road then the Beach, to the Eastward the land is fertile and the low land broader then on either side, but the West end is rocky and barren. Off this part the Water is in general very shoal, and the reef nearest the Shore—the lowland is in general Coral Sand, or rock Covered with a Fine Black Mould which in many places is not more than a Foot thick tho in some places it runs to a good depth—Near the Foot of the Hills, are Numbers of large Flat Stones and the earth is of a reddish Collour Covered with Fern, Reeds & Bamboo and on the top the ridges, are Naked rocks of hard brown Stone, tho the water is Shoal in some parts, yet in others there was no bottom with 40 fathom of line

It produces Breadfruit, Cocoa Nuts, Yams, Taro, Plantains, and almost every thing Common to the Society Islands and the reef affords Plenty of Fish and large Turtle

The Cloth tree here grows to a larger Size then in the Society Isles, tho they do not Cultivate it; they have Most of the Trees in Common with the Other Islands, they have also a Species of the Primrose. The Island is Watered with innumerable rivulets from the hills, which being bankd up for the Cultivation of Taro, affords Shelter to the Wild Ducks, which are here in plenty & affords also plenty of Fine Eels Shrimps prawns & a fish like the Millers thumb[26]–

The Island is full of Inhabitants for its size and my Contain 3000 souls,[27] their Collour is nearly the same as that of the Society Islanders; but they are more robust and have a more savage appearance, and this is hieghten'd by the Turmerick & the oil that they Use to Collour their Cloth, which gives them a Yellow disagreeable look[28]–

The Men wear their Hair and beards in different forms as they please, and the Young Weomen wear their hair Long flowing in ringlets to their Waist and dress it with the White leaves of The Fara[29] or Palm like ribbands and Odoriferous Flowers. They also make necklaces of the Seeds of the ripe palm apple & flowers Elegantly disposed; which not only Sets their persons off to advantage but afford a Continual Nosegay[30] to themselves and all who sit near them and they are in General handsomer Weomen then any we saw in those seas—nor do they make use of the Lewd Motions or gestures in their dances so much in Use in the Society Isles tho they are equally good at that diversion and move with a becoming grace, and their dances seem Nearly those of the Friendly then the Society Isles–

Children of Both sexes go naked till they are 5 or 6 years old; the Boys have their Heads mostly Shorn; but the Girls hair is Sufferd to grow long which, as it is not of a strong Wiory nature but flows in ringlets, when they arrive at 14 or 15 sets them off to much advantage,—the Old weomen Cut off their Hair when they Mourn the loss of their relations but we observed no marks of this kind on any that appeared Capable of Child bearing. They never kill their Children here as at the Society Islands, nor do they know any thing of Societys;[31] they are Careful of them and use them very tenderly.

They have no Marriage Ceremony, but Join and live as Man & Wife while they agree; nor is virtue deemd of any consequence among them. While they agree they live on the Estate of either, & if they part after having Children the Man takes the boys and the Woman the Girls, & each retire to their own estate, the Children being No Obstacle being no hindrance of their getting other partners.

They Have no Tattowing[32] nor do they Cut the Forskin but keep away all superfluous hairs from the Body; as they Seldom bathe in the Sea they are but indifferent Swimmers or Divers, the rivers being too Shallow for that exercise and few or none of the Weomen know how to swim at all–

Their Dress is similar to that of The Society Isles & both Sexes wear pearl shells in form of a Gorget with Collars of Hair Neatly plaited, these shells are Common but as we Saw No pearls, it is possible, as they always find them on the reef frequently dry, that the Oysters may loose their pearls while they lay open and half dead with the heat of the Sun after the Surf has thrown them up[33]–

Their Temper appears in many respects Similar to the Indians of North America then any of their Neighbours; they seem rather Serious then lively and appear to be always ruminating on some Important business

When they go abroad, they have each a large piece Glazed Cloth of a Purple Collour which they Carry folded up, except it happens to rain, when they wear it by way of Cloak; if the rain Continues they Strip & tye a Girdle of Grass & leaves about their Middle; if they have no matting on, and Wrapping their Cloaths up in their Cloak proceed home, or to the next house when they have Dry Cloaths to put on–

Their Cloth and Matting are made from the Same Materials and after the same manner but is much Coarser, but they have a Method of dying & Glazing it so as to make it Turn the rain and Scenting it with sweet flowers & perfumes, they prefer the Cloth plant or Chinese Paper Mulberry to any other tho they have several other trees & Shrubbs fit for that purpose but this is the most durable;[34] they do not bleach it so well as the Society

Figure 9. Pearlshell necklace, Tubuai, Austral Islands [990.2.1477]. Reproduced with permission of Musée de l'Histoire Naturelle, Lille

Islanders and their principal Collours are purple, Red & Yellow, the latter they extract from the Turmerick which grows in abundance here, but we could not learn how they prepared the others

Their Houses are built of an Oval form and at a distance resemble a long hay stack, They are from 40 to 80 feet long, and from 15 to 30 broad and about as much in height—the ridge is a Strong Beam, supported by two or more pillars, Chiefly Toa, and the Sides and top are a frame of Strong timbers Squared to 5 or 6 Inches and firmly lashd together, the Thatch is neatly made and Well put on is of the Fara or Palm leaves and will last several years; the Thatch reaches the Ground on the Back & Ends and on the front within about 6 feet, the Front is Closed with Timber

Neatly Carved & painted with a redish Collour and has several Openings about 4 feet high & 2½ Wide which have shutters, answering the double purpose of Doors & Windows, these Shutters are also Carved with rude figures of Men & Weomen and the Inside is Neatly lined with reeds, about 4 or five feet up—the Floor is Covered with Grass, to a good thickness, and a division in the Middle with a tier of Stones to part the Men & Weomen, at the end belonging to the Men is a place seperated from the rest for the purpose of Burying the Males of the Family;[35] this place is fenced by a teir of Flat Stones set up on end four or five feet high, and here the Weomen must not Come—in this place they keep the Images of their Fore fathers or Tutelar deitys, as they beleive that their Souls are fond of seeing respect paid to their remains, and that they always hover about the place of these representatives. They are Curiously Carved and decorated with human hair, & the teeth and Nails of the departed friends, red feathers, & Pearl Shells neatly disposed–

The Chief of their furniture is Matts for sleeping on Baskets of Several Sorts and Neat platters of different Sizes for Holding their provisions, Stools for Beating pudding on and a Stone or pestle for that purpose, the Stools & Platters are Made of the Tamanu, or *Callophylum Mophylum,* with the Nut of which they Scent their Cloth—and when they go to Sleep they beat the Musquettoes out and make a fire at each Door to keep them out—as they are very troublesome and together with Fleas & lice keep them employd till Sleep gets the better of them, and the Rats run over them all night in droves, but as we left several Cats it is possible that in time they may reduce their Numbers. They have No Snakes or any thing more Venomous then a Centipede or Scorpion, and their Birds & insects are Common to all the Society Isles–

Their Food is Chiefly Breadfruit (which they preserve as the Society Islanders do making it into a sour past Calld *Mahi*) Yams, Taro, Plantains, Cocoa Nuts, Wild Roots & fish which they Bake in the Same Manner as at the Society Isles, they always Cook out of doors and the Weomen & their Servants are under the same restrictions Nor Can a Woman toutch What her Child has toutchd while the Child remains Sacred, and the Weomen are prohibited eating the Turtle, Cavally Dolphin & Albicore but may eat all the rest,[36] they have abundance of the White Salmon, and plenty of delicious rock fish with Shell fish of several kinds, among which are a sort of Cockles which are excellent when Stew'd–

The Turtle is also Sacred to the Men and is only Used as Sacrafices or eaten by the Chiefs & Priests–

Their canoes are differently built from any of the other Islands which we have seen, and are from 30 to 40 feet long and Carry from 12 to 24 men; they are narrow at the bottom, Spreading out to 16 or 18 inchs at the Gunnel, and Carry their bearings to the top, they are about 2 feet deep, and Sharp toward the head & Stern the Head resembling the Head of some Animal with a large mouth, and the Stern rises into a Scroll neatly finished and Carved.[37] The Canoes are built of Several pieces well trim'd & Joind together by Seizings of the Fibres of the Cocoa Nut, the whole painted with a redish paint, and on the Sides are stuck with breadfruit Pitch, the Scales of the Parrot fish & Small Shells, in a number of arches, which have a handsom appearance, they are Built of Tamanu & Breadfruit and are Well finished, Considering their tools, Which are no other then a Stone or Shell adze, bones, & Sharks teeth with Coral & Sand to rub them Smoothe—after which the Skin of the Stringray, Nourse[38] & Shark Serve to pollish the Work, which were all the tools We Saw them use, their paddles are from three to four feet long, and the blade is Circular, having a ridge on the one side like our Oars, but the other is hollow'd out instead of being flat. Their Fishing Geer are Hooks and lines, large Seines, Spears of different kinds pointed with Toa which evry fisherman makes for Himself; their Hooks are of Pearl Shell, Which they grind into form with a Stone & Sand, and drill a hole with a piece of a Shell or a Sharks tooth fixd in a long stick which they they Work between their hands after the Manner of a Chocolate Mill after which different sizes of the Branchy Coral Serve for files to Cut the hollow of the Hooks to their fancy; they have no beards to their Hooks but turn them with the Bow more rounding & the Point Close to the Back—they are of different forms as the Fisherman fancys—their lines & Netts are Made from the Bark of the Roa[39] and are well twisted in three Strands

They have no sailing Vessels and Never leave the land except they are blown off as all the Islands of which they have any account are at too great a distance for them to hold any intercourse,[40] and when they fish within the reef seldom use their paddles but set along with long poles or staves to prevent frightining the fish, they may be in Chace of; the White Salmon and the Turtle they Catch with their Nets some of which are very large and they have Several fine white Beaches to haul their Seines on–

They have abundance of the 'Ava or Intoxicating peper which grows without Cultivation, and they use it in the Same Manner as the Society Islanders prefering the method of Chewing it to any other

They Cultivate nothing but the Taro,[41] a root of the Nature of a Yam which Grows in Watery Ground, the tops of which Make excellent greens, in the Cultivation of this root both Men & Weomen labour, taking great Pains to level the Ground and bank it up, so that the Water May Cover the Whole of it, their only Method of digging being with a pointed Stick and hauling the Brush up by the roots and when they find it Necessary to level a piece of Ground, they Carry the earth about in baskets saving the Stones for embankments, and find whether it is properly leveled by turning a Stream of water into it; as some of them are always employd weeding or planting, they always Carry with them a long staff or wand, with which they knock down the Ducks which they come within reach of, at this they are expert and frequently Come on them unperceived the large leaves of the Taro keeping them from the sight of the ducks till they are within reach–

Their war weapons are made of Toa, they are Spears or Lances 18 or 20 feet long, and regularly taperd from within about 12 or 14 inches of the Heel to the point, Clubs which answer the double purpose of Clubb & Spear; these are from 9 to 12 feet long, 2/3rds of which is a round Staff about the Size of the Common Spunge Staves, the remaining part is flat blade about 4 inches wide in the Middle and tapering from the Middle, each way; the point being Sharp enough to peirce a Mans body; on the head of the Staff where the blade Commences is wrought a Double diamond all wrought from the Solid and the Whole polish'd & finishd in a Stile that some good artists would be surprized at

The old Men have Walking Staves & handles of Fly flaps made of the same wood, highly finishd, on the Top of their Staves they generally have Carved a double figure of a man representing a figure with one Body & two Heads & some of two, standing back to back, their Fly flaps are made of the Fibers of the Cocoa Nut twisted & platted very Curiously[42]

When they are Accoutered for War, they bind a piece of red Cloth or Matting, or both, round their Waist with a Sash Made of the fibers of the Cocoa Nut Platted into Sennet, at each end of which hands [*sic*] a tossel of the Same. Round their waist they fill all the folds they Carry a Number of Flinty Stones; the Shoulder is Mostly bare, on their Breast a pearl Shell

Figure 10. *Tahiri,* flywhisk, Austral Islands [990.2.2548]. Reproduced with permission of Musée de l'Histoire Naturelle, Lille

hangs in a Collar of braided hair, and their head defended by a Cap made of the fibers of the Cocoa Nut wrought after the Manner and something in the form of a Bee Hive; they are covered with White Cloth, and on the top, a Bunch of black feathers from the Man of War Bird, and with a Spear or Club are Complatly equipt. Some of these Caps have a pearl shell on the front with a Semicircle of Feathers from the Wild ducks Wings round it, but these are more for Show then use but the Others will resist a severe blow, and a Cutlass will make no impression on them–

The Use Neither Slings, nor Bows, in War, and tho their Weapons bespeak them to be Warriors, yet it does not appear that they distroy the

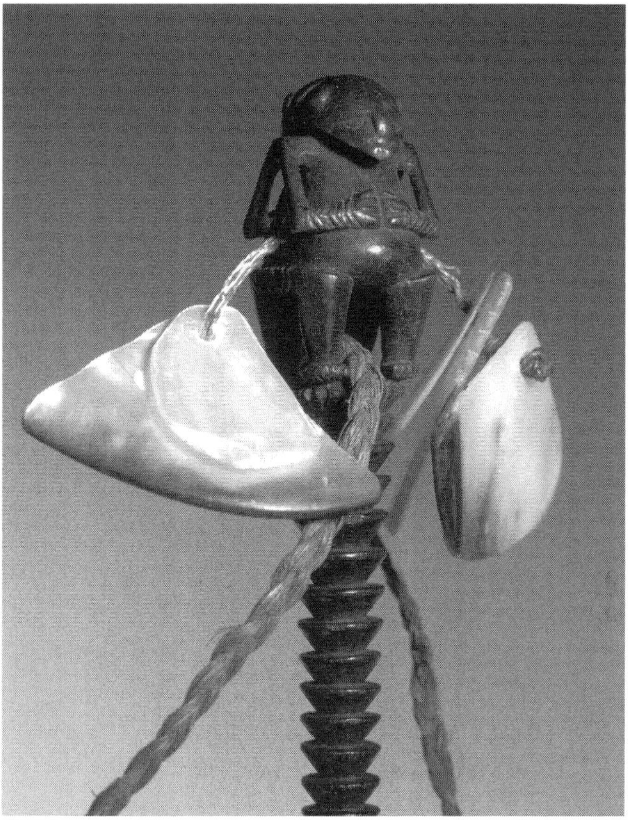

Figure 11. *Tahiri,* flywhisk (detail), Austral Islands [990.2.2548]. Reproduced with permission of Musée d'Histoire Naturelle, Lille

habitations of each other as in other Islands: many houses appear to have Stood Several Years, but they perhaps satiate themselves with blood for they appear to fight furiously.

Their Music are drums made of about 12 inches diameter and 4 feet long hollowed out after the Tahiti Manner and Covered with Shark Skin, others of about 18 or 20 inches high, & 10 diameter, Conch Shells with long tubes, Flutes of a larger size then those of Tahiti but Used in the same Manner—and the Sound of the Whole of them is more harsh and disagreeable then those of The Society Isles; tho the Workmanship is superior.

Their Marae's or places of Worship differ from these of the Society Islands, being all Flat pavements and having a number of large Flag Stones placed on end in tiers or rows in the Center,[43] they are planted with the *Ti* or Sweet root having a long Stalk of about 6 feet long,[44] and as thick as a mans finger; these places have each a little house on on Side, and bear some resemblance of a burying ground; here they offer Sacrifices of Men and Turtles. when a sacrafice is to be made all the Males in the district assemble at the Marae and the Old Men and the Priests (who are Numerous) always bring their Walking staves in one hand and a young Plantain Tree in the Other, these are thrown in a heap with long prayers when (if the sacrafice is to be a human one) the Victim is pointed out, & knocked down, When they soon dispatch him with their Staves which are sharpened at the point for the purpose the Body is instantly dissected with Bamboo knives, and each takes a part which he wraps in the leaves of the *Ti* and each Carries it to his own Marae, where it again offered, with a plantain tree—the Head, bones & bowels are Interd in the Morai, and a Stone put up, not to perpetuate the Memory of the Man but as a mark for the Number that have been Offered there. Some of these Morals has Numbers of those Marks. A Feast is then made, and eaten in the Morai, by the priests, of Fish, Bread, Taro &c—part of which is also offered with long prayers. The friends of the Victim, if he happen to have any, put up with it quietly for fear that they should follow him, on the Next like occasion. We knew of no more then two being Offerd during our Stay both of which were Young Men–

Besides the General Marae, each Father of a Family has one, Where they Make frequent tho not regular Prayer and Offerings, and if they are taken Sick they beleive it to proceed from the anger of the atua (or Deity) or from Some of their relations; or Should they go to War in a Wrong Cause they think that any Sickness which befals them at the time is sent as a punishment on them for their fault—On our first anchoring in Bloody bay Most of the Inhabitants of the Island flockd to that place, the land about which is an Uncultivated Swamp, and In the Course of the Few days that they remaind there for want of their Usual Bedding, they Caught Colds, Agues, & Sore Eyes Running at the Nose &c.—and all these they said fell on them through our means, and on this Account it was that we found Such an Alteration in their behaviour when We anchord the Second time[45]–

But the Priests, who Seemd to have all the Athority and be Nearly on a footing with the Chiefs, Seeing that we were no Other then Common Men and liable to accident like themselves, Could not bear to see such superiority as the Europeans in general usurp over those who differ from themselves, and became jealous of us with respect to their religious authority to which they saw that we not only refused to take notice of but even ridiculed, for this reason they used all the Means in their power to keep the Chiefs from making Friends, thinking perhaps that if we staid in the Island, their Consequence would be lessen'd, which in all probability would have been the Case[46]–

The Island is Govern'd by three Chiefs, Tinarau, Tahuhuatama & Hitirere before Named,[47] each of whom are absolute in His own district and of these two are related by Marriage, Tinarau having The Sister of Tahuhuatama to Wife. Yet they do not agree; and notwithstanding the Smallness of their territories they are continually at War. There Are Other Chiefs, who reside as private Gentlemen of those we found Tamatoa to be one, Who on our first Coming Acted for Hitirere, and Taʻaroatehoa acted for his Father; one of these are always as it were in Commission and the other on Half Pay and if one is removed by War, Death or otherwise the other always Supplys his place, receiving his honors nor does the deposed Chief suffer no more than the loss of Command & is always treated with respect, but no man can ever arrive at that dignity unless his Father Was a Chief. Their Classes are the Same as at the Society Isles, but the Priests seem to have more Influence and appear to be next to the Chiefs in point of Authority[48]

Their Language is a dialect between the Society & Friendly Islands but not so much different from either as to prevent its being understood by both; and it is more then probable that they are all decenced originally from the same stock, tho so much Different in their Manners Customs and Appearance. In Other Countrys it is observed that the Inhabitants of the Northern & Southern Climes are more robust in general then those within the Tropics but it is to be observed in those Seas in Islands at an Inconsiderable distance from each other in a North & South direction.[49] Perhaps this may be occasioned by the different degrees of Fertility of the Islands, which are generally more Fertile near the line then at a distance from it and the Inhabitants of those Isles where evry Necessary is Supplyd by Nature have no occasion to Cultivate the Earth and are less robust and vigourous then those Who have Exercise and Labour in procuring their Food

The Inhabitants of Those Islands drive about in their Canoes to an amazing distance and I am therefore led to think that the whole of the Islands in these seas might have been peopled from South America, Notwithstanding the difference of their Language Manners & Customs all which are liable to Change in length of Time yet the present language of all the Islands in these Seas differ no more then the English dose in different Countrys.[50]

On one of Their Maraes we found part of a Canoe which we knew to belong by its form to some of the Society Islands; and on making enquirey, one of our Tahitians (Named Tupairu, Colemans Friend) declared that She was the same that had been drove off From Tahiti with Six or Eight More, of which he related the Following Story.—

Some years before our arrival at Tahiti the Districts of Hitia'a, Matavai, Ha'apaiano'o, Puna'auia, Tiarei & Pare (Commonly calld, Te Porionu'u or Te Aharoa) being at War with Atehuru, Sometimes Calld Te Oropa'a, each district furnish'd their proportion of Men & Canoes; to one of which He (Tupairu) belongd; being then resident in Ha'apaiano'o, the Canoes being assembled at Pare, they proceeded to a place in Atehuru Calld Taiarapu, where they landed, and attackd Te Oropa'a but were repulsed, and forced to retire to their Canoes; however, they brought off several of the Enemys dead, one of which was put into Tupairus Canoe, in the Meantime the Oropa'a Fleet came up and Closed them so vigorusly that they were forced to Fly, and at last to Jump overboard and take to the Shore at Ta'apuna (another part of Atehuru) leaving their Canoes to the Enemy who followed them on Shore without seizing their Canoes, where they were forced to fly to Pare; the Wind being off shore Some of the Canoes were drove on the reef and dashd to pieces and Eight or nine drove to Sea among which Tupairus was one and these they saw no more of,[51]

This story agreed exactly with the account of the Natives of Tubuai and we had no doubt of the part of the Canoe found here being the same that Tupairu described, as the time of Her Coming on Shore agreed, and part of a man being found in her with the Flesh decayd, and eaten off the Bones by the Birds, She must have been some days in drifting here as the distance is Nearly 6 Degrees of Lattitude but nearly on the same Meredian of Longde

This Circumstance led us into further enquirey to know if any such thing had happened before; when we found that the Present Tamatoa was Great great Grandson to a Chief of the Island of Ra'iatea (an Island 120 Miles N W of Tahiti) who had been driven off in a fishing Canoe, and after being drove about for some time, had landed on this Island which was then but thinly inhabited by some people, who had been driven to it in the Same Manner from an Island which they Calld Rurutu[52] which they described to be at a great distance to the Westward and some others from an another which they Call'd O Hiva to the Eastward.[53]

On his arrival he settled himself not knowing his way home, and was acknowledged as a Chief by these people,[54] he also Gave Names to three Districts from the three Islands of Ra'iatea, Taha'a, & Huahine, which they still retain.

This was further Confirmed on our return to Tahiti, where we learnt from Purea, the present Queen Dowager, and Mother of Tu (or Mate,) who informd Us that Her Great gt Grandfather Named Tamatoa, a Chief of Ra'iatea, was lost or blown away in a Fishing Canoe and had never been heard of since, and the Young Tubuai Chief was imediatly acknowleged as her relation and adopted the Friend of Mate who wishd to make a voyage to Tubuai to Claim his kindred with Tamatoa, the time of these Circumstances agreed so well with both their Accounts that we remaind in no doubt of their being Facts–

This, with an account of several Islands which they discribed in different directions, were the Principal information we were able to Collect from these people; and tho from their Savage Appearance we at first supposed them Cannibals yet we found that tho they had no animal for food that they detest the Idea of eating human Flesh,[55]—and now to return to the Ship—

3 *Return to Tahiti*

We stood to the N N E with a fine Breeze an fair Weather and during the passage Coleman was employd in making trade. On the 20th we made the Island of Me'etia under which we hove too and devieded the Trade, Amunition, Arms, Wine, Slops &c in lotts which was put into the Cabbin in Safety till the Ship should Come to an anchor, and on the 21st we bore away, and anchord on the 22nd in Matavai Bay, where evry thing being Settled the Following Men went on Shore,

Viz—

1	Chas. Churchill	do Mastr at Arms
	George Stuart	do Mid
	Peter Heywood	do.
	Jas. Morrison	do Boatswains Mt
5	Jno. Millward	do. Ab
	Chas. Norman	Carprs Mte
	Thos. McIntosh	do. Crew
	Wm. Muspratt	Ab
	Mathw. Thompson	do. do.
10	Richd. Skinner	do. do.
	Thos. Ellison	do. do.
	Thos. Burkett	do. do.
	Jno. Sumner	do. do.
	Michl. Byrn	do.
15	Josh. Coleman	Armr
	Heny. Heildbrandt	Cooper

Those who remained in the Ship were

1	Fletcher Christian	Act. Lt.
	Jno. Mills	Gunnr Mt
	Isaac Martin	Ab
	Willm. Brown	Gardiner
5	Edwd. Young	Mid
	Willm. McCoy	Ab
	Jno. Williams	Ab
	Mathw. Quintrell	Ab
	Alexr. Smith	Ab

and with them the Two friends of the Young Tubuai Chief who were now become very fond of Mr. Christian and would not leave him, They and the Young Tubuai Chief were also instantly Joined by a Number of Fresh Tahitians both Men & Weomen which increased their Number to 35 in the whole.

As soon as the Ship was at an Anchor those who intended for the Shore began to land their Chests, Hammocks &c—but having only one Boat that would Swim and a tolerable high Surf going, we made it night before we got all on Shore, being affraid to venture much in the Canoes of the Natives, at one time, tho they made a much better hand of landing them in the surf then we could have done with the Boat.

As we were fearfull of the Canoes we were forced to wait for the Boat to Carry the Amunition, which was not landed till evry thing else was on Shore and then not more than two Mens together.

Having landed our Baggage, We found the Tahitians ready to receive us with evry Mark of Friendship and hospitality; amongst us we found the whole of them striving to outdoe each Other in civility towards us and we found our Old friends ready to receive us with open Arms and all were glad when We informd them that we intended to Stay with them–

Among the things which we carried on Shore was the Carpenters Mates & part of the Armourers tools;—a pig of Iron for an anvil, a Grindstone, Some Bar Iron, a Suit of Collours, some Iron pots, & a Copper kettle, about 3 Galls of Wine pr. Man, and, (except Byrn) each Man a Musquett, Pistol, Cutlass, Bayonet, Cartridge Bos, 17 lbs of Powder & a quantity of lead to make ball, and some Spare belts, and having a Musquettoon & two Spare Musquets the Former was left in my Care & the Musquets fell by lot to Chas Norman & Thos. Burkett, and Byrn being blind and of a very troublesome disposition it was thought that arms put into his hands would be only helping him to do some mischief and he was therefore kept without, we wanted the Saws, of which there were a Whip & Cross cut in the Ship, but Mr. Christian told Us He wanted himself, and gave us some trade in liew, he also Gave us two Spy Glasses, and an old Azimuth Compass for which I provided Cards & Glasses privately, he also told us to take the 10 Swivels on Shore but they were no use to us; the Sails which he thought he would not want and Canvas was also devided among us, and the Tubuai Images were put into my hand as a Present for the Young King. It being late before evry thing was landed, Mr. Christn told us that He intended to stay a day or two, and hoped that we would assist him to fill some water, as he intended to Cruize for some Uninhabited Island where he would land his Stock (of which the Ship was full, together with plants of all the kinds that are Common in these Islands) and set fire to the Ship, and where he hoped to live the remainder of His days without seeing the face of a European but those who were already with him.

I having formerly made Poeno, (Chief of Matavai) my friend, and Millward having made Friends with Poenos wife, [1] we were now invited to Live with them, which we accepted and were treated like the rest of the Family, but with more attention & respect; the others also went to the Houses of their Former Friends where they were treated in like manner.[2]

In the Night we found the Ship under way, standing out of the Bay,

Figure 12. "On Matavai River, Island of Otahytey," George Tobin, 1792 [Call no. PXA 563 no. 35]. Reproduced with permission of the Mitchell Library, State Library of NSW

but it proving Calm in the Morning She was not out of Sight till Noon during which She stood to the Northward on a wind.

We were all much surprized to find the Ship gone, as Mr. Christian had proposed staying a day or two to give us time to get on shore what things we might want or had forgot to take on Shore; this Gave us reason to suppose that He either was afraid of a Surprize or had done it to prevent His Companions from Changing their mind.

On the 23rd. Muspratt, McIntosh, Norman, Heildbrandt & Byrn went to live in Pare with Ari'ipaea (uncle to the Young King), & Chief of that district, and the Others remaind in Matavai, Mr. Heywood & Mr. Stuart living together on the land of Stuarts Wife whose father was also Mr. Heywoods Friend—Coleman & Thompson at Colemans friends, Churchill by himself at his Friends, Skinner by himself, at his wifes Fathers; & Sumner, Burkett & Ellison at Sumners Friends.

Immediately on landing they informd us that a Vessel had been there lately, and had left a man who they Call'd Brownee who was then at Taiarapu with Mate settling some business with Vehiatua, Chief of that Pininsula,[3] and as we heard they told strange storys of him, We wishd to know what had been the true Cause of his Stay, and therefore appointed Churchill & Millward to go to Taiarapu & take presents to Mate and at the same time See who this Man was.—and on Hearing our story now in the proper manner Vaetua, (Mates Brother) who had been Mr. Haywards Friend told us that it was by his order that the Cable was Cut at Pare[4] He being angry with Lieut. Bligh for Putting Mr. Hayward in Irons; and said if Mr. Hayward had been punnished with Churchill, Muspratt & Millward that he would have killd Lieut. Bligh, haveing taken his Station behind him armd with a Clubb for that Purpose, and on his describing the Circumstances we recollected seeing him On board and Close by Lieut. Bligh on that day.—They also informd us that the Captn had told Mate of Captn Cook's death and had left them the Picture of it and on which Score they were angry that we had not told them before, and accused Mr. Bligh of imposing on them by saying that he was alive in England, that He was Capn. Cooks Son which they were informd to the Contrary of by Captn Cox, who told that Captn. Cooks son was then in England.[5]

He said that as Soon as he had seen Mr. Hayward receive the First Blow he intended to level the Lieut. and escape by Jumping overboard, and diving till He reached the Shore, which he said he could reach in one dive and be out of Sight before any one could know who it was that had done it.

He said his reason for Cutting the Cable was to let the Ship Come on shore, where he hoped that She would bilge, or at least receive so much damage as to prevent Her going to sea, and by that means he hoped to get His friend out of Mr. Blighs power as he supposed all hands would be forced to live on shore if the Ship received much damage, and Cursed Mr. Christian for not killing Lieut. Bligh which he said He would do himself if ever he came again to Tahiti.

On the 27th, having appointed that We should meet at Pare, and make out presents to the Young King, We marchd in a body under Arms to Pare, taking with us the Tubuai Images and several other presents of red Feathers, Friendly Island & Tubuai Cloth, Matting and War Weapons Iron Work &c.—and were Joined by those who were at Pare and after being Welcom'd to the District by the Priest Making a long Oration and presenting each of us with a young Plantain tree with a Sucking Pig or a Fowle.

Having made known our business to Ari'ipaea—who told us that we must not approach the Young king as he was yet Sacred, unless we Strip'd the Clothing off from our Head & Shoulders, which we refused telling him that it was not Customary to remove any part of our Dress except our hats and if we were under arms it was not our Country Manners to remove our hat even to the King.[6]

However that we might not seem to be deficient in point of Good Manners each was provided with a piece of Tahiti Cloth to put over their Shoulders and take off in the Young Kings Presence, when we March'd to his House in procession each attended by a friend to remove the Tahiti Cloth which we had on,[7] all of Whom Stripd as they entered the Sacred Ground, the Men to the Waist, and the Weomen uncovering their Shoulders and tucking their Cloths up under their arms, and our Tahiti Cloaths were removed. We were followed by a Multitude of both Sexes, all of whom observed the Same rules in their Homage; having got to the opposite bank of the River facing the *Fare Ra'a* or Sacred House, the Young King Appeard, sitting on the Shoulders of a Man; and having a large piece of White Cloth round his Shoulders and his Head almost Hid with a Garland of Black & red Feathers. As He approachd the Bank, he saluted us with the Word Manoa (Welcome) which he repeated to each, calling us by the Name of our Tahiti Friends; and having placed himself over against us, Hitihiti Strip'd himself Naked to Carry the presents, and the Party drew up on the Bank for the Purpose. The Tubuai Images were first sent in the Name of the whole, with which Hitihiti told a long Story and which from the Number of red feathers were thought a Valuable present, and produced a general exclamation of wonder when they were held up to publick View on the opposite bank of the river.

After these were delivered, evry one sent his present seperatly, which Consisted of Red feathers Cloth &c.—and the whole being finishd, the Party formd three divisions & dischargd their arms, at which the Young Chief was so much pleasd that He told us to follow our own Country fashion in evry thing, and take no heed of their Ceremonies, when we retired.—we were Now Conducted to Ari'ipaeas house where a Feast was provided for us of a Baked Hog, Fish, Bread, Taro & Cocoa Nuts, Plantains &c.—after which a Proportion of land was pointed out for the Use of the Whole when in this district, and in the Evening we returned to Matavai, and Next day the 28th a Messenger arrived from Mate with a Hog and a Piece of Cloth for each of us and pointed out two pieces of land for the use of the Whole; the One (Pt Venus) for Cocoa Nuts and the other well stockd with Breadfruit Trees near the Spot where Poenos House stood; these were ordered for our present use, tho we stood in no need of His Care, having abundance of evry thing supplied by our Friends.

However as Millward & Churchill Set out this day for Taiarapu, they were loaded with Presents for Mate that we might not appear to be behind hand, among the presents were several large roots of Tubuai 'Ava, & a Bottle of Wine, the 'Ava was a Grand present, & the wine he gave to a Sick Man, as he had been informd by some one that it was good for sick people.

They were well received by all the Chiefs at whose houses they Stop'd on their way, but particularly by Mate & Vehiatua, who loaded them with presents, Mate desiring that we Should make his land our own, and Vehiatua giving Strong invitations to Come and see Taiarapu. Temari'i, Chief of Papara, also used them extreamly civil, disiring them to send some of the Others round that He might form an Acquaintance amongst them, they missd Atehuru, (having but an unfavourable account of it) altho Te To'ofa the Chief Sent to invite them while they went past in a Canoe[8] and they returned to Matavai on the 10th of October bringing with them the Englishman who Calld himself Brown alias Bound, and Said he had been left on Shore from the Brigg Mercury, T H Cox Esqr, Commander of London. He said he had stayd at his own request having had a dispute with some of His Shipmates and Cut one of them a Cross the Face with a knife, this and Some other things which he related of himself was sufficient to give a very good idea of his Character and to put us on our Guard against one who appeard to be a dangerous kind of a Man; however we each gave him some addition to his Stock of Cloaths and he soon Musterd as good a Stock as any of us had, what he brought on Shore were either very slender or soon expended had got from Captain Cox an augur, some Gimbles & a Plain which were the whole of his tools tho as he had no work to do, these were more then he had any occasion for,

He also informd us that Captn Cox had given Mate a Musquet, & some pistols, with Flints and Amunition, but had left none with him nor had he an Ax or Saw tho Captn Cox had left numbers of each in the Island.—He set out on the 18th in Company with Burkett who went to Taiarapu to See Mate.

When he was gone, Poeno produced a letter Signed T H Cox wherein the Vessel is Calld His Swedish Majestys Armd Brig Gustavus Illrd and wherein he Calls Brown "an Ingenious handy Man when sober but when Drunk a dangerous fellow". This Letter was put on Shore at Tetiaroa and brought to Poeno, and this agrees with Browns account, as he said she was bound to the Sandwich Isles & from thence to China. as Brown found this letter in Poenos possession afterwards He secured it Himself to prevent it from being of any further Use in pointing out His Character, Which according to His own account was black enough. He had according to his Story been a Serjeant in Portsmouth Division of Marines but being broke had gone to India in the Euryidice Frigate where he Left Her, and staid in the Country and was Cook to Col. Bailly when He was taken by Hyder Ally, into whose Service he entered and turning Musselman[9] was made an Officer; this Service he soon left, & Coming down to Fort St. George soon found an Opportunity in Compy with some others to Seize on a Small Vessel loaded with Companys Goods which they Carried off. He was afterwards taken and tryed but for want of the evidence against him he escaped punnishment, but was sent to England, where he soon found the Country too hot for Him and Having made a Cruize in H M

S Pomona, he left her, and got on board the Brig Mercury from which he was put on Shore in this Island.[10]–

Finding ourselves Settled I began to think it would be possible to build a small Vessel In which I had hopes of reaching Batavia & from thence to England. I communicated this to McIntosh and Millward, and the Mater was agreed on; but we resolved to keep the real motive a Secret, and to Say that she was only for the purpose of Pleasuring about the Island; and for this purpose, I having observed that Mathw. Thompson had got a Quadrant (formerly Mr. Hallets) and some of Mr. Haywards books,[11] tho He could neither read nor write, I was determined if Possible to get possession of them, and with a little perswasion I got the Quadrant for Six small trade Adzes (Calld here loeys) & a Gallon of Wine but when I wanted the Books he began to have some suspicion, and was sorry that He had let me have the Quadrant, which I told him was only for Amusement. He said He had No Cartridge paper and the books would answer that purpose, I told him that I would give him paper in lieu which would answer that purpose better, but this only served to Confirm his Oppinion, however as I had a Seamans Daily Assistant I took no further Notice,[12] and affected to be easy about them tho I was sorry that I could not get them.

Norman & Heildbrandt having agreed to be of our party, McIntosh and them removed to Matavai on the 1st of November bringing their Effects with them and having got Houses prepared on a Square piece of Ground raised above the level where we fixd a Flag staff to Hoist the Collours on Sundays; we were also Joind here by Burkett (who returned on the Second, & brought Brown with Him) Sumner, Ellison, Churchill & Byrn, and having appointed Divine Service to be read on Sundays evry thing at present seemd right.

I now made a publick proposal to build a small Vessel to Cruize about the Island which was agreed to, as McIntosh said it was possible to put one together and He had no objection, Norman & the Copper being both Workmen, and the rest of us Could Chop off the rough parts ready for their Use–

Having agreed on this Head, I informed Poeno that we intended to build a little Ship, as we did not understand the Method of Handling Canoes, and in which I told Him that we could carry Him & Mate with some of our Friends to the Neighbouring Islands. He was well pleased, and told us to Cut down what timber we pleased, as there was plenty in Matavai.

On the 6th Brown & Ellison Set out for Taiarapu, and returnd on the 11th. Brown having taken Ellisons Cutlass had been playing some tricks with it at Atehuru and had it taken from him by the Natives, one of which had Cut him a Cross the Hand with a piece of Bamboo, and in the Scuffle he had lost his Cloth, which had been part of the tick of a Bed[13] which he wore in the Country Stile, on their return Brown applied to us to recover the things, but on enquirey we found that he had been the Aggressor, and as we did not think the Natives to blame we told him that He must endeavour to live peaceably and not bring himself into trouble, otherwise He must stand to the Consequence and as he found that we would not support Him he Contented himself for the present, and Poeno having given him a house and a piece of Ground he remaind quiet in Matavai for some time; the Natives never troubling him as they supposed He was under Our protection, tho they knew he was a Stranger to us, and he often Used them very ill, which on our Accounts they took no notice of and they always allowd for His not understanding their language or Customs–

On the 11th we bigan to Cut down Trees for our Intended Vessel, and having Cleard a place near the Square under the Shade of some trees, we laid the Blocks, and on the 12th laid the Keel which was 30 feet.

The Plan being drawn to the Following dimentions,—Length of the Keel 30 feet, Length of Deck 35 feet, Length of the Stem post 6 f. 6 in., Stem 7 f. 2 in., Breadth 9 f. 6 in. on the Midship frame; depth of the Hold 5 feet; breadth of the Floors & Timbers 4 inches to 3½ thickness 3¼ to 2½; Keel Stem & Stern post 8 inches by 4

Saturday the 14th, Employd trimming Stuff for Molds & Cuting trees down for Planks.

16th. Having got some Molds made, I took part of them and got some of the Natives to assist me when I procured three or four floors & some timbers. Churchill also took some & went to Pare & Tetaha on the Same Errand, and returned on the 20th. with Some Pieces of Purau but only one answer'd to the present Molds—in the mean time McIntosh Superintend the Cutting down trees and Splitting them for Plank, and I had Collected several more pieces of Purau which was the Best to answer the purpose of Timbering, and the Bread fruit for Plank–

20th. Having Colleted Several More Floors, we set about triming them for Use, in Which I assisted, by doing part of the rough Work, while McIntosh & Norman fitted them in the Mean time the rest were busy in Cutting down Trees, and Splitting them For Plank, which were laid up to Season but at this the progress was but Slow, it being as Much as we Could do to trim one plank of 30 feet long in two days; and what work We had now Cut out lasted us all the Week.

Monday 30th. This day we errected a Shed to work under, to keep off the heat of the Sun, which we found very intence, and to prevent us from being interrupted by the rain which we now began to expect from the appearance of the Weather.

Decr 1st. this day we received a Present of Hogs and Provisions from Poeno by order of Mate and this day according to our expectation the rain began, and lasted with some few intermissions for near three weeks, during which time no work was done out of the Shed Mean time and we fitted what Floors & Timbers we had trimd, the Stem & Stern post, & Plank of 2½ inch for the Stern.

21st. the Weather being Fair, we set to search for more Timbers, and set up the Stem & Stern posts. It must here be observed, that as we had but few Molds, we were under the necessity of altering them to evry Frame, and the timbers being Scarce in the low lands, we were only able to procure One & some Knees, nor was this the only difficulty that we labourd under; for We found that Several of those which were already trim'd & fitted, had started, & became Straight, so as to alter their form some inches, to remedy which we found it answerd our purpose best, only to Side them for the present, and let them dry before we took in hand to finish them, or put them in their places. The removing of those timbers which had started, & siding the Others kept McIntosh & Myself Employd till Christmas, while Norman and the rest were making Plank.

We kept the Hollidays in the best manner that we could, killing a Hog for Christmas Dinner, and reading Prayers which we never Omitted on Sundays, and having wet weather we were not able to do any thing out of doors for the remainder of the Year–

We informd the Natives of the reason of our Observing these Hollidays, and espiecally Christmas Day; all of which seemd to regard with attention, and readily believed all that we could inform them of, never doubting that the Son of God was born of a Woman, and they always behaved with much decency when present at our worship; tho they Could not understand one word; yet several were desirous to have it explaind to them, and some of them wishd to learn our prayers which they all allowed to be better then their own those who were constantly about us knew when our Sunday came, and were always prepared accordingly, seeing that we rested on that day they did so likewise and never made any diversions on it. One of them was always ready to hoist the Ensign on Sunday Morning, and if a stranger happened to pass, and enquire the meaning, they were told that it was *Mahana Atua* (Gods Day) and tho they were intent on their Journey, would stop to see our manner of keeping it, and would proceed next day, well pleased with their Information.[14]

On the 4th the Weather being fair, I set out to the Hills accompanied by some of Poenos Men, & one who lived with myself Constantly, in quest of timbers, and returned with several, the Purau[15] being plenty in the Mountains; but Mostly at a Good distance as they always take the first at hand for their own Use—these We sided as usual and laid them to dry, the Natives Frequently assembled about us to see our work, and seemd much surprized at our method of building, and always assisted willingly to haul the Trees to hand, & hew off the rough; they are very dexterous at Spliting, but as they have no Idea of working by rule, they could be of no use in triming the Plank.

Amongst our visitors Came a Blind Man, who they led to the place, and he examined the work by feeling evry part and asking the use and intention; and seemd amazed at the Construction of the Vessel of which he Seemd to have a good Idea and said to His Country Men "our Canoes are foolish things to this one". He askd us many questions, and received answers, with which he went away well satisfied.

7th. This day we got more timbers and trimmd them as before. Norman and the Others Still making plank, and as we wanted Irennails the Cooper (Heildbrandt) was set to work to Cut Amai, this being the best wood which we could find for that purpose

11th. Went in search of More timbers, & had tolerable Success. The business of searching for timber always took up a whole day, having Several Miles to go before any Could be found to answer our purpose, and when We found them we frequently had the misfortune to breake them by tumbling them down the precipices, which we could not avoid; it being impossible to Carry them along the Steep Clifts, and what we Cut in one day would keep McIntosh & Myself employd for three or four, having as before Observed the Molds to alter for each frame.—Nor was the making of Plank less troublesome, having no Saws (except hand-saws) the largest tree would afford no more than two thicknesses of Plank, Some of the trees Cut for that purpose measuring six feet round which took a deal of Labour to reduce into plank of Inch & a quarter with axes & adzes; and as we had but two Adzes we were forced to make the Small trade hatchets (such as sold in London at 9d each) answer that purpose, by lashing them to handles after the manner of the Natives, which answered our purpose very well.

And here I may also observe that a deal of Labour might have been saved by workmen, who understood their business, by trimming the Timber in the Mountains, which would have made a Considerable Odds in the Weight, but of this I was not a sufficient Judge, and was therefore obliged to bring it home in the rough, and Trim it afterwards, however this appeard but trifling in point of difficulty and was not Sufficient to make us abandon our project.

18th. Brought home some more timber; and having got several dry enough to Work, we Cut up a plank for Ribbands and set up several frames to guide us in our work, and as we had but little Iron Work, we made shift with Irennails, putting a Spike in evry other Floor, and Irennails in the rest.

This kept McIntosh & myself employd till the 30th as Norman could not be spared from making Plank it being necessary to keep one workman in each branch of the Business.

On the 1st. of February our attention was drawn from our Work by a *Heiva* which according to Custom was performd in our Neighbourhood before the Chief of the District, to see which all the Inhabitants of the district were Assembled.[16]

evry thing being ready Captain Cooks picture was brought (by an Old Man who has the Cahrge of it) and placed in front, and the Cloth with which it was covered being removed, evry person present paid the Homage of striping off their Upper Garments, the Men bareing their bodys to the Waist, Poeno not excepted, and the Weomen uncovering their Shoulders. The Master of the Ceremonies then made the *Utu* (or usual offering) making a long speech to the Picture, acknowledging Captn Cook to be Chief of Matavai and placing a Young Plantian tree with a sucking pig tyed to it before the Picture–

The Speech running to this purpose—"Hail, all hail Cook, Chief of Matavai, Chief of Air Earth & Water, we acknowledge you Chief from the Beach to the Mountains, over Men, Trees & Cattle over the Birds of the Air and Fishes of the Sea &c. &c."[17]

After which they proceeded to perform their dance, which was done by two young weomen Neatly and elegantly dressd in fine Cloth, and two Men, the whole was conducted with much regularity and exactness, beating drums, & playing flutes to which they kept true time for near four Hours.

On a signal being given the Weomen Slip'd off their dresses and retired, and the Whole of the Cloth and Matting which was spread to perform on,[18] was rolld up to the Picture and the Old men took posession of it for the use of Captn Cook.

Several Baskets of Provisions Consisting of Fish, Plantains Breadfruit Taro & Cocoa Nuts were bought and presented to us, and at Poenos request we fired the Musquettoon which we Charged with Slugs & firing into a large Apple tree brought down several of the Fruit at which they expressd much wonder and departed well pleased–

On the 2nd Came another *Heiva,* which Poeno brought to the Square this was Conducted in the same manner, and attended by the Inhabitants as before, but Captn Cooks picture was not present, Poeno receiving the Cloth and Matting which we devided amongst us, the Whole Amounting to near one Hundred Fathoms–

After the people were departed we Missd the Flat haulyards, a pair of Trowsers & three Pigs from the Stye; and on enquirey found that the Thief was in Pare where we followed and apprahended him, finding the Haulyards in his posession but the Trowsers & pigs were gone. We brought him to Matavai where we gave him 100 stripes; and Brown having lost a hog Cut of His Ears[19] tho he Could not be sure that he had stolen it. Poeno advised us to Shoot him saying he will now go and Steal from evrybody without fear, however we thought he had been punnishd sufficiently and let him go and he quitted the district amidst the shouts and Jeers of his Countrymen.—Another having stolen a knife some days before, was also brought to the Tree & received a smart flogging.

We soon found that this Method of Proceeding had the desired effect and few instances of the kind happened after, tho they had many Opportunitys to steal our tools they never medled with any of them, as they knew that we would find them out, as they cannot keep anything to themselves and we began to get hold of their language so fast that we could understand evry thing they said, and make a good shift to discourse with them–[20]

On the 3rd We returnd to work as before Collecting more Timbers & making Plank.

On the 6th we received a Visit from 'Itia who was come down to visit her Son the Young King at Pare. She brought presents of Cloth for each as did also her Sister Teano (wife to Vehiatua, Chief of Taiarapu) who accompanied her. She Staid at the Square some days, and the Vacant space Near the Square was made use of for Dancing Wresting & throwing the Javlin; and the young Men & Weomen frequented this place for their amusement afterwards when the weather permitted, so that we were entertaind with a dance almost evry evening while we remaind here without going from home to see it.[21]

When She saw the Vessel Which now began show in Frame, she told me that she had got a handsaw from Captn Cox which she would give Me, and a Man was sent away to Taiarapu to bring it, who returnd with in a few days and it proved to be a very Good one; we supposed that it Cost at least 5 Shillings in London; it was quite New and had not been used, and was what we stood in great need of as our own were much the worse for wear.

As the Frame of the Vessel began to assume some form, We had frequent Visitors, who were all desirous of examining evry part, and curious to know how evry part was secured, but most of them were doubtful whether ever she would be finishd, Saying the Jobb was too long, and wondering how we could keep at it without being tired.

Before 'Itia took her leave She gave orders that we should be well supplied with provisions, of Hogs, Fish &c, but this was needless, as evry one who Came to visit us brought Something with them; so that we never wanted for any thing.

8th. We had hithirto gone on with our Work without any thing to obstruct us except Rainy Weather but now an accident happened which put a Stop to it for some time—

The affair was this, Thompson who resided with Coleman at Point Venus had ill used a young Girl, for which her brother in revenge knock'd Him down, and Fled. Coleman was at this time Just recovering from a Fit of Sickness, when Thompson came home vowing revenge on the first that Offended him.

A Number of Strangers had arrived at the Point, (where they generaly stop on their passage round the Island to take the Opportunity of getting to windward in the morning before the Sea Breeze sets in), and had flackd round the House as usual to see the Englishmen, Thompson Ordered them away; but as he Spoke English they did not understand him, and paid no regard to the Order, on which, he took His Musquet, and firing amongst them Killd a Man & a Child which he held in his Arms, and the Shot passd through a Womans lower Jaw breaking both the Bones, & Grazed another Man on the Back, on which they all fled. The Man was one of Vaiuriti, who was going round the Island on a party of Pleasure with his family, of which the Child was one. We expected that this would be revenged; but no notice was taken of it. Mr. Heywood Gave the Mans Wife a White Shirt, & Churchill (who had always been aspiring at Command) thought this a Good time to Offer himself as head of the Party in Case an Attack should be made upon us by the Natives, but as we all lookd upon the affair as Murder, we declined either Making him our Chief or taking any part in the business; on which he sent Brown to Taiarapu, to Vehiatua for Canoes to Carry him to Taiarapu, where he intended to Stay. The Canoes Came and on the 20th He set out accompanied by Brown & Thompson.

22nd. Finding the Natives made no stir and blamed None but Thompson for the Murder, we set to work again and Collected more Timbers and Trim'd them as before, making Plank.—Ellison's Pistol was Stolen this day out of the House.

Peter Heywood having set out on a visit with His Friend, we were this day informd that He was killd at Vaiuriti; but He returned to Matavai on the 6th of March bringing with him part of the Barrel of Ellisons pistol which he had found at Hitia'a, but the Thief had escaped. He informd us that He had stoppd one night in Atehuru where he was well received by *To'ofa* the Chief, but heard some of the People propose to plunder him, on which he made the Chief a Present of His Hat & a Knife which was all the English things He had about him, and he was sufferd to pass unmolested. He next went to Papara, where he was well received and staying one Night with Temari'i he set out for Vaiuriti for the purpose of Seeing Purea who was there. When He arrived in Vaiuriti he was Seized by the Hair by one of the Natives who held a Stone in one hand with which he was about to knock out his brains but was prevented by another who seized His arm, the Man had mistaken Mr. Heywood for Thompson, and was brother to the Man that Thompson killd, but the other who prevented him was brother to His wife and remembered Mr. Heywood at Matavai when He came to see the Man & his Child and had Made the Wife some presents when she was weeping over Her Husband & Child. As soon as the Man found his Mistake, He was very sorry, and begd that He would not be angry, inviting Him to His House; but He refused & Proceeded to *Pureas.* He stopd there all night, & proceeded to *Taiarapu,* Calling at *Moananuis* as he passd thro Vaiari, where he was well received.—When he Arrived at *Taiarapu* He was kindly received and loaded with presents by *Vehiatua,* who pressd him to Come & live with Him.[22] He then proceeded to Mate's, who treated Him in the Same Manner, but beggd that He would not quit Matavai as he understood that Churchill Thompson & Brown were Come to live there. Mr. Heywood promised him that He would not quit *Matavai* and persued his Journey homewards by the North side of the Island, being well received by evry person where He stopd in his way.

8th. This day went in quest of more timber with tolerable success. Employd as before & this day arrived a Messenger from *Vehiatua* with Presents and an Invitation for Myself and Millward to come to *Taiarapu* making us large Offers; and a letter from Churchill containing the like invitattion and seconding Vehiatuas request and promising us large posessions in Taiarapu; and at the Same time telling us that Thompsons arms had been Stolen by the Natives, which was but bad encouragement for Strangers to go there—but as we were glad to be rid of them we declined the kind invitation of *Vehiatua* and sent him presents in return.

This Morning a Messenger came from Pare to request our attendance there, as Metuaro was expected there from *Mo'orea* with a Fleet which having on board a large quantity of Hogs & Cloth for the Young King the *Atehuru* men had threatened to Plunder,—we repaird to Pare under Arms and a Feast was made ready for us.—the Fleet arrived without being molesteed and we returned to Matavai; in our way we were accosted by the Young King who to thank us for our attention to Him desired us to take fish out of His Canoes when ever they came to *Matavai* & to make no Ceremony about taking anything that belongd to Him; in return for which Complement we fired our Musquets–[23]

12th. Still Employd as before. In the Night between 10 & 12 Came Thompson and having made known his loss of His Arms; on which Norman supplyd him with his Spare one, and he set off before Day for Taiarapu, having told Norman that he had been informd that some of Mate's men had taken his arms and swore that He would put the man to Death as soon as he found Him out. He said that his reason for returning so soon was to prevent the News of his being at *Matavai* from reaching *Taiarapu* before him; but the true reason was that he did not whish to be seen by Coleman who He had robb'd while he was sick, he also said that Churchill & Him had quarreld and parted, and that they lived seperate, He at *Tautira* and Churchill at *Vaiaotea* at the distance of 18 or 20 miles and as his Arms were taken away in the Night, He had no suspicion that Churchill had any hand in the Theft tho the Natives said Publickly that He had taken them away, and on my enquiring of Poeno about it He informd me that *Vehiatuas* Man told him that Churchill had them.

On the 14th arrived a Messenger from Mate desiring that None of us might quit *Matavai* or *Pare* and he Also Confirmd the Account that Churchill had taken the Arms, we were satisfied of the truth of this and promised the Messenger that we would not go to *Taiarapu.*

Monday the 15th. The Frame being now Compleat, we began to trim the Timbers fair for Planking, and Coleman being quite recovered, we proposed to Him to make the Iron Work for the rudder Bowsprit &c.—to which he agreed on Condition that a pair of Bellows could be made and Coals procured to get sufficient heat, having no objection to assist, himself in making the Bellows, & getting the Forge in order.—We immediately fixd on a plan for making the Bellows; and Heildbrandt was set to work to assist Coleman; the Breadfruit planks made a tolerable set of Boards. Canvas supplyd the place of Leather, and the Iron handle of a Sauspan made the Nozzel, a Frame of Plank filld with Clay was made for the Forge, and Coleman Cut a hole through a stone to point the Nozzel of the Bellows through, the Pig of Ballast made a good anvil & the Carpenters maul answerd the purpose of a Sledge.—in the meantime we got Charcoal Burnt, and the Forge was got to work, but we found it necessary to keep the Canvas constantly wet to make it keep in the wind, which answered the purpose very well and Coleman having Hieldbrandt to assist him soon Got some part of the Ironwork into form, Making eye Bolts instead of Braces for the Rudder with a Bolt to go through the Whole.

16th. Sumner set out for *Taiarapu* on a visit to Mate, and did not return till the 26th during which time the Work still Went on well; and by this day, we had got to planking, and had got four Streaks on the larboard side. Sumner brought Churchill with Him who informd us that Thompsons arms were restored, and he had brought Normans Musquet with Thompsons thanks for lending it. He said that the Arms had been taken by some of the Natives who were Stopd by *Vehiatuas* Men going a Cross the Isthmus; this passd very well as we did not depend on what the Natives said. He also informd us that Vehiatua had died suddenly, and that He Churchill was put in full Possession of The Sovereignity of *Taiarapu* by the Name of Vehiatua his Friend who died without Issue,—He made us all promises of large posessions in Taiarapu if we would go and live with him but all refused seeing what he aimd at, which was no other then making himself Great at our expence and when I told Him that I had rather be one of Poenos friends, then Chief of *Taiarapu,* he dropd any further perswasions–[24]

During Sumners Absence he had made friends with *Temari'i* Chief of Papara and he being in alliance with Mate He had no objection to His going to *Papara* to live; and He brought Canoes from Temari'i, for the Purpose of Carrying him & Burkett there, they being both tired of the Work, and seemd to think, like the Natives, that it would never be finishd.–

April 1st. Burkett, Sumner & Churchill set out for Papara, and Byrn & Ellison went to live at *Pare,* and our number being reduced, we devided ourselves thus—Norman & Millward to make Plank, McIntosh & Myself to put them on, & Coleman & Heildbrandt to make the Ironwork.—and by Easter Sunday we compleated Six Streaks on the Starboard side, our Manner of Proceeding was this, after McIntosh had fitted one Plank, and placed it, he left me to bore it off, and prepared another, when it was bored off he secured it by driving one Nail, and one Irennail in each timber, and three Nails in each butt,—during the Holidays we learnt from the Natives that Churchill had fired upon some of them at *Tetaha* for frightning away some ducks which he was about to fire at. one Man was wounded in the Back and a Boy in the Heel, the Boys wound Mortified and he died soon after.

On the 12th arrived Muspratt from *Taiarapu,* on his way to *Pare* where he resided still, he informd us, that He had set out with Burkett Sumner and Churchill, & Confirmd the report of the Natives and told us that Churchill had his Collar bone broke at the Same time, and that He had left them at *Papara* on the 4th and proceeded to Taiarapu to see *Mate*; where a dispute had taken place between Brown who was now with *Mate* and one of Muspratts Men, wherein Brown got one of His Arms broke which Muspratt Set for Him and took his leave, he related the Story to this purpose

On his arrival at Taiarapu he was feasted by *Mate* according to Custom, and had invited Brown to partake. After dinner the provisions were deliver'd to His people, and some of them being absent it was taken care of by one of the others, to whom Brown went and demanded some for his dog: the Man told him that the dog should be served when the rest of the Men Came, which much displeased Brown, and He attempted to strike the Man, who warded of the Blow so effectually that Browns arm Broke against his, on which He ran for a Pistol to Shoot the Man but He escaped before He could find it.

As we were like to be Soon out of Plank it being now a whole weeks work to make one of 30 feet, we therefore set about the Beams and Knees till there should be some more plank ready, having now Compleated 8 Streaks on each Side. For the Knees I was forced to go to the Mountains while McIntosh fitted the Beams. In the Mean the *Mo'orea* People haiving rebell'd against *Metuaro,* Chief of that Island & Brother in law to *Mate,* he sent to us to know if He should send his arms over to quell them, to which We agreed, but told Him to send His own people to use them; and Hitihiti being present was appointed to the Command. The Arms being brought to us we Cleand them and put them in order when they set off and Arriving at Mo'orea soon brought them to subjection, Hitihiti having himself killd the Inspired Priest of the Rebels[25] and their Chief, (the adopted Son of the late Mahine) Teri'iamoeatua, forced to fly to Atehuru, leaving the Island in possession of Metuaro whose right it was, but from which he had been kept by *Mahine* his Uncle and His party, till the Bounty had Saild in April 89, when he having formed a strong party was Calld Home from Tahiti where he then resided and having strengthend his party from Tahiti was admitted as Joint Chief with Teri'iamoeatua who now became Jealous of His power, and had taken up arms to drive him out again, but the fire arms gave Metuaro such strength that He was forced to relinquish all Claim & fly to *Tahiti* for refuge. From Atehuru he went to Papara where

Temari'i gave him land and where he now resides private with His Mother & Aunt (Vahine) who was the Wife of Mahine deceased–

15th. Employd fitting the Clamps and getting the Beams ready, making Plank &c.—this day we received a letter from Burkett informing us of the Death of Churchill & Thompson, also a letter from Brown to the same purpose. Next morning the 16th Came Brown himself, Having been Sent by *Mate* to inform us by word of Mouth, as he thught that He could not explain it by letter; and He now gave us the following particulars—

Soon after their Arrival at *Taiarapu* they had a quarrel (which we were sensible Brown Had Fomented) and parted. Thompson making friends with *Ti'itorea* the Chief of *Tautira* & uncle to *Vehiatua,* and Churchill went to *Vaiatoea* to a house prepared for him, Brown going to live with Mate who was then at *Tautira.* Thompson growing Jealous of Churchill threatened to Shoot him if any difference or distinction was made between them. this Coming to Churchill's ears he got a Canoe & came down in the night when Thompson was asleep, his men soon found Thompsons Arms, and brought them out to him, but being sent in for the Powder Thompson waked, but the Night favourd their Escape when they returned to Churchills House.—Thompson missing his Arms soon got a light, and went to his Friend who lay in a House Close by, desiring him to Mann a Canoe, & telling him what had happened, the Canoe was got ready and he reachd *Vaiaotea* by Sunrise Churchill being informd of His approach, was up, and desired him to keep off, and Thompson replyd you have nothing to fear, for I have no arms, and I am only come to tell you that I lost them last night, and desire your assistance to recover them, on Churchills appearing convinced that He had no evil intent and by shewing his bayonet as the only arms he had, he was permitted to Come in and their former Annimosity being dropd, (they began to reason with each other, and found that Brown had been Active in promoting their Quarrel.) They now agreed to live together, and Thompson set out for Matavai to borrow Normans Musquet, while Churchill promised to use His endeavours to recover the Arms. Thompson returned, and they soon Came to a right understanding, when the Arms were recovered, as if by Churchills interposition, & Thompson being told that they had been taken from some of the Natives Crossing the Isthmus was perfectly satisfied and made no farther inquirry about the business–

Soon after Churchill, being bound on a visit round the Island, left

Thompson to take Care of the House, who also Sent Normans Musquet by Churchill with His thanks for His civility in lending it, in the mean-time one of the Natives, a Man who had been at Lima (Calld *Maititi*)[26] and who had been beaten by Churchill, came to Thompson and told Him evry thing relating to the taking away of His Arms, *Maititi* being one of the principal hands Concern'd. This exasperated Thompson, & he resolved to Shoot Churchill, which He put into execution immediately on his return, for which the Natives had put him to Death.

Burkett wrote thus "Churchill having broke his Collar bone shooting at some Ducks, I perswaded him to Stay with us, till he should get well, but He refused, and desired me to accompany him home on the 10th which I did and we went together to Vaiaotea, where Thompson received us in a Friendly Manner and we supp'd together, after which Thompson dropd a hint that He had found out the Thief but said no more. Next morning I went to the Beach to put my Canoe in order as I intended to return home after breakfast; while I was getting the Canoe ready I heard the report of a musquet, on which I ran up to the House but was stopd by Thompson who stood in the door loading his Musquet askd me if I was angry: as I had no arms I saw it was in vain to say Yes, and therefore Said No, and said I hope you dont mean to take the advantage of me; He told me "No—not without you are angry" and then Said "I have done him." Upon my nearer approach, I saw that Churchill was dead, the Ball having passd below the Shoulder through his body, entering at his back. as I now thought it high time to be off, and interr'd the Body as fast as I could—Thompson seized on his effects, I askd him for some of his books, but He refused, and I left Him and returnd home.—I intended to have askd your oppinion about the affair, but have since heard that Thompson is killd by the Natives in revenge for His having killd their Chief, and his body Carried to the Marae."

We knew not what to think of this business as we were inclined to think that Thompsons death was more on account of His having the property of both, then for Killing Churchill, but the Natives insisted that it was for killing him who they Acknowleg'd to be a Chief in consequence of His Friendship with the late Vehiatua whose Name he also bore.–

As I wishd to be particularly informd of the manner of their Deaths and to See *Mate* about getting Some rope & Mats for Sails, I set out for *Taiarapu* on the 17th, in Compy with Brown and Arrived at *Tautira* where He lived on the 20th I was well receivd by Mate who begd that I would not think of Coming to live in Taiarapu, which he said would prevent the people from Submitting to His Son. I promised him that I would not quit my Friend *Poeno* and told Him I had only Come now to see him, and hear how Churchill & Thompson were kill'd. I told him also that I wanted some rope & Matts for the Vessel which I described to Him, and he promised they should be made. On enquiring into the manner Churchchills & Thompsons death a Man was Calld whom I knew to be one of Churchills favourites, and he related evry thing in same manner that Burkett had done, as he was with Churchill & Steerd his Canoe in his Journey round the Island. I then askd Him how Thompson was Killd and by Whom at which he seemd rather doubtful and saying to me "dont be angry, it was I that killd him seeing that He had killd my Chief & my Friend". The Manner was this, *Pataea* (for such was the mans name) being sorry for his Friends death, was determin'd to be revenged on Thompson, and having got five or six More (who when they knew the Cause were equally enraged), they went to Thompsons house and saluted him by the Name of Vehiatua and told him that he was now Chief, and such like flattering stories till Pataea got between him and his Arms, and being a Stout man, knockd Him down. The others whipd a short plank (which happened to be at hand) across his Breast, and Placed one on each end, while Pataea ran for a large Stone, with which He dashd His Scull to pieces, they then Cut off His head, & Buried the Body. In the mean time Maititi secured their Arms and the House was plunderd; the Head *Pataea* brought to the Marae at *Tautira,* where he had left it and where he said it then was, and if I had a mind to see it, he would shew it to Me. I accordingly went to the Marae with him, when he produced part of the skull, which I knew by a scarr on the Forehead. I asked him why they had not brought him to us at Matavai, when He replied "the distance is too great, and our anger would be gone before we could get there; and we should have let Him escape when we were coold & our anger gone so that He would not have been punishd at all and the Blood of the Chief would have been on our heads".

I Promised the Man that he should not be hurt by me for what he had done, as I lookd on Him as an instrument in the Hand of Providence to Punnish such Crimes–

I Staid here three days during which time I was Feasted evry day by

Mate who also infomd me that the Nephew of *Vehiatua* (a boy of about 4 years old) was appointed to His name & Honors, and His father *Taipo* as Regant during his minority, (the People of *Taiarapu* refusing to acknowledge Young Tu, who they said was a Bastard and not the son of Mate.)[27]—however as He had some possessions given to himself he was resolved to keep footing in Taiarapu, and had hopes of gaining a party of His Sons favour.

When I took my leave He presented me with a large Hog, 3 bamboos of Scented oil & quantity of Cloth and I returnd to Matavai on the 24th, having been well received at evry place I stopd at, on my way both up & down.–

The work had gone on very well during my absence and by the 30th both sides were plankd up, the Ceiling in, & the Beams Secured, but now Norman and Heildbrandt left off Work and did not return to it till the Middle of May, However as the heavy Iron work was done and Coleman was now able to proceed by him Self with making nails & small work, and we set about Collecting Bread fruit Gum, Which we Boild into a very good Substitute for Pitch and with What rope had been brought (by ourselves and the Natives) from the Ship, we Musterd Oakum Sufficient to Caulk the Vessel all over. We were now visited by *Metuaro* who presented us with a Couple of Baked hogs, & some Cloth. He said that he had been making presents at all He could Muster or else he would have brought us more; he brought with Him the Dog Bacchus which had been left with Poeno together with a Bitch Calld Venus when We saild in April 89, and tho the animal had never seen us since we had been here He knew us immediately and Came fawning about us, at which the Natives were much surprized.

The dog & Bitch were seperated as soon as the Ship was saild and had never been together since, by which Means Mr. Blighs intention of getting a breed of Large Dogs on the Island was in some measure frustrated. Poenos sister having taken a fancy to the Bitch took her to Vaiari & Metuaro taking the Dog to *Mo'orea* when he was Calld home.

As we found it a tedious Jobb to gather the Gum or pitch, we Employd a Number of Natives. Dressing a Large Hog we made a feast for a Number of the poorer Sort and desired evry one that partook, to bring in his proportion of Gum, which they did not fail to perform according to the quantity of Pork they had received, as we found this answerd our purpose we repeated it till we had sufficient for our Purpose. We found that by

Boiling it down it made Good Pitch and Hogs lard being Mixd with it made it answer the purpose of Tar.

Tho the Method of Procuring this gum was dear yet the Hogs Cost us Nothing, and the people were not over paid for their Labour, and a Hog of 200 lbs weight would not bring 50 lbs of Pitch. Their Method of Procuring it is this—they take a peg made of *Toa* which with a Stone they drive through the bark in several places and having served a Number of Trees in this manner they let it stay till next morning, when the Gum is run out and hardend. This they scrape off with a shell, and make it up in a Ball; but a Man can hardly get a pound of it by himself in two days.—no other tree affords this Pitch but the Breadfruit and when it first runs is as white as Milk and as thin but it soon hardens and looks like white wax and when Boild becomes black and is in all respects like pitch extracted from pine; tho' this Comes from the Bark only and not from the Tree.

17th. Norman & Heildbrandt having returned to work, we got about laying the deck, which was finishd by the 1st of June, and in the Mean time Heildbrandt set about making Casks out of a White Wood Calld by the Natives Faifai, the grain of which resembles White Oak; the Young Chestnut trees which grow in abundance in the Hills making Hoops—we also Cut Masts Boom Bow Sprit & Gaffs intending to rigg her Schooner fashion and made a Kellick[28] with *Toa* and Weighted it with lead.

4th. This day We fired a Volly & Drank a Keg of Cyder which had been prepared from the Apples Calld *Vi* on purpose for the Occasion. We were also visited by Byrn & Ellison who had come to Point Venus in their way to Tetiaroa. We now Set about Caulking, Making rope, Blocks &c. The Purau answerd for the Shells of the Blocks, and the Toa for Shievs & Pins. The Bark of the Purau being Cleand made very good rope, & a sheet of Copper made a Barrel for a Pump, with Colemans Assistance.—in Caulking the Vessel we observed that an insect Calld here *Huhu* had eaten into a part of the Stem Which we found it Necessary to shift & put a new piece in its place. The Rudder being fixd, & the Vessel Caulkd all over, We paid Her with pitch, and by the 1st of July She was ready for Launching with Masts Boom Bowsprit & Gaffs Compleat.

We had frequent visitors while She was building Who examined her inside and out and viewd each part with surprize, wondering how it was possible to make such a Vessel, and what seemd to draw their attention most was the Method we used of twisting the Plank which sometimes proved an over match for us, and we broke several, after expending a whole weeks labour on them, and being Assisted by Fire, Water and a good workman who understood his business—notwithstanding which, and all the Schemes which Necessity could invent we were frequently forced to throw the Planks away which with Iron work would have been of Use.—We lost only one pair of Compasses during the time She was in hand, and them we supposed to have been lost in the rubbish, and now put up our Tools and prepared for Getting her afloat.

With what rope we Could Muster we slung the Masts on the Sides making a kind of Cradle under Her Bottom, and having done with Most of the augur Shanks we made use of them as Bolts & Clenchd them through the Keel & Kelson to strengthen that Department.

And being all ready on the 5th We applied to Poeno Who told me that the Priest must perform His prayers over Her, and then He would have her Carried to the Sea.—the Priest being sent for and a Young Pig & a Plantain given Him When he began Walking round and round the Vessel, stopping at the Stem & Stern, and Muttering short sentences in an unknown dialect; and having a Bundle of Young Plantain trees brought to Him by *Poenos* Order, he now and then tossd one in on Her deck. He kept at this all day and night and was hardly finishd by sunrise on the 6th. When Poeno & *Teu, Mate's* father, Came with Three or four Hundred Men, and having each made a long Oration, their Men were devided in two partys, and the Servants of Teu having received a Hog & Some Cloth which was provided by Poeno for the Occasion, one of the Priests went on board and Several plantain trees was tossd to him from both sides. He then ran fore & aft, and exorted them to exert themselves, and on a Signal being given they Closed in, and those who Could not reach by hand got long Poles. A Song being given they all Joind in Chorus & She soon began to Move and in Half an hour She reachd the Beach, where She was launchd & Calld the *Resolution.*[29] Tho Several Trees were Cut down which Stood in the Way, yet She received no damage, except breaking the Masts in a passage of about 3/4ths of a Mile.

Having to the Ropes from under her & a Canoe afloat with her, we towd Her round point Venus into a small Bay to the Eastward of the Point, and Moord her with the Killick, & a warp on Shore in a Good birth, and under the shelter of a Point within the Reef.

And having the Scooner Affloat, we were now employd till the 12th, fixing Houses & getting our things removed when we got two houses fixt and Coleman Came to live with us at the Point, which we Calld Cockroach point, according to its own Name.—and boiling Salt took up the rest of our time this Month.—Having an Iron pot and a Copper Kettle we built a furnace of Clay and fixed them in; and filling them up Continually as the Steem evaporated we kept them at work night & day, devinding the Night into Watches of 2½ Hours, which we could Judge very well by the Stars, but the Salt water proved So weak here owing to the fresh water river which emptys itself at the Point, that we could not make more than one pound per Day.

2nd. We now Cut trees down for Masts, and in the Mean time Covered the Schooner over with Cocoa Nut leaves, wove like Matts.—Employd Boiling Salt:—Making the Masts, & the Cooper Making Casks, and the Weather being fine we began to Kill hogs and Salt them, taking out the Bones and Curing none but Prime Meat, as we cured Sufficient to fill a Cask it was stowd away on board, putting about 100 lbs in a Cask.—this we had no method of Weighing, but Cut the Meat by guess to resemble good four pound pieces, taking Care not to have any too small—this, with making rope &c. lasted till Near the end of the Month, when we receiv'd from Mate about 400 fathoms of Rope which being Mostly Small we laid and made Cable &c. for Shrouds & Stays, and got the Schoner Masted & riggd.—While other Maters were going on I took in hand to repair my Watch, the Chain of which was broke and by the help of a Pair of Compasses & a Nail which I filed up for a turn screw I took her to pieces & with much dificulty at last got the Chain repaird, but in a rough Manner and for want of Tools and Skill, it Cost me much pains and trouble to get the work together again which however I at last accomplished and with such good success that Stuart would have me take his in hand, and try what I could do. I took her to pieces and found about two inches of the inner part of the Main Spring broke of, to remidie this I softened the broken part of the Spring and cut a new hole for the ketch, and having put the work together found that she went very well.–

We also prepared a Log reel and line and Cutting a Glass Phial in halves with a Flint and fixing a leaden Center Cast on purpose, made a tolerable good half Minute Glass, Counting the Seconds by the Musquet ball slung to a thread, between which and the Watch we made it tolerable correct.

The Box of the Azimuth Compass being too large to be conveniently kept, we got a small gourd which answerd to the size of the glass, and made a Compass box of it, slinging it in Jymbals in the Bittacle where it was intended to remain for the purpose of Steering only,—and the spare Glass answerd to fix in the Bittacle to keep the Wet out, and a lamp made to burn oil over the Compass, which answerd very well, we also made some Candles of Goats fat which we had saved for the purpose–

A Cabbouse was next wanted, and this McIntosh built of Plank; & Coleman Cut stones square to line it in side and Contain the fire, these were placed & plastered up with Clay instead of Mortar.

evry thing seemd to be had without trouble or Dificulty except sails, and how to procure them we Could not tell, Matting being scarce and at the Best very unservisable, and tho we had Cut up our Cloaths, we had not sufficient Canvas amongst us to make her one Sail which would be fit to set at sea.

However we Continued at Work preparing such things as were in our power, and trusting in providence for the rest—Salting Pork Boiling Salt & making Casks, and getting ready evry thing that we Could think we might want. During this time the Vessel was afloat, and Still Continued to be tight, nor did the Sun hurt her as she was continually covered.–

12th. this Day a Messenger arrived from the Young King desiring our Immediate Assistance to quell the People of the District of *Tetaha* who had rebelld, and made an inroad into *Pare,* burning all before them; the Messenger also informd us that the *Pare* people had repuls'd them forcing them to leave two of their Dead behind them which were brought to the Young Kings Marae, and that they were preparing for another attack, being set on by the People of *Atehuru.*—he told us also that *Ari'ipaea Vahine* the Young Kings Aunt who had been at *Ra'iatea* for some years, was arrived at Pare with a Numerous Fleet which were all ready for War.

As we did not know that ever we should be able to effect our purpose, tho evry thing was getting forward, we found it necessary for our own sakes, to assist them, and therefore returnd for Answer that we should be at Pare Next morning—and Armd Accordingly on the 13th, leaving one to take Care of the Schooner, we marchd to Pare, where Ari'ipaea-Vahine received us, and a Dressd Hog was presented to us.—Byrn & Ellison being at Tetiaroa and Musprat on a Visit to *Papara* with his Friend *Ari'ipaea,* we were now only Eight in number, but were her Joind by Brown, who informd us that the Atehuru people had made war on *Temari'i;* which was further Confirmd by a Letter from Burkett desiring our assistance. Having made our breakfast we proceeded to Tetaha Surrounded By a Multitude (with *Poeno* & *Paitia* two Chiefs at their head) from Matavai.

before that we had proceeded half a Mile We found the *Maro e atua* or Sigl for War (which is several Fathoms of Cloth in one piece passd round several Trees, crossing the path several times)[30] and a Hog tied to each tree which the Maro passes round; this is generally Put up with some Ceremony, and the Enemy was defied to take it down.

On seeing this our party ran instantly and seized on the Maro & hogs, when the Enemy who lay conceald till now, made their appearance, and a Fray instantly commenced and Several heavy blows exchanged before We were observed by them—on our approach they Fled, but this Confused Mithod of engageing prevented us from knowing our own people, who were so scattered that we were not able at a distance to tell them from the Enemy, and we were therefore of No use but to look on while the Enemy retreated to the Mountains & our party returned with a deal of Plunder, & several Canoes which they had not been able to remove

We Now informd the Chiefs that they must alter their mode of Fighting, and bring their people under some Command, in Case they should have occasion to go to war again, which they promised to do; and having demanded Matts to make sails for the Schooner, we took our leave of *Fa'ataua,* or *Ari'ipaea Vahine,* and returned to *Matavai.*—This woman being the first Born has the right of the Sovereignity of Tahiti but having no Child she had Transferd the right to her Brother during her Absence, and now Continues it to his son; tho she is not out of Power herself by it & when she visits *Tahiti,* being always honord and respected, and always holds the reigns of Government when present.[31]—She paid much regard to us; and soon had matts collected sufficient to make Three Sails, viz M. Sl. Fr Sail & Jibb.—She was very active in the business, and took care that we were well supplied with provisions. the Young King also sent us a Double Canoe of 48 feet long, & for each a Hog a Piece of Cloth and a Bamboo of Oil.—Brown set off a Cross the Mountains to join Burkett and Sumner at *Papara,* and we promised to Join them as soon as the Sails were made.

Coleman having made two Needles, we set about making the Sails, using the bark of the Purau for twine, quilting the Matts, & seaming them at evry foot distance to strengthen them.—Mean while the *Tetaha* & *Atehuru* people had united their forces & were began to Commit Hostilitys both on *Papara* & *Pare,* and on the 20th we were demanded to assist again, which for our Credit we could not refuse, nor was the Sails any excuse, as we were wanted on Shore, and the Enemy looking on our peaceable inclination as the effects of Fear, sent us word that they would Come to *Matavai* & burn the Schooner and a Challenge sent to each Separately by their Warriors, who bid us defiance, telling us that each would have his man to Carry to the Marae, and much more such language.[32]—and they had also entered *Pare* again burning and destroying all before them.

On the 21st early in the Morning, leaving one as before to take care of the Schooner, we got into our Canoes and paddled to the Lower end of *Pare.* Here we were Met by *Poeno, Teu,* & *Fa'ataua,* and almost all the Men of *Matavai* with *Paitia,* & Matahiapo, at their head who were both principal men & their head Warriors. We were now but Eight in Number, and having given the Chiefs such directions as we thought necessary, they promised to observe them, and being willing to take the Cool of the Morning, we set forward in Good order, surrounded by Multitudes of all ages from both Districts, but the *Matavai* men kept Close to us, claiming the preeminence, and keeping the others in the rear.—on our approach the Enemy retreated to a high steep eminence in the Mountains, which Commanded a narrow pass, which was the only one by which they could be approachd, and as this place had resisted all Former attacks, they had got all their property to the place in readiness, & had formd an encampment of Huts ready to dispute the Pass; however we determined to proceed, as we could not hope for Peace without driving them from their strong hold: but it being some miles up in the Mountains it was Noon before we got near enough to see the pass & the situation of the enemy, who we found well posted. The heat became so intense that we should have been in a bad plight had not our friends brought with them plenty of Cocoa Nuts which we found very refreshing and tho we had Marchd at a slow pace, we now stood in great need of—having halted a few minutes we proceeded to the Pass, which was along a Narrow ridge where two men could scarcely pass in safety.—the Tahitians made a full stop when they came to the place, but seeing us proceed they followed, and Paitia & Matahiapo came in the Van[33] to be our guides over.—in crossing the pass we found ourselves open to their Stones with which they plyed us briskly from the Eminence above our heads, where our Musquets would not reach to do execution, tho we were forced to walk over at an easy rate for one Hundred yards or more, none of us except Coleman was hurt, and he only received a blow of a Stone in the leg which did not disable him.—However his Tahiti friend received a blow between the Mouth & Nose that brought him down, & having English Cloaths on was Mistaken for one of Us and they gave us a loud Shout & redoubled their Vollies of Stones, by which upwards of twenty more wer wounded before we could fire a Shot. However we got over and with a warm fire advanced up the Hill; when they soon gave way. As soon as this was observed by our Party they rushd in, & three of the Enemies Head warriors having fallen by our shot they fled; and our party persued them down the other side of the Mountains. Mean time the Plunder of their Camp was seized by the *Pare* Men, the *Matavai* people being more intent on driving their Enemies; the Chief part of their Houses being burnt, and distroyd, we returned in the evening to Matavai.—The Number of Hogs taken here were incredible; several of the largest died with the fatigue of coming down, their own weight & fat being more then they Could support.—the Party in Atehuru, being Yet in arms, the Young King was desirous that we should assist him to quell them, and force them to Restore the Maro ʻUra, or Royal sash; together with the Marae Taputapuatea,[34] being the Movable place of sacrafice;—the Peha rea or Sacred Chest wherein their Images are kept with the Valuables belonging to the Deitys; the *Fare Atua,* or house of God, with several other things which belongd to them, which the Father of the Present *Toʻofa* Chief of *Atehuru* had taken in war from *Tu* or *Mate,* and which had been kept in Atehuru ever since, but we found it so fatigueing that we Got the Sails ready in Order to Shorten our marches.—We had by this time between 6 and 7 hundred weight of fine Pork Salted, & got it on board, and having bent the sails and Got our Amunition on board, on the 26th we saild for *Pare* leaving the Houses in charge of the Natives with what things We did not want and leaving only Skinner in *Matavai* who was bad with sore eyes, which made our Numbers still but Eight. At Pare we found Hitihiti who had come from Papara where he had been with Burkett & Sumner, Who with the Assistance of Muspratt, Brown & Himself had repulsed the *Atehuru* & *Tetaha* people with a great slaughter; but as they would not submit to *Temariʻi,* they Had Sent him to us to desire that We would keep them in play and appoint a day to let the

fears we told him He should not be Hurted, telling him that Englishmen never used those ill who the Chance of War made their Prisoners; at which he seem'd easy, and promissed that evry thing in his posession should be restored, and that He would submit to evry thing we demanded in favour of the Young King.—To'ofa's friends soon Came after him to the Schooner, and he gave them Orders to go and Bring evry thing that belongd to the Marae; which they Obeyd.

He was a handsome well made Man about 22 years old, about 6 feet high, but *Pohuetea* is a very Corpulent old Man between 60 and 70.

4 *From Tahiti to England*

On the 1st of October the Canoe bearing the Marae, Ark &c.—was brought and deliverd into charge of the Priests of *Matavai* and *Pare;* who proceeded with her directly to *Pare,* and Orders were now given for the Fleet & Army to return home, when they accompanied the Sacred Canoe escorting it Carefully to *Pare,* and in the Afternoon a breeze springing up we Weighd, having Poeno & the Two Atehuru Chiefs, and run up to *Tetaha* where we anchord for the Night, & were Joind by Burkett and Amo who came to assist at the Peace we weighd at 9 Next Morning the 2nd. and worked up to Toa Roa harbour where we anchord in the afternoon. We landed the Chiefs and Went with them to the *Marae,* where the Peace was Concluded, and by our advice they were continued in possession of their Land; and *Pa,*[1] an Old Chief who was out of Commission, was put into the District of *Tetaha* as a Substitute for *Metuaro* to whom it was voted, the *Atehuru* Chiefs promised on their parts that they would always honor the Young King as their Sovereign, and by way of strengthning the Peace each of them took one of us as his Friend. Great feasting now took place a Volley of Small arms was fired on the occasion and all the Chiefs of *Tahiti Nui* or Substitutes for them attended.[2] Much feasting now took place, & on the 4th we weighd and workd up to *Matavai,* where we arrived by Noon, having Carried away the head of our Fore Mast, which being made of Bread fruit we found would not answer, and therefore Condemnd them Both. 6th. We were visited by Burkett & Amo (the same mentioned by Captn Cook) *Temari'is* father, who stayd three days, and returned to *Papara.*—

Norman & Millward new set out in quest of Masts to Hitia'a, where we were informd some grew of a Better sort of wood, and in the mean time we landed evry thing, and Cleand the Schooners bottom and paid it with Pitch.

We were now visited by *To'ofa,* who staid some time in Matavai, but he died soon after of an ague, and was succeeded by his nephew, a boy

Figure 13. "Morai Point, at Oparrey, Island of Otahytey," George Tobin, 1792 [Call no. PXA 563 no. 42]. Reproduced with permission of the Mitchell Library, State Library of NSW

of the age of about 4 years, Calld by his Name.—He is the Son of *To'ofas* sister, who now takes upon her the regency or Guardianship during his Minority.

26th. Norman & Millward returned, having cut two Masts one of *Faifai* and the other of Toi, with Spars for a Gaff, Boom & two Sweeps & new railing—which were brought down on the Next Morning, by two of the Natives, who made a raft of them with some Bamboos to help to float them, and saild them down with a temporary Sail made of Cocoa Nut leaves,—we went to work immediately to Make the Masts &c. and at the same time boiling Salt & Salting more pork; but had the Misfortune to break our Iron pot when we were forced to desist, & save the Kettle to Cook in, and we had now near 8 Cwt of Pork cured.

1st Novr. The Masts being finishd we got them in, Riggd them & Blackd the Mastheads & rigging, and gave them a Coat of Grease. We found them very heavy but were in no dread of Carrying them away.—The Oars, Gaff Boom & rails with a Squaresail Yard were now made, and evry thing Got on board, we also got a Small Canoe to answer the purpose of a Boat.

9th. Muspratt Came to the Point in his way to the Islands of *Tetiaroa* and on the 10th having got evry thing on board, we Got under way in order to visit *Tetiaroa,*[3] leaving Muspratt to follow in his own Canoe, but the Natives were better acquainted with the Weather then Us and did Not come out. We stood to the Northward with a Fresh breeze at ESE which Freshend to Gale & forced us to heave to, the Sea running very high and no anchorage near the Islands, forced us to keep at a Distance—at 4 in the afternoon we wore & hove too with our head to the southward still blowing hard and a high seas. In the Morng of the 11th it Moderated, and we made sail standing in for the Land, having only seen the Islands not daring to venture near them, the Vessel behaved remarkably well, but the Sails suffered by the Weather.

12th. at 4 in the Afternoon we got inside the reef at *Tetaha* and run down to *Ta'apuna,* intending to sail for Mo'orea as soon as our sails were repaired, here we came to an Anchor, and *Pohuetea* came on board, and brought two roasted hogs & some Breadfruit, Yams, & Taro, we also met with *Poeno* here, who had left Matavai the same time we did, bound round the Island, we got one of his Men as a Pilot, and having repaird our Sails, in the Morning, Weighd and run over to Mo'orea, Where we anchord in Vaiari harbr on the same day; the distance being little more then 10 Miles.

We were well received here by Fa'ataua who was here on a visit, and Next Morning *Metuaro* sent a Messenger to desire we should come round to *Opunohu* or Captn Cooks Harbr near which place he lived, to this we agreed; and on the 14th Weighd and went round, accompanied by *Fa'ataua* in her Canoe—one of *Metuaro*'s Men piloted us into a small cove to the Westward of the Harbour, where we Came to an anchor in the afternoon, and Metuaro and His Wife Terereatua came on board with several of our old acquaintance, and we saluted them with 6 Musquets. after welcoming us to the Island they enquired what our business was, to which we replied, to see our friends, they then desired that we should not be in any hurry to leave them, and ordered us to be well supplied with evry thing that the Island afforded, and having settled Matters so as to leave one on board evry day to take care of the Vessel the rest went on shore to see their friends.

My principal look out here was for Matts, but these were scarce, and we could hardly get sufficient to keep the sails in repair but this scarcity of Mats We supposed to be owing to their unwillingness to part with us; and as they knew we could not leave them without sails, they kept the Mats out of our sight, but evry thing else they gave us freely, and loaded us with presents.

While we were here we went to see the Cattle, which were about 6 Miles distant on the West part of the Island—the whole that now remaind were One Bull, Five Cows, & one Cow Calf, and one of the Cows big with Calf—the Bull had some time ago slipt his hip bone out on the left side, which wasted the leg and thigh which was occasioned by a Fall Jumping over a ditch—but Metuaro inform Us that he had got the Calves since, they are all very large and in good order, but quite wild, being only kept as curiositys—they have plenty of fine Grass, and it is possible they may increase now, which they could not do before, the Bull being kept by himself till *Metuaro* was calld home, who observing that Lieut. Bligh had been at some trouble and expence to bring the Cow & Bull together at Tahiti resolved to do the same here to try if they would increase, which he found to answer, and as we told him they were valuable, and would bring a good price if a Ship should come here, He promised that they should stay together while he held his authority in *Mo'orea.*[4]–

As we began to think our visit long enough, and some of us thought we had been too long from home, we weighd on the 25th having on board Metuaro, his Wife Fa'ataua and several men of distinction, and workd up to Vaiari where we anchored the same day. *Metuaro* was very desirous that we should stay some time longer, but we thought short visits best, and promised to come again, He made us each a present of Hogs & Cloth, and Norman having a fancy to Stay a while at *Mo'orea* he took him at his word and taking his leave of us set out the same night on his return homeward and we prepared to sail next day having on board 48 hogs & a large quantity of Cloth &c. &c.

Coleman, having gone on shore to fetch some sand for the arms which he had found to answer the purpose of Emory at about 2 miles from the Schooner, was seized by a Man (who knew that He was the Man who wrought among the Iron) and threatened to Kill Him, having a large stone for the Purpose in one hand; he said that Coleman had had his wife on board and had used her Ill, but some others coming up as if by Chance prevented him, and settled the Matter on Condition that Coleman should make him a handsome present, by which means he got off & Came on board with the sand; when he told us the Story we saw that it was only a scheme to get the trade from him, and if we overlookd it we should only encourage them to do so again, and that to prevent being robbd it would be necessary to go arm'd, and therefore resolved to punnish the Offender if we could find him.

Early next morning the 26th Coleman, Millward, McIntosh & Heildbrandt went on shore armd, and proceeded towards the place, but before they reachd the House where they supposed to find him, notice was given of their approach and those who had been Concerned Fled, but not so fast as to prevent the Shot from overtaking and wounding two of them, one in the Thigh & body and the other in the Arm, both of which acknowledg'd the scheme they had been concernd in, and begd for quarter, but the principal one Escaped. On enquirey they found that the House belongd to him that had first seized Coleman and demanded the trade, and as he was not to be found they plundered the house and returned to the Schooner with some Cloth, Hogs, Oil and a Canoes sail which they found in it, and which we wanted to repair our own with, leaving the wounded to get themselves dressd. On their return on board a Messenger was sent to inform *Metuaro* of what we had done, who sent and turned the Man off his land, and told us when ever they offered an insult to shoot them, and was sorry that the men who were wounded were not kill'd out right, which he said would deter others from such attempts. Mean time a peace offering Came to us from the Landed Men of the District,[5] desiring that we should not be angry with the whole, for what one bad man had done. We accepted the Offering and told them that we did not wish to hurt any one, but that we would always punnish such offenders as we were able to find out, but that we never wishd to punnish the Innocent for the Guilty, and would therefore proceed no further in this Affair. We wrote to Norman to inform Him how we had settled the Affair, and desiring Him to acquaint us if they made any further Stir about it, and Weighd on the 27th for *Tahiti*.

Vaiari is a snugg little Harbour on the East part of the Island, the entrance is a Narrow break in the Reef which lies half a Mile from the Beach; the Channel is deep, and a Ship may ride in 7 Fathm within half a Cables length of the shore, and tho the Harbours Mouth lies open to the sea breeze the swell never reaches the Shore, as may be proved by the Trees

& Grass growing close to the high water mark, and as the land breeze which blows evry night, affords an opportunity to get out evry 24 hours, I should prefer the Harbour to any that *Tahiti* affords for a single Ship as all kind of Provisions are found there. Common to both Islands, and equally plentiful, and wood and water are to be had much easier at *Vaiari* then at any part of *Tahiti* as both may be had here within hail of the Ship. Captn Cooks Harbour is large & spacious, but being to leeward, is subject to heavy rains (from the Clouds gathering round the tops of the Mountains) while *Vaiari* enjoys fine Pleasant weather, and is always dry except in the proper season.

The Wind being light we did not reach *Ta'apuna* till the 28th, when we entered the reef and worked up inside of it to *Pare,* here we landed the Hogs, and sent them up by land. on the 29th *Ari'ipaea* Presented us with a large baked Hog and Accompanied us to *Matavai* the same day, together with several of his Friends.

As soon as we could see the Beach at the Point we saw it lined by the Inhabitants who had Flockd to the place to see us as soon as the News of our approach began to spread; and when we Anchord could scarce get from the Schooner to the *Houses* for our old Friends, who flockd about us and were as eager & seemd as much rejoiced as if they had found some of their lost relations.

We now landed evry thing, and Coleman went to live at His freinds house, where he fell sick of a Feverish Complaint, but as we had neither Skill nor Medicines the disorder was suffered to take its Course, and after having brought him nearly to the Brink of the Grave, it left him and he recovered.

Byrn and Ellison being returned from *Tetiaroa* went to *Mo'orea* to reside some time with *Metuaro.*

Having got evry thing on shore by the 10th of Decr and expecting the Wet season now to set in shortly,[6] we got the Schooner hauld up and housed over to shelter her from the Weather.

Coleman having declared that he would not have any thing to do with the Schooner, and our finding that our hopes of reaching *Batavia* or any other place without sails, and finding that even Matts could not be had, we dropd any further attempts that way, and devided the Pork, which on examination proved excellent Meat, and superior to any that had been salted in the Ship, which we imputed to a powder Cask which we had used to saved the pickle in, and by this means the Salt Petre contain'd in the Staves had been communicated to the whole of the Pork.

23rd. This day arrived Byrn from *Mo'orea* who staid with us to keep Christmass and returned to *Mo'orea.*

The Weather being now Wet we had nothing to do but prepare for it, by securing our houses and screening them in.

27th. This evening a man came into the House and unperceiv'd Carried off the Box containing all my writing Utincils paper &c—with the Compass Cards & Glasses watch &c. The Box being Missd, pursuit was made, but tho evry Means was instantly taken, no account could be heard of it till near noon the next day, when it was discovered by a Young Man who was our Neighbour, who being up on a Cocoa Nut tree getting Nuts, he saw the Box, and getting down as far as he could, he ran and took it from the Place and returnd to us with it unhurt, at which I was very well pleased, and offered him a present, which he refused, saying he was glad he was so lucky as to find it.

In about 2 days after, we learnt that the thief was a Lunatic who had come to the Point with a Number of People belonging to the *Ra'iatea* Fleet who came over with *Ari'ipaea Vahine,* and were now bound round the Island, and had Come to the Point in their way, intending to go to Windward as soon as the Weather permitted.

The thief was soon apprehended, but did not appear to be so mad as he was represented—having seen the Box open the day before he took a fancy to the things that it Containd, and as it stood on a table with out any other security then its own lock he found means to escape with it, but it being instantly missd, he heard the noise that it occasioned and had put it into the Bush, where it was found, and made off for fear of being taken, but having informd one of our friends of the affair, he made known to us the thief and we having now got him in our possession we gave him a good smart Whipping & let him go, when he promised that He would never steal any more from us or any body else.

We had now frequent Visitors from different parts, & particularly from the *Ra'iatea* people, who made much inquirey about Captn Cook, Sr Joseph Banks &c. &c.—and as we were also Visited by several people of note from *Huahine,* the Island where Captn Cook had left *Ma'i,* we learnt of them that he died (of the *Hotate,* a disorder not much different from the Fever & Ague) about four years after he had landed, and the

New Zealand boys both died soon after, they greived much for *Pounamu* their Native Country, and after *Ma'i* died, they gave over all hopes & having now lost their chief friend, they pined themselves to Death.—They also inform'd us that *Ma'i* was one of the Lowest Class (Calld Manahune) and had been condem'd to be sacrificed for Blasphemy against one of the Chiefs, but his Brother getting wind of it sent him out of the way, and the Adventure arriving at *Tahiti* at the Time, he got on board her and came to England, and his Friendship with Captn Cook afterwards, made him more respected then his riches, and the meaness of his birth made him gain very little credit with his countrymen tho he kept them in awe by his arms.—His Horse was killd soon after his landing by a Goat who Gored Him in the Belly which they knew no remedy for, and the only revenge he could have was to kill the Goat; the Mare remains yet at *Huahine,* and part of the House which Captn Cook had built for him. His Goods were devided after he died, & he distributed many before his death, the Musquetts are in possession of a Chief who was his Friend (Calld *Tenania,* brother to *Teri'itaria* king of *Huahine*) but are of no use being both disabled; these Accounts we had also from a very intelligent man who lived with *Ma'i* some time as a servant, and who informd us that he was very careful of His property till he died, when it was distributed among his friends—they also informd us that His Arms and the Manner in which he used them made him Great in War, as he bore down all before him, and all who had timely notice fled at his Approach and when accoutrd with his Helmet & Breastplate, & Mounted on Horse back they thought it impossible to hurt him, and for that reason never attempted it, and Victory always attended him and his Party. Nor was he of less consequence at sea, for the enemy would never attempt to come near the Canoe which he was in.

They informd us that his Garden was destroyd by the Hogs & Goats &c.—having no body to look after it and the poultry were all dead except one Goose, being devided and kept in different parts of the Island as Curiositys after His Death and many being taken to *Ra'iatea, Taha'a, Borabora &c.*[7]

On the 10th arrivd here *'Itia* from *Taiarapu,* bringing with her *Teano* her sister & a Number of Attendants. She Congratulated us on the Success which attended us in the War which had proved very beneficial to Her Son, who was now to be invested with the Royal *Maro,* for which purpose she had now come to prepare.[8] She made each of us a present, and next day we were entertained with a Boxing Match by the *Ra'iatea* Men, & Wrestling and Dancing by the *Tahiti* Men & Weomen.[9] *'Itia* was Mistress of the Ceremonies, and the Number of Spectators present was very great, and among them came *Ari'ipaea Vahine* who had returned from *Mo'orea* to assist at the Ceremony of Investing the Young King with the Royal *Maro.* Next day the 12th I attended *'Itia* at her request to *Pare* on a visit to the Young King; at entering his bounds she was forced to Change her Cloaths, and put on those which belongd to him, before she could Inter his house, but he desired me to wave that Ceremony, and received Me very Courteously. A hog was prepared for Me, but *'Itia* could not partake of any Provisions under her sons roof; nor could she eat in a house or Canoe where he had been till all His Ceremonies were performed, and he is restricted within particular bounds, to prevent his rendering any thing sacred which is not intended for his use; and for this reason he was never permitted to come near the Ship, as his presence there would have rendered evry thing Sacred so far as to prevent not only his own family, but evry body else from either eating on board, or using any thing that Came from the Ship, by which means all their presents would have been rendered useless to any other but himself.[10] After we took our leave of Him, I went with 'Itia and Air'd the Powder which I found in Good Order, and having Cleand the Arms which were here, returned to Matavai.

14th. Arrived here Burkett on a Visit, with whom I set out on the 17th for *Papara,* having heard much of His friend *Temari'i* who I had not yet seen. We reachd *Papara* next day, where we were received by *Temari'i* himself. He is a Handsom wellmade man of about 27 or 28 years old and about 6 feet high. He received me with evry token of Friendship, and desired me to be one of His friends; we soon became perfectly intimate, and during my stay he feasted me evry day, and begd that I would be in no hurry to return home.

Whiel I was here the Young Kings Flag arrived, and was received by *Temari'i* and Conducted to His *Marae,* but kept by the Beach close down in the Surf till those who Carried it were abreast of the *Marae,* when they turnd short round and proceeded to the Marae—as the Flag passd, the Inhabitants hid themselves, and all Fires were put out—we attended them to the *Marae,* where *Temari'is* priests having set the Flag up, made the Usual peace Officering of a Hog and a Plantain tree, the Priests repeated it and several young Pigs & Plaintain Trees were Offered with long

Harrangues; and *Temari'i* made a long speech declaring *Tu-nui-e-a'a-i-te-atua* to be his Chief, and ordered a feast to be provided for those who bore the Flag—this Flag was the Union Jack which they had got from Captn Cox, and was Slung a Cross the Staff with a stick in the tabeling as we sling a Pendant, it was decorated with Feathers Breast Plates Tassels &c.—as the Chief People of the District were present, we honord the Ceremony by firing our Musquets,—which was received as an honor, and some of those who were present interpreted this into a declaration on our part to support it in Circumventing the Island, as it was Composed of English Collours, and they made no scruple to say that War would be instantly made on those who should attempt to stop it.[11]

It was kept one Night in the *Marae,* during which time prayers were Constantly saying by one or other of the Priests which attended it; and when it proceeded they returnd to the Water Side, where they had before been, & proceeded along by the edge of the Surf towards *Taiarapu.*—On the 23rd I took leave of *Temari'i* who gave me a pair of Canoes & several Hogs Cloth &c. and Burkett accompanying me we set off for *Vaiari,* where we were received by *Tutaha, Poenos* brother & *Moananui* his brother in law—who entertains us civilly and we set out for the Isthmus where we hauld the Canoe a Cross, this part of the Island is a low level spot about 3 miles it is thick of Wood, but as the Inhabitants frequently travel this way there is a Good road, and it is much easier to haul the Canoes a Cross, then to go round the Peninsula when they are Bound to *Tautira.*

As soon as we reachd the North Side we were met by Messengers from *Mate* desiring us to come up to Him at Afa'ahiti about 6 Miles from the Isthmus; we accepted the invitation, and leaving the Canoes at a house Close by set out by land, and arrived there in the same afternoon, (the 25th,) when a feast was prepared for us, and Mate was glad see us.

He now informd us that the people of *Taiarapu* had used him very uncivil, although the Flag had been received, and passd with all the Ceremonies; which he said was only for fear of us and not their regard to His son. He told us that we had yet a right to Chastise them for Killing Thompson, and said that if we once made our appearance in Arms in *Taiarapu* they would never make any resistance and he would be at the Expence of the Amunition, that his Son might be Sole King, he also told us that He had conversed with *Temari'i* who was ready to furnish Men & Canoes when ever we thought proper to take it in hand.

27th. having told him that we would Consider of the Matter we signified our intention to go homeward, when he ordered his Canoe & went down to the Isthmus with us, when we launched our own and set out in Company for *Hitia'a,* and having landed at *Tetuis* (a Man of Rank) we had a dinner prepared, and we then proceeded to *Avaimais* where a Feast was also provided, and we remain'd here all Night.

And on the Morning of the 28th a hog & some Cloth being prepared for me I took my leave, and leaving Burkett to return to *Papara,* and Proceeded to *Matavai,* where I arrived on Saturday the 29th and found Numbers assembled at Matavai and Pare to attend the Approaching Ceremony and among them Metuaro with Norman, Ellison and Byrn from *Mo'orea,* and all the principal Men of the Island, and the beach was filld with Canoes.

Feby 1st. Millward and McIntosh set out for Papara, for the purpose of seeing Temari'i, and Conversing with him about the War with *Taiarapu.*

10th. 'Itia brought the Amunition Chest with evry thing in it, and with a pair of Pistols delivered them into my Charge, and gave me a Bayonet (which she had got from Captn Cox) which I fitted to my own piece, my own being broke. *Metuaro* also paid me a Visit and invited me to go and live a while at *Mo'orea.*

13th. This day the Ceremony of Investing the Young King with the *Maro 'Ura* or Royal Sash took place; the Sash is of fine Network on which Red and Yellow Feathers are made fast, so as to cover the netting; the sash is about three yards long, and each end is devided into six tassels of Red Black & Yellow feathers, for each of which they have a name of some Spirit or Guardian Angel, that watches over the Young Chief while the *Maro* is in his Possession and is never worn but one day by any one King; it is then put into the Sacred Box and with a Hat or Shade for the Eyes Made of Wicker & Covered with feathers of the same kind and never used but on the Same occasion it is delivered to the priests, who put it Carefully by in the Sacred House on the *Marae,* where no person must touch it.[12]

This Ceremony was performed at Pare on the New Marae which was built for the reception of the Movable Marae &c. which we had brought from *Atehuru* and where these things were now kept. The Chiefs (or their Substitutes) of *Te Porionu'u* and *Mo'orea* attended and Tu-nui-e-a'a-i-te-atua the Yong King being placed on the *Marae,* a Priest making a long Prayer put the Sash round his Waist and the Hat or Bonnet on his head & haild him King of *Tahiti. Metuaro* then began by His Orator making a long Speech and acknowledging him his King, when three Human Victims were brought in and offered for *Mo'orea,* the Priest of Metuaro placing them with their head towards the Young King and with a long speech over each, he offered 3 Young Plantain trees. He then took an Eye out of each, with a Piece of split bamboo, and placing them on a leaf took a Young Plaintain tree in one Hand, and the Eyes in the Other Made a long speech holding them up to the Young King, who sat above him with his mouth open; after he had ended his Speech & laid the Plaintain trees before the Young King, the Bodys were removed & buryed by his priests in the Marae, and the Eyes put up with the Plaintain trees on the Altar—the rest of the Chiefs then brought in their Sacrafices in the Same Manner, going through the like Ceremony, some bringing one Victim & Some two according to the bigness or extent of their district, after which large Droves of Hogs and an immense quantity of other Provisions such as bread, Yams, Tarro, Plaintains, Cocoa nuts &ca. were brought and presented to the Young King. Several large Canoes were also hauld up near the Marae on the sacred ground; these were dressd with several hundred fathoms of Cloth, Red Feathers, Breast plates &c.—all which were secured by the priests & Young Kings attendants—the *Maro* being now removed and taken Care of by the Priests, they all repaird to feasts prepared for them, which lasted some weeks, the Number of Hogs destroyd on this occasion were beyond all conception besides Turtle, Fish &c. &c.—

I enquired the Cause of the Eye being offered, and was thus informed. The King is the Head of the People for which reason the Head is sacred; the Eye being the most valuable part is the fittest to be offered, and the reasons that the King sits with his Mouth open, is to let the Soul of the Sacrafice enter into his Soul, that he may be strengthened thereby, or that He may receive more strength of discernment from it, and they think that His Tutelar Deity or Guardian Angel presides to receive the Soul of the Sacrafice.[13]

Several Large Hogs were placed upon the Altar and the Human sacrifices offered this day were 30, some of which had been Killd near a Month.

These were the First that had been offered since our coming to the Island. They never offer Men but such as have committed some great

Crime Nor then, but on particular Occasions, but Hogs Fish &c. they offer without Number and on evry trifling affair.

20th. Arrived Millward and McIntosh who having settled the Matter relative to the War, we determined to put it into execution, as None of the Chiefs of *Taiarapu* had assisted at the Ceremony of investing the Young King with the Royal sash. *Temari'i* had proposed to Make a Grand Feast, under Cover of which he Could have his Men and Canoes collected before he told them what he wanted them for, and by that means would prevent it from being blazed about—the English were to be there as partakers of the Feast, and when we were ready to attack them we could be in their Country before they knew what we were at, and by this means make an easy conquest.[14] This appearing to us a very good plan, we agreed to prepare for it as fast as possible, and began to get things in order for Launching the Schooner; but from the Number of Visitors which daily came to see us, owing to the Number collected together in the two districts, we were not able to make any Progress, and it was the 1st of March before we Got her Launched. We filld the Water for Ballast and Stowd the Casks with Stones and Wood, we also got the Pork on board, masted and rigg'd the Vessel, but still kept our intentions a secret.

Among our Visitors We often Had the Young King, but as his presence in any House would render it useless to any of the Natives he Never came in.

Sunday the 13th. He was Carried round the Beach of *Matavai* on Mens Shoulders dressed in a Cloak of Black feathers and his Head almost Hid in a large Garland of Black and Red Feathers—he was attended by the principal people of the District carrying the Union Jack horisontally over their heads, but as all could not get under it, several Fathoms of painted Cloth was added to it. His Ceremonies are not all performed yet, for which reason he can only pass by the Beach, and cannot go inland, except on sacred Ground leading from the Beach, he made us presents, and appointed each to a portion of Land, being very fond of the whole of us, and desired his Subjects to treat us as his relations, calling us his Uncles (or *Metua*'s).[15]

14th. Bent the Sails and got evry thing on board and on the 21st Weighd & saild for *Pare,* leaving in *Matavai* Mr. Stuart, Mr. Heywood, Coleman & Skinner. We anchor'd at the lower part of *Pare* where we were Join'd By Norman, Ellison and Byrn, making our number now seven, being McIntosh, Millward, Heildbrandt & Myself.

22nd. Weighd & saild for *Papara,* but having light airs we anchord at *Ta'apuna,* and weighd on the 23rd, sailing along Atehuru, which from its White Beach and the Narrow border of Flat land Covered With Trees, (Chiefly *Purau* and *Fara*) we thought much resembled the North side of *Tubuai.* We were invited to stop at several places where the Natives were very Civil, and *Pohuetea* begd us to Stop at his house, but the Anchoring being bad at *Taitapu* (that part of *Atehuru* where he now lived) we declined, and stood on, the wind being still light; it was night before we reach'd *Papara,* we anchord for the Night with in a break of the reef about a Mile from *Temari'is* house. Some went on shore to Temari'is to Sleep, & he Came down to View the Schooner as soon as he had notice of Her Arrival. Next Morning we Weighd, and workd up to the *Marae,* and Came to an Anchor, here we found Burket, Sumner, Brown & Muspratt, we went on shore to *Temari'is* to Breakfast but was scarcely sat down when a Friend of *Hitihitis* arrived in haste, telling us that a ship had anchord at *Matavai* since we had left it, that those who we had left there were gone on board, and that the Boats Mand and Armd were then at *Atehuru* in their Way after us, that Hitihiti who was their Pilot had sent him to give us Notice that we might know how to act.[16] No time was not to be lost in fixing on the best plan, and it was agreed to avoid seeing the Boats: and for this reason we got on board leaving Brown & Byron on shore, and Got under way stood out with a fresh Breeze at ESE standing to the Southd on a Wind.— we hoped by keeping out of sight of the Boats to reach the Ship and go on board of our own accord, hoping there by to have better treatment then if we stayd to be made prisoners, and Hitihitis Messenger had given us a very unfavourable account of the Treatment of those who went on board from *Matavai.*

When we were about a league from the land we saw two sail to leeward, but could not disern whether they were Boats or Canoes, but as we left them apace we thought they could be no other then Fishing Canoes. Soon after noon we lost sight of them, and at 4 oClock we hove about & stood in, but it was Sunday the 27th before we could fetch in, owing to the Contrary winds & light airs which prevailed.

When we Anchord we were informd that Mr. Hayward, formerly of the Bounty, was Officer of one of the Boats, which proved to be the same we had seen, who finding they were not like to come up with the Chase had returned to the ship; we also learnt that Byrn had gone to the Ship and Brown having plunder'd Burketts house of all that he could, was gone on board also.[17]

Temari'i, seeing Brown seizing on all that he could find, had sert evry thing back into the Mountains where Burkett, Sumner, Muspratt, Heildbrandt, McIntosh & Millward, went after them, leaving Norman, Ellison and Myself to take Care of the Vessel; in the Mean time I went on shore to get some Cocoa Nuts & some provisions dressd, leaving Norman and Ellison on board, and as the surf run high on the Beach I took no arms with me, when I left the Vessel, when I went to *Temari'i* he promised that I should have what I wanted Imediately. I told Him that we must go to the Ship; when he said "if you do Hayward will kill you for He is very angry". He ordered some hands to carry off Cocoa Nuts and in the Mean time pressd me to stay with him, saying if you will go into the Mountains they will never be able to find you; but I still denyd him; telling him that I must go to the ship. He then unbraided me with deceiving him, and told me that I should not go, and at the same instant I observed several of the Natives on board the Schooner (where they had gone by *Temari'is* order and under pretence of carrying Cocoa Nuts on board) had taken the Opportunity of Seizing Norman and Ellison and throwing them overboard. I then Begd *Temari'i* to prevent them from being hurted, when he told me that there was no fear of them, and in a few minutes after they landed and were Conducted to Me amidst a Thousand or More of the Natives, when they Pourd so fast on board the Schooner that they bore her down on one side and she rolld the most of them overboard; however they soon stripd her of evry thing that they could remove and brought the things on shore, unbending the Sails & unreeving the rigging which they brought away with them.

We askd Temari'i what was the Meaning of this Treatment, and seeing nothing of our Companions and being unarmed ourselves we hardly knew what to think of our situation; he told us it was because we wanted to leave Him, and told us we must go and secure ourselves in the Mountains and keep away from the Ship and we should have our arms and evry thing restored, and he would make good all our damages. We still refused; when he said then I'll make you go, and his men Seized us and was proceeding in land with us when we begd of *Temari'i* to let us see some of our Shipmates before we went; which he agreed to & a Guard was placed over us, till he should return. We were conducted to the house of Teri'iamoeatua where we had provisions prepared in abundance. We staid here all Night, and next day, When we proposed to make our escape, and a Trusty friend who had lived with me all the time I had been on the Island, being one of *Poenos* Men found us out and promised to have a Canoe ready by Midnight to carry us to *Matavai,* where he said that Poeno waited with impatience to see us. As soon as it was night, he took his station on the Beach, and about 10 oClock brought Brown into the House; we asked him if he had any arms, when he produced a Pistol which he said he had brought from the Ship with two hatchets & a knife, these He delivered into Normans hands, and asked us what we meant to do, & where the rest were, to which we answerd that we had not seen the others since they landed and we were going to the Ship and askd Him the Name of the Ship & her Commander; but the only account he could give was that she was an English Ship of War and Could inform us No farther. He also Produced a Bottle with some hollands[18] of which he offered each a Dram, but the smell proved sufficient for Me and the other two draink but sparingly. Brown told us that He had been Landed at the North Side of the Isthmus by the Ships Boat of which Mr. Hayward had Command, and was sent to *Papara* with presents for *Temari'i,* but had not seen him, he said he had been beset near the *Marae* and narrowly escaped being Killd, his Pistol being wet would not fire, and was forced to shelter himself in the thick Brush near the *Marae,* and was proceeding to return to the Ship when he was met on the Beach by our Man.

The Canoe being ready we armd, Norman & Myself with a hatchet each Ellison the large Knife, and left the Pistol with Brown, who fresh Primed it, & we set forward; having got to the Canoe without interuption we got in and paddled to *Atehuru,* landing about 6 Miles from *Papara* on a sandy Beach, which being white was of some help to us in Travelling; here we left the Canoe and proceeded alongshore for 12 or 14 Miles and reachd *Pohueteas* House at *Taitapu* about 4 in the Morning of the 29th. Here we found a launch at anchor near the beach and some Canoes hauld up near the House. We haild the boat but received no answer; those on board being all fast a sleep, as were those who were on shore in the Canoes. On Enquirey we found that the Canoes belong'd to *Ari'ipaea,* who was Here with them, and the Officer Commanding the Boat was Mr. Robert Cornor (Second Lieut of His Majestys Ship Pandora Captn Edward Edwards) who being asleep in one of the Canoes we waked him and delivered our selves up to Him, telling Him who we were, and delivering the Hatchets to Brown when he came up, also the Pistol and amunition which he had given to Norman by the Way.

Having informed Mr. Cornor where the Schooner was, and what had happened to us, he left us in the Launch with Mr. Rickards, Masters Mate of the Ship, and Six Men, and with 18 more he set out (as soon as daylight enabled him to proceed) by land for *Papara,* taking Brown with him, we remain'd here till two in the afternoon when Mr. Hayward (who we found was Third Lieutenant of the Ship) arrived with the Pinnace and 20 Men Armd, and by his orders we had our hands tyed and Mr. Richards being ordered into the Pinnace, Mr. Sevill a Midshipman was put on board the Launch & ordered to proceed to the Ship then 25 or 30 mils distant. Mr. Hayward askd us no other question but where the others were, which we could not answer not knowing ourselves. We parted from the Pinnace about 3 oClock, and during the Passage up, Mr. Sevill gave each of us half a Pint of Wine and from Him we learnt the Fate of the Bountys Launch, and he also informd us that Lieut. Bligh was made Post Captain, he also enquired what was become of the Bounty and who was in her, which we answerd to the best of our knowledge, and we reach'd the Ship at 9 oClock when we were handed on board and put both legs In Irons, under the Half Deck, after which our hands were cast loose, there being no Marines, two Seamen & a Midshipman were posted over us with Pistols & bayonets–

Here we found in Irons Geo. Stuart, Peter Heywood, Josh. Coleman, Richd. Skinner, & Michl. Byrn, who informd us that Handcuffs were Making by the Armourer which were next day put on, and orders Given to the Centinals not to suffer any of the Natives to speak to us, and to shoot the first Man that spoke to another in the Tahiti Language. We remaind under the Half Deck some days, during which time we had full allowance of evry thing but grog, which we did not then want, having plenty of Cocoa Nuts provided for us by our friends, who were not suffered to speak or look at us, any who lookd pitifully toward us were ordered out of the Ship–

In the Meantime a hammock was given to each to spread under us and a shirt & Trowsers given to each of us but these were of no use as we could not get them on and off, our Irons being Clenchd fast–

The Carpenters were now set to work to erect a kind of Poop on the Quarter Deck for our reception.

On the 9th of April the Schooner was brought to the Ship by Mr. Hayward, and in her came Thos. Burkett, Jno. Sumner, Thos. McIntosh, Willm. Muspratt, Jno. Millward, & Henry Heildbrand who were Iron'd Hand and foot in the Same manner as we were as soon as they came on board.

The Poop or Roundhouse being finishd we were Conveyd into it and put in Irons as before. This Place we Stiled Pandoras Box, the entrance being a Scuttle on the top of 18 or 20 inches Square, Secured by a bolt on the top thro' the Coamings, two Scuttles of nine inches square in the Bulk head for air with Iron Grates, and the Stern ports bar'd inside and out with Iron; the Centrys were placed on the top while the Midshipman walkd a Cross by the Bulkhead. The length of this Box was 11 feet upon deck and 18 wide at the Bulk head; and here no person was suffered to speak to us but the Master at Arms, and His orders were not to speak to us on any score but that of our provisions–

The Heat of the place when it was calm was so intense that the Sweat frequently ran in Streams to the Scuppers, and produced Maggots in a short time; the Hammocks being dirty when we got them, we found stored with Vermin of another kind, which we had no Method of erradcating but by lying on the Plank; and tho our Freinds would have supplyd us with plenty of Cloth they were not permitted to do it, and our only remedy was to lay Naked,—these troublesom Neighbours and the two necessary tubs which were Constantly kept in the place helpd to render our situation truly *disagreeable.*

during the time we staid, the Weomen with whom we had cohabited on the Island Came frequently under the Stern (bringing their Children of which there were 6 born, Four Girls & two Boys, & several of the Weomen big with Child) Cutting their Heads till the Blood discolloured the water about them, their Female friends acting their part also and making bitter lamentations,[19]—but when they came to be known, they were always driven away by the Captns orders and none of them sufferd to come near the Ship. notwithstanding which they continued to come near enough to be observed, and there performd their Mourning rites which on the day the Ship Weighd, were sufficient to evince the truth of their Grief

It being Customary for the Officer of the Watch to examine our Irons before he was releived, McIntosh happening to have a large Shackle had got one of his legs out in the Night, which was reported to the Captain and a general examination took place, when the leg Irons were reduced to fit close, and Mr. Larkan the First Lieut. in trying the Handcuffs took the Method of setting his foot against our breasts and hauling the Handcuffs over our hands with all his Might, some of which took the Skin off with them, and all that could be haul'd off by this Means were reduced, and fitted so close, that there was no possibility of turning the Hand in them, and when our wrists began to swell he told us that "they were not intended to fit like Gloves"–

however Colemans legs being much swelld he was let out of Irons as was also Norman & Byrn on their falling sick, but they were always handcuffd at night. McIntosh & Ellisons arms being much galld by their Irons Had them taken off till they should get well, but their legs were still kept fast–

The Schooner being fitted, & the Water Compleat we saild from *Tahiti* on the 19th of May[20] and on the 20th had our Grog served in full allowance.–

We stood to the NW and next day made Huahine[21] & *Ra'iatea, Taha'a* &c. and laid off & on here several days, sending the Schooner in with the land, and here *Hitihiti* was landed having come from *Tahiti* in the ship, we next proceeded to *Aitutaki* and Palmerstons Isles and in the examination of them the Jolly Boat with Mr. Sevill & four hands (one of which the Son of the Boatswain of the Pandora) was lost, by being blown off when going to the Schooner which lay at anchor near the Reef; the Ship & Schooner both run to leeward in quest of her but to no purpose, on these Islands was found Part of the Bountys Driver Yard which was in the raft that went a drift from *Tubuai.*[22]

Standing to the Northward several Islands were discovered and at one of them Calld Chatham Island[23] the Schooner was Missed and given over for lost.

We Cruized some time in search of Her but without success & stood for the Friendly Islands, where meeting with wet weather, the roughness of the Work made our Habitation very leaky, and when any rain fell we were always wet, we applyd to the First Lieut. to have something done to remedy it to which he replyd, "I am Wet too and evry body on Deck and it will dry when the Weather Clears up".

Our miserable situation soon brought sickness on amongst us and the Surgeon (Mr. Hambleton), a very humane Gentleman, gave us all the Assistance in his power, but at the same time informd us that Captn Edwards had given such orders that it was out of his power to be of any service to us in our present Circumstances, however between him & the Second Lieut. a Copper Kettle was provided to boil our Cocoa in which was served with Sugar in Lieu of Butter & Cheese—and this with the Divine Providence kept us alive–as the place was washd twice a week we were washd with it, there being no room to shift us from place to place and we had no other alternative but standing up till the Deck dried (which we could but very badly do when the ship had any motion) or lying down in the wet, and when the roughness of the weather gave the Ship any Motion we were not able to keep ourselves fast, to remedy which we were threatened to be stapeld down by the Captain, but Mr. Cornor gave us some short boards to Check ourselves with which he made the Carpenters secure; and thereby prevented us from Maiming each other and ourselves–

We anchored at *Nomuka*[24] where we wooded and watered and returned to the Northward again in quest of the Schooner, leaving a letter with one of the Chiefs for her if she should come in our absence, and it is possible that if she had Come here that She would have been plundered by the Natives who behaved very indifferently even to the Ship; the 2nd Lieut. being knockd down on shore by some of them and some of the Men stripd stark Naked, and Some of them having got into the Cabbin jumpd out of the Windows with several of the Captains Books &c.—but being persued they left the things and escaped, one of their Canoes was seized for the Captain & brought on board.

At Chatham Isles the Natives were also very dexterous at theiving, and one of them made a shift to get out of the port in the Lieutenants birth under the Half deck with a New Uniform Jacket belonging to Mr. Hayward, which he put on as soon as he was a stern of the Ship and paddled off with it.

We Cruized 10 or 12 days and returnd to *Nomuka* without hearing any tidings of the Schooner, and her and her Crew were both given over as lost.

The Natives of the New discovered Isles seem to differ very little from the Friendly Islanders; their Language seems to be the same, and the Construction of their Canoes is very near alike, they have hogs, but they are remarkably small—these Islands are high, but do not appear to be very fruitful, and are about 2 days run to the NE b N of *Nomuka*.

Yams were now purchased by the Purser to Issue in lieu of Bread, which were served at the rate of 3 lbs of Yam for one of Bread while they lasted, and having Compleated the Water Saild from *Nomuka* about the 1st of August steering to the NW,[25] and it was now known that her destination was for the Island of *Timor.*

Several Islands were discovered on this passage, and on the 22nd, made the reef which Crosses the Streights in the Lattd of 9°, having narrowly escaped running on a Patch about a Mile long, which lay by it self but a few days before—this was Calld *Wells's Reef* from its being discovered in the Night by a young man of that name.–

Finding no opening in the Reef, we hauld to the Southward working to windward some days, and on Sunday the 28th of August the 2nd Lieut. was sent to find an Opening in the reef with the Yaul and the Ship hove too—and on Monday the 29th at 7 PM the Ship went on the Reef. Just at the time the boat returns within hail and warnd them of the Danger, but it was now to late, the Current running fast towards the reef caused a heavy surf in which the Ship was forced for to the reef with Violent and repeated strokes and we expected evry surge that the Masts would go by the Board. Seeing the Ship in this situation we judged she would not hold long together, and as we were in danger at every stroke of killing each other with our Irons, we broke them that we might be ready to assist ourselves and keep from killing each other, and Informed the Officers what we had done when Mr. Cornor was acquainted with it he Came aft and we told him we should attempt nothing further, as we only wanted a Chance for our lives; which he promised we should have, telling us not to fear. In the Meantime the Ship lost her rudder and with it part of the Stern post and having beat over, between 11 & 12 she was brought up in 15 fathom with both anchors, and the first news was nine feet water in the Hold. Coleman, Norman and McIntosh were ordered out to the Pumps, and the Boats got out, as soon as Captain Edwards was informd that we had broke our Irons he ordered us to be handcuffd and leg Irond again with all the Irons that could be Mustered, tho we beggd for Mercy and desired leave to go to the pumps; but to no purpose, his orders were put into execution, tho the Water in the Hold was increased to 11 feet and one of the Chain pumps broke—the Master at Arms and Corporal were now armd with each a Brace of Pistols and placed as additional Centinals over us, with Orders to fire amongst us if we made any Motion; and the Master at arms told us that the Captn had said he would either shoot or hang to the Yard Arms those who should make any further attempt to break the Irons, we found there was no remedy but prayer, as we expected never to see Daylight and having recommended ourselves to the Almighty protection we lay down and seemd for a while to forget our Miserable Situation, tho we could hear the Officers busy getting their things into the Boats which were hauld under the stern on purpose & heard some of the Men on Deck say I'll be damnd If they shall go without us. This made some of us start, and moving the Irons, the Master at Arms said fire upon the rascals—as he was then Just over the Scuttle I spoke to him and said for gods sake don't fire, whats the matter there is none here moving—in a few Minutes after, one of the Boats broke a drift and having but two Men in Her she could not reach the Ship again till another was sent with hands to bring her back, and now we began to think they would set off together, as it was but natural to suppose that evry one would think of himself first, however they returned, & were secured with better Warps, and now we learnt that the Booms being Cut loose for the purpose of Making a Raft one of the Topmasts fell into the Waist and Killd a Man who was busy heaving the Guns overboard and evry thing seemd to be in great confusion—at daylight in the Morning the Boats were hauld up and most of the Officers being aft on the top of the Box we observed that they were armd, and preparing to go into the Boats by the Stern ladders—we Beggd that we might not be forgort, when by Captn Edwards's Order Joseph Hodges, the Armourers Mate of the Pandora, was sent down to the take the Irons off Muspratt & Skinner & send them & Bryn (who was then out of Irons) up, but Skinner being too eager to get out got hauld up with his handcuffs on and the other two following him Close, the Scuttle was Shut and Bar'd before Hodges could get to it and he in the Mean time knockd off my hand Irons & Stuarts. I bed'd of the Master at Arms to leave the Scuttle open when he answerd "Never fear my boys we'll all go to Hell together". The words were scarcely out of his Mouth when the Ship took a Sally and a general cry of "there She Goes" was heard, the Master at Arms and Corpl with the other Centinals rolld overboard, and at the same instant we saw through the Stern Ports Captn Edwards astern swimming to the Pinnace which was some distance astern, as were all the Boats who had shoved off on the first Appearance of a Motion in the Ship. Burkett & Heidbrandt were yet handcuffd and the Ship under Water as faar as the Main Mast and it was now begining to flow in upon us when the Devine providence directed Wm. Moulter (Boatns Mate) to the place. He was scrambling up on the Box and hearing our Crys took out the Bolt and threw it and the Scuttle overboard, such was his presence of Mind tho He was forced to follow instantly himself. On this, we all got out except Heildbrandt and were rejoiced even in this trying scene to think that we had escaped from our prison tho It was full as much as I could do to clear my self of the Driver boom before the Ship Sunk—the Boats were now so far off that we could not distinguish one from the Other, however observing one of the Gangways Come up I swam to it and had scarcely reachd it before I perceived Muspratt on the other end of it, having brought him up with it, but it falling on the Heads of several others sent them to the Bottom here I began to get ready for Swimming and the top of our Prison having floated I observed on it Mr. P. Heywood, Burket & Coleman & the First Lieut. of the Ship, and seeing Mr. Heywood take a short plank and set off to one of the Boats, I resolved to Follow him and throwing away my trowsers, bound my loins up in a Sash or *Maro* after the Tahiti Manner, got a short plank & followed and after having been about an hour and a half in the Water, I reachd the Blue Yaul and was taken up by Mr. Bowling, Mrs Mte, who had also taken up Mr. Heywood. After taking up several others we were landed on a small sandy Key on the Reef about 2½ or 3 Miles from the Ship. Here we soon found that Four of our fellow prisoners were drown'd, two of which Skinner and Heildbrandt with this Handcuffs on, and Stuart and Sumner were struck by the Gangway. Burkett being landed with his handcuffs on, the Captn ordered them to be taken off, we also learnt that 31 of the Pandoras Ships Company were lost, among whom were the Master at Arms & Ships Corporal—but all the Officers were Saved.[26] a Tent was now erected for the Officers & another for the Men, but we were not suffered to come near either, tho the Captain had told us, that we should be used as well as the Ships Company but we found that was not the Case, for on requesting of Captn Edwards a spare boats sail to shelter us from the sun being Mostly naked It was refused tho no use was made of it and we were ordered to keep on a part of the Island by our selves, to windward of the Tents, not being suffered to speak to any person but each other, the provision saved being very small this days allowance was only a Mouthful of Bread, and a Glass of wine; the water being but a small quantity, none could be Afforded.

We staid here till Wednesday morning the 31st, fitting the Boats during which time the Sun took such an effect on us, who had been Cooped up for these five Months, that we had our skin flead off, from heat to foot, tho we kept our Selves Covered in the Sand during the heat of the Day, this being all the Shelter that the Island affoards, the whole of it being no more then a small Bank washd up on the reef which with a Change of wind might dissapear, it being scarcely 150 Yards in Circuit and not more than 6 feet from the level at high water. There are two More of the Same kind of which this is in the Middle; between it and the one to the Southds is a Deep Channel through which a Ship might pass in safety. These Keys are laid down by Captn Edwards and their Lattd is between 10° and 11° South, about one Days run from the Nd. Cape of New Holland

during the Night as we found the Air very Chilly and having no covering, we threw up a bank of sand to sleep under the lee of, which proved but an indifrent barrier as we had frequent flying showers of rain sufficient to make our lodging Miserable to not sufficient to save any to allay our thirst which was very great, we tryd for water but found none, & Mr. Cornor Making a fire got a Copper Kettle which he filld with Salt water and Making it Boil, attended it all Night saving the Drops which the Steam causes in the Cover which he put into a Cup till a spoon full was mustered

and one of the Pandoras people (Named Connell) went out of His senses drinking salt water

On the 30th the Master went with a Boat to the Wreck, to see if any thing had come up, the Topmast heads being out of the water, the Top Gallt Masts struck. He return with part of one of the Top Gallt Masts which he saw'd off to get clear of the Cap—and a Cat which he found sitting on the Cross trees, one of the Ships Buoys drifted past, but was not thought worth going after tho we had no vessel to Contain water when we should find it.

The Boats being ready, on the 31st at 10 AM we embarkd in the Following Manner, McIntosh, Ellison & Myself in the Pinnace with Captn Edwards, Lieut. Hayward and 19 Officers and men, making her Compliment 24; in the Red Yaul went Burkett & Millward, with Lieut. Larkan and 19 officers & men, making her Comp 22; in the Launch, Peter Heywood, Josh. Coleman & Michl. Byrn, with Lieut. Corner & 27 Officers & Men, her Comp 31, and in the Blue Yaul Norman and Muspratt, with the

Master & 19 Officers and Men, Making Ninety nine souls in all—and in this situation we had a passage of between four & five hundered leagues to run before we could reach the Dutch Settlement on *Timor* with the Scanty allowance of 2 Musquet balls weight of Bread & hardly a Jill of water & Wine together for 24 Hours, in a Scorching hot sun now nearly vertical–

We left the Key (which was named Wreck Island) & proceeded to the NW and next morning, the 1st of Septr, we made the land which we supposed to be Part of New Holland and the Two Yauls were sent in with the land, while we stood on towards an Island, where we hoped to get water & in the Afternoon we were Joind by the Yauls who had got Water and having filld their Vessels followed us; they having Joind us we stood into a bay to search for Water and having as we approachd the Beach found that there were some inhabitants on it, tho it was but small and did not appear very fruitfull the natives appear'd on the Beach to the amount of 18 or 19 men, women & Children, who appeard to be all of one Family; they came off freely to the Boats when we found that the Collour of their skins was heightend to a Jett Black by Means of either Soot or Charcoal, they were quite naked and their hair long & Curling but Matted like a Mopp and some had holes in their ears which were stretched to such a size as to receive a Mans Arm, we made signs that we wanted water which they soon understood, & a half ancker being given to one of them & some trifles by way of encouragement, he soon returned with it almost full, which being started into a brecco[27] and gave it to him again. He then Calld a Young Woman who stood near him and sent her for the Water, she soon returned, and with her a Mean with a Bundle of Spears, when she came to the Beach the Man who had sent her went and received it, and standing up to the fork in the water, made signs for the Boats to come in, which was declined and He kept retreating. Mean while two of the Men began to prepare their Weapons, & a Javlin being thrown, struck the Pinnace, and an Arrow fired which fell close along side, & both were taken up & several Musquets were fired, at which they dropd, & the Man who had the Keg let it fall & fled, but finding himself not hurt, he returnd and took it with him; they soon dissapeared and Captn Edwards ordered the Boats to follow him, putting off and standing to the westward to some other Island then in sight, at this the First Lieut. seemd displeased, and spoke his mind so loud that Captn Edwards heard him, and desired him to be silent and obey his Orders and at his Peril to say no more about the Matter—we reachd the Islands & Examined them but they afforded no water nor any thing eatable, except a sort of plumb which contains a Glutinous Gum which sticks in the Mouth teeth Throat &c.—& were by no Means a delicacy, however they were eaten; but Shell fish of which we had brought some from the Key, we could not toutch for want of Water—among the shell fish found on the Key were two large Cockles of the Gigantic sort which Measured about a foot the longest way of the Shell–

Finding no water here, we bore away to the Westd and at 3 next morning made an Island where we hoped to get water, & standing in came to an anchor till day light when we weighd & got Close in, seeing no natives a Party was sent on shore to Water which at least they found by digging and evry vessel was filld, the Kettle was boild with Portable soup, & a pint served to each Man with as much water as we could drink, but we were reduced to many shifts to Contain water having made Canvas bags, filling a Pair of Boots & evry thing that would contain water if but for a day was filld and then the whole did not amount to 200 Gallons; a scanty allowance for 99 Men to subsist on who did not expect to reach *Timor* in less then 14 days and knew of no place where we could recruit till we reachd it and tho we had got an additional stock of water it was no addition to our allowance as we knew not how long the passage would be—having filld our Water we saild to the Westward and for fear of Parting Company in the Night the Pinnace took the other Boats in tow all night which was the Case evry Night through the passage–

The Heat of the Weather made our thirst insupportable and as the Canvas bags soon leakd out, no addition of allowance could take place, and to such extremity did thirst increase, that several of the men drank their own urine, and a booby being caught in the Pinnace the Blood was eagerly suckd, & the Body devided and eagerly devoured; two others were Caught by the other Boats which shared the same fate as the distress was general.

We kept a line constantly towing, but never caught any fish tho we saw several.

On the 9th as I was laying on the Oars talking to McIntosh Captn Edwards ordered me aft, and without assigning any Cause ordered me to be pinnioned with a Cord and lasshd down in the Boats Bottom, and Ellison, who was then asleep in the Boats bottom, was ordered to the same punnishment—I attempted to reason and enquire what I had now done to be thus Cruelly treated, urging the Distressd situation of the whole, but received for answer "Silence, you Murdering Villain, are you not a Prisoner, You Piratical Dog what better treatment do you expect," I then told him that it was a disgrace to the Captain of a British Man of War to treat a prisoner in such an inhuman Manner, upon which he started up in a Violent Rage & snatching a Pistol which lay in the Stern sheets, threatened to shoot me. I still attempted to speak, when he Swore "by God if you speak another World I'll heave the Log with You" and finding that he would hear no reason & my mouth being Parchd so, that I could not move my tongue, I was forced to be silent & submit; and was tyed down so that I could not move–

In this Miserable Sitaution Ellison & I remaind for the rest of the passage, nor was McIntosh suffered to come near or speak to either of us; however we made ourselves as easy as we could and on the 15th we made the Island of Timor, when the Boats seperated & Stood in for the land, having had a fine Breze & fair Weather all the way.

We try'd for Water at several places, but could find none till the 16th in the Morning when we found a Well near the Beach & here the Launch Joind us again when we proceeded in Company to Coupang which we reachd at Midnight and came to a Grapnell off the Fort till Morning. We found a Ship in the Road, and a Number of small Craft, and at 8 in the Morning the Captain went on shore to the Governor. About 10 we were landed, and Conducted by a Guard to the Governors house, & from then to the Castle where notwithstanding our Weak Condition we were put into Stocks and on the 19th the Yauls arrived & we were Joined by our fellow prisoners whose treatment had been better, but their fare the same—Immediately on our landing Provisions were procured which now began to move our bodys and we were forced to ease Nature where we lay, which we had not done during the Passage and some were now so bad as to require repeated Clysters, but the Surgeon of the Place who visited us could not enter the place till it had been washd by the Slaves, we had laid 6 Days in this situation when the Dutch Officer Commanding the Fort, being informd of our distress came to visit us & taking Compassion on us, ordered Irons to be procured, and link'd us two & two; giving us liberty to walk about the Cell, and now a Guard of Pandoras Men were placed before the Door in addition to the Dutch Soldiers–

As we were Yet Mostly Naked, we got some of the leaves of the Brab Tree, and set to work to make hats, which we sold to procure us Clothing;

but evry article being dear we could purchace little here; and thread and Needle being very dear we made but little progress; however we made shift to supply ourselves with Tobacco and some little refreshments–

We found that there were prisoners in the Fort, Seven Men a Woman & two Children who had escaped in a Boat from Sidney (or Port Jackson, Botany Bay) they had passd some time on the Governor for Part of the Crew of the Ship Neptune which they reported to have been cast away, but not being able to keep within Bounds, they were discovered to be Cheats, and Confined in the Castle till they should pay the Debt they had Contracted.

We remain'd here till the 5th of October when we were removed on board the *Rembang,* ye Dutch Ship then in the Road—and Mr. Larkan, being the Officer on this duty coming to the Prison with a Guard with Cords for the Purpose pinnioned us with his own hands, setting his foot against our backs, and bracing our arms together as almost to haul our arms out of their sockets; we were tyed two & two by the Elbows, & having our Irons knockd off were Conducted to the Beach and put on board a long Boat to proceed to the Ship but before we reachd her some of us had fainted owing to the Circulation of the Blood being stopd by the lasshings—When we got on board we were put both legs in Iron, and our lasshings taken off–

The Botany Bay men were now brought on board by a party of Dutch Soldiers and put in Irons with us, in the Same Manner, and the Ship Weighd in the Evening for *Batavia* and Next day McIntosh Coleman & Norman were let out of Irons with liberty to walk the Deck.

Our hands being now at liberty we expected now to find some little ease, & prepared to go to work on hatts having brought our stuff on board with us, but happiness is not to be always found where it is expected and is every of a short duration–

The ship was very leaky and were ordered out of Irons two at a time, for two hours in the fore noon, & two hours in the afternoon with Centinals over us to work the Pumps—this new liberty, as we thought it, we gladly embraced, but soon found our strength unequal to the Task—and I one day told Mr. Larkan that I was not able to stand to the pump at Spell & Spell (the ship requiring the pump continually at work) to which he replyd Tauntingly, "You *dam'd Villain,* you have brought it on yourself and *I'll make* you stand it; if it is was not for you we should not have been here nor have met with this trouble", to which I replied "trouble often comes unsought" and he then ordered me to be silent–

However this work was soon at an end for hard work at the pump, and the deck where we lay being Constantly wet, and having no Cloathing under, or over us, soon put us past labour; and we were then kept below, the pumps being now left to the Dutch Seamen and *Malay* Slaves–

This ship was badly found and Worse Managed and if Captain Edwards had not taken the Command and set his Men to work she would never have reached Batavia, having Split Most of Her Sails in passing the Streight of *Bally*[28] and having none to bend in their stead very narrowly escaped going on shore–

However we reachd *Samarang,* a Dutch Settlement on the Island of *Java,* by the 30th of Octr where we came to an Anchor, and here we found the Schooner, which had arrived at this Island 6 weeks before, with all her Crew, consisting of a Masters Mate, Midshipman, Quarter Master and Six men, one of which died since their Arrival. They were Joyfully received by their Shipmates and the Schooner being brought out of Harbour accompanied us to Batavia where we anchord on the 7th of Novr.

We were now put on board an old Hulk in the Road with the Pandoras Officers and Men & here McIntosh, Coleman & Norman had the liberty of the Deck as before and here we received 10/- per Man for short allowance in the Boats, with which we purchased some few refreshments in addition to the Ships Allowance, being Still Victualled by the Purser of the Pandora.

The Schooner being put up for Sale the Captn Purchased her, and sent her as a present to the Governor of *Timor* & devided the Mony amongst the Ships Compy.

Nankin Cloth was here purchased and served to the Ships Company, and as we had now recovered our health we commenced Taylors as well as hat makers, and by Working for the Ships Company got some Cloaths for ourselves which we stood in much Need of, but this was prohibited by Capt. Edwards as soon as he knew it

We remaind here till the 23rd of December during which time we were not permitted to come on Deck but twice, each for about half an hour at a Time to Wash ourselves, and here we enjoyd our Health, tho the Pandoras people fell sick and died apace.

With respect to the City of *Batavia* I can say nothing, not having had a view of it, but it makes no shew from the Road, the Church & some storehouses being the only Buildings that can be seen from the Shiping. It is situated at the Bottom of a deep Bay or Inlet and surrounded by low and to all appearance Swampy land which has no appearance of Cultivation—the small river by which its Canals are filld emptys itself into the Bay and teems with such filth that the Road where the large Ships lye is little better then a Stagnate Pool; during the Night the Dew falls very heavy and the Morning is generally darkened by a thick Stinking fog which continues till it is exhaled by the Heat of the Sun–

As the Sea Breeze seldom reaches the Road till afternoon and some times not during the Day the Weather is Close & Sultry and the land Wind coming off in the evenings brings with it a sickly disagreeable smell sufficient to breed Distempers among Europeans—to prevent being infected by this, we apply'd for liberty to smoke tobacco which being Granted, all our leisure time was thus employ'd but particularly in the Mornings & Evenings, which we found very beneficial and freed us from headaches &ca. which we supposed to be occasioned by the pestilential vapours–

The Climate of *Batavia* is by no Means calculated for Europeans and together with the New Arrack (a most pernicious liquor) carries off Great numbers daily and such a havock had Death made within the last 6 Months that the Fleet now in the Road were forced to send to Holland for Hands to Navigate them and even now they were not half Mannd, tho the Crews of the outward bound ships were put on board as fast as they came to an Anchor, it was said that 2,500 Officers & Seamen had been carried off this season exclusive of the Inhabitants—The Chinese & Natives of the Island do all the Labour in loading & unloading the Ships as the Dutch seamen are mostly removed as soon as the ship is made fast–

Provisions here are Neither cheap nor Good, the Beef being all small and lean and Rice is the only substitute for bread, at least all that can be the fare of the Ships Company. Cloathing of all kinds and especially the Manufactures of Europe is dear also, and in fact I could find Nothing Cheap but Arrack which is as bad as poison; but nevertheless it is plentifully used by the Dutch, and it Cost the Pandoras Officers some trouble to keep their Men from using it also–

20th Novr. The First Lieut., Mr. Larkan, saild in a Dutch ship for Europe with part of the ships Company and on the 23rd of December the remainder were devided Lieuts Corner & Hayward taking each a party and with them the Botany Bay men—and we were put on board the *Vreedenbergh* in which ship was Captn Edwards with twenty three officers & men and on the 24th she weighd and dropd down to a small Island in the entrance of the Bay Calld *Onrest* on which the Dock Yards is, and to this place they send their Convicts where they are employ'd making Rope & Careening the Ships–

We weighd from this place on the 25th, tideing it out through the Straights, and it was this afternoon before We got any Provisions, having been Victualled no longer then the 22nd by the Purser of the *Pandora,* and when we got it it was served after the Dutch Method which was thus—two drams of Arrack pr Day, equal to 1/3rd of a Pint—three Pounds of Flesh (Beef & Pork) one & a half of Fish—do. of Sugar, do. of Tamarinds, half a Pint of Gee half a Pint of Oil, & a pint of Vinager with Rice in lieu of Bread to serve each Man for a fortnight—the rice was little better then Grains, most of it having the husts on it, and the Oil & Tamarinds were fit for no use that we could put them to—Such was our food, and two Quarts of water a day gave us plenty to drink, but our lodgings were none of the Best, as we lay on rough logs of Timber, some of which lay Some inches above the rest and which our small portion of Cloathing would not bring to a level, the Deck also over us was very leaky, by which means we were continually wet, being alternatively drenchd with Salt water, the Urine of the Hogs or the Rain which happened to fall–

We passd the Streight of *Sunda* on the 1st of Jany 1792 and met with Nothing Material during our passage to the Cape except burying two of the Pandoras Men & several of the Dutch Seamen—this and the Method of Issuing the Provisions was the only thing that occur'd worth Notice, and which as is Shews the true Character of Dutchmen diserves Notice, they made *Ranson,* or fortnights allowance, to serve us Sixteen Days and by the time we reached the Cape they had gaind upon us nearly a fortnights allowance–

March 14th. this day we were let out of Irons two at a time to walk the Deck for two Hours each, but were Scarce able to stand on our feet we were got so weak by living or rather existing on Our Miserable allowance—this was the First and last Indulgence of the kind we had during the Passage, except one or two Who had been let out for a few hours in a day by the intercession of the Dutch Surgeon, and we now found the weather Sharp and Cutting

15th. Made the Cape of Good Hope and on the 18th came to an anchor in Table Bay, where to our inexpressible joy we found an English Man of war was riding which we were soon informd was His Majestys Ship Gorgon from Port Jackson,[29] and on the 19th we were sent on Board her, where our treatment became less rigourous and 2/3rds Allowance of Provisions was now thought Feasting

Shortly after arrived the other Ships with the rest of the Pandoras men We learnt here that the First Lieut. of the Pandora had saild some time and having left one of his men behind he was sent on board this Ship by Captn Edwards. McIntosh, Coleman & Norman were here at liberty as before and the Rest of us only one leg in Irons, and evry Indulgence Given & Lieut. Gardner of this Ship, in the absence of Captn Parker, very humanely gave us a Sail to lay on which by us was thought a Luxury; and was indeed such as we had not enjoyd for 12 Months before

And here being supplyd with Shirts & Trowsers we laid what trifle of Cash we had out in refreshments and began to get our health & strength very fast having the Benefit of the fresh air which for some time before we had been strangers to, being removed from between Decks to sit on the Fore Castle for 6 or 8 hours evry day–

On the 4th of April Captn Edwards came on board in order to take his passage in the Gorgon and on the 5th she Weighd for England and on the 10th we were ordered full allowance.

18th. Made the Island of St. Helena which we passd near enough to show our Collours and see two Ships in the Road who returned the Compliment by hoisting theirs.

22nd. Made Assencion and anchord the same day—found riding here an American Schooner belonging to New Providence and having got on board 28 fine turtle Saild on the 24th—after Crossing the Line we spoke an American Brig bound to Bengal, and an English Brig the Prince William Henry, bound to the South Fishery.

19th of June. Anchord at Spithead. On the 21st we were removed to His Majestys Ship Hector where we were treated in a manner that renders the Humanity of Her Captain and Officers much Honor and had Beds given us and evry Indugence that our Circumstances would admit of allowed

On the 12th of September our tryal commenced on board His Majestys Ship Duke in Portsmouth Harbour and to the Minutes of the Court

Martial I refer the reader for a more particular account of that Transaction. Mean while I shall endeavour to give some account of the Island of *Tahiti* or King Georges Island and of the Manners and Customs of the Society Isles in General with an account of their Language such as I was able to procure during my stay on shore there of Nineteen Months, exclusive of Near five Months which elapsed while the Bounty lay there under Lieutenant Blighs Command and five Months More which we expended after the Taking of the Ship before we landed most part of which time We were conversant with the Natives.

PART II

The Account

The Island of Tahiti

5 *The Tahitian World*

The Island of Tahiti is better laid by Captn Cook then I with an indifferent Quadrant could be able to ascertain. Its Lattd is between 17° 28' and 18° South and its Longitude about 211° East. (According to Captn Cook Pt. Venus is in Lat 17° 29' 30" So, Long 149° 32' 30" West.)[1]

It Consists of two Peninsulas both of which are of a Circular form with an Isthmus of Low land about 2½ or 3 Miles a Cross—the larger Peninsula is Calld *Tahiti Nui* or Great Tahiti, and is about 80 Miles in Circumference and the Smaller, which lies to SE of Tahiti Nui, is Calld by the Names of *Tahiti Iti* (Little Tahiti) and *Taiarapu* and is about 30 Miles in Circumference according to my Computation having no aperatus for surveying I can only give the Distance according to my own oppinion[2] it is in most parts defended by a reef of Corral, in some places a Mile or a Mile & a half from the Shore, within which is several small keys—the Beach in some places Black & others White.

Both peninsulas are Mountainous, and Covered with Trees of different sorts—having each a border of Flat land (except where it is seperated by Mountains rising out of the Sea) which is likewise Covered with Trees Chiefly the Bread fruit & Cocoa Nutt—Several of the Mountains rising out of the Sea rise Gradually till they form one great or general pile in the Center of the Island which may be seen at 20 leags dista; they are intersected by innumerable Vallys all of which are Cloathed with Verdure—the Ridges are covered with reeds which at a Distance resemble Grass while they are Green, and the tops of the Hills are for the Most part Covered with large trees—and the Highest Mountains teem with innumerable Cascades forming a Delightful prospect and thirty of these may be Counted pouring from a high Mountain lying behind Matavai Calld *Orohena*[3] which water the neighbouring vallys—and before it reaches the Sea forms many small rivers & Brooks all of which are Excellent Water, being produced by Springs some of which Issue from the Solid Rock.[4]

The Climate of the Society Isles differs very little from that of the Leeward Islands, and may be calld (after Changing the Seasons one being in Nd & the othe So Latitude) the same—during the Six Months that the Sun is to the Southward of the Equator, the Weather is unsettled and the Wind Variable and when the Sun Draws nearly over head the Rainy Season begins and continues with intermissions while it is passing to the South & repassing to the North which is Generally from October till April—in this season the Westerly Wind is the most prevailing and it sometimes Blows very hard & brings with it a heavy Sea, and when the North or South Wind happens to prevail it generally brings much Thunder & Lightning with it, and the rain falls in deluges, swelling the rivers so as to overflow the low land in a few hours, bringing large trees from the Mountains, and tumbling Huge Rocks before it—and frequently Carrying away the Houses of the Natives into the Sea, however the loss they sustain is not great and they are generally supplyd with plenty of Timber for Fuel without the trouble of going to the Hills for it—as the Westerly Winds bring a heavy sea with them, this Season of the year is the worst that a Ship could Choose to visit *Tahiti* as the Bay of *Matavai* is by no means a safe Road being entirely open to these Winds, Nor is there any place about the Island that Affords a Good Harbour except Pare, where the Bounty lay, and the entrance of this being narrow & rocky it is necessary to have buoys placed to steer in by; and the advantage of a Calm must be taken to tow out, as the trade wind blows right in and the Westerly Winds always bring bad weather.

Pare Harbour is the only one which *Tahiti* affords where a Ship may ride in safety at any season of the Year—(*Matavai* Bay Cannot be Counted safe more then Six or Seven Months in the Year) the Anchorage is Good in 8 to 16 fathoms Black sand—To the Westward of the reef which defends Point Venus about a Cables length lies a bank of Coral which is Calld the Dolphin bank—The shoalest part of it is bare 13 feet but between it and the reef is a Good Passage with 22 fm water; and this passage I would recommend before going to leeward & by keeping the reef aboard, and coming no nearer than 10 fathom—You may run in and anchor in Safety—but by going to the Westward You are liable to meet with sudden puffs thrown off in a Southerly diriction from One tree hill (a Bluff Commanding the Bay) which is sometimes followed by a few Minutes Calm before the true wind recovers its force—and a ship may be baffled and if weakly mand, as is often the Case after a long Voyage, forced to bring up in foul ground or be driven out and obliged to work to windward again but this is not always the Case & with a Fresh Sea Breeze there is no fear, but by keeping to the Eastward of the Bank all trouble may be avoided—There is another Rock in the Bay but it is in sight and close to the East part of the Beach

Water is plenty all over the Island but Wood for Fuel is not, as there are few other trees in the lowland except the Bread fruit & Cocoa Nut, with which it is Covered; but evry tree has its owner, & must be either purchased or leave obtaind to Cut of the Natives—

While the Sun is to the N. of the Equator the air is Clear and the Weather fine, and the SE wind blows regularly, the low land being covered with trees affords an agreeable shade and the Heat is not felt to any excess and during this season the Natives pass though the Mountains from one side of the Island to the other which they cannot do in the rains and are then forced to keep to the sea side if they have occasion to travel–

The seasons differ much on the opposite sides of this Island, partly owing to the Island of *Mo'orea* or *Eimeo* lying in a N. & S. diriction a cross the west part of it and while the Trade wind blows on the North side the West wind blows fresh on the South, but when the Wind gets to the Southward of S.E it prevails against the West wind and then the south side is deluged with rain from the Clouds which settle on the Mountains of *Taiarapu* while the Nd. side enjoys fine pleasant weather with scarce a shower of rain for 6 Months—this makes a material difference in the Breadfruit Harvest, which generaly begins on the N. side about Novr and is over by January; but on the S. side it is sometimes over by November at one Season and does not begin till Jany at another–

The Tides in this as in Other Tropical Countrys are not Great, and the Highest tide which I observed at Point Venus was Eighteen Inches and the time nearly two oClock at Full & Change–

The Soil of the Country is rich and fertile, and in the Valley & low land is a fine Black Mould, but near the Isthmus on both sides it is Coral & sand and rather Barren, producing little else but *Fara* (or Palms) Trees—the Hills Consist of several Strata of Red, White, Black Yellow & Blueish Collours—With several kinds of stones; the Red is a kind of Clay, and in it, is found a stone something like the Cornelian, that will strike fire, but is full of veins & Joints & will not stand a second stroke—the White is a kind of Pipe Clay without Stones, the Black a fine fat mold & the Yellow of a Gravelly Nature with large stones and the Blue is a Strong tough Loam, all of these are found in a Depth of ten or twelve feet from the Surface, and under that a soft sandy rock of a Brownish Collour intermixed with some that is hard & Black, there is also large Cliffs of a Black stone in the Mountains which runs in squares from two to Eight or ten inches, & several feet in length of which the Natives make their Adzes–

The Mountains are rocky to the Tops, but covered in most places with earth to a good depth and produce a Number of Large trees, the Clifts in the Mountains bear evident marks of having been burnt by fire, tho there is no account among the Natives that ever a Volcano subsisted here—in one place in the Mountains of *Ha'apaiano'o* a whole Hill appears to have been Overturned but the Natives say it was done by Thunder, but more probably by an Earthquake—the Beds of the Rivers are Gravel, and large stones part of which appear to have been washd from the Hills. Some are hard pebbles, other contain a Glassy substance and will melt in a hot fire, and many appar full of holes like the pummise stone but are heavyer

The Vallys are fruitfull & run in some Miles, but far up the Mountains are Inaccessable being very steep & frequently drenched with rain, and the only road to ascend the Mountains is from the sea side along the ridges by which rout those who Travel them must proceed

The produce of these Islands in General are Hogs which are large and Plenty, and their flesh excellent—Goats which are also Plenty & good food—Dogs which are here esteemd a Delicacy, and are allowed by former Voyagers to equal an English Lamb[5]—these are all the quadrupeds which they esteem good Food; they have also Cats & Rats but eat neither—and what Black Cattle has been left there they hold in no esteem. Fowles are plenty and good, and if killd young are equal to those of Europe either for tenderness or Flavour;[6] they have a number of Birds & fish which shall be described in their places. Their Vegetable productions are Fruits & Roots of Different Sorts and are these[7]

Yams Calld here *Uauaai*—these Grow wild in the Mountains, and are from one to six feet in length but not more then five or Six inches round, they are very good but as they take Much trouble to dig them out they are seldom sought after, except when the Bread fruit is Scarce, they never take the Pains to Cultivate them.

Taro, another Root which they Cultivate these grow in Water and the Ground must be leveled for that purpose & bankd up to keep the

Water Constantly on it—they Grow to 12 or 14 Inches long and as much round—and are little inferior to Yams the root when dressd is Mottled inside with Green blue & White—and the leaves make excellent greens having a tast something like our Asparagus; but if they are not sufficiently dressd they cause an Itching in the Fundament for several Hours after they are eaten–

Umara, a kind of sweet potatoes, diffirent from those of America or the West Indies they are of an Orange Collour & somewhat near the size of those in England, and are plenty they are produced by planting slips from the stalkd, which taking roots produce the Potatoes.

Ape these are large Mountain roots something in shape like the *Taro* but much larger they are also Coarser and more insipid, and if eaten without being properly dressd Cause a disagreeable Itching in the Mouth and throat which does not suddenly go off, to remedy this they are kept all night, in the oven which takes away the Itching & biting quality

Mapura—this is a kind of small *Taro* which Grows in the Mountains and is hot & biting but made eatable in the same manner as the *Ape*—and with this they make past for their Cloth.

Teve—this is another hot biting root like a large turnip radish which Grows in all parts of the Island and must be dressd in the same Manner–

Pia–this is a root resembling a Potatoe but is bitter to the tast and cannot be eaten till it has been grated down and steepd in Water, but it answers best for Paste by roasting & beating it up with a little water the Method of Preparing it for food is thus; they having gathered as many of the roots as they want get a rough stone which they wash Clean & Grate the *Pia* into a trough filld with Clear Water, mixing it up and when it settles the water is pour'd off and more apply'd for five or six days, when the Water is strained off and the *Pia* dryed for use it being then like fine Flour and makes excellent puddings or Pancackes–

E'huoi is a kind of Fern Root growing in the Mountains only, it is good eating when dressd—many other roots are found in the Mountains which are good food but seldom sought for, except bread is scarce.

Ginger & Turmeric grow in abundance all over the Islands as does also Tobacco, Sugar cane Indian Corn Pumpions Red pippers &c.

Among the Fruits the Bread fruit of which there are near thirty Sorts diservedly takes the lead—This Tree (calld by the Inhabitants *Uru*) Grows to the Size of an Oak, and afford Food, raiment, timber for Houses &

Canoes, & pitch for their seams—The leaves also are of use serving to wrap up their provisions when they dress them—the leaves are of different sizes some of them not more then 9 inches & others 2 feet long, they are broad and of as much substance as a Cabbage leaf, notchd on the edges with 4 or 5 notches of about 6 inches deep and the Collour a dark Green—it never sheds all its leaves and appears Constantly in bloom, as the Leaves which fall are forced off by Young ones making their way out—the Branches are large and spreading and on the ends of them the Fruit Grows, singly or in pairs, but seldom more—some of them are round, and others long and are from 3 to 6 inches Diameter; the fruit while unripe is a bright Green and rind is rough; as it ripens the rind becomes smoother and the Collour changes to a brownish with a Yellow tinge and appears spotted with White, from the Gum which forces its way through the rind and drys on it, and the fruit is then fit for use, & if it stays but a few days on the tree after the Gum has made is appearance it Grows Mellow & falls, and the tast becomes sweet & is too luiscious to eat till it is mixed with some which has been made into *Mahi,* but if Gathered before it falls its Collour inside when baked is Yellowish and its Consistence like that of a Potatoe tho the Taste is not like any thing that I recollect in Europe America or India, but it is nevertheless pleasant and agreeable, and tho when dressd it will not keep good more then two Days, yet it is so plenty as to answer evry purpose of Bread and is here the Staff of Life, The Method of making it into Mahi for store shall be described in its place–

The *Ha'ari* or Cocoa Nut is the next Fruit and is a Very Serviceable tree; the Nuts when Young are excellent drink and when Old Make Oil, Sauce for fish puddings &c.—the Shells make Cups for eating and drinking—the Husk makes lasshings for their Canoes and with the leaves they make temporary huts, screens for their houses, baskets &c.—and the trunk when past bearing makes fuel, tho they stand many Years Good except they Chance to loose their top by lightning which they often do—more then any other trees—they are always Green & shed some of their leaves, or rather Branches evry Year, still Growing taller as they Grow older–

The *Vi* or Yellow Apple is fine Delicious fruit growing to the size of an English Apple but different in smell taste & Substance, the pulp being Contained in a stringy substance round the seed—it has a thin tough rind like a plumb and its Collour when ripe is a fine Gold, its Flavour superior to the Pine, and it has no bad quality tho eaten to excess. It Grows on a fine Stately tree which sheds its leaves regularly, the leaves begin to fall in Sept and by Christmas the Fruit & leaves appear, and the Fruit is full ripe in June. Some of these trees are 9 feet round, but the wood is soft & spungy & fit for no use but fuel it will either Grow from the Seed or by lopping of a Branch, which when stuck in the Ground takes root and soon bears fruit–

The *Eheia* is another kind of an Apple, more like the English, but the taste is more watery & insipid, when ripe it is of a fine red & white, and the Tree is about the size of a Common Cherry tree; it sheds its leaves in the same Manner, but the fruit is not ripe till October—These two trees, & another bearing a red flower like a honysuccle, are the only Trees on the Island which shed all their leaves at one time or before any others appear–

The *Rata* or *Ihe*—is a kind of horse Chesnut in shape like a Broad Bean about 2 inches over the Trees are large and serves for fuel &c.

The Shaddock, Calld here *Uru Popa'as* (or English Bread): these trees were planted here in Captn Cooks time but the Fruit has never arrived at any perfection, the trees have been planted in different parts of the Island by the Natives merely as curiositys–

The *Me'ia,* which is the General Name of Plantains, Grows here in abundance and in the Highest perfection. The large Horse Plantain Calld here *Paparua* Grows to nine inches in length and as much round, and with *Taro* & Cocoa Nuts Makes excellent Pudding–

The *Orea* or Maiden Plantain is the best of all the small kinds of which these Islands produce twelve different sorts—not named here, but no Bannanas–

The *Fe'i* or Mountain Plantain is different from all the Others, and is Calld Mountain from its Growing Chiefly there as I never saw any of them in the East or West Indies I suppose they are peculiar to these and the Other Islands in the So Seas—the stalk or tree is of a Dark purple or Blackish Collour, the leaves much longer and the Collour Much darker then the Common Plantain and the fruit does not hang down but grows erect and Clustering thick round the stalk from a kind of Pyramid If Gathered Green they make a substitute for Bread, and if Cut while raw they Smell like a Cucumber—But when ripe they smell like Yellow Paint, and the Inside of them when bruised is something like it in Collour & Appearance—the Skin is then of a reddish Brown—when Baked & Made into a Pudding they are as Good as Custard the root also when dressd is equal to a Yam—as they Grow in Great Plenty in the Mountains they want no labour but that of Bringing home–

Among their Forest trees are the following, with shrubs plants &c.—The *Toa* or *Casuarina* a very hard wood with which they make their War Spears & Clubbs, Beetles for Making Cloth &c.[8]—and with its Bark they make a fine Brown dye—this wood is too hard for any tools which we had, yet the Natives work it with Stone tools, but it Costs them a deal of labour

Tamanu or *Calophyllum Mophylum* is a very large spreading tree, which they use for Building the large Canoes, making Stools for Sitting on, Pillows and Pudding stools, with Dishes, & trays, some of which are Six feet long, intended to Hold a large Hog when Dressd these are wrought out of the Solid and neatly finishd the Wood being something like Walnut, receives a fine Polish, and the Nut which Grows to the Size of a Walnut and as plenty, makes a very sweet perfume for their Cloaths–

Mara is a large tree the wood of which is hard and white, and the Grain close; when it grows old the Collour Grows brown—this is Chiefly Used for Building the War Canoes, making Cloth Beams, Long Steering Paddles and makes Good Ax & Adze handles–

Faifai—this Tree is as large as an Oak, and in Grain something like White Oak, it answers for several purposes—as building Canoes, making large Chests &c–

Amae—this is a hard Close wood of a reddish Collour which they also used in Building their Canoes, making Ax & adze handles &c—with this tree they Generally plant their *Marae*'s or places of Worship, and leaves of this tree are always used in religious rites

Toi—this is another large tree of which the Wood is White & hard, and used for Building both War & Common Canoes Planks for Scraping the Cloth plant on &c–

Purau or Hibiscus Tiliacous [*sic; Hibiscus tiliaceus*] is somewhat like Elm bearing a Yellow flower—the Body of the Tree serves for Building Canoes, making Paddles and we found it to answer very well for Timbers & Knees while building the Schooner Some of the Young Shoots run Straight for a Good length and of them they Chiefly make the rafters of their Houses, Sprits for their Canoes, Bows &c—and the Bark being Cleaned make neat washing Mats, of a fine texture for wet weather—it also makes rope & line and we found it, of much use in making our rigging–

Aito—this is another large tree the wood of a reddish Brown nearly as hard as Toa, & answers several purposes in their Canoes, with the Bark they Dye or tan their Cloth, Nets & lines, which tho only done by steeping in Cold water gives it a strong Collour which will not wash out and the Bark of the Toa has the same property

Torotaia this is a hard Tough white Wood and is Used for Outriggers for their sailing Canoes, and being durable is preferd for the Purpose of railing their Houses–

Hutu this is a large tree which answers the purpose of Building Canoes, but is not durable, it bears a Nut about the Size of a Sheeps heart of a Black Collour which has the Property when put into the Holes in the reef where the fish resort, to stupefy them; so that they never attempt to escape but suffer themselves to be taken but it is not much used for their purpose–

Tutui, or Candle Nut Tree, Grows to the Size of a Walnut tree, bearing a fruit exactly like a Walnut but of an Oily nature and if eaten Causes almost an immediate vomiting, but the Kernels after being roasted till the Shells come off make a Good Substitute for Candles (by being Strung on the Stem of the Cocoa Nut leaf)—burning with a strong blaze—the Bark of the root makes a fine light Brown dye, and the trunk fuel.

Tou (or *Cordia Sebestina Orientalis*), the wood of this tree is soft & white, and of this they make Scoops for Bailing their Canoes—the Leaves Mixed with the Berries of the *Mati* makes a beautiful red for Painting their Cloth

Mati is a species of Fig about the Size of a Common Cherry tree, the Figs or Berries are about the size of a small Cherry and are of a Brownish Collour; and being Squeesed on the leaves of the *Tou* produce a fine Scarlet die The Bark makes excellent fishing lines, twine for Nets, and a fine Matting for sashes or *Maro's*—It also makes a good strong Cloth

Nono or *Morinda citrifolia* this is a Small tree bearing a fruit like a small Soursop but not so pleasant to the tast and seldom eaten, the Bark off the Root makes a fine light Yellow die for their Cloth–

Eaua is a kind of Wild Fig, or Sloe tree of the Bark of which they make an excellent Grey Cloth, Calld Aroa, which is the most durable of any they have, and is therefore Highly esteem'd

Pua is a handsom tree Calld by Cn Byron the *Barringtonia* it bears odouriferous flowers of a Yellowish hue, with which they make Garlands for their Heads, and The *Tiare* a tree bearing White Flowers of a fine Smell answers the same purpose

Evavai, or ye Silk Cotton tree, Grows in abundance all over the Country but is made no use of–

Roa (*Urtica Argenta*) is a Shrub the Bark of which answers the purpose of hemp and is used for their Best lines & Fishing tackle—it Grows as high as hemp, and the leaves are not unlike each other

Aute (Morus papyrifera) or the Chinese Paper Mulberry tree of which there are two sorts, Calld here *Mairi* and *Purau*—of the Bark of these they make their finest white Cloth, and they Cultivate large plantations of it for that purpose to these Plantations the Goats are distructive animals eating the Bark off and spoiling the Young Plants & are not to be kept out by the Ditch & fence with which they are encompassed for this reason the Goats about the Plantations are either kept tyed fast or drove back into the hills, where they run wild—as they are not esteemed of Great value–

Ohe or Bamboo grows here in abundance some of which are 60 feet long but their substance is not very strong—however they serve when Cut into lengths to hold Oil and for those who dwell far from the Beach to carry their Salt Water in which serves evry purpose of Salt in this Country—it also serves for making Fences, Fishing rods, knives &c—and of a small hard sort they make their Arrows while the large makes quivers

Aeho or Reeds these Grow in abundance on the Hills and are servicable for many Uses, as fixing the thatch on for their Houses, making Fences, and for Burning at Night when Fishing, and they frequently burn them to Clear the Ground of them–

Oporo, or the Chili Pepers, were planted here in Capt Cooks time, and with the *Tobbacco* may now be found in all the Islands being carried about as Curiosities

Eaute this is a Shrub about the size of a rose tree bearing a red flower with which they dress their Heads, it is also used by them as a Medicine for Sore Eyes, which is common among Children, it is no way disagreeable and is taken in their Food–

Fara, or Prickly Palm, Calld in India *Pandanus,*[9] Grows here in abundance, generally near the Beach in Barren Ground; the roots of the trees grow above Ground, and support it like shores standing round to the height of 5 or 6 feet—the Outside of the tree is hard & with it they point their Javlins, but the Inside is soft spungey & fiberus—the Leaves Grow

Figure 14. *Tapa* or barkcloth beater, Tahiti [1925.376]. Reproduced with permission of University of Cambridge Museum of Archaeology and Anthropology

in a Special manner round the Branches and are about 6 feet long and 4 inches Wide with long prickles on their edges & Center—with these they make their Thatch by sewing the leaves on reeds—they also make mats for their Sails & for performing their Heivas or Dances on; some of which are of a large size—the Blossom is a large Bunch of Flowers of a Buff Collour yeilding a Fragrant Smell—with this they Scent their Oil & Cloth—the Seed is Composed of a number of nuts which grow upon a round Core and have the Appearance when ripe of a Pine Apple—their taste is sweet & pleasant, and they are frequently put into the Earth with Plantains when they are put to ripen to give them a fine Flavour.

Papa this is a kind of Palmeto the leaves something like the *Fara* but without Prickles, and of this they make their matts for Sleeping on and for wear in Wet weather this grows Chiefly in the Mountains and here also is found the *Ahi* or Sandal Wood which has a Smell like Cedar and with this they Scent their Oil &c

Hoero Tumu or Cabbage Tree Grows also in the Mountains, but are small & not very Plenty—they seldom exceed 30 feet in heigth—the Bark is rough & hard pointing over like Scales from the Earth to the top of the tree where the Cabbage Grows singly, and the leaves or branches look like fern forming a Circle Horisontally—they seldom eat the Cabages as it is some trouble to get them–

Pirepire is a small shrub growing to the Size of Heath, and with the bark they make a very fine Matting for Sashes or *Maros*–

'Ie'ie is a king [kind] of running shrub or vine of which they make Fish pots, & other Wickerwork, and it is used in the Construction of their Houses, answering better then line for securing those parts that are exposed to the weather

To or Sugar Cane Grows here without Cultivation to as large a size as any in the East or West Indies, and I make no doubt but if Cultivated would be much larger, the Natives make no use of it except to Chew as they pass where it Grows and when it becomes too thick, they Clear the Ground by Setting it on fire–

To popa'a or Indian Corn was first Introduced by the Bounty—and is now to be found in all the Islands—it Grows here luxuriantly and We have produced three Crops from the same seed, and a fourth well on in a twelve month—it may be produced in any of the Islands with little trouble, as the Soil of the Whole is in general good from the Beach to the top of the Mountains, but the Natives tho they are fond of it never take the pains to Cultivate it, in any quantity; alledgeing that they have plenty of Food, and it is therefore no use to labour for what Nature has abundantly Supply'd them—and Such is their Oppinion respecting evry other Article of Food Introduced amongst them by European Ships which are either distroyd by Shifting from place to place as Curiositys, or suffered to run wild for want of being Cultivated and taken Care of—Some of the Cobbs of Corn which we produced were 12 inches long and well fill'd–

They have several sweet herbs for scenting their Oil & Cloth—and a kind of Cresses which makes excellent sallad are to be found in all parts of the Country, all the English Garden seeds planted on our first arrival were nearly gone to decay, and destroyd as before described tho with care they might be had in tolerable perfection

'Ava, or Intoxicating peper, is Cultivated here with much Care and pains with the roots of this, they Intoxicate themselves they always drink

it before they eat and it is prepared thus—several hands have each a proportion of the root given them to Chew which when they have done sufficiently they spit it into a large Platter, Some of the leaves are then Infused and Squesed to pieces in it, and in the mean time another prepares a Strainer from the Stems of Coarse Grass Calld *Mo'u,* something like hemp, and the whole being well mixed is wrung through the Strainer and the leaves & Chewings thorwn away—and the Juice is then devided according to the Number who are to drink it, by dipping the Strainer into the Platter and wringing into each mans Cup his Share—they now drink their dose which as it is of a tolerable thick Consistency and smells something like a Mixture of Rhubard & Jalap[10] can be little better to take—almost Imediately deprives them of the use of their limbs & Speech, but does not toutch the Mental Facultys and they appear in a thoughtful mood and frequently fall backwards before they have finishd eating, some of their attendants then attend to Chafe their limbs all over till they fall asleep, and the rest retire and no noise is suffered to be made near them—after a few hours they are as fresh as if nothing had happened and are ready for another dose—a Jill[11] of this Juice is a Sufficient dose, but if they eat any thing immediately before it, it has no effect–

After about a fortnights Constant use the Skin comes all over with a white scurf like the land scurvy and the Eyes grow red & firey and the Body lean and Meagre but on being left off for a few days the Scales fall off the Skin then becomes clear & smooth and they soon grow fat & wholesom to view this gives me reason to think that this nauseous draught must be very wholesom as those who use it are Seldom afflicted with disorders of any kind; and those who use it regularly are some of the oldest men in the Country—It is Common to all but is more used by the Chiefs & their Familys, Servants &c than by the Common people—they prefer the method of Chewing it to any Other—it is in much request among people of rank but even some of them never tast it–

Ti is a plant Growing in the Mountains the root of which is sweet and this they roast & eat the leaves are about 14 or 16 inches long and 5 or 6 wide and serve for thatching temporary huts, lining their pits for *Mahi* & makes a temporary Garment for Fishing in &c by platting all the stems together to reach round the Waist, and Splitting the leaves which depend to the knees–

All these Grow in the lowlands but the largest timber Grows far back in the Mountains—the Bread fruit is to be had at all seasons, but it is most plenty in the Harvest when they Gather it in and lay it up in store Making it into a sour past by fermentation Calld *Mahi* which shall be described in its place—the Cocoa Nuts, plantains & almost every sort of Food are plenty at all seasons alike–

Their Cultivation does not extend to any great degree the Chief Articles of it are the Cloth Plant, *'Ava, Taro* & Sweet potatoes and some times they plant Cocoa Nuts & Plantains but these plantations are generally the labour of the Chiefs and if they make one in their lifetimes they sufficiently do their duty—they seldom plant any Breadfruit trees as they grow up wherever the root is Seperated, by the Hogs or otherwise and they have often to root the young ones out, to Clear the ground of them, but the Plantains want Planting sometimes after the Westerly winds which if they are not secured are often blown down and these are the only things they take any pains with, nor can this be said to Cost them either Labour or Toil and as evry part of the Island produces food without the help of Man, it may of this Country be said that the Curse of Eden has not reachd it No Man having his bread to get by the Sweat of his Brow nor has he Thorns in his path–

They have Many Birds, for which we could find no names, but among those we knew were these—Herons Blue & White, Wild Ducks, Parroquets; Green, Blue & White—Fly flappers, Wood Peckers Doves, Wild Pidgeons, a Chatering bird like a Jay, Sandlarks, Plover, Martin, Men of War & Tropic birds with several other Aquatic Birds and the Mountains produce birds of Different kinds unknown to us, among which are a large bird nearly the size of a Goose, which is good food; they are never seen near the Sea nor in the low lands–

They have no venomous reptiles or Insict except the Centepedes & Scorpion; the Former are large & plenty but the latter small and scarce and I never heard of any harm being done by them. The Natives think nothing of them and will handel them with a little Ceremonys as we do earth worms &c.—the Lizards are of two sorts, one a fine Bright shining Collour and an Innocent harmless look, the other of a Black or dirty Brown and of a most forbidding appearance, they are both harmless and are seldom more then 6 inches long—Butterflys, Moths and Common Flys like those of Europe, they have also a Fly which differs very little from the Common Black fly, which bites very sharp and is sometimes very troublesome, these they say were first Brought here by the *Lima* Ship.[12] the Musquettos are not very troublesome, the other insects, such as Grasshoppers Crickets, Beetles &c are the same as in other Countrys

These Islands abound with the greatest variety of Beautiful and delicious Fish besides the Fish Common to other Countrys within the Tropics the reefs afford some of the most beautiful Collours that can be conceived and these rich colours are allways fine Fish, among those found Near these Islands are the Grampus a Young Whale, Porpoise, Swordfish, Shark, Turtle, Albicore, Dolphen, Bonnetta, Skip Jack, White Salmon, Cavally Old Wife—Snappers White & Red, Garfish, Barracoutta, Ballihoo Leather Jacket, Yellowtail, Ray, Sting & Common, Parrot or Rainbow fish, Flying fish, Squid, Spray, Eels Sea & River; Hedge Hog fish, Sea Cat, Mullet White & Red, Stone Brass, Blochan Founder or Sand Dab, Warrior fish, Doctor Dogfish, Nourse, Millers thumb Sea Chub, Sea Roach, Sea Gudgeon and innumerable others[13] for which we could find no names, among these the Whale, Turtle, Porpoise, Shark, Albicore & Dolphine are sacred, and the Weomen must not eat them and the Turtle is either presented to the King or Eaten on the *Marae* as they are not caught in great Numbers, besides these they have Shell Fish with which the reefs abound among which are Small Conchs, Pearl & Small Common Oysters, Crabbs Cray Fish, Prawns & Shrimps, Cockles Common & horse, Tygers, Wilks & Winckles of different Sorts, Clams, Muscles, & Sea Eggs with a thousand other Shells for which we could find no names they have also land Crabbs but few eat them. I never found in those Islands the Grooper, King fish or Jew fish which are Common in the West Indies–

Their Fishing tackle Consists of Seines of large dimension lines & hooks of all sizes, Spears, Snares, Pots &c—evry Fisherman makes his own hooks lines twines and evry article of His Geer, which are not to be equal by any thing but their Skill in using them, they make their lines from the Bark of the *Roa* (and others already described) twisting it (in either two or three Strands as it is found to answer best) on their naked thigh and make ym with great Judgement & regularity; but not half the size in proportion to the Fish for which it is intended that ours are and their hooks are made of Pearl Shell, Bone, Wood &c of different Constructions for the Different fish, some being made to Answer the double purpose of Hook & Bait, they make their hooks by Grinding them into form on a stone with water and Sand and with a drill made of a Sharks tooth, they make a hole into which they introduce a Sprig of the Coral as a file and work out the inside part; and as they have no beard they make the point to round, in toward the back of the Hook inclining downward, and seldom loose a fish after they get it once hookd

They have a Number of Methods of Fishing and are expert at all—the First is With Seines from 5 fathoms long and one deep, to Sixty fathoms long and twelve deep—these large ones have a bag or Cod in the Middle and when they haul them in Deep Bays they never land them till they are done fishing, but cast off the Cod on the outside of the surf, and bring the Fish on Shore in their Canoes when they haul the Sein into a Canoe and having laces on the Cod Shoot it afresh, in this Manner they Catch a great Number of fine fish and some turtle—while they are fishing in this manner the Net is always surrounded by Swimmers how dive down and secure such fish as are like to escape and tho the Sharks often attend them yet they seldom interrupt their work and if they Catch the Sharks in the Surf they Surround them and force them on shore which is so far from being deemd dangerous that it is Counted fine Sport—the Sharks here are not very large seldom exceeding five or Six feet in length—with their Small Seines they Catch the Flying fish having Small Canoes for that Purpose, which will Carry two men, the seines for this purpose are 15 or 20 fathm long, and 9 feet deep, these they Shoot amongst the Fish and Splashing the water about with their paddles frighten the Fish till they dart into the Net and Mash themselves, they then haul in their net and take out the fish, and following the School shoot it afresh as they fish for them for Bait for the Dolphin they frequently take the Night for it and Choose the Dark in preference to the Moon light, when the fish cannot see to avoid the Nets—in Calm Weather they follow the School with a number of Canoes and Surround them with other Nets in a Circle and having drawn them into a small Compass make the Canoes fast to the Nets and Jump overboard, diving under the Nets and Seizing what fish they Can by hand and Frequently bring up one in each hand besides what get Mash'd in the Nets, the fish being prevented from rising by the Sight of the Canoes, and keeping Close together never attempt to escape till the men come among them–

They have Cast Nets also for Small fry, both Square & Circular and throw them with great desterity and when the Fish Comes into the Shoal water they get a quantity of Cocoa nuts leaves from which they take the

Stems and tying them together, twist them the inside forming a kind of rope with the leaves all round it this they Call *Rau* and with this they Sweep the reefs & Shoal Water and bring whole Schools of Fish to the Beach where they apply their small Seins and lade Nets to land them—they also sweep the Beaches with those small Seines with a Man at each end who wade out till they are up to their Necks together, and then seperating to the length of the Net walk in & often (especially in the Night) and at the Mouths of the rivers have good hauls–

They Catch plenty of Fine rock fish in pots, and Wares; and are excellent hands at diving after them and I have seen a Diver in Clear Water and Calm weather pursue a Fish from one hole in the rocks to another without coming up to breath; but in rough weather they cannot see to follow them, the bottom being darken'd by the ripple on the Surface—the most curious part of this fishery is that of taking the Hedgehog fish and Sea Cat; the one being so full of prickles that they can take hold no where but by the Eyes, which is the Method by which they get them as very few are caught any other way—and the others adhere so close to the rocks, that it is as much as two men can do at times to haul them off and I have seen them in 3 or 4 fathom forced to quit them, and come up several times before they could accomplish their end; if a Stone lies handy below, they kill the fish there, and then they get it off easy this may seen an odd Method of Fishing but I have seen it attended with good Success and the Divers return in a few hours with large Strings of fine Fish. In the Night they fish in Canoes & on the reefs for different sorts of Fish, which they Draw round them by lighting bundles of reeds, and have nets made to scoop them up and put into their Baskets–

In the rainy season they Catch large quantitys of Small Fry at the Mouths of the rivers by means of a large bag made of the Membranous Stratums of the Cocoa Nut tree sewed together, the Mouth of the bag being made with two Wings to Spread the river, they place it and lay stones on the lower part to keep it down they then sweep the river with a *Rau* and bring all the Fry into the Bag; and in this Manner get several Bushells at a haul, in the Mean time the Weomen have their part of the Fishery and each being equipt with a bag & a Basket, form themselves into three or four lines across the river up to their Middle, & keeping the lower part down with their feet hold the upper part in their hands alternately searching it and putting the Fish into their Baskets till they are either tired or Satisfied when they leave off and go home to Dress them, it is No disgrace for any woman to be thus Employd and if the Queen is present she generally makes one and they are Generaly paid for their labour with Good Sport & plenty of Fish—another method is when the rains are over and the waters subside, they dam the River up with Stones and Grass, leaving several sluices to which they fix their Bags or Nets, and going to some distance up along the Bank they all plunge in together and drive the Fish before them who flying to the Sluices fall into the Nets—but this Method is not used till the fish grow scarce–

When they angle in the Sea, they generally used *Baked bread fruit* for Bait, and Stand up to their neck in water, having a long Bamboo for a rod and a Basket hung round their Neck to put the fish in, they Catch in this Manner several fine fish—the White Mullet they catch with hand lines, and the red in Small Nets; these latter tho delicate fish are here used as bait for the *Albicore* and *Bonnetta* which are Caught thus—they have a Double Canoe carrying Six or Eight men, and in the Bow is fixd a long pole like a crane to lower and haul up on a Cross piece or Roller at the heel by means of a Back rope, on the Head of this they fix two pieces spreading like horns to which they bend the lines, on the top of the Crane they fixd a Bunch of long Black Feathers from the Cocks tails the Motion of which when lowerd near the Water attracts the Fish and draws them round the Canoe, between the Canoes they sling a kind of Basket with their Bait which admitting the Water keeps the Fish alive till they are wanted, when they See any fish they paddle toward them till they come round the Canoe and then they keep the Stern of the Canoe to windd and paddle from them, a Man is then placed to throw Water with a Scoop, and make a continual Spray like rain, and the Hooks being baited the Crane is lowered so as to let them Just under the surface. The Man on the Bow who attends to bait the Hooks keeps throwing now and then a small fish while the other with the Scoop keeps a Constant Shower about the Hooks; the Fish soon fly at their prey and get hookd when the Men who attend the Crane rope, having notice given them, haul up and the Fish swings in to the Man who attends to receive them and bait the Hooks afresh—Some of them fish are very large, and often run the Canoes under water when they do not haul up briskly, but this is attended with no evil, except the line should break, when they loose the Hook which if it Chance to be an Iron one is as Great a loss to them as we should think an Anchor

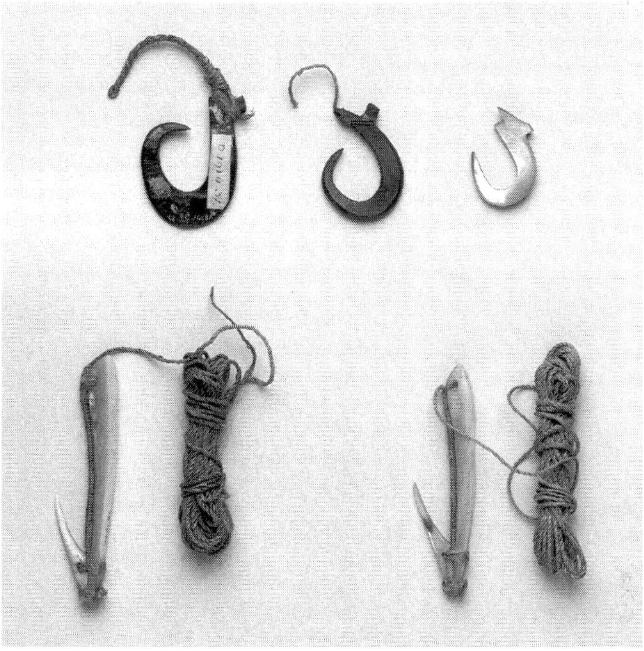

Figure 15. *Matau,* fish hooks and lures, Tahiti [D 1914.29–32]. Reproduced with permission of University of Cambridge Museum of Archaeology and Anthropology

The *Skip Jack* is Caught by a hook made to resemble a small fish, with some Hogs Bristles fixd for a tail and are drawn after the Canoe in the same manner, but caught by a long bamboo for a rod which the fisherman works with the heel in the bottom of the Canoe, and plays it by hand while another paddles the Canoe, the Canoes for this Fishery are mostly Single, with some one and some 2 men, but those with one Man can do nothing if there is any wind but let their hooks tow while they paddle to windward, but they always loose ground while they stop to unhook a fish and put their hook over again by which time the School are got to some distance, while those who have two always keep up with them—of these as well as the *Albicore* & *Bonnetta* they Catch great numbers—they also Catch the *Cavally* and *White Salmon* in their small Canoes but without rods; these fish they are forced to play and the Canoes being light, when they have hookd a Fish they steer after it, till it is tired & drawing their line in gradually, get it along side when they watch an Opportunity and Seize the Small part next the tail in their hand and whip it into the Canoe, Seldom trusting the Strength of the line to haul them in by, as the lines used for these fish are in general not bigger then what we use for *Mackarell.* Nevertheless they Seldom loose any—in this Manner they also Catch the Shark and Other large fish with small lines, their Canoes being extreamly light, soon weary the Fish, and by this Method make them easily taken

They always fish for Dolphin four or five leagues from the land in sailing Canoes plying to windward—when they reach their distance they Bait with Flying Fish, and are very fond of Iron hooks; their lines for these Fish are generally two strands and of a Good length, some of them Measure 100 fathms. They Choose the two Strand lines as they are less apt to get foul by Twisting then those of three and as the Dolphin Jumps and twists about when hookd they are not so ready to breake and easyer Cleard after running out; they never wet their lines till they see a Fish, and then they make sure of it, tho they are often deceived; as the Fish will sometimes leave part of their Jaws behind them if too Suddenly Stopd in their Carreer, they are forced to play them some time before they haul them alongside, to get them in which they always do by laying hold of the tail part with one hand & the line in the Other; the Canoe being low for that Purpose—These fish Follow the Sun and are therefore most plenty when the Sun is to the Southward of the Equator, during which season there are Not less then Sixty sail of Canoes from *Matavai* only, employd in the Fishery—the Fish Spawn about March after which they seldom look for them, but get ready for the *Albicore* & *Bonnetta* fishery that then Commences and the Sailing Canoes ply between *Tahiti* & *Tetiaroa* for them Fish which are caught in great quantitys about the reefs of *Tetiaroa*–[14]

While the Dolphin season Continues they Catch a number of Flying Fish of an Extraordinary size which are in general so large as not to fear them these they catch with Bait in this Manner—they get a Number of Wands of 6 or 8 feet long from which they strip the Bark and balance by Slinging a stone to one end so as to swim upright with one half their length out of water, to the lower end they fix a hook (made of fish bones & baited with Cocoa Nut) with about a Fathom of line; these being all prepared (they generally have as many as they Can Conveniently Stow in the Stern of the Canoe) they stand off to their proper distance and throw the Wands over board at a distance from each other, and Standing in they pick them up again when they frequently find Fish at each, so that if they have no luck of Dolphin they seldom return empty as they often take Sharks & other fish on which the Shark preys, who flying to the Canoe for Shelter, are often taken by hand—and the Shark they often Catch in a Noose prepared for that purpose seldom having occasion to bait a hook for them, when they get the Shark fast they haul his head out of water and beat it till they see no signs of life in it with heavy *toa* Bludgeons which they Carry for the Purpose and when he is dead they get him into the Canoe

They frequently meet with the Swordfish while they are out who never fails to Attack the Canoe and if the Bottom or side is Not of very hard Wood, he strikes the Sword into her in several places before it sticks fast enough to hold him, but as soon as he sticks they are overboard and secure him with the Noose, and having freed him from the Canoe kill him with their Bludgeons and get him in—but are frequently forced to Steer homewards and Stop the leaks which he Occasions—Their days Sport being then Over as they are sometimes closely put to it to reach the shore, seldom Carrying anything with them that is fit to stop a leak and their only recourse is to Bail

Besides other Methods of Fishing they have Spears which they throw with Great exactness, these are 14 or 16 feet long pointed with two prongs of *Toa*—they use no line but if they Strike a Fish they swim after it; they have others with Several Prongs which they throw at random among the Schools and frequently kill two or three at a time

They seldom kill any whales but young ones which get entangled among the reefs, and thrown over by the surf into Shoalwater; when they find one in this situation they attack him with their war Spears & kill him, tho they sometimes get their Canoes dashd to pieces by him–

Among the Fish there Is a kind of Conger Eel of a Brownish Collour with a Green border round the Fins from Head to tail, they are Caught about the reefs and are of different sizes from one to Six feet long, these Fish are of a Poisonus Nature to some and if eaten gives the most excruciating pain while others who eat of it feel no effects nor do the Natives know who will be affected by it till they have eaten it, as they have a remedy for it they take no account of the matter and eat them at a venture. I partook of one of these Fish without feeling the smallest effects from its poison, while another who eat of the same Fish was almost raving mad,

His Body and limbs swelld to a very extraordinary degree and Covered with red blotches and at the same time the Hands & feet itching in Such a Manner as to be unsufferable and burning as if on fire, the Eyes welld and firey and to appearance fit to start from the Sockets, this Continued with short intermissions for Eight Days but in the Course of a Week more by the assistance of some of the Priests who procured Medicines he got quite well, but often found a great itching in the Palms of the Hands & follow of the feet—These Fish are Calld by the Natives *Puhe Pirirauti* and as they don't know the Good from the Bad they are loth to throw them away and therefore eat them to make sure of them—they have also a small red Crab, not bigger then a small horse bean, which say will kill a man Instantly if he eats it these are the only poisonous things we ever heard of except the *Hutu* or *Hutunut* beforementioned, but this tho is Stupifies the Fish will not effect a Man–

As to Minerals, there are few in these Islands but Iron and that scarce, tho in fact there were few who were sufficient Judges amongst us to know any other–

It is on all hands allowed that Necessity is the Mother of Invention and tho the Divine bounty has rendered Art almost useless for procuring the Neccessarys of life in this Country yet the Ingenuity of these people is highly Conspicuous in evry article of their Manufacture, of which their Cloth Matting and oil are particular Articles of their Trafic, if it may be so Calld, but this is Genrally carried on by making presents rather then by Exchange of Commoditys[15]

Their Cloth, of which the General Name is *Ahu,* is of Different sorts and made from the Bark of different trees but the process of all is the Same–[16]

The Best and finest white Cloth Calld *'Opu* or *Parauai* is made from the *Aute* or Cloth Plant and is made thus—The plants having to their proper length (10 or 12 feet) are cut by the Men and brought in by them which is their part of the work—the Weomen then Strip off the bark by entring a pointed Stick between the bark and the Plant and ripping it the whole length on one Side, & the Bark peels off after they have Stripd all the Plants they take the Bark to the Water, where they wash it, spreading it on a board for the Purpose Scrape it Clean, taking off the Outside rind with a large Cockle shell and having freed it from the Sap and Slime, it is wrapd in plantain leaves and covered with Grass, where it remains for two three or four days—when it becomes Clammy and glutinous, & is then fit for working, it is then spread of a regular thickness of several strips forming a band of 7 or 8 inches broad and of what length the piece is intended to be and the Ground where they intend to work is spread with plantain leaves to keep it from the dirt—the Beams are then placed at equal distances about 6 feet asunder & at each of them two weomen work, having the Piece between them, beating it with square beetles to its proper breadth; this they perform by a Song given by one & Chorous'd by the rest, and keep regular time and Shifting the Piece backwards and forwards till it is all beat out to a regular Breadth and thickness—it is then spread in the sun to Dry for one Day, after which it is bleachd in the Morning Dew till it is perfectly white, being kept from the sun till it is sufficiently bleachd, and then it is spread one or two days in the Sun to dry it and put up for Store or Use

Sometimes they notch the Outward bark with a stone and wrap the Plants in leaves for two or three Days before they Strip them, which makes the Cloth beautifully Clouded with several shades of Brown.

They also Mix the Cloth plant with Breadfruit bark, but this is of a Coarser kind and does not bleach so well tho the Cloth is equally strong—Some of this cloth is very fine, and neck cloths made of it might be mistaken at a small distance for the labour of the Loom–

If a landed Man wants a large quantity of Cloth made at once, he informs his Tennants when he means to Cut his plants and on the Day appointed all the Weomen attend with each their Beam & Beetle and a proportion of Breadfruit Bark being prepared they bring the Work together and some times to the Number of 200 strike off together, making as much noise as so many Coopers, the piece is finishd in one Day and is sometimes 40 or 50 fathoms long and 4 fathoms wide–

They make another sort of several Thicknesses which are not placed regular or above half beaten this is Calld *Maro* of this they make their Upper Garments by Striping from one part and pasting on to another till they bring it to a regular breadth & thickness and trim the Fragments off with a piece of split bamboo which answers the purpose of a knife—These they Paint with *Mati,* a Beautiful red extracted from Berries of that name, & leaves before discribed, which they prepare thus—the Berries & leaves being gathered several hands begin & Nip them till they emitt a drop of Yellow Juice which they put on a leaf and so proceed till all are done the leaves with the juice on them are then put into a platter and sprinkled with Water when they are wrought up by squeesing till they become red and after they are sufficiently squeesed they are thrown out and the Juice put into a shell for use, a Bunch of the Fibers of the *Mo'u* is then procured to dip in the paint and Wet the leaves and Sprigs they mean to imprint on the Cloth which being placed on it and pressd by the hand leaves the print behind and in this manner they paint it in many fanciful forms[17]

besides this method of Paitning they dye the *'Opu* of Several Colours—as Brown of several shades from the Bark of several trees, scraped off and infused in Cold water into which they dip the Cloth and the Sun heightens the Collour, twice dipping and 6 or 8 days Sun is sufficient to produce the highest shade, which never fades till the Cloth is worn out the Black is produced from the Sap of the Mountain Plantain or *Fe'i*—or by soaking the Cloth under the root of some particular Cocoa nut trees which Grow in Swampy Ground where in a Nights time, or three or four separate dippings, it becomes Jett black. The Brown is Call'd *Hiri* or *Puhiri* and after it has been Worn some time makes a Good Black, being then better then Clean White for receiving the Collour. The Black they Call *Uere*

The Yellow they extract from Tumeric & the roots of the *Nono*—and with the latter, being a pale light collour they dye the lining of their Brown Cloth which they past in very Curiously, and paint the border with red which gives it a very showy appearance this is now Calld *Hapa'a*—they also take of Red, Black, Yellow & White a piece of equal dimentions, and paste them together Cutting them in Curious Forms so as to shew all the Collours—another Method is taking old brown Cloth, which they tear in pieces and Mix with some New bark, beating the Whole into one piece and when finishd it is spotted all over, this they dip in the Yellow dye and line it in the Same Manner, Infusing Sweet Scents in their dye this is Calld *Opotapota.*

The Ora is a Grey strong Cloth made of the Bark of the Sloe tree. Large quantitys of these trees grow in the Mountains, particularly Near *Vaiuriti,* where there is a great lake which they Call *Vaihiria* from a large kind of Eels which they say is produces as big round as a Man, to the Banks of this lake resort Numbers of the *Arioi* (Who are Generally good Cloth Makers tho it is Chiefly the Weomens employment) to make the Cloth, it being held in great esteem being the Strongest & Best for wear.

They Generally stay some months on the Banks of this lake where they have plenty of Provisions—some few Inhabitants live Constantly there and are mostly employd making Cloth—the lake emptys itself into the Vally of *Vaiuriti* and they say that they have never yet found bottom, to it they Waft themselves from side to side on rafts made of the trunk of the Mountain Plantn.

They Make Cloth of several different trees but these are the most common, it is Chiefly the Work of the Wiomen tho the *Ariois* are very excellent hands in evry branch of the work but especially at Dyeing & Painting—the only tools requisite for making the Cloth after the Plants are Strip'd, are a Shell to Scrape the Bark, a Board about a foot wide and two feet long to scrape it on—a Beam of 8 inches Square and 10 or 12 feet long to beat it on, and Beetle of 2½ or 3 inches square and 14 or 16 inches long to beat it with—the Beam is made of *Mara,* a hard wood, & the Beetle of *Toa* having Grooves on each square of 4 different sizes, for the different kinds of Cloth they are intended to work, the Beam is Calld *Tutua* and the beetle *Ie*

The Cloth serves them for Dry weather and they can wash and dress it often as they please, scenting it with the *Tumanu* Nuts, which are bitter to the tast but of an agreeable Smell and by infusing them (when pounded) into water and dipping the Cloth into it the Smell will remain for several weeks, and generally till the Cloth wants dressing afresh–

Matting Is No Inconsiderable branch of their Manufacture. Of this they make Sails for their Canoes,[18] Bed Mats, Cloathing for Wet Weather, Sashes for Dress and Carpets for Acting their *Heiva* or Plays upon—Those for Sails, Carpets & Bedding are made from the leaves of the *Palm* & *Palmetto* the former is Calld *Moea* and the Latter *Evane.* Some of which are ten twelve & fourteen fathoms long, and two fathoms wide and are wrought with great regularity, and are Coarse or fine as the Makers fancy being from two to Sixteen parts to an inch—Those for Dress are known by the Name of *Ahu* with the name of the Bark &c of which they are made perfixd, they are made of different sizes, for the different part of Dress, and from the Bark of the *Purau, Mati, Roa* Cocoa nut leaves &c and Some are very fine, and have from twenty to thirty parts to an Inch, they are all made by the Weomen who work them by hand, without the Assistance of any machine except a Muscle shell to split the stuff

The Weomen also make matt Bags or Baskets, with Black and White, neatly disposed, and of Many different Patterns–

The Wicker Baskets are made by the Men, from a running Vine Calld *Ieie* and are equal In workmanship to those of Europe–

Their Platters, Stools, Chests &c are all neatly made and Well Finished; and are the more admirable when we consider their Tools, which are no other then Stone Adzes of Different sizes, Shells, Sharks teeth, Bones, Sand to scower, and Fish Skins to polish, and with these tools they Build their Houses, & Canoes their Toil and pains have been much lessend since they have known the Use of Iron then which they esteem nothing most Valuable—they work the Pearl shells into Many forms for Fish hooks, having a different Shaped hook for evry different Fish, with this they Compose the Ornaments of their Mourning Dress which are Neatly disposed and it is surprizing to see with what exactness and dispatch they put it into form and drill holes with a Sharks tooth (fixd in a long stick which they work between their hands) which will scarce admit the point of a Common pin–

Their lines for Fishing &c are made from the Bark of several Shrubbs, but the Bests is made of the *Roa* and are Equal if not superior to any in the World, they twist them on their thigh in two or three Strands for their different purposes, and Ball them up as they make them–

The rope for their Canoes, Fishing Sceins &c is chiefly made of the Purau which being strip'd of its outside rind and laid in water to Steep for Three Days, to take off the Slime, is then Dryd and twisted by hand, making two strands first, and then laying in the third—they make the Strands as they lay them by supplying them with more Bark as they twist up and when it is finished is smooth and as regular as if spun on hooks in a rope Ground, and with the Help of Tar, would be good rope and is nearly as strong as Common hemp they seldom make any larger then three Inch, but to any length they have Occasion for and for particular occasions they lay three of these together–

Their method of making Oil is this—The Cocoa Nuts being full grown, are Gatherd in and freed from the Husk. they are then Broke in halves and the Milk which is then sour is thrown away and the Inside of the Nut grated into a Trough made for the Purpose—a piece of Coral tyed on a kind of Horse on which they sit to steady it serves for a Grater. the Nuts being all grated, the trough is hung up, or fixd on a stand and the stuff left to disolve, and in a few days the Oil begins to run, then Grate into it *Sandal wood* and mix into it the Dust from the Palm blossoms and other sweet flowers herbs &c—and when all is disolvd they strain it off, and put into Bamboos for Use. the Oil retaining the Scent while it is kept Close stoppd—this Process of making it takes up near three Weeks, during which time they mostly turn it over and Mix it evry day—Another Method is by placing the Nuts in the sun to melt, which is done in a few days, but the Oil thus made is always rank—the Cocoa Nut is the only oil they make and the Chief use of it is for Dressing their Hair or anointing their Bodys where they Chance to be sunburnt—it is Calld *Monoi.*

Their Manner of Trafic which they Call *Tarahu* & *Ihoa* is this. If a Man has occasion for more Cloth then he can procure from his neighbours, he takes a large hog or two, to the house of some of the People who Inhabit the Valleys and whose Chief Employment it is, and agrees with him to make the Cloth by such a time and in such quantity as shall be deemd the Value of the Hogs—which being settled, the Undertaker calls his neighbours together, and tells them He wants so much Cloth made by such a day, and those who Choose to be concerned signify it to him, the Hogs are then killd and a feast made, after which each Furnish their proportion & the Weomen meet and put it together, and when finished it is delivered to the purchaser—but should the Undertaker not fulfil His agreement, or delay the time, through Negligence the other may if He is able plunder his house as for a theft

If a Man wants a house or a Canoe built, he employs one or more Carpenters paying them before hand one half of what shall be Judged the Value of the Work they are to perform, in Hogs, Cloth, Oil, Matting &c—and finds them in provision all the time they are at work and when the Work is Compleat he pays the remainder, according to Agreement, but should he refuse, or neglect and the Neighbours think the labour worth the stipulated agreement, then they may plunder him of all that he is worth

If a Man wants to be Constantly Supplied with Fish He takes a Hog to a Fisherman and according to the size He agrees with the Fisherman to supply Him with Fish for one or more Months, which they seldom fail to perform, Weather permitting for the stated time. What they look upon as fulfiling the Agreement is bring as much Fish evry day as the Family can Eat, and for Failure of Promise they may be Plundered as before. Sometimes they agree for a supply evry other day and when the Fisherman fulfils His promise well they make Him a Feast—and the Fish they bring are sometimes equal to ten times the price at a Fair exchange–

Such is the Method they use in trade, and if a Man wants help to Cultivate a piece of Ground for Cloth, 'Ava, *Taro* &c—he Employs his labourers in the same manner, always paying them the whole or one half of their hire before hand, but their Principal Method is by Gifts and Presents to each other, and it is not Common to refuse the Greatest Stranger any thing he stands in need of whether Food raiment or any thing else–

6 *Tahitian Society, History, and Culture*

The Island of *Tahiti* is devided into Seventeen Districts Calld *Fenua* (or Lands) with the name of the Head Chief of each annex'd. These are again divided into Chiefs Shares (or *Patu*) and these again into lesser Divisions calld *Vahi* which are the Squires Shares and the Lord of the Mannor holds three *Vahi*

The Names of the Districts of *Tahiti Nui* are, 1st *Pare,* 2nd *Matavai,* 3rd *Ha'apaiano'o,* 4th *Puna'auia,* 5th *Tiarei,* 6th *Hitia'a*—These six are always in alliance and are Calld by the General Names of *Te Porionu'u* and *Te Aharoa* and Extend from the Isthmus along the North side of the Island Westward to *Tetaha*—7th *Vaiari,* 8th *Vaiuriti,* 9th *Papara*—these Three extend from the Isthmus Westward on the South Side to *Atehuru,* and are known by the name of Teva-i-uta—they are always in alliance with Te Porionu'u–10th *Atehuru,* 11th *Tetaha*—these two Districts lye on the West side of the Island and were ever rebelious to the reigning King till they were reduced in our time into Subjection. *Tahiti Iti* Contains six Districts which are 1st *Afa'ahiti,* 2nd *Tautira* (Calld by Captn Cook Oheitepeha), 3rd Tepare, 4th Vaiaotea, 5th *Mataoae,* 6th *Vaiuru*—the First beginning at the Isthmus on the North Side and the last ending at the Isthmus on the South Side—these Six were also rebellious and never suffered the King Flag to pass till our time—for a list of the Present Chiefs of *Tahiti* See the Vocabulary[1]–

The Chiefs of *Tahiti* are of two Houses, which are *Te Porionu'u* and *Teva-i-uta,* each being absolute in their own dominions but only one can be *Ari'i Nui* or king and the other lives in Friendship with him till Death or War dispossesses Him of His Honors and title which then devolves on the other. they are supported by Voluntary Contributions and Free Gifts which however the People must not refuse to make if they have wherewithal to supply the Demand; if they have not it is not expected—The present Ari'i Nui (or King) is the Son of *Mate* or O Tu, his name is *Tu-nui-e-a'a-i-te-atua* which may be thus translated, "Tu, the Great begot-

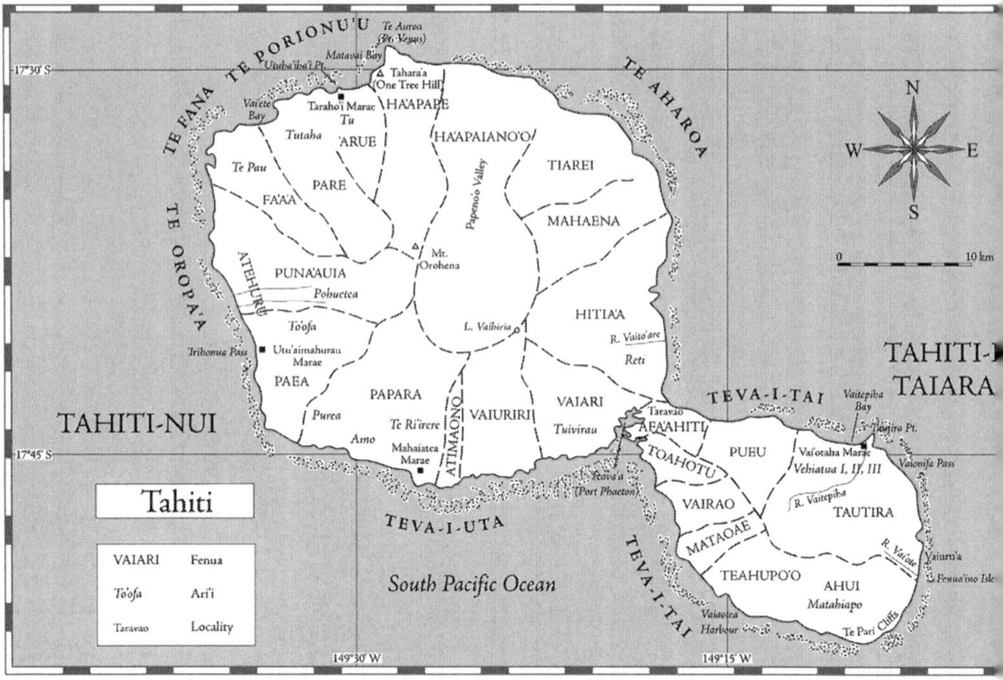

Figure 16. Map of Tahiti showing political districts, groupings, and key sites. Courtesy of Nick Keenleyside at Outline Draughting and Graphics Ltd.

ten of God", and his title *Atua Ra'a* or Sacred God—which Sacraligous Name and title He obtained by His Mother declaring that the Deity (*Tane*) Cohabited with her in her Sleep and proving Pregnant soon after, the Child was declared to be the Offspring of the Deity and is rever'd as something supernatural—the only Male of the House of Teva-i-uta is *Temari'i* Son of *Purea* (Calld Oberea by Capt. Cook) deceased, and *Amo,* and Should both lines become extinct the Royal *Maro* becomes elective and evry Chief in the Society Isles becomes a Candidate–

The Chiefs are Numerous and evry district has two or three besides others who reside as private Gentlemen on their own estates while out of Employ being still regarded as Chiefs tho residing as a Squire under another and when they are Calld into Office they leave their estates to the Care of their Friends who have no rent to pay except supplying such demands as are made by the Chiefs in Common as if the land belongd to any other person

Before I proceed any farther it may be requisite to the better expanation of their Manners & Customs, to discribe the Different Classes into which they are Devided which are Four viz 1st Ari'i rahi or Nui or King—Ari'i, Chief of a District, which are Greater or less according to their Possessions, 2nd *To'ofa* which answers to Lord of the Mannor, 3rd *Ra'atira*—Esquire, & 4th *Manahune* or *Mata'eina'a* Tennants—amongst each of these classes are Some *Ra'a* or Sacred and some *Noa,* Unhalloed or Common. servants are Calld *Teuteu* in General but those who wait on Weomen are Calld *Tutae* by way of derision—tho it is not uncommon to find Young Men of the first Familys and the Younger Brothers of Chiefs in the Service of the Fair Sex but by debasing themselves thus, they are rendered Incapable of assisting at any religious Ceremony[2]–

The Chiefs have each Personal estates and when in Office have either a District or Part of One Calld a *Patu* which maintains them by Contributions—under them are the *To'ofa* & *Ra'atira* each holding his land independent of the Other, any Ra'atira can put a *Rahui* on his own division (which is so named from their power to prohibit the expenditure of any species of Provisions on his own land)—the Chief on His *Patu* and the King on the Whole, or any Number of Districts, but if the Chiefs should not act up to the Dignity of their Office they may be devested of their Office, but they are still Chiefs, and tho the King may be stripd of his Government he still retains his royalty and none but one of the Two Familys can ever enjoy that Dignity while they are in being so that it is no more then a Change in the Ministry, with the other Chiefs it is the same and they often Change stations. When a king is invested with the Maro *'Ura* or red sash of Royalty, he sends two Flags round the Island by different routs and those who acknowledge his Supremacy pass them with Ceremony, and attend his Corronoation with evry Chief a Human Sacrafice, but if they refuse to acknowledge him they Break the Staff and trample on the Flag as soon as it enters their Territory; upon which war is declared against them and if they cannot reduce them by War they enjoy their Independance, but the King is King still—While these Flags are passing no fire is made near the Beach; nor must any Canoe be launchd for any Purpose the bearers of the Flag Passing Close to the surf the whole way any breach of this would be punishd with Death and forfeiture of Estate, the Beach being made Sacred by the Royal Flags, it would be a Crime of the Highest Nature to launch a Canoe over it or make a Smoke nearer then 2 or 3 miles of it

When a Chief is present in any Company the Men strip their Bodys to the Waist not suffering any Covering on their Head or Shoulders in His

Presence—and all the Weomen present uncover their Shoulders tucking their Cloth under their armpits, to Cover their Breasts in token of obediance and respect, to his presence. the Men are not always particular in this point except Upon the Chiefs Heredetary land or that of His adopted friend, where any neglect would be deemed as Insult and punishd accordingly—but in presence of the King the Chiefs themselves must strip—Nor do they stop to see him first if they Have Notice of *His approach* either by land or in a Canoe, Nor must any person pass his land by walking over it or Sailing by it without paying the Compliment–

If a Chief takes a liking to any thing in the Posession of any Person and they don't like to part with it immediately, he then Curses it, or Calls it by his own name or any of his relations and it is sanctified so far that the Owner cannot again make use of it upon Pain of Death or Forfeiture of their land tho they may keep it if they will, which however is seldom the Case—nor Is the Chief often obliged to make use of this alternative, as they make it their Study to anticipate the Wishes of their Chiefs, and leave them nothing to ask for, giving them whatever he seems inclined to have and when the Chiefs do ask for any thing it is Given freely at the first word

If a Chief should enter or even toutch the House of any Female of a lower Class, it is rendered sacred by his presence and She Can never eat in it any more (but any man may) and she must provide herself with a new house and new furniture—for this reason if the Chief should be caught in the rain, he must not take shelter till he comes to a Mans house, or one of His own (of which He has several for that and such like purposes) tho He should be a mile from one, and for this reason also No woman except of equal rank, can eat on board a Ship after the Chief has been on board, under pain of severe punishment, which accounts for the Women Calling the provisions on board *Ma'a Ra'a* (Sacred food) every thing on board being made sacred by his presence, yet nevertheless when they were right Hungry would eat in private, tho even then they will hardly ever eat in company with other Weomen except they are well acquainted

The Chiefs are in General taller stouter and of a different appearance from the Common People and their Weomen are also larger and fairer then the lower Classes. They have in General a more serious and thoughtful turn and are more accomplishd, they are always superior to them at all things either Labour or diversion, and the Ari'i *weomen* are by far the Best Clothmakers. in labour they are always first, it being no disgrace to know how, but a great one not to know how—and they always bear a part in the Cooking Provisions for their Guests—they are Company for their meanest Subject or Servants who nevertheless pay them due reverence & respect and their poverty never renders them despicable, as they never loose their rank nor can any who are not born a Chief ever arrive at that Dignity, and tho when a Child is born the titles & honors of the Father immediately fall to it, Yet the Father is still a Chief, and is always regarded as such, tho out of Office by the birth of a Child to which he is sometimes a Guardian or Regent[3]–

Their only pride is Cleanlyness and Generosity for which they are remarkable, and I may say they have no equals in these points—Their retinue Costs them nothing as they pay their attendants no wages, and Change them often, no man staying in their service longer then he pleases, tho they have some who stay their whole lives in the service of the same family—and these old servants are always considered as one of the Family and by them the Household is Managed and they, like other Courtiers have as much to do in the Government as their Masters–

Few of the Chiefs are shorter then Six feet, but many of them exceed that height by some inches, for this reason they readily beleived Captn Cook and such of His Officer as were tall stout men were Chiefs, but they have no Conception that a short man can be a Chief

If any Person speaks disrespectfully of a Chief he is sure to suffer death, and should one Chief speak ill of another it would instantly bring on a War and this has been the occasion of several bloody battles and is at present the subject of the annimosity between *Taiarapu* and *Tahiti Nui,* the late Chief of *Taiarapu* having refused to acknowledge *Tu-nui-e-a'a-i-te-atua* who he said was not the son of the Deity nor of *O Tu* but of a Favourite Minion and that his Mother had only raised that Story out of Her own head that her Son might not be disinherited if he did not attain his proper size–

The People in general are of the Common size of Europeans, the Men are Strong well limb'd and finely shaped—their Gait easey and Genteel and their Countenance Free Open and lively, never sullied by a sullen or Suspicious look—their motions are Vigourous active & Graceful and their Behaveour to Strangers is such as declare at first sight their Humane disposition, which is as Candid as their Countenaces seem to indicate, and their Courteous affable and freindly behaviour to each other shews that they have no tincture of Barbarity, Cruelty, Suspicion or Revenge—they are ever of an even unruffeld temper, slow to anger and soon appeasd and as they have no suspicion so they ought not to be suspected, and an hours acquaintance is sufficient to repose an entire confidence in them[4]–

The Men Wear their Hair in different forms Some have their hair Cut short & others wear it long and flowing over their Shoulders in Waves and others tied in a bunch on the top of their Heads, and their beards neatly pickd, which they do with a fish scale & here a Painter might take an excellent copy of a *Hector* or an *Achilles.*[5]

The Weomen are finely Shaped and the Natural Collour is a *Brunette* tho some who are moe exposed to the Sun are very dark, especcially those who are fishermen and Constantly exposed to its rays, but those who are not exposed are of fine bright Collour, and a Glow of Blood may be seen in their faces their skin is as tender as Europeans and they scorch as soon in the sun. They are in generall handsom and engaging, their Eyes full and sparkling and Black almost without exception. their Noses of different descriptions their mouths small, lips thin and red, and their teeth white and even and their Breath sweet and perfectly free from taint. The Hair of Both sexes is mostly Black or dark Brown, in some Coarse and others fine, which the Weomen wear Short and Neatly Cut in waves in their Neck. They take much pride in keeping it in exact order and decorate their head with sweet flowers they are careful to keep it free from Vermin, and for that purpose were exceding fond of our Combs, as they also were of Scisars trim it, a Sharks tooth being the only intrument they have for Cutting hair—tho the Weomen hate to have Vermin in their heads as much as we do yet the men are not so delicate and many eat them–

Tho the fashion in which the Weomen wear their hair is contrary to the Inhabitants of other Countrys it is no ways injurious to their beauty as neither Sex wear any thing on their heads but Garlands of Flowers nor dress their hair in any other Manner then by Combing and oiling but all are particular to have it regularly trimm'd; and some trim their Eyelids and brows and pick them into form.

Their limbs in general are neat and delicate and tho they go bare-footed their feet do not spread like the inhabitants of Africa and other Hot Climates and many with the help of a Fashionable Dress would pass for handsom weomen even in England–

The Number of Inhabitants in *Tahiti* are Near 30,000 of which their warriors may be reckoned at near one third of that number.[6] Their Chief Strength consisted formerly in their Naval force, which at present is but triffling, their Navy being but on a very indifferent footing, *Tu* thinking it better to keep peace then make war. at present his whole Naval force does not exceed 20 sail of War Canoes & for the most part of these he is beholden to his Sister *Ari'ipaea Vahine* who brought them from *Ra'iatea*—but he stands in no need at present of large Canoes as *Mo'orea* is now under him. *Metuaro* having adopted His Son to be Heir to *Mo'orea*

At the time the Island was discovered by Captn Wallis *Temari'i,* the Son of *Purea* (since deceased) and *Amo,* was *Ari'i Nui* and *Amo* being an *'Arioi* had left Her but not till the Boy was born when *Purea,* who was a Stirring active woman and regent for Her Son, got him declared king and invested at Pare with the *Royal Maro* and Mate or *Tu* who was then about 7 years old was forced to fly to His Fathers Estate at *Papara* where he lived private tho the *Maro* was his right, but soon after Captn Wallis saild, *Mate* made a party in *Atehuru* and soon forced *Temari'i* to exchange stations, and take his own possessions, but *Te To'ofa* and *Pohuetea* Chiefs of *Atehuru* at the Head of their men Seized on the *Marae* and Carried it and the *Maro* to *Atehuru* where they forced *Mate* to come to have his Ceremony performed and at the same time laid him under restrictions that made him rather a Dependant to them then their King and all the releigeous rites were now to be performd at their *Marae* where all the other Chiefs were under the Necessity of Bringing their offerings and were often Plundered of them before they reachd the *Marae* and of this they were affraid to Complain, fearing the *Atehuru* people who being mostly renegades supported by *Te To'ofa,* had gaind themselves a Great name in the War and they at last became very troublesome neighbours; keeping both *Mate* & *Temari'i* in Awe of them. *Tahiti Iti* taking the advantage of the situation of affairs revolted, and as they lookd upon themselves seperated from Tahiti Nui by the Isthmus, they declared for *Vehiatua* and made him their king, but Could not obtain the *Maro,* being forced to retire to their own Country, *Temari'i* and *Mate* having united to keep their right in their own Families and repulsed *Taiarapu* With Great Slaughter but could never reduce them to subjection by reasons of the many Strong holds which they Posess–

About the same time *Mo'orea* revolted and *Mahine* (the Uncle of *Metuaro* proper king of that Island) seized on the Government and Forced Metuaro to fly to *Mate* for refuge together with his Sisters *'Itia* & *Teano,* where they were on Captn Cooks Arrival at the Island when a truce was made–

This may in some Measure account for the Situation in which he found the Island, and for his finding Purea living retired with Her husband with whom She then lived they having parted before on account of a Quarrel but had now made matters up. *Temari'i* is the same Captn Cook Calls *Teridiri*—probably *Te ari'i rahi* or head Chief, which title he assumes evry where but in the presence of *Tu-nui-e-a'a-i-te-atua*—he being Calld *Ari'i Nui* or the Great Chief; the Young Woman *Taumata* was his cousin, and sister to His Present Wife *Teri'itahi; Purea* having no other Child but *Temari'i,* having killd all that came before him

Tu or *Mate* is the eldest son of *Teu* or *Hapai,* who is also mentioned by Captn Cook. these two are now on Freindly terms and *Temari'i* having no Children, adopted a Daughter of *Tu* but she died young, but it is probable he may have Issue by his present wife, if not the right falls to the present King, who is a boy about 10 or 12 years old–

On or about the time of Captain Cooks arrival at *Tahiti* the last time Tu was engaged in a War with *Mo'orea* and with the assistance of *Temari'i* and *Te To'ofa* & *Pohuetea,* who joind their Forces to his would have reduced *Mahine* to obedience or forced Him to relinquish his Claim to the Island to Metuaro the Proper Heir, but *Te To'ofa* began to grow Jealous of *Tu*s Growing Power; and envying the rich presents made him by Captn Cook—determined to lessen it if possible and for that Purpose kept back his supplyes, and after Captain Cook saild, he turned his force back his supplyes, and after Captain Cook saild, he turned his force against Tu [repetition in original—Eds.] and joind with *Mahine,* who between them destroyd *Tu*s fleet and plundered him of evry thing, killing and destroying most part of the Cattle & Stock which Captn Cook had left and carrying of the rest–

Mahine was now suffered to remain in quiet possession of *Mo'orea,* and Metuaro & his sisters were forced to remain at *Tahiti,* where *Tu,* taking *'Itia,* Metuaros sister to Wife, *Metuaro* took *Tu*s sister *Terereatua* to be his wife, but *Mahine,* who was against these Matches, and supposed they would at one time be the means of driving him from the posessions he had seized upon, was detirmened to set them to work if he Could not seperate them but finding he could make nothing of them tho he set *Taiarapu* & *Temari'i* by the ears and now he declared war against *Tu* who was forced to make an effort with the small Fleet he had left—these he put under the Command of *Moana, Tutahas* brother, & Vaetua, *Tu*s own brother, and a bloody fight took Place in *Matavai* Bay when *Mahine* had brought his Fleet but being himself Killd by *Vaetua,* the Fleet was mostly destroyd and His men fled home where they placed His adopted son *Teri'iamoeatua* on the throne of *Mo'orea* where he remaind till after the Bounty saild in Aprl. 1789, when having made a party in the Island, he got posession and by the help of the Arms left with *Tu* he obtaind his right and forced *Teri'iamoeatua* with his Aunt & Mother to fly to *Tahiti* for refuge where he now resides private–

Their Genius & Temper being before described I shall now describe their Manner of Making War[7]–

War in this Country often happens from mere trifles however what we may think a trifle may seem to them of Great Consequence—The Districts have all a parting or Boundary line, frequently a river, which separates their lands from each other. If any dispute happens the party Who happens to be the Occasion of it are Calld upon to make good any damage or defeciency which if they refuse to do war is declared in this Manner. The Priests and the head Men of the Contending Party being Assembled near their Bounds, and having consulted the Preists—if they give a Favourable Answer War is then the Word and the party who think themselves most Injured send out a Slinger to the Boundary line, where having Charged the Sling he discharges it *over* the Heads of the Opposite party Crying out "Ua afa te vai" which Signifies the War is declared but litterally "The Water has borne down its banks" This is answerd by a Slinger from the other side who slings a Stone and Calls out in the same manner, they then Cry out to each other "Ia ora te atua i te tama'i ra" (God save you in your War)–they then return home seemingly in peace, and make a War Feast, killing a Number of Hogs for the Warriors, and sometimes make a human Sacrifice & Next morning repair to the Appointed Ground they are always attended by inspired priests who before they come to the Charge encourage them to Fight manfully and there is no fear of Victory and Spirits them up by blowing their Conch Shells which they always use on these Occasions having a bamboo tube which they blow through like a Trumpet, they always send or offer conditions of Peace to those which are deemd the weakest party which if they refuse & they are Worsted they are drove from their posessions and the Conquering Chief puts a Subordinate Chief of his own in to Command the Conqud Country and if the Vanquishd people will promise to pay obedience to the New Chief they are permitted to remain and enjoy their lands as before but this they seldom will do they having so great an affection for their Chiefs that they had rather partake of his disgrace and loose their Estates then enjoy their property under another, should they act otherwise they would be very Meanly lookd on & be made a bye word among their Countrymen, and their lives be a torment to them afterwards

They take No Captives nor give any quarter, unless a man falls in with one who has formerly been His adopted friend, a breach of which they were never known to make—they are not forced to Fight any longer then they please, and a man never obtains the Name of a Warrior tho he kills his Man, should he receive any wound himself, as they think that a Man Who suffers himself to be wounded does not know how to defend himself, and tis more Honor to return with whole bones then broken ones–

Tho they are not Imediately under the Authority of the Chief in Battle yet they Fight furiously, knowing that in case of being Vanquishd they loose all their posession yet tho this seems of small account where it is but ask and have yet they all prefer the having to give then being forced to receive—and when they make a present, it is so freely done and so graceful that Christianity may blush at the action and be ashamed to be surpass'd by those whom we Call Savages—This is the Chief reason that a *Tahitian* has to Fight for and in Some of their Sea Actions Much blood has been shed as they Frequently lassh Bow to bow & fight it out, when the Strongest party generally get the day and the Weaker are forced to save themselves by Jumping Overboard

Their Weapons are Spears of 12 or 14 feet long pointed with the Stings of the Sting *Ray,* Clubs of 7 or 8 feet, both of which are Made of Toa a hard heavy wood, Slings made of the Platted fibers of the Cocoa Nut, they have bows and Javlins for Sport but never use them in War

Some of their War Canoes are very large, and carry from one to Three Hundred Men, they have often one Hundred paddlers all of which have heaps of Stones and each man a Sling, besides Spears & Clubbs, and when the one party becomes too strong for the Others they are forced to Fly and the Conquerors Carry off their prize in Triumph—Such was mostly the Fate of Tus Fleet after Captain Cook left him, and since that time his Navy has gone almost to ruin, tho he has still been lucky, and often Conqueror yet he always prefers peace to War–

They always bring of the Dead if they can, by any means, as all that they leave are Carried to the *Marae* where the body being offered as a Sacrafice the lower Jaw bone being Cut out and placed in the *Marae* as a Trophie—and the Body is interrd in the Marae the Man who killd him now takes his name, this being the only Method by which they attain to the Charracter of a Warrior they must bring off their dead, which is often severely disputed, by the living and especially the Friends of the Fallen Warrior who fight more furious to protect the body when dead then they did to assist him while living—If the Conqueror Should prevail and Maintain his conquest he takes the Name of His Adversary as a Title of *Honor*—after the Peace is Made the relations of the Deceased Warriors, soon find out the Men who killd them and each Family sends a present to the Man by Who their Freind or Relation was killd, & hire a Set of (*Uraeva*) or a Sort of People somthing similar to our Morris dancers and a Principal part is acted by the Daughter or Nearest Female relation of the Deceased Warrior in a Dance at the House of the Man who killd him, the Dance being Finished the Cloth, Matting & Dresses are all presented to Him and He Now entertains all the Deceaseds Relations, sumptuously for Several days and they Declare that they Owe him any Grudge or animosity for killing their Relation and their Sorrow is now turnd to Joy and evry thing is most amicably Settled and the Conqueror, to Make the Friendship more Firm on his part adopts the Nearest relation of the Deceased as his Friend, and by bearing his Name becomes one of the Family and is ever after Treated as such and is as much beloved in the Family as if he had been born in it

Their Relegion is without Form or regularity and tho in many respects peculiar to themselves yet it may be in many respects be compared to that of some of the Antient Jewish tribes[8]—and their Traditions which are Numerous may be compared to theirs and in many respects correspond with our books of the Old Testament—They have Images but they offer them no kind of Adoration—their Deitys are three which are Calld by the General Name of *Atua* but worshipd as three distinct persons and spoken of seperately are Calld

Tane, the first or Father of Gods, somtimes Calld *Atua Nui* (Great God) and somtimes *Atua Mana* Tremendous or Awful God, Maker of the

World and all things and the Cause of all things, light Darkness, Thunder Lightning and rain &c–

'Oromatua, or the Son who presides over War and peace who punnishes Chiefs with Sickness and Death for any Neglect of their Duty–

Ti'ipa huamanu—the *Hoa* or Friend of Both and is their Messenger to Earth—these they style *Atua fanau po,* (or *po roa*)—Gods born of, or brought forth from Darkness or Eternal Night; to these they never apply but in time of War, or when any Sickness befalls their Chiefs, as they deem them too great to intrest themselves, in any Trivial or insignificant affairs and are very Cautious how they attempt any thing that may offend them, for fear they should destroy the World intirely as they were near doing when they were offended; having overset the World and broke it to pieces, which is they account they give of the cause of so many Islands as they are acquainted with

Besides these, they have a number of inferior Deitys evry Man & Woman having a Garudian Angel who they suppose to be the souls of their Departed relatives who have been Deifyd for their good works and whose business is to watch and protect them, While on earth—and as they beleive that evry man shall be rewarded with happyness in the Next world, so they take leave of this without any anxiety, and when they Die take leave of their Friends with as much composure as if they were going on a Journey–

As they believe in a Future state so they also beleive that those who have been good Men and have been liberal to the Gods shall have the highest place, but think of none worse then Earth—they say when they Dream that the soul is absent, and talking of Dreams they say "My soul saw such a soul &c"—and when any one Dies they say their soul is fled, and that it Flies to the Deity who (as they express it) eats it—that it then comes out through him and partaking of His Divinity is sent to take care of some other Mortal who may be born at the same time, or suffered to roam at large through the Heavenly Mansions where it wants for Nothing they also beleive that there is an Evil Deamon whom they call *Ti'i* but that his power extends no farther then by being able to punnish them on Earth by getting into them, and causing Madness, Fits &c but that he cannot enter without the leave of their Angel who can also drive him out—for this reason as soon as they fall sick they instantly apply to the Deity to remove the Cause by prayer and offerings and apply to the priests for their assistance—and enquiring of themselves, they endeavour to rectify any little affair that may have caused a misunderstanding by sending a peace offering to those who they think they have offended, and when they have given all they have away to the Priests & Deitys and cannot appease their anger they Call their Friends about them and recommend them to the Care of their Guardian angels, desiring them to be careful how they should Offend them and to be mindful that they make much of their Chiefs and be generous and Good to strangers; and frequently dye without a Groan to reduced to the last by pain & Suffering

They beleive that the Sun & Moon are the original parents of all the Stars, and when they are in eclipse they say they are in the act of Generation and that evry thing on earth is produced in the same Manner and that evry thing made by the Deitys at first is disolved and drop'd away and that others are produced in their rooms and that the whole systim of nature

Figure 17. *Ti'i,* carved double figure, Tahiti [Oc, TAH.60]. © The Trustees of the British Museum

keeps constantly Changing and in support of these arguments they say dont we see some Die, and some born evry day, the rivers run to the Sea, the Trees rot, and the Rocks fall from the Mountains all which has Continued From the begining of the world and yet they are not diminished but others supply their places

Their traditions respecting the Creation are in many respect the same as we find in the Bible they do not limit the time but say that God produced all things from nothing and set evry thing in Motion by his Command—and some of their accounts of the Stars may be said to Correspond with the Greek fables they have Names for Most of them, into which Men & Weomen have been translated for Good & evil Works, they say that a Girl Calld Taurua, of Great Beauty but a Great Whore, was for Cursing Tane sent into the Planate Venus where she must remaind for her punishment and of several others of the same and such like discriptions. Castor & Pollas they say were two brothers, who begd of *Tane* to be taken away from their parents who had refused to give them some fine Fish—upon which they went away from home and praying to *Tane* a White Cloud came and took them away they are Calld Pipiri Ma or the Pipiris–

As they are superstitious in all their Customs and think that evry transgression against God or Man is attended with punnishment, so they have but few that may be calld real Crimes among a People who have no other law but that of Nature, they firmly beleive what they are taught by their priests and Forefathers and which they suppose to be the Command of God—they know that from him all their blessings proceed, and when they approach their places of worship, it is with a Reverential Awe, that would be an honor to Christianity, and when in the Act praying always behaves with due Decorum–

Yet tho they maintain that their Method is right as they are taught, they allow that another is as good, and are Charitable enough to allow that evry Man if He worships his God as he is taught is in a fair way of happiness and will meet such reward as he deserves, but that this World is the only place of punnishment they all hold and think it impossible that ever there can be an other

Their Weomen bear no part in their religious rites, and neither them nor their Male servants ever partake of their Ceremonies, they have no place of worship for themselves, nor do they ever enter one but at their Birth, but any priest may Officiate for them when any thing ails them, and they are no less in the Eyes of the Deity then those who are admitted to be partakers of religious rites

Their Ceremoneys Consist of Innumerable Sacrafices, prayers, Feasts &c held on the *Marae,* at which their Priests always preside but before I proceed to the ceremonies it is Necessary to Give some little Account of the *Marae* & Priests.

The *Maraes* or Places of Worship are Oblong Square pieces of Ground planted thick with trees, and inclosed by a Wall of Stone some 4, 5 & 6 feet High and as much thick, some are piles of Stone rising in large Steps and are Built solid and Firm and the largest in *Tahiti* is at Papara—See Captn. Cooks Voyage, he having given an Account of it I need not here Further describe it, they are of different dimentions, and are built without Mortar, in the Center is a table or Altar on which they make their Offerings, and on one end a House for the reception of the Priests, when they Come to offer sacrifice and Feast on the *Marae*–

Figure 18. "The Morai at Oparrey, Island of Otahytey—Looking towards Matavai," George Tobin, 1792 [Call no. PXA 563 no. 39]. Reproduced with permission of the Mitchell Library, State Library of NSW

In one of these *Maraes* which is their Grand and principal one and is in the district of *Pare* they keep a movable one something similar to the *Ark* of the Jews, and which is the occasion of as many quarrels as it formerly was, this *Marae* is calld "Taputapuatea" thus translated "Sacrafise the White hog", and is the place to which evry Chief on the Island, and those who are subject to them on Other Islands must repair to offer their sacrafices, as they think it the only residences of the Deity on Earth

This Movable *Marae* is a Box about 3 feet long 2 feet wide and one deep in which is kept the Three Deitys or rather the Images to represent them as they are only for the purpose of remembrancers and are not Worshipd, Nevertheless they bear the Names of the Deitys on the top of this Box is raised several peices of rude Carved work on the tops of which are represented Birds with extended wings as the Deity is fond of Birds and makes use of them to come on Earth in—and the whole is decorated with bunches of Red & Yellow Feathers, which to them are as Valuable as Gold, this, with a Movable House which is part of the *Marae* and Fixed on a strand together, is Calld (Fare atua) "the House of God" they are Screend in and kept Covered with the best Cloth the Island produces, painted in different Collours and Here also is kept the Royal *Maro* &c and none must approach, but the Priests on pain of Death, and even they are obliged to divest themselves of their Cloaths to the Waist, whenever they enter a *Marae* and when they enter the Fare Atua they strip Naked leaving their own Cloaths outside, and while there they Cover their Nakedness with Cloathing belonging to the sacred place, which they pull of at their return leaving them there, & resume their own—

This *Marae* is the principal place of Worship & Here only they offer Human Sacrafices. It has ever been the object of Dispute each desiring to have it in their own posession it was seized from Tu about 20 Years before our coming to the Island by Te To'ofa Chief of Atehuru who had assisted him to recover it from *Temari'i*—*Te To'ofa,* finding Himself of some Consequence insisted on having posession of the *Marae* &c and keeping them in Atehuru which He had done till our time, and having in our time made war with Tu and refused to acknowledge his son, Tu Demanded our Assistance and by our Help *Te To'ofa* was reduced as before described and the *Marae* brought to *Pare* where a New Stone one was built for its reception and there were made the First and last Human Sacrafices which they made during our stay on the Island and these we were informed had been found

Figure 19. *To'o,* god image, Tahiti [Z 6067]. Reproduced with permission of University of Cambridge Museum of Archaeology and Anthropology

Guilty of Blasphemy against God or the King and these were Not Burnt, nor do they burn any

The Walls of the *Maraes* are as before said built without Cement and tho the Stones appear some round and some exactly squared, yet no tool except stones are used in the construction of them—When a *Marae* is to be Built the Chief Gives Notice thereof by sending a piece of Cocoa Nut leaf to evry Man under him, with orders that at the time and place appointed he shall appear with a Stone of the dimentions that he shall find described by the Priests and they accordingly attend if the Stones are not Judged sufficient the order is renewd, these leaves are Generally made up by the priests with knots, tied in a Manner peculiar to themselves, and Contain the Dimentions of the Stones that each man may work without the assistance of another when the stones are all Collected, the Priests give notice that they are ready and a part of each day is set aside for the Work—a Sacrafice is then made, and they proceed in their work during which time no fire must be lighted in the District till they leave off Work each Day—after the work is finished and the Alter errected, they expend two or three days in the Consecration of it which is done by making many Sacrafices, Human & Common, with prayers & feasts, and during the time the religious part of the rites are performing no fire must be lighted, and this is observed in all rites wherein the Generality of the People are Conserned.

The Priests are of two Classes and are formed out of all ranks of People according to the Ability they Posess they are the only People who have any knowledge and it is their business to keep the lower Classes in Ignorance tho some are of the lowest Class themselves yet they gain esteem according to their knowledge, or rather from their being lucky in the business they profess–

The first of These are Calld *Tahu'a Marae* and their business is to make the Offerings at the *Marae* and have the Charge of the Holy place, their prayers or Hymns they Chant out in an unknown tongue which the Natives or at least such as are not of their profession do not understand nor do many of the Chiefs, tho they are all considered as Priests and they seldom Officiate but on particular occasions when they are forced to assist for want of others but as they are Plenty they are seldom under such Necessity

The others are Calld *Taura e atua* and pretend to Devine Inspiration, and are Consulted on all Occasions, whether in War, Sickness or otherwise and through them the Will and Pleasure of the Deity is known, few of them pretend to be inspired by the same Deity and those who claim the Superior ones are Men of Great Art and address, and from their Skill in their Art make themselves of great Consequence they never attempt to apply to their Deity, but when a Chief is taken sick, or to know the event of any War which they may have in hand and as they are well acquainted with most of the Circumstances before they begin they Can tell events of this kind to a Certainty if their skill proves ineffectual in sickness they never fail to accuse the Friends and relations of the sick for their want of Relegion and Neglect of their Duty in the performance of it, but should he recover while under their care their Charracter is firmly established, and tho' of the lowest Class become the Bosom friends of the Chief or

Party in whose behalf they used their skill, and are sent for on all Occasions and Carress'd, even tho their skill should afterward fail–

When they are Consulted with respect to the Event of War &c they dress themselves in a Fantastical form and decorate themselves with Red and Black Feathers, of which they suppose the Deity to be immoderately fond as he always makes use of Birds when he decends on earth and having his Head bound with *Rauava* he goes into a close place screend in Near the *Marae* for that purpose, or into some thick bush where he remains a few Minutes, and comes out sneezing two or three times when he begins to look wild, his eyes staring, and his body distorted into many forms and in a moment he seems to have undergone a most amazing Change—these postures, they attribute to the contest between their own soul, and that of the Deity endeavouring to take its habitation which it at last effects and they appear as if stupid and do not know any person. His Colleague, who is Generally a Tahu'a then Compliments him by the Name of the Deity which he professes to be inspired with, and asks him such questions as he or the party Conserned wish to have Answered & he returns him answers in a low squeaking tone of voice but should he be questioned while struggling with the Deity he somtimes utters half sentence in a Curious Manner as if both souls endeavourd to speak at the same time and somtimes speaks with his natural, and sometimes in a Squeaking Voice—When the Spirit leaves him he begins to Gape and Yawn and often falls backward with a loud shriek and lays speechless some Minutes, when he awakes as if from a sleep and his body being reoccupied by his own Soul He resumes his own voice, and seems to know nothing of what has passd, he Generally times it at the flight of one of the Birds from the Marae and his Colleague does not forget to inform him of what Demands the Deity has made & those Concerned seldom fail to furnish him with evry thing he required, if they have it, or Can by any Means get it–

This is the Method by which they always proceed and Several Weomen pertend to the same office and make their enquireys for their Own Sex in Sickness, and Child birth, and such is their belief in them, that they think if one of them is present, and not applied to, that the Mother would never be delivered—but instead of one they have sometimes half a Dozen who facilitate the Birth of the Child by their prayers and offerings and in return Strip them of Half they posess without giving them any other Assistance

When a Priest or Priestess enters a house for this purpose they always bring with them a Young Plantain tree, and having taken one of the leaves from it throw the tree on the top of the House and then enter making several short prayers, in different parts of it and stick the leaf up over the Door or entrance, they then proceed to enquire into the particulars of the business and are always perfectly acquainted with evry Circumstance before they proceed in any thing, by which means they know what answers to make whether there is any hope of Success or fear of Disapointment before they begin

When they make an offering to the Deity, the Hog is brought to the *Marae* where it is killd and Cleand as if for eating, it is then besmeard with its own Blood and placed on the alter to rot and they suppose the Deity is Gratified by eating the Soul of the Victim as he also does of those who die Whether Man or Beast, but those who are killd on purpose for him have always the effect of procuring favours for the Maker of the Sacrafice, the Priests then Dress the intrails with Bread fruit & Roots, and eat them on the *Marae,* and as they observe the Birds often eat the Plantains they frequently lay a bunch or two of the Best sort on the Alter together with Fish, Fowles &c and they are scarce ever without some thing on them

The first Fruits of all kinds are offered to the Deity, next to the Chief and to the Lord of the Mannor, before they eat any themselves, and the Fish in like Manner, if a Man has a Fishing seine to Wet or a New Canoe to launch he makes a Feast on the *Marae* for the Priests, who offer up Plantain trees and prayers for their success, and the First fish always goes to the *Marae* where the Priest offers it with prayers, the Next to the Priests, the 3rd. to the Chief, and the 4th. to the Lord of the Mannor or landlord; and till all these are served they never taste the Fruits of their labour–

The first pig is always offered at 8 or ten Days old and a Chicken of the Brood is also offered, and for their Children they always make an offering according to their ability and is either a Pig or a Fowle

If any thing toutches the Alter, or even the Sacred Ground about the Marae, let the Value be ever so great it is deemd Sacred, and for that reason can never be brought into unhallow'd ground, or toutchd but by the Priests & should a Hog or Dog &c run into any of the Sacred Grounds they are killd for sacrafice

When a Feast is made on any *Marae* it is always from a Freewill Offering (& of which they have many) and the Whole of the Victuals must be eaten there & not removed from the Sacred Ground, let the quantity be what it will the Breast & one shoulder of evry hog is the Chief's share but in his absence they fall to the Priests with the Head & Intrails which is their own share, nevertheless if any person at hand is Intitled to eat on the *Marae* and has not been served they invite him or them to partake

When the priest or preists (as beforesaid) attend these Feasts they and all who enter on the *Marae* Must be Naked to the Waist, but when they attend any Ceremony off the *Marae* they have their Shoulders Covered and their Head anointed with Oil, a kind of Turban bound on with Secred leaves a Breastplate (Calld *Taumi*) on their Breast and their Cloaths bound on with a Sash or Girdle of Braided hair or Cocoanut Fibers neatly platted of a Great length, and Made up in Bights or doubles, with a Tasell at each end—

The Provisions brought to the *Marae* must be dressd on it, and near the House where Baskets are kept for keeping it in, should it last three or four days–

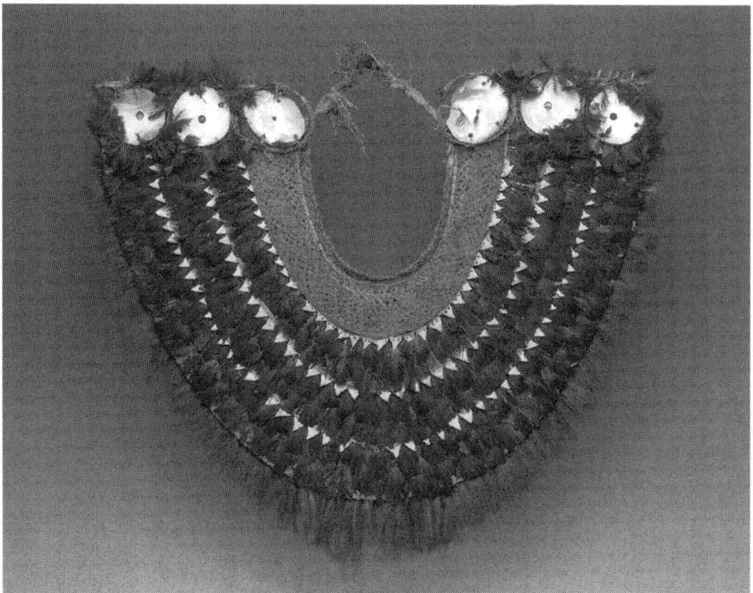

Figure 20. *Taumi,* feather gorget, Tahiti [D 1914.10]. Reproduced with permission of University of Cambridge Museum of Archaeology and Anthropology

They always wash themselves before, and after they eat, and should a Dead lizard, Mouse or rat toutch them they would wash before they handled any Food and shoud they happen to find one in or near their oven or toutch any of their Culinary Utensils they would use them No More—Notwithstanding which the will eat a Hog which has died if they know of No disorder which might be the Occasion of his Death–

If any person toutches a dead body except of those killd by War, or for Sacrafice, is rendered unclean, and can toutch no provisions with their hands for one Month, during which time they must be fed by another. If the Man killd in War be toutched by a relation they must undergo the like but otherwise Washing is sufficient

If any person have a running sore or large Ulcers they are toutchd by no person else and if they die, the House wherein they lived is burnt with evry thing belonging to it–

When Mourning for the Death of any relation they Shave the Fore part of their heads and sometimes the hind part together with their Eye brows & beards, and Cut their heads with Sharks teeth in excess of Grief or Joy. See the Mourning Ceremony

They always Venerate the Grey heads, and are kind to Strangers, and protect the Fatherless & the Widow–

A Child may Curse its Father, Mother, Uncle or Aunt but it would be Blasphemy for them to Curse it the Child may not Curse its Grand Father, Grandmother, Brothers or Sisters but the Grand Father or Grandmother may Curse their Grand Children with Impunity but it is Death For any Man to Blaspheme or revile the Gods or the King

When They Marry they Never Join with their Blood relations but a Man May take two Sisters, and a Woman two Brothers at the same time if they are all agreeable and it is lookd upon a piece of Great friendship for a Man to Cohabit with the Wife of His adopted freind if She is agreeable: the Adopted friend being always accounted as a brother

If a woman has husband and he died without Issue the Husbands Brother takes her, if He has no wife, and should he have Issue by Her the Children are Calld by the Former Brothers Name, & take his estate; but should he have a Wife he keeps her at his house till she gets a husband and she is still acknowledged as one of the Family

If a Man has a reason to part with his Wife he inform her of it to which she mostly agrees, deeming it reproachful to remain after such notice, He then Devides all His Goods and Chattles with her, and she leaves him and takes the Female Children with her leaving him the Males, if she lives single she always Claims the rights of a Wife, and tho they do not Cohabit, always look on each other as Friends and Apply to each other for any little property which at any Future period of their seperation they may stand in need of and each enjoys their own estate but should they Choose to live together after such seperation it lies at their own option and they may return to each other at any time. If the Woman takes an other husband she relinquishes all claim to her rights in her first Husband, and Can demand No More of Him, but Her own estate and her part of the Goods as before discribed

If a Man finds his Neighbour, or one who is not his adopted Friend in the Act of Adultery with his Wife he has the Law in His own Hands and may if He thinks proper put One or both of them to Death with impunity or punnish His wife with Stripes, and Plunder the House of the Offender, The latter is the Most Common but I have known two Men killd, who were taken in the Fact, and no further enquirey made then the Acknowledgement of the partys present to Certify the Fact

Their Marriage are no other then an agreement between the Partys and their Friends, and tho the Young are uncontrouled, they Generally take the Advice of their parents and Friends; which being settled, they Join and are Calld Man & Wife without Ceremony, except the Greeting of their Friends who present them with Hogs, Cloth and Sundry Necessary Articles. If the Woman is a Virgin Her Friends Must perform an *Amoʻa* (a Ceremony to be hereafter described) to their New Son in law, before the Males of her Family can eat any provisions with Him, or that He has toutch'd, the Young Man exchanges Names with his Fatherinlaw, and the Woman with Her Motherinlaw, if she has had a Husband before, the Exchange of Names and presents is the only Necessary Ceremony, the Husband then Claims his Wifes Posesssions, which are delivered to him without reserve, and they Having Houses on each live where they think Proper (but should they part, then the Wifes property returns to herself as before said), if they Have Children they proceed thus

When a Child is born whether Male or Female it is taken to the Family *Marae* (of Which evry Family have one) by a Person who is employd to attend it while the Mother Goes into a Warm Bath—and the Father and Priests repair to the *Marae* and offer a Young Pig or a Fowle or two to the Deity, and a Priest, who is well paid for His trouble Cuts off the Childs Navel String within Six or eights inches of the Belly with a piece of split Bamboo and while the others are praying buries it in the *Marae* a Temporary hut is then prepared Near the Marae to which the Mother repairs, and the Child is brought to her by the servant appointed to attend it and who must remain there with the Mother & Child till the rest of the Navel string drops off, which may be either kept in a house Sacred to the Child, or buried in the *Marae.* If the Child is Male, they May bury the Navel string as soon as it Comes off, which may be Six or Eight days, but if Female it is sometimes kept a Fortnight or Three Weeks; during which time the Mother toutches no kind of Provisions herself, but is fed by another person, and whosoever else toutches the Child must undergo the Same restriction till an *Amo'a* is performed to take it off, previous to which an offering Must be Made of a Plantain tree and a Young Pig, or a Fowle or two for the Mother which is done as soon as the Navel string is buried or the time fulfild for the removal of the Child from the *Marae* nearer the Fathers House which is built for and sacred to the Childs use, but still they Can not enter that House nor toutch the Child with the same Cloths on which they wear when they their own provisions—to take off which from the Father and Uncles, a Second *Amo'a* must be performed and from the Mother & Aunts a Third before the Child may Come into a house where its Father and Uncles Eat, a Fourth and for the Mother & Aunts a Fifth–

If the Child is Male there is one More which is performd when He adopts a Friend, which is the whole required to make his head Free, evry thing he toutches being in his Minority or Sacred State is made Sacred by his toutch and rendered useless to any other. If the Child is Female there are two others, one when she gets a husband that Her Male relations may Eat of the Provisions which he has toutch'd, and another that they may eat out of the same Dish and then her Head becomes Free also but she is generally free before these two except her head should toutch any thing

These Ceremonies when performed for the Males are Calld *Amo'a* only, but for the Females they add *Oeahou,*[9] signifying something more, as they have one more then the Males—for the Males Hogs or Fowles and Cloth are always but for the Females if they can not raise them, a Fish will do—but however this is seldom the Case, and they are No way sparing in the performance of these rights and much Feasting then takes place

Evry thing the Children happen to toutch before these rites are all performd is rendered sacred and thrown in a place adjoining to the House in which they live, and raild in for that purpose, they are always Careful how they Go about and should a Childs Head touch a Tree by the Carelessness of the attendant, the Tree tho ever so valuable is Cut down and destroyed roots and branch, and if it should break a limb of another or bruise the Bark in its fall that tree Must be destroyed also; nor must they use the timber for fuel–

Some of the Weomen are 16 or seventeen Years before all their rites are performd, which makes them very cautious what house they go into or what things they toutch—but the Men are Generally Made free as fast as the Father can get it done which is sometimes by Six Years old and sometimes not till twelve, the Children of People of rank are generally longer before they have all their rites performed, then the lower sort as it has a Grander appearance by being long about & they always make large Feasts of these Occasions

The reason of all these Ceremonies are that as soon as a Child is born it being the Fruit of the Father and Mother is superior to either, as Much as the Fruit is to the Tree for food, for which reason the Child is as soon as born the Head of the Family and the Honor and Dignity of the Father is transferd to the first born Child whether Male or Female, and before all these rites are performd the Parents are not thought worthy to partake of its Food, but as they have always a sufficient provision for themselves and have the ruling for their Children those of High Rank defer the performance under Collour of it being Grand to have their Children longer in a Sacred State, tho in fact it is that they may Continue longer in Power, but those of low degree have no intrest in it and therefore get it done sooner, and as soon as the Childs head is free it then becomes perfectly its own Master and May act for it self—Where this uncommon Custom so contrary to nature took its rise, we could never learn it having been with them from time immemorial but it may in some measure account for the difference in stature between the Higher and lower Classes of People—the latter Class having sooner their liberty have earlier Connections with each other then the Higher and the chiefs in particular, are Mostly arrived at years of Maturity and Manhood before they Cohabit with their Weomen

The Amoʻa we saw thus performd at a Marriage Ceremony, and differs very little from that performd through the different degrees of Childhood–

The Friends of Both parties being assembled at the *Marae* the Young Man and his Wife were placed on a large quantity of Cloth spread for the Purpose near the *Marae* alongside of each other, the Man on the right of His Wife—opposite them at the Distance of 30 or 40 Yeards and at the other end of the Cloth sat the Father Mother Uncles & Aunts of the Bride, a Priest then having Furnishd the Mother with several pieces of Sugar Cane and some leaves from the *Rauava* (or Sacred Tree) she takes a sharks tooth and Cutting Her head on the Fore part, lets a Drop of Blood fall on each piece of the Sugar Cane and placing a peice on a leaf gives *two* to the Father and each of the Uncles & Aunts, and keeps two for herself, these they place on the Palms of their hands and holding them up to their Foreheads rise up and proceed slowly along the Cloth till they arrive where the Young Couple sit, keeping their bodys half bent all the way; and having deposited the leaves and Sugar Cane at the Feet of the Young Pair they retire without speaking in the same Manner to their Seats, the Priest then advances with a Branch of the *Rauava* in his hand and Makes a long Prayer; which having Finishd, He goes to the Young Couple and biding "God bless them in their Union" (or as they express it in their Sleeping together) he takes up the leaves and pieces of Sugar Cane and proceeds to the *Marae,* where he burys them with prayers and makes an Offering to the Deity of a Hog &c—and in the Meantime the Couple rise and go to their Parents and they Embrace them and bestow their blessings on them. The Cloth is then gathered up, and Presented to the Son in law, who generally throws part of it out for the Young People present to scramble for, and they are proud that can get a Narrow Strip of it to put on in Honor to the rite and wear it till it is expended telling all they know how they obtaind it—the Company then return to the Bridegrooms house and he sends three or Four Hogs to his Father in law, who has them immediately killd, and a Feast Made of which all the Males of both Familys partake a Feast is also prepared for the Weomen and all partake of the Festivity

The Father of the Bride then delivers her portion to Her Husband as before described and an exchange of Names takes place

When a Man adopts a Friend for his Son the Ceremonie is the same, only placing the Boy in the place of the Woman, the Ceremonie is ratified, and the boy & his friends exchange Names and are ever after lookd as one of the Family the New Friend becoming the adopted son of the Boys

Father—this Friendship is most religiously kept, and never disolves till Death, tho they may separate, and make temporary Friends while absent, but when they meet, they always acknowledge each other–

And should a Brother or one who is an adopted friend become poor or loose his land in War, he has nothing more to do but go to his Brother, or Friend, and live with him partaking of all he posesses as long as he lives & his wife and Family with him if he has any—or if any relation or Friend tho not in immediate want, comes to the House of his Friend, he is always fed while he Stays and is Not only welcome to take away what he pleases but is loaded with presents–

They are ever Courteous to the Stranger and Hospitable to the Wayfaring Man and what they have is always at the service of their Visitors—and when a Stranger enters a House he is Saluted by the Master and perhaps all the Family With *Manuia* (Welcome) *Ia ora te atua i te'aria mai* (God save you in your Coming) & *Ia ora i te tere ra'a* (God save you in Your Journey) and the like Compliments at parting–

When they meet each other, after but a short absence, they embrace each other as we do but instead of kissing each other they Join Noses and Draw in each others breath through the Nostrils sometimes in token of great love, they almost suffocate each other by their long Continuance of their embrace—this Method is common to both Sexes, but if they have been long absent the Weomen Weep and Cut their heads with a sharks tooth till the blood flows copiously, which is always the Case in either excess whether of Grief or Joy to show their love they always perform this Ceremony on the slightest accident happening to their Children and Evry Woman is provided with one or two as soon as she is Married, as they never Cut their heads before and have them wrappd in Cloth, and fastened with the Pitch of the Bread fruit, so that the points stick out about a quarter of an inch like lancets–

People of Note always travel by Water about their own Island, and as there is a number of Houses Built by the Chiefs of each district, for the reception of strangers they are never at a loss for an Inn; some of these Houses are 150 feet long 50 or 60 wide, and 30 or 35 high. As soon as they land they Haul up their Canoes, near their Inn and send Notice to the Nearest of the same Rank, who repair to the place Immediately with provisions for them—and if they stay long enough evry one of the same Class in the District supplys them with one days provisions for all their

Company—In fine Weather they put up any where, and erect temporary sheds in the Most convenient place–

If any person of whatever Class he may be should be travelling by land and Meets None who Invite him or should happen to be unacquainted in the District he is passing through and has occasion for provisions, he enquires the Name of the fi[r]st *Ra'atira* and repairs to his house—on his entring he receives the usual Compliments and having made known his business, the Master of the House Immediately orders provisions to be got ready for him, and the Mistress entertains his Wife in the same Manner & they enjoy a secret pleasure at having had the good fortune to have the Strangers come to their House and they are for ever after deemd friends tho they had never seen each other

When a Chief or Stranger of rank from other Islands Visits them they perform a Ceremony Calld *Utu* which is a Peace offering, which is done thus the Chief or Stranger having taken up his residence in One of the Houses built for the reception of Strangers (of which there are several at convenient places in evry district) the Chiefs and people of the District Assemble near the spot with their presents, each Chief being attended by a Priest with Young Plantain trees & Pigs, they then take their places opposite the Stranger about 30 or 40 yards from Him, and the Priest of the First Chief begins by tying a Young Pig and a small bunch of Red Feathers to a young Plantain Tree, makes a long speech, welcomes the Stranger in the Name of His Master and the People, and then lays the Plantain & Pig down at the Strangers feet who takes the red feathers and sticks them in his Ear or hair a Number of Hogs Cloth &c are then brought in and presented to Him by the Chiefs Men—and the inferior Chiefs and landed Men go through the same Ceremony, each presenting him with a pig or Fowle with a Plantain tree, which is the Emblem of Peace on all occasions, and used in all civil and religeous Ceremonies, and their present of Hogs & Cloth and when the Whole have made their offering and presents the Stranger is invited to a Feast prepared for Him of Baked Hogs Breadfruit &c &c—of which none but himself and his retinue partakes. I have seen at one of these Feasts 50 Hogs Baked and as much provisions as one Hundred Men could Carry prepared for a Stranger of Quality for one Day; and repeated for several days in the same District, each Person of the same rank providing one Days food–

But nevertheless it is better to visit in quality of a private Gentleman then of a Chief tho both fare sumptuously yet the gentlemen are the Most Numerous and they may expend more time in One District in a Continual feast sometimes they make a Months stay in one District but seldom Hurry when they are on a Visit

The lower Classes always entertain those of their Class or Society in the same Manner, according to their abilitys but they Mostly prefer the Method of Visiting in the retinue of Cheifs and Gentlemen and this Method of living draws many Young People into the roving Society of the *Arioi,* which shall be discribed in turn and as they always find plenty of Food, and raiment without Much trouble they Never think of Settling till they Arrive at Mans estate, if they do then

When People of equal rank visit each other in their own or other Districts they are always made welcome by Greetings as soon as they enter the House as before discribed and as soon as they are Seated, the Master of the House orders a feast to be prepared for them, and enquiries the Cause of their Visit, What they want &c to all which they Answer without hesitation or Preface and their Wants being made known they are instantly promised to be supplyd if the other has it His power, and in the Meantime they are presented with a piece or two of Cloth and one or more live Hogs by way earnest to their being supply'd; and if the Man of the House has not what his Visitors Want, He begs them to stay at His House till He can procure sufficient to supply their Wants among his Neighbours–

All the Provisions dressd for the Visitors they Must take with them, it being accounted no treat if any of the Family partake with them nor do they Call any thing a present which Nature produces, except accompanied by something which is procured by the Assistance of labour or the Art of Man; for which reason they always give Cloth or some thing else with their Gifts, Provisions being held of No value being produced by Nature, and they think it not proper to make store of them–

They never return thanks, but by *deed,* having no Word in their language expressive of it and when they part they always use Compliments—they always beg their Visitors to remain with them till they are perfectly well satisfied with their treatment for should any depart unsatisfied they would get at bad Name, those who are not well treated never failing to declare how they have been used and in this Manner they frequently make a Visit of several Months getting a little from one, and a little from another till they get what they want before they return Home

The Tennants (or *Mata'eina'a*) hold their lands of the *To'ofa* (Lord of the Mannor) or *Ra'atira* (Squire) to whom they pay their rent by Making Cloth, when they want it, or supplying His demands in hogs, if they have them, if they have none, he requires none, and never forces them to find what they have not—It is no disgrace for a Man to be poor, and he is no less regarded on that account, but to be Rich and Covetous is a disgrace to Human Nature & should a Man betray such a sign and not freely part with what He has, His Neighbours would soon put Him on a level with the Poorest of themselves, by laying his posessions waste and hardly leave him a house to live in—a Man of such a discription would be accounted a hateful Person and before they would incur such a Name as that of Covetous or Stingy, they would part with the Cloth off their back, and go naked till they got more–

If any Man is Caught in the act of Theft and is immediately put to Death, the Person who killd him is brought to No account for it. But if the Thief escapes & the Property is afterwards found on Him, the Person whose property it is, may plunder him of His Goods and Chattels which the Theif always submits to, the Owner leaving with Him the property which he stole and taking all the rest, but should be absent himself, and take His goods off His land, the Person Injured may oblige the thiefs land lord to deliver to Him the House, & land, which the Thief did posess till the damage is made good or ransom it with Hogs to the full satisfaction of the Party Injured, this latter Mode is mostly practised: for if the land was once put into posession, the Party so holding it could never be removed except by War, or the Commission of some Crime against the Chief; after such ransom is paid the Squire may if He pleases compromise Matters, with the Thief, and let him return, on Condition that He pays the Ransom or gets Friends to do it for him, or give it to some other who has been distressd by War and the Theif must go and live on His Friends–

They Have Carved Wooden Images of Men which they call *Ti'i* set up as boundaries of their Estates, not to pay devotion to but to remind passengers below & of equal rank to the Posessor and owner of that land, to strip the Cloths off their shoulders & heads, as they pass by in Compliment to the Owner—All ranks of People must pay this Homage as they Pass the land belonging to the *ari'i rahi* or King—The Ti'i or Image denoting the Kings land is remarkably larger then the Common size, and the To'ofas or Ra'atiras land is known by a Number of little White Flags being fixed in different parts beside the *Ti'i*—any neglect or refusal of these Honors are the occasion of Disputes and often are the occasion of Wars or Houshould Broils between the partys, if the owner is a Minor, the affront is the greater, the Mother instantly applys the Sharks tooth to Her head in Grief that Her Child should be insulted, & the Father flys to strip by force those who have offended, if the offender makes a Concession by offering a Plantain leaf and declaring their Ignorance, the Matter is settled but if they continue obstinate Blows ensue which increase the Friends of each party become acquainted with the Affair, who repair Armd to the place and the Battle becomes general and often ends with the loss of some lives, and often involvs whole Districts in a War With each other, and a Chief and his people may be driven from the land through the means of a quarrel arising from the neglect or refusing to pay the proper Compliment to a poor Mans Child, tho the Father might have been beaten with impunity by one who might quarrel with Him, but no Man must presume to treat the Heirs of large estates with such contempt or neglect on pain of Death and such insults often end in the total extripation of one of the Familys concernd, it being deemed Blasphemy to Call them by a Wrong Name

Their Chiefs are accounted the Head not only of the people but of the Priests, and evry other Society that are instituted amongst them and being accounted more then merely their superiors none refuse to pay them the proper Homage and they are always particular in performing their part strictly where it is due evry Chief paying that Homage to the Child of another

They have few law disputes; and Private disputes between Men relative to themselves only seldom produce a Blow, and I cannot say that ever I saw a Blow given in consequence of a quarrel which did not arise from such grounds as before discribed,

If any dispute should happen about the boundarys of their land, as they have No Records nor any deeds of Gift they always refer to the Neighbours for a decision, who new Mark the bounds of each Mans land, and None disproves of such decision, as they are very superstitious in religious rites they would rather submit to let the whole be Common to both, then either would undertake to Mark his own bounds, fearing that he should be punishd with sickness or Disease if He incroachd on the property of His Neighbour–

This and all other Dipsutes is settled by the Neighbours and the party who is declared to be in the wrong, almost always submits at the first word and making a Peace offering to the Man offended, declares himself in fault, and desires he may think no more of it–

No Man ever Claims a right to any land but his own, or His adopted Freinds, which he may use during his friends life and should his friend die without any other Heir the Adopted friend is always considered as the right owner and no man disputes his right–

If a Man bequeaths the Whole, or a part of His land or property to any Person before His Death, and there are Witnesses to prove such bequest none objects to it—tho the Heir himself should be absent and know nothing of it till the Witnesses inform him of the right he has and call him home to take possession

These rules are handed down from the Father to the Son and they want no law to keep them in force and Nature has taught them to use all Men as they would be used by them, which is their common standard, and tho there are some exceptions Yet that I may with no more then truth is their General Character

They have a Ceremony Calld *Rahui* which is a Kind of Jubilee[10] but have No fixd time allotted for keeping it—It is a Prohibition or Embargo laid on the Provisions, & Stock, in Whole or in Part, in any one or More Districts to prevent a Decrease by consuming the Provisions or Stock in, or transporting them out of the Districts so *Rahui'd,* which they are forced to observe under pain of being driven from their land. The Chiefs, To'ofas, & Ra'atiras may at their Will and Pleasure *Rahui* the whole or any particular Species of Provisions, Stock, Fish &c within Their own limits and When they think Necessary to prevent a great decrease of Hogs they can *Rahui* them thro the whole District—but the King can at his own discretion Rahui several districts—and sends his orders accordingly to the Chiefs To'ofas & Rat'airas to prohibit the expenditure or removal of such Provisions as he shall name within their Several Districts, and Estates for the Time Specified by Him; but he generally takes the advice of the Inferior Chiefs, Priests &c—and they have always timely Notice before it takes place, and know the Reason why it is to be take place and on the Day fixd proclamation is made by Cryers for that Purpose and a large Bundle of Bamboo leaves hung up to the first tree at each end of the District, or part *Rahui'd,* to give notice to all passengers that all within the limits are under such Circumstances & to inform them what treatment they may expect in them a Hog and part of such provisions as are *rahui'd* are hung up near the Road in some Conspicuous place, the Hog being killd and hung up by the Heels—When the *Rahui* is taken off the leaves are taken down, and a Feast of the Jubilee takes place after an Offering has been made at the Cheifs *Marae,* which lasts Three Weeks or a Month, to which the Chiefs and People resort, and they are all entertained by Contributions laid on the People, of the District, or Districts, which have been *Rahui'd* who resort to One to keep the Feast and each of them Get ready daily by two o Clock or thereabouts one Hog with a proper proportion of Vegetables, which is brought to the Place of Rendezvouz and there Devided into Seventeen proportions, one for each District, which being delivered to the Chief of Each, it is taken to their seperate Rendezvouses, and divided by the Servants, giving each of To'ofas & Ra'atiras their share, and *they* again divide it among their people and every thing is carried on with the Greatest Harmony no quarrels ever ensuing at these Feasts—The Feast is Calld *Taurua Ari'i* (the Cheifs Feast) after dinner they amuse themselves with Wrestling Dancing, Throwing the Javlin, Running for Hogs, & Scrambling for Cloth &c—which are Given by the Chiefs or holder of the Feasts

Many of the *Ariois* always attend at these Feasts and as they are Mostly Young Men who are active and lively they help the sport, the things put up for the Scramble are Canoes, Hogs, Cloth, Bamboos of Oil &c, which being brought into an open Space by the Servants of the Chiefs who keep the Hogs fast till the time appointed and they are always the wildest they can pick out, that they may Make the Better sport, the Canoes have Masts fixd to hang the Oil up to, and being placed at equal distance from each other have the Cloth hung up by the ends between them, a Priest then advances, and Makes a long prayer at the end of which He throws a young plantain tree into one of the Canoes, and the Hogs being turned loose the scramble is begun by all ages & sexes, and as they are frequently numerous they afford some sport before they are all taken—the Canoes, except they happen to be seized by a whole family, are Generally torn to pieces, the Cloth is generally torn in ribbands, which are worn as Trophies, and preferd to whole pieces obtaind any other Way, the Fowles are frequently torn in pieces and the Hogs and Goats often Get Kildl in the Scramble—but if a Man takes a Hog fairly, it is his own; and none will attempt to wrest it from him except two or more happen to lay hold at the same time; and should a Man receive a bruise or breake a limb by being thrown he never blames any person, as they never willingly hurt each other–

Tho the Chiefs or Ra'atiras have power to put on these Rahuis on their land, without the Consent or approbation of each other, yet they seldom do except to prevent a scarcity—and then Hogs are the principal objects to it, tho it frequently extends to several other kinds of Provisions, but when the King sees it necessary to prevent a scarcity by a Number of People being Collected in one district, such as the Arrival of a Ship or of a Fleet of Canoes when Numbers resort to see the strangers; after the first feasting is over he puts on a *Rahui* till they shall return home or the Concourse of People shall lessen and the Visitors be distributed, otherwise they would distroy the whole stock and breed a Famine there—and at such times the Reefs are *Rahui'd* to prevent the Shell & other fish from being distroyd, which would otherwise be the Case as they flock from all parts of the Island to view the strangers without bringing Provisions for their Own Use, generally giving to the Strangers all they bring with them, and trusting to the District they come to for food—which the owners are ashamed to refuse while they have any for themselves, when the People return homewards the *Rahui* is taken off, that the Strangers may be suppld, who are nevertheless plentifully fed from the Neighbouring Districts where the *Rahui* has not been put on–

The *Rahui* on the reefs is signified by placing Bushes along the part *Rahui'd,* with bits of white cloth tied to them and after they appear there No person dare fish there on pain of forfeiting their Lands but they may fish with Nets hooks &c in their Canoes by which Means they procure good Supplys, if the Beach is *Rahui'd* they Must not lanch a Canoe off to fish, or any other purpose; but this never Happens but when the Kings Flag is passing–

Besides the Feast of the Jubilee, or *Rahui,* they make a Feast on the *Marae,* at which none can be present but *Ra'a* or Sacred Men this always Consists of one or more hogs and other Provisions, with plenty of 'Ava, these are Mostly Held on Family *Maraes* belonging to the *Ra'atiras,* and are Calld *'Opu Nui*—at them the Chief of the Patu and all the Ra'atira and priests attend, and when the Provisions are taken out of the Oven, the Preists make a long Prayer by Way of Grace, and taking a Piece of Bamboo for a knife (if they have knives they must not be brought there else they Could not carry them away again) and taking a part each sort with a bit of ʻAva puts them on a Plantain leaf and with a Prayer offers them on the alter or on top of the House, Mean time some of the rest Desect the Hog or Hogs and distribute them as before discribed and they begin, but should a Stranger pass at the time, they send to invite him and if he is not known to any present, they enquire if He be a *Raʻa* or *Noa* man, to which he answers truely and if he be *Raʻa* or Sacred he partakes of the Feast if *Noa* is unhallowed he refuses, none ever attempting to impose on Strangers in such Matters as they are liable to be found out afterwards, when Death would be the result of the Fraud

The Weomen have also their Feasts, which are Calld *Oehamu* they are Generally of Fish, of these *their* Male Servants May partake—and so may any other Man, they are held on the Common Ground in such place as they find Convenient–

7 Arts, Rites, and Customs

Their Buildings are principally the *Marae's* or Places of Worship, which have been discribed by Captn. Cook and some of them are amazing large piles of stone that must remain as Monuments of their Ingenuity for ages, they regularly and exactly built without tools, or Cement, and can receive No damage but from time, of these evry family of note have one of proportionable size to the Wealth of the Owner, and In them as beforesaid they perform their relegious rites with becoming decency and awful Reverence[1]–

Their Houses are Neat Thatches Made of the Palm leaves and Supported on posts and are of Different sizes according to the owners abilitys the Dwelling houses are Mostly raild round with Wattles,[2] and in bad weather they screen them in with Cocoa Nutleaves wove into a kind of Matting which they remove in fine Weather, they are exactly Calculated for the Climate and want no other fence but to keep the hogs out—the common size is from 30 to 40 feet long 18 or 20 High and about the same broad of these each family has two, on for the Males and the other for the Females, & some have their Hogstyes in the Middle—they are generally of an Oval form, and the Eaves come within 9 feet of the Ground Which is always raised somthing from the level to keep the floor Dry, the Floor is always laid with Grass or Hay to a good thickness, on which some of the family sleep on Mats, others who take the trouble, have bedsteads raised with little Stools Neatly Carved out of the Solid for Pillows and sleep on Cloth, & Matts, their Furniture Consists of a large Chest or two[3] to hold their property in, and on one of these, the Master of the House and his Wife Sleep on Cloth and Matts, and those who have not stools for Pillows use the seats of the Canoes—one or two large Stools for the accommodation of their Guests, stools for Beating Pudding on, with a stone or two Neatly Cut for a Pestle, Platters and trays of different sizes, baskets of several sorts and a post or two to hang their provisions on–

The unmarried Weomen generally Sleep Near the Parents and the

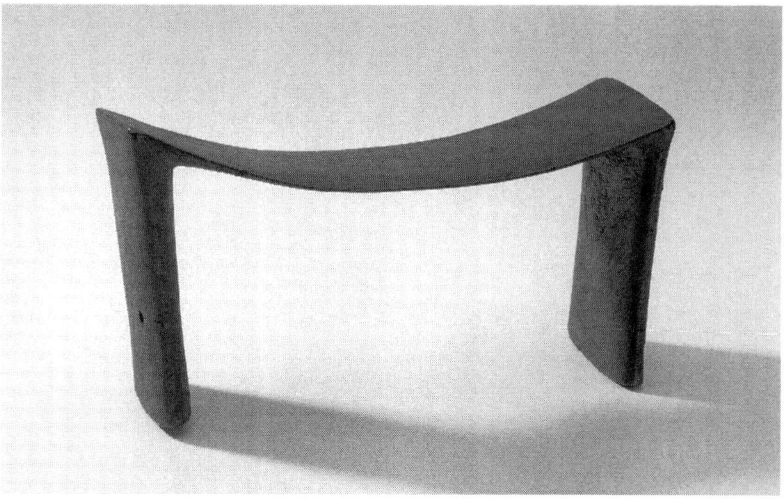

Figure 21. Headrest, Tahiti [Z 6040]. Reproduced with permission of University of Cambridge Museum of Archaeology and Anthropology

Unmarried Men and Servants generally sleep in the Weomens eating house, but in fine weather they prefer the Open Air, as the Grass with which the floors are Covered if not frequently removed produced abundance of Fleas for which reason they sleep out of Doors to avoid these disagreeable companions—they always divest themselves of their Wearing apperal when they sleep but most of the Young Men and servants make their wearing apperal serve for Bedding also, as they seldom take the pains of keeping too many Cloaths at one time, except an extra suit for Dress, which they do not Wear in Common, this way of Proceeding has its Conveniency as they have always their Bedding with them, and have nothing to take Care of—they Have also small houses for Kitchins, as they never dress provisions in the House they eat in, the smoke being not only disagreeable to them, but Spoils their Cloths–

The Houses of the Chiefs are not remarkable for being better furnished then those of the Common people tho they are somthing larger; and like the Houses for the reception of Travelers are generally Open at all sides, having a low fence of Plank forming a square about them, and the part within the fence either spread with small pebbles or laid with Grass—but if they intend to reside long in one house or place, they have a Neat small house raild in for their use, but they frequently sleep in poor mean huts and eat in the Open Air, hanging their provisions to a Tree–

Their Canoes may be also Comprehended in the article of Building and those for War are Certainly curious machines when We consider the tools with which they are Constructed—which before they had Iron introduced amongst (and of which they have now but small quantitys) Consisted of No other then Stone Adzes of different sizes, leg or Arm bones of Men for Augur, Chisel & Gouge, Coral and Sand to smooth with and Skins of Fish to polish,[4] and where Fire Could be of any Use in burning off the rough it was also used but now they that have Axes for the rough work and small hatchets, which they convert into Adzes by lashing them to handles, make quicker work; they have also a number of saws but Can make no Use of them, and Nails of different sorts makes Gimblets, Chissels &c and are even Converted into small adzes for Carving with, the Adze being their principal tool at all kinds of work–

Some Stone tools nearly of the Same Construction are in use among the Natives of New Holland and it is not Improbable that these were the original and only tools in use among other Nations before the use of Iron was known—[5]

The length and Size of the War Canoes having been before described I shall proceed to describe their Construction and equipment

Each Canoe (of which there are always two lashd together) is at her Greatest breadth about 4 feet wide and 6 feet deep and the whole length from 60 to ninety feet, the bottom is sharp and projects in a straight line to the wale[6] where the extream breadth is where the round is sudden turning into the side which rises about 14 or 16 inches of one Plank in an upright Manner, which makes the Midship Frame form the figure of a Spade the Mark on Cards known by that Name, they are built of several streaks securely lashd together with platted Cocoa nut fibers, the Keel pieces forming the two lower streaks, on which another is raised and on it another which is mostly the Wale, which falling as suden as the quarter of a Circle the Side is raised on its inner edge, each streak consists of Several pieces of 3 or 4 inch Plank well lashd together, and the Keel is generally Composed of two or three lengths, inside they have three or four timbers of the Natural Growth to answer for Floors & timbers, or rather knees which are firmly lashd to each side as high as the wale—the proa or bow projects with a great rake forward, having no Stem, and is

Closed in with round pieces on the top and the top side is Closed in with a square piece answering to the side, like the end of a Chest, and in the same manner abaft where the stern rises suddenly from a full buttock; and being Closed in on the Uper part, forms a spire or Cone regularly taperd to a point, and becoming nearly round as it rises, on the Bow and top of the Stern are rude figures of Men for ornaments the height of the bow, being somthing more then the level of the top of the Gunwale, which is without sheer, and the height of the Stern nearly 24 feet, the Image being 18 inches or 2 feet higher—When the Canoes are ready for putting together (for they cannot be used singly by reasons of the narrowness of their Construction) they are placed alongside at a regular distance fore & aft, which is commonly about 6 feet asunder, and are secured by eight or ten square beams of 5 or 6 inches square which are fixed on the upper part of the Wale of each at equal distance and firmly lashd and are partly let in to the Wales and part into the topside—and the whole being made secure by lashings the frame of the stage is laid with other strong Beams on the top of the Gunnel projecting without the wales on either side, being about 20 feet wide, and secured firmly to the lower Beams by lashings, the stage is then laid with plank, like a Deck, with scuttles or openings on each side, & in the Middle, for the paddlers, who are often 100 and upwards, on the fore part of the stage is raised a Breast work of Plank about 4 feet high, over which the Warriors fight, and when they are equipt for War, the decks are filld with heaps & baskets of stones, and evry paddler has a sling, they are often Managed by Sails, the Masts being placed on Steps on the top of the Stage, and Supported by the rigging and when under Sail take Four Men with long paddles to steer them and Sail at a good rate in smooth water, but in rough Weather they Make less way and more water, the motion making them soon leaky—when at Sea they often keep 6 hands bailing with scoops they having no other method to free them of the Water with which they are often filld by the Surge rolling up between them, but they are nevertheless in no danger of sinking but drive till they are freed—and in port they are always forced to Haul them up to prevent their sinking—When they Sail in Fleets the Chiefs Canoe has always an alter on Board–

In these Vessels they Frequently go from Island to Island in large partys, somtimes 10 or 12 Sail, and by Means of them the Iron work left at *Tahiti* is distributed among all the Islands they are acquainted with; in

Figure 22. "A double Canoe with the Eotooa (God) and provisions on the prow—Island of Otahytey," George Tobin, 1792 [Call no. PXA 563 no. 41]. Reproduced with permission of the Mitchell Library, State Library of NSW

return for which get Pearls, Pearl shells &c—Some of the Islands they sail to are at the Distance of more then 100 Leagues.[7]

The Chief of *Taiarapu* keeps one of these Vessels constantly plying between *Tahiti* and *Me'etia,* Calld by us Osnaburgh Island, 27 leages SE of Taheite, which is Subject to Him, and in her, he sends Iron Work and What European Commoditys he Can raise as presents to the Chiefs, who in return send back Pearls, Pearl Shells, Stools for Seats, Pillows & Pudding Stools Made of *Tamanu,* with Dishes & Trays of the same wood, Matting, Cloth Oil, Hogs &c &c—and she seldom returns without a Cargo by Means of this Island they have Communication with several others to the NE of Tahiti and taking the advantage of the Northerly Wind reach *Me'etia* where they watch Wind shifting to stretch to the Northward to a Group of small Islands, the Capital of which is Calld *Tapuhoe*[8] which appears to be the same by their account where the African Galley one of Commodore Roggeweins Squadron, was lost (he was fitted out by the Dutch West India Company and passd these Seas early in this Century and His ships afterwards Seized by the Governor of Batavia) from this Island the first Iron was imported to *Tahiti* and a Beam of Oak which we saw at *Tetiaroa* (a Number of Small Islands 8 leagues N of Taheite) is I have no doubt (from the Account of the Natives some of whom are now living, who remember the loss of the ship, tho they Could form No Idea of Her but from the description of the Natives of Tapuhoe, but saw the Beam Come on Shore which they supposed to be part of the ridge of a House) a part of that ship which may account for their knowledge of the Use of Iron when that Island was discovered[9]

It may seem strange to European Navigators how these people find their Way to such a distance without the Help or knowledge of letters Figures or Instruments of any kind but their Judgement and their knowledge of the Motion of the Heavenly bodys at which they are more expert and can give a better account of the Stars which rise and set in their Horison then an European Astronomer would be willing to beleive which Is nevertheless a Fact and they can with amazing sagacity fore tell by the Appearance of the Heavens with Great precision when a Change of the Weather will take place and prepare for it accordingly when they Go to Sea they Steer by the Sun Moon & Stars and shape their Course with some degree of exactness[10]

at the Distance of 8 Leagues N. or N½W from Point Venus lies the Islands of *Tetiaroa* in number ten, incompassd by a reef about 10 or 12 leagues in circumference. They are all low and for the Most part Covered with Cocoanut trees which is all they Produce, they are the Property of *Tu*s Family who keeps the Inhabitants in subjection by keeping them from Planting the Breadfruit or other Trees and suffers nothing to grow there except a few Tarro for His own use under the Charge of one of His favourites—and as these Islands cannot be Approachd by large Canoes He makes them His Magazine for all His riches, a Number of Canoes are kept for Fishery and Near 40 Sail of small sailing Canoes which they Haul over the reef are kept constantly plying between them & *Tahiti* they bring Fish for the Kings houshould, and return loaded with provisions—and besides these the Dolphin Canoes trade there when the Fishing season is over Carrying Provisions, and Returning With Oil which they Make in large quantity, a Variety of Fine Fish and a Sauce Made of Ripe Cocoa Nuts Calld *Taiero,* the Nuts being gathered before they are too old and

Grated in the same Manner as for Oil which being Mixed with Shrips and left a day or two to ripen becomes like Cruds and is excellent sause for Fish, Pork or Fowle—this is also made at Tahiti and a Basket of it always accompanys a Fish or Hog when dressd for a Feast, the Nuts must not be too old or it will become oily & rank—

Their Travelling Canoes are Different from those of the War Built, having low sides, Broad sterns and a flat Plank projecting over the stem, which is upright they are about three feet Deep, 18 inches wide and 50 or 60 feet long, the bottom flat and rounding, and the sides Flat and rather falling in, the stern rising with a regular rake for 10 or 12 feet on the top of which are placed pieces of rude Carved Work of a Cilindrical form of two or three feet High they are hollow and the Open work represents rude figures of Men Supporting each other on their hands forming several Teirs and have some resemblance of an old round tower, the size of those denote the quality of the Owners, these Canoes are also Double, being secured by two or three strong barrs lashd to the Gunnels of each—and on the Broad planks of the Bow they fix a Movable House or Awning for the Owner and His Family to sit in out of the Weather—Canoes of this size are paddled by 20 or 30 Hands and answer the same purpose as a Gentlemans Coach in England—in them the people of Note travel from place to Place—They have these kind of different sizes and the small ones, some of which Carry only one or two Men, may be used Double or single occasionally with or without Masts

The Single Canoes have a float supported by two out riggers; one Forward and one aft, the Float being nearly the length of the Canoe, these are Chiefly used for Fishing and Other Uses[11]–

The Canoes of this Built, used for Sailing, are nearly of about 30 feet long and are either Double or single as the Owner fancys they are raised with Wash boards and the Masts stepd on Cross peices above all, the Double ones have two Masts placed one in each Canoe at equall distance one from the Stem and the other from the Stern and a like distance from each other, being nearly at the thirds of the Canoes length, the Masts are Supported by the Shrouds and Stays, of which they have always one to shift to Windward, on the Mast Head they Have a kind of Funnel basket fixd by way of ornament—The Sails are made of Matting, and are long and Narrow, being mostly as long as the Canoe and the Mast one Third Shorter, the breadth not exceeding 5 or 6 feet, the foot of the sail is spread by a

Short Crooked boom having an elbow or knee on the after part to which a spreet is securely lashd and to which the sail is laced all up the after leech and being secured at the Mast Head by a rope to keep it from spliting the Sail, it forms a sweep in which form the Sail is Cut & the end of the spreet Comes directly over the Masthead where it is Confined in form of a Fiddle Bow, by the rope which supports the Weather leech of the sail, the sail being extended on a frame is quite flat, having no belly but what the Wind gives it—at the Spreet end hangs a long Pendant of Feathers, wove on three lines which reach the Heel of the Mast, the Sheet is generally made fast to the Splice or Joint of the Boom & Spreet, and is at the Command of the Man who Steers, if a Single Canoe, but if a Double Canoe they must have others to attend them—the Sails of the War Canoes are Made in the same Manner but they being larger, have a frame ladder to go to the Mast head, while the others have only a few short sticks seized a cross the Mast to get up to fasten the sail and the line which keeps the Spreet in its place–

The single Canoes riggd for Sailing have only one Mast, and are riggd with a large Float paralel to their Keel or Middle line and two Thirds of Her length from the side supported by an Outrigger a little before the Midships, Consisting of several strong pieces or Spars of a proper Size, & Steadyed by a single one from the Stern to keep it fore and aft, on the top of the Fore Out rigger the Mast Stands and two spars are fixd one third of the Canoes length, supporting a stage of two Planks on the Opposite Side to the Outrigger, and serve also to Support the Mast by making the Shrouds fast to them and on their Stage they sit, when Fishing for Dolphin, to keep their Cloaths Dry when sailing, these Canoes Have Wash boards of 12 or 14 inches as well as the Double ones, and are preferd to them for Fishing, but none of them will sail at a great rate, seldom going More then 5 or 6 knotts pr. Hour and if the Floats are Not Straight or Well adjusted, which is somtimes the Case, they will not sail so well as that–

They have No Method of reducing their Sails but by Casting off the lower part and rolling it up, and should that not answer, as it frequently will not, they must take their Chance and as they Cannot reduce the sail at Head but by Casting it off intirely for which purpose a man must go to the Mast head, and it would be next to impossible to get them up again from the quick Motion of the Canoe, for which reason they let them stand at all events and had rather Overset, or loose the Mast, then Strike the Sail, and in Squally weather both these Accidents often happen, but they are so accustomed to them, that they think nothing of either, tho by being dismasted they are frequently blown off and heard of no more—When they are taken in a Squall they luff Head to it and shake it out, but should the squall Continue too long & the Vessel is like to fall off they all hands Jump overboard & hang her head to windward till the Squall is over, when they get in & steer their Course, but should they not be able to hold her on and she gets overset their First Care is to secure evry thing, and Make their Fish Cloth, Paddles &c fast and when the squall is past they tow the Canoe round with the Mast head to Windward and making a line fast to the upper part of the Spreet all hands get on the Out rigger, and hauling the head of the Spreet out of the Water, and the Wind getting under the Sail lifts it, when they all swing off with their whole weight together & right her Some hands then keep her head to windward till the others free her of the Water and then get in and proceed on their Voyage—this frequently happens on their return from Fishing, when they endeavour to out carry each other till they are overpowerd by the Wind & get overset—of this they think the danger so little that they never require any Assistance except to take in their Cloth, or such things as may receive damage by being long wet, but they frequently loose so much ground as to be forced to run for *Mo'orea* and somtimes for *Huahine* and *Ra'iatea* and We have known some of them who being dismasted have been 9, 12 and 15 days at sea with scarce a Mouthful of Provision and No Water, as they seldom Carry more then a Few Cocoanuts and a bread fruit or two Sufficient to Serve as long as they intend to Stay out, and trust to providence for a Fish—Those who sail in the large Canoes are better provided, and are in no danger of such distress as they Can never overset and should they Carry away their Masts are better able to get them put to rights again, having plenty of Cordage & Matts to repair their damages–

In Building their Canoes they hollow out the Bottom or Keel pieces, and having fitted them they smear each part of the Butt with Pitch Made from the Gum of the Bread fruit Tree, which being wrapd round a Number of Candle Nuts reeved[12] on Sticks for the Purpose and being lighted and held over a tray of Water the Pitch drops in and being taken out of the Water & made up in balls is fit for use—with this as before said they smear the Edges and Buts of the Plank, & having a quantity of

Cocoa Nut fibers beaten up like Oakum they lay it between the pieces and bringing them together with Sets & Wedges, lash the parts firmly together with plat made of the same and after they have passd as many turns as the holes will admit, they Caulk them with more of the beaten fibers, over the Seams in the wake of the lashing they Spread more Pitch & Oakum, and lay a piece of Bamboo split & soakd for the Purpose, and having formd the Bottom they proceed to bring on the next peice or Streak, pitching the seams and securing it as before—they never pay the bottom or sides, tho it would be of much service to them, but they cannot bear to toutch the pitch, which would be often the Case as they haul all their Canoes up as soon as they land–

They have no rule for Building, but the Eye and have no Idea of working by a line; yet nevertheless some of them are built with as much exactness, as if they had been pland by able builders; and according to the oppinion of some good Workmen they are well finishd

The War Canoes (and those Made presents to the Deity which are occasionally Used for that purpose, and are in fact built for it only by the Contrivance of the Priests who are in the intrest of the King and tells the other Chiefs that the Deity wants Such a Number of Canoes of Such a Size & they set about building them Immediately) are Built by levying Contributions and are done thus—Each Chief who has one to build, Calls the *To'ofas* & *Ra'atiras* together to a Feast and informs them of the Request of the Deity and desires them to Collect Hogs, Cloth, Oil &c to pay the Carpenters,[13] to which they readily agree and the Carpenters are Employd who go into the Mountains and Mark their Trees, the Ra'atira on whose land the Trees happen to be sends hands to assist in Cutting them down, and hewing out the peices in the rough according to the Carpenters directions, that it may be the easier brought down, as they form each part out of a Solid Tree, and often at some Miles distance in the Hills–

When they have Sufficient collected to Make a beginning they fix a day to fetch them down and a house is erected to build the Canoe in, when the timber is brought down a Feast is made and an Offering of a Hog to the Deity to prosper the Work, a Feast is also made for the Workmen at evry Piece they make Fast, and when the Bottom is Compleated a Grand Feast and Offering is Made, which is repeated at the Finishing of evry Streak till the Whole is Compleat, when a greater Feast is Made, and the Canoes being Dressd with Cloth, Breastplates, Red and Black

Feathers, Fine Matting &c—they are Brought to the Grand *Marae,* and a Man is killd and put on board and Offered as a Sacrafice, when the Canoes are hauld up near the *Marae* where she is Covered with Thatch till Wanted, the Priests securing the Feathers for the Deity and the other Decorations for the King, to whom they are presented in Form, as before, the Eye of each Sacrafice being presented before him and the Body interd in the Marae. The War Canoes are Offered in like Manner but Hogs serve instead of Men

When Men are Wanted for Such Occasions the Chief assembles the *Ra'atiras,* at the *Marae* and a feast is Made at which none must be present but those who are by birth intituled to give their Oppinion, he then informs them of the Business which they however know beforehead they then agree among themselves about the Fittest Man and if any have been Guilty of Blasphemy or has been a Most Notorious thief and has escaped punnishment they fix on him and one of themselves undertakes to kill him and watches his Opportunity, the business being mostly kept a secret till he is killd, which is generally in the Night when the Man appointed to kill him, finding where he sleeps, knocks him in the Head with a Stone and gets his servants to make a large Basket of Cocoa Nut leaves into which they put the body and Convey it to the Canoe to be offered into which they put it—and they careful not to disfigure the Face as that would make them unfit for an offering and an other must be got in stead, for which reason they mostly strike them on the back of the Head or Neck—If they can fine none whose Crimes deserve death they tell the Chief & a hog must be killd in stead—and will not kill a Man to gratify a Private pique of any Man even tho the Chief insists upon it, and if he persists in having one he must kill him himself, and should He be killd in the Attempt the Man so killing him comes to no harm. If such a thing is insisted on, they never fail to give Notice that such as think themselves in danger may keep out of the Way and should any Man be killd without sufficient Cause (tho they Never admit them to be present at their Tryal) His Friends instantly make War on the Offenders but if He is known to be guilty of the Crimes laid to his Charge No Notice is taken of it, as evry one deems it right and the Man who kills him is Justified as having been the Executor of Justice–[14]

If a Man of Property is found Guilty of a Crime which deserves death he is punishd as well as the Poorest in the Island an Instance of this we saw at the time the Young King was invested with the Royal *Maro*—one of the first Men in *Mo'orea* being sacrificed for attempting to stop the Flag from Passing through his land on that Island–

During the Celebration of that Ceremony Numbers of Human sacrifices were made and many who knew themselves Guilty, took Sanctuary about our houses where they knew themselves perfectly safe, as they knew our aversion to such Horrid practises but we could not protect all tho we often tryd in vain to diswade the Chiefs to drop their Barbarous Customs, who always gave for answer, "If we do there will be no Chiefs". However we protected all who took sanctuary with us and tho surrounded by the Most Notorious thieves on the Island our Property was always safe

But this was only a temporary respite as they seldom fail at one time or other to bring them up and should they Fly from one District to another their Charracter always follows them and should a Sacrifice be wanting, the Chief of the district in which they have taken shelter always points them out before one of His own People by which Means he secures the love of his own and is dreaded by others

If a Man under such Circumstances submits himself to be bit by a Woman so as to Draw blood he is thereby rendered unfit for a sacrafice and saves his life but can never be admitted to partake of any religious rite, being ever after deemd on an equality with Weomens food, and must be a Womans servant everafter—they never sacrafice a woman nor is she or any of Her Servants as before said permitted to be present at or partake of a Feast made on the *Marae* nor must she eat of any Food which has been toutchd by a Sacred person, tho it were her own Husband–

In their Common way of life their food is the Animals & Vegitables before discribed, but is Chiefly Vegetables and Fish of which they have abundance and their Cookery is simply baking and broiling, having no vessel that will stand fire Nor do they understand the Method of Converting Clay to that use, however they loose little or none of the Substance of their food by baking, and Fish Dressd in that manner are preferable to boild–

the Men and Weomen eat separate, and for this reason each Family has two houses except a Man Chooses to reside in his Wifes house and then each take one end–

The Children eat with the Mother till their restrictions are taken off,[15] tho she Cannot eat of the Food which is the Childs nor that it has toutchd nor must the Childs provisions enter the House by the same entrance at which the Mothers comes in at and in traveling they Must have separate Canoes for the Men & Weomens food, of which the Children may partake

the Weomen have their own particular trees for Bread, and can eat no other and Must have particular People to Catch fish for them and should a Shark, Turtle, Porpoise Albicore Dolphin or Cavally which are Sacred Fish be Caught by their Fisherman they Cannot Eat of them, but may dispose of them to whom they Please–

It has been supposed by Most Former Voyagers that they were also forbidden to eat Pork, but in this they were most certainly Mistaken for if any Woman has an Inclination to keep her Hogs Pennd up and prevent them from feeding on any other ground then their own they may eat pork—but as this is troublesom (and should the hogs get loose, and run on the land of their Male relations they become unfit for them to Eat, or should any of their Male relations or the Chiefs toutch the Hogs it is the same) and attended with difficulty they seldom attempt it as they Have the Greatest Variety and abundance of fine Fish—yet nevertheless they often kill and eat pork under that denomination taking Care to keep such Men as are not of their retinue out of the Secret, their Servants always agreeing on this score are sure not to want for part of what the Mistress posesses

the Men may partake of any of the Weomens Food but must not toutch any but what is given them and tho they enter the eating house of their Wives they must not toutch any of Her Culinary Utensils, otherwise she must not use them again but He may apply them to his own Use and she must provide herself with a New set or as many as he has toutchd

No Woman Can eat in a house where a Chief has been, unless she is of the same rank and authority with Him and then she may Eat in his presence—and if any Woman of Inferior rank should tresspass in eating in any House, Canoe or Ship where a Chief Had been they would not only be severely striped but loose their posessions, for which reason they are Careful how they these laws as they know that few are given to keep a secret for which reason they always refused to eat when invited before Men, but would take the Food offered them and give to their relations, this may also account for a Number of the Chief Weomen who refused to Dine at Table yet eat Hearty with the Servants

They Eat Fish of all kinds which the Sea or rivers Produce, as they hold that nothing unclean Can be the Produce of Water but from our being so fond of Flesh they at First Conceived that We were Cannibals as they have an account of the Inhabitants of an Island to the East of them who eat each other and it was with some difficulty that were able to perswade them to the Contrary as they were in some Measure Confirmd in their Oppinion by Brown (the Man left by Captn Cox) who threatend to put a Child into the Oven and the Mother of it Could Never be perswaded to beleive that he was not in earnest and would never Suffer the Child Near him afterwards, they were also further Confirmd as some of our People had said fooshly that they Had eaten part of a Man[16]

They Make Three regular Meals in a Day when at Home and eat Hearty and nothing can give them more satisfaction then to see a Stranger do the like, when they invite them to eat, which they are ever ready to do, always parting what they have Cheerfully, be it little or much but when they are from home, and Numbers are Met in one District, Provisions grows scarce from the Rahui before describd and are sometimes whole days without any and when they Get any they Eat so large a quantity as would readily give a Stranger an Idea that they were mere Gluttons and it would Certainly Appear more so to those who were perhaps Sated with the abundance of Good Provisions arround them which these People had most likely stinted themselves to supply them with & which they always do by endeavouring to surpass each other in their presents & giving away what they stand in Immediate Need of themselves

In general they Cannot be Calld (except at such times) immorderate eaters tho their Method of Stuffing their Mouths as full as they Can hold, has the appearance of it–

They sit Cross leggd and having a place spread with leaves (often under the shade of a Tree in fine Weather) for a Table Cloth and sit at a distance to prevent offending each other by Flapping the Flies away which are often troublesom, always Swarming where any provisions are especially Fish which draws whole swarms about them and having some Clean leaves laid for Plater & dishes the Provisions are set before them & They Cut their Meat or Fish with a piece of Bamboo or knife, and put it into a Cocoa Nut Shell with Salt water, and the Sause before Discribed and having washd their Hands in another shell they proceed sucking the flesh or fish & repeatedly dipping it in the sause, Eating large quantitys of Breadfruit or Taro drinking Clean water or Cocoa Nut Milk and after their Pork or Fish is done they have a sort of Pudding made of Bread

Fruit Calld *Popoi* of which each has a Shell which when they have eaten finishes this and they then Wash their hands and Mouths using a Piece of the Husk of the Young Cocoa Nut to Clean their teeth of which they are particularly Careful of

When they drink *'Ava* they are forced to eat as fast as possible after it, or they would not be able to eat at all, it takes such Immediate effect, it is no disgrace for either Men or Weomen to be intoxicated with this Root but the Weomen seldom take the pains to Cultivate it and the Chief weomen who Use it, can procure it without that trouble–

They have several sorts of Pudding besides the *Popoi,* the Method of Making which is this—The *Popoi* is made of Baked Bread fruit and *Mahi* (Bread fruit of the last season Made into sour past) being beaten together on a Stool with a Stone, Both kept for the Purpose and mixd with Water and when done is Not unlike what We Call Flumery, and is eaten with Water or Cocoa Nut Milk—it is made of either seperately, but the Mixture is preferd by Most and it is excellent food and may be made either Hot or Cold–

another sort is made with the Mountain Plantains & *Mahi* Mixt which when made ready is equal to if not superior to Goosberry fool & may be made of any Consistence either for Knife or Spoon this is Calld *Popoi Fe'i*

Paipai is another sort made of the Bread Fruit that gets too ripe on the tree, which being Beaten up with Cocoa Nut Milk and baked is delicious food

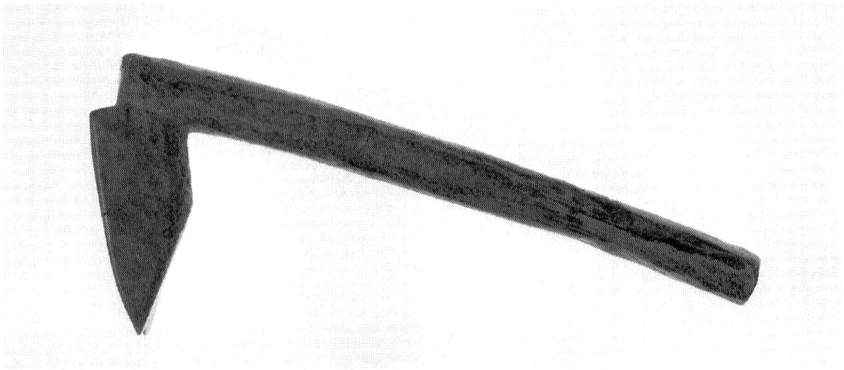

Figure 23. Breadfruit splitter, Tahiti [D 1914.19]. Reproduced with permission of University of Cambridge Museum of Archaeology and Anthropology

Poe Atutare is another sort made of the Bread Fruit before it gets too ripe—which being Baked & the Core & rind taken away (as for any other use it is) it is Mixed with Juice squeesed from Hard Cocoa Nuts which is White & thick as Cream and being wrappd in Plantain leaves is put into the Oven and Baked again

Poe Taro is Made by grating the Taro down on a rough stone, and Mixing it with some of its own young leaves, & sweet herbs, & the Juice of the ripe Cocoa Nut before discribed

Poe Pia is made in the same manner by mixing the Juice of the Cocoa Nut as before, the Nut being grated as for oil & the Juice wrung out with the *Mo'u* which serves for a Strainer on all occasions—this being mixed in a Tray they throw in some Hot Stones which hardens it in the same manner as batter is hardened in a frying pan but if this is eaten in large quantities it Causes a giddiness in the head from some time after, tho it has no bad effect attending it, another Method of Dressing the *Pia* and which takes off the cause of the Giddiness, is by mixing the Pia & the

Figure 24. *Penu,* pounder, Tahiti [D 1914.16]. Reproduced with permission of University of Cambridge Museum of Archaeology and Anthropology

Grated Nut together with Water and baking them in the Oven, & when done this way its taste and Appearance is not unlike a Yeast Dumplin but something sweeter

Tuparu or *Teaparu* is an Excellent pudding made of *Taro* (or Bread fruit), Ripe Plantains & Cocoa Nuts Grated & Squeesed & wrung out as before, the whole being strained through the Mo'u (or Fibers of the Stem of the Cyprus Grass) to [t]ake the strings of the Plaintains from it, and being baked in leaves is as good as a Custard, the Juice of the Cocoa Nut being Mixd with some of the Milk answers the purpose of Milk and Butter, the Milk being tart, takes off the luscious sweetness of the Plantains and gives the whole a pleasant taste

as they make this in large quantitys they make the leaves of the Plantain tough to contain it by searing them over the Fire; and tying up 5 or 6 quarts in a bundle, put it in the oven where it remains all night, and being taken out is put by for Use, it will keep for several weeks

as they seldom have plantains sufficiently ripe for this purpose they gether them a few days beforehand and bury them in the Earth (with some ripe Palm Nuts which gives them a fine Flavour) putting Grass all round them to keep the dirt from them—and in this Manner they ripen all their Fruit when they Have Not sufficient for their purpose ripe on the Tree—and in this they have a superstitious Notion that should they bathe in the Sea while the plantains are in the earth that they would never ripen properly—this only extends to the Person who puts them in the earth—nor could we perswade them out of this foolish notion tho we shewed them to the contrary—and they always insisted that we had more then Common power to prevent the fruit from spoiling—and tho we perswaded themselves to try they still affirmd that it was on our Account and that were they to try on their own heads the fruit would Certainly spoil or rot before they were ripe–

They Get fire by rubbing two Sticks (Commonly Dry Purau but Breadfruit or any other Dry wood will answer the Purpose) together thus, they take a long piece sufficiently large that they may hold it fast by sitting with their feet on it and Cutting a Groove on the Upper part 5 or 6 inches long with a shell to receive the point of a smaller piece which they hold between their hands and begin Chanting a Prayer (without which they suppose they Could not get the fire) and rubbing the point of the Small piece in the groove of the larger one and shoving from them increase their

Motion from a slow easy strike to a quick smart one when the Dust made by the Friction takes fire, which they put into a leaf with some dry Grass and wave it about till it communicates to the whole when they have more leaves & Wood to make their fire–

When they Make an Oven they Make a hole in the Earth of a proportionable size to the Provision they have to dress and Making on their fire build it up with wood which they pile round with stones throwing the bottom ones up as the top falls in till the wood is all burnt to Coals and the stones red hot they then level the stones and the Coals being free from smoke they spread the oven over with leaves or the trunk of the Plantain and the Provisions being wrapd in and Coverd with leaves is Covered with Grass and the earth thrown up on top and the provisions left to Bake a proper time according to the quantity mean while those who were employd at it go to the water and wash themselves all over and when the oven is opened it is done so carefully that the least particle of earth or Sand does not come to the provisions which are taken out clean and well dressd

They are very expeditious in preparing their food and will dress a Hog whole (which they always do never cutting them to peices till they are baked) and let it be sufficiently well done in two Hours tho it were 300 lbs weight, they like their food well dressd tho they frequently eat fish raw—and then they dress a large Hog for a Small Company they never dress it thoroughly, that the Visitors may not have it spoild for a second dressing, as they always take away whatever has been provided for them–

When they kill a hog they strangle it or drownd it the former Method is preferd and is done by putting a rope round its neck which they heave up with a stick or leaver till the Hog is Choakd they then Stop its Nose Fundament &c with leaves or Grass and the Animal afer a few Strugles expires, they then wet it all over and lay it on the fire or make a fire round it if it be large with Dry leaves and Grass and scrape it Clean with Sticks and Cocoa Nut shells—after which they take it to the Water and Scrubb it Clean with rough Stones and open the belly with a piece of split Bamboo or knife and take out the Bowels and Blood which having burst its Vessels runs out of the Flesh and is found in the Belly—with the Blood they mix the fat of the Guts and putting it into Cocoanut shells put hot stones into it and Make a kind of black Pudding which serves the Cooks with some other fragments for a relish while dinner is dressing—the Hog is Clean washd and laid on leaves till the Oven is ready, the pluck is either Broild or Washd, and wrapd in leaves and put in the Oven, the Guts are also Cleaned and baked, and as they have plenty of assistance the whole is soon ready. the Guts, being kept fast to the Crow, are ripd from end to end and well washd when they are laid on the hot stones to scald being shifted alternately from the Stones to the Water till they are perfectly sweet, & Clean and being wrapd in leaves the whole are put in the Oven with Bread fruit Split & Scraped which is all the preparation it wants *Taro, Mahi* &c and Covered up as before and in this Manner they dress all their food. the Breadfruit will broil or roast on the fire which Method they use for a small quantity, and Fish wrapd in the Breadfruit leaves and put on the fire are better then Boild, being dressd by their own Moisture which is prevented from evaporating by the leaves which have as much substance as those of a Cabbage If they have a Pig of 10 or 12 pounds to bake they will dress it sufficiently in half an hour–

In the time of Gathering in the Harvest of Bread for Store they make an Oven in which they Bake 15 or 20 Hundred weight of Bread which when baked becomes sweet like gingerbread, of this they make a sweet pudding, and on this the Children (Male & Female of or belonging to the family who make it) Feast while it lasts, which is generally six week or two months—during which time they are kept Covered from the sun and are restricted within their respective bounds which are houses fences round in square for that purpose—and at the end of that time they are liberated but are so fat that they can scarce breath and are some Weeks before they can Walk to any distance during this time they loose the Tand[17] Collour of their skin and assume their own natural one which is agreeably fair & Clear but are so tender that the sun scalds them as fast as it would the Fairest European and those who expose themselves to the Weather soon alter their Complexion.

When a Chief or *Ra'atira* wants one of these Ovens of Bread made, they inform their Tennants who go in a Body and bring Wood from the Mountains, while others Collect the Stones and while the fire is Burning evry Man brings his load of Bread which is put into the Oven whole and without further preparation and being Covered with leaves is thatchd over with Grass & the Earth thrown up over it and do not open it for three or four days, when they take it out for use evry day as it is wanted, keeping it covered till the Whole is expended, and this they Repeat evry harvest–

The Bread thus dressd is Calld *Opio* and has a very agreeable tast and the Collour is Changed to brown throughout

The poorer people are not excluded from this Method of Feasting their Children tho they have not sufficient Bread for the Purpose, having nothing more to do but signify their intention to their Neighbours, who bring their proportions of Bread and Assist them to Collect Wood and Make their Oven, Somtimes they Join two familys making one oven between them–

At this Season they make their *Mahi,* a sourish past made by fermenting the ripe Bread by which means they keep it till next harvest while the Bread (which they have the whole Year round but not in such plenty as to serve) is scarce they may be eaten by itself or by being beaten up in puddings, and when mixd with the new bread makes the Best *Popoi*–

The process of making it is this—the bread being gathered in, they scrape off the rind with shells ground sharp for the purpose and lay it in heaps to grow Mellow where it lays for 3 or 4 days—pits are then made in their Houses or Near them, and being well lined with Grass and leaves, the Bread is thrown in being first split in peices with a Wooden Adze made for that use, and with it a few of the ripe fruit which have fallen from the Tree to hasten the Fermentation and the pits being filld and heaped up are Covered with leaves & Grass & large stones put on the top to press it into the Pits in this Manner it foments and when it settles they shift the leaves that are bad and taking the Core or harts out fill one pit out of another and Cover it up for Use–

Some take out the hearts at first but tho that Method renders the *Mahi* whiter then the other yet the Bread will not ferment so soon without the assistance of some old *Mahi*—nor will it keep so well—the Men and Weomen having each their own trees have also their own *Mahi* and should a Man who is not the Servant of a Woman toutch even the Covering of the Womans *Mahi,* it is rendered unfit for Her Use which at once accounts for Sr Joseph Banks's having spoild a quantity which belongd to a Woman by his being desirous to see the nature of the Process of making it and examining the Contents of the pit—which was not only rendered of no use to the Woman but the place in which it was underwent the same fate and no woman Could ever use it afterwards[18]

If the Crop on any individuals land should run short of His expectation and He has not sufficient to make as much Mahi as he wants or thinks will serve He makes a Number of Garlands of a shrubb Calld *Piripiri* and takes One to evry House or as Many as he thinks proper and throws them in without saying any thing except to till the day he intends to send for it or have it brought home evry one knowing what is Meant by the Garland. If He has hands sufficient to Scrape the whole at once it is brought home to the House, each Man bringing the Garland left at his house as full of Bread as it Can be Made fast and laying it down at the Door returns without any further Ceremony then bidding God bless his Work if He has not sufficient help to take the whole in hand at once he makes it known and either Goes himself for it when he wants it or has it brought at the time he nominates to those who supply him who are ever ready to assist evry Man according to his Abilitys. If he goes for it himself he always finds the Gardlands ready filld at the appointed time—By this Method of assisting each other they never feel the last Inconveneince from having a Scanty Crop and if a Chief wants a Supply for the purpose of Making *Mahi* he sends a Bit of Cocoa Nut leaf to all, or as Many of the Inhabitants of his district as he shall think proper, and on the appointed day they Bring each a load, which is generally accompanied with a hog by some and fish by others according to their several abilitys but this they have seldom occasion to do as they are always well supplyd and when supplys are raised this Way the people bring it in such a Manner as bespeaks at once their regard for their Chiefs and fear of displeasing them always testifying their sorrow that he should be so far neglected as to have the trouble of sending for bread

They Make an Offering of their First fruits to the Chiefs besides those Made to the Diety[19]—this Ceremony is Calld *Ihi Ari'i* and is thus performed, the Fruits being ripe the *To'ofa* or Lord of the Mannor informs the *Ra'atira* or Squires that on such a Day the Offering is to be made & it is Proclaimed through the District by a Cryer to inform their respective Tennants, the *Mata'eina'as* or *Manahune's,* who on the day Appointed, each gather some of evry species and having put them into a Basket, which is hung round with a piece of Cloth, is tied to a pole, which is ballanced on their Shoulder by a sucking pig hung by one foot to the other end, and repair to the House of the respective *Ra'atira* who then heads his own people and proceeds to the House of The *To'ofa,* who with His priest and Orator heads the whole and the procession proceeds to House of the Chief, sometimes four or five Hundred in a body, before being arrived the To'ofa by means of His Priest and Orator (who always attend on such occasions) makes a Peace offering of Young Pig a Plantain tree & a small tuft of red Feathers these the Priest offers as usual and the Orator makes a long speech in behalf of the *To'ofa* & *Ra'atiras* expressing their loyalty and the love they have for their Chief, the *Ra'atiras* having by Means of their Priests (each Family having One or More in or depending on it) made their Peace Offering, the Fruits are deposited before the Chief and they retire and return home—When this Ceremony is performd to the King the Chiefs of the District always head the procession

This Ceremony is then performed by the *ra'atiras* to their respective *To'ofa* and afterwards by the Tennants to their *Ra'atiras,* after which they Carry in as Much Bread as they think will be sufficient putting it in large Baskets made of Cocoa Nut leaves which when filld are as Much as two Men Can Carry—with each of which they send a small Fish, intimating that they do not offer bread alone, with this a Baked hog and several small baskets of Bread, Taro, Cocoa Nuts With the Husks peeld off, Plantains &c are Carried to the House of the Chief, *To'ofa* or *Ra'atira* each in their due proportion

Such Presents as this they are Continually Making to their Chiefs &c—and never send a Fish, Hog or Fowle without a proper quantity of Vegetables with them and When the Bread is Scarce they substitute *Mahi* in lieu, tho they always shave some, the *Mahi* being wrought up like Dough, is rolld up in leaves to the size of a Penny loaf or roll and baked with the other provisions, Fe'i or Mountain plantains are also substituted for Bread, and when gathered green answer very well, being much Superior to the Common plantain to eat as bread.

When they Go into the Mountains which they often do in Companys to Cut Timber Gather Herbs & sandal wood for their Oil, Cut rafters for their Houses, Paddles for Canoes, &c. and for the Purpose of dying Cloth, which takes them up several days, they subsist themselves on Birds fish &c Using the Mountain Plantain and Wild Roots for Bread, the land producing plenty of Birds and the Springs plenty of Fish, they catch the birds by fixing the Gum of the bread fruit on long Bamboos, and setting them up, take the Birds which perch on them, as we do with Birdlime, others who are used to this Method of living can with much exactness knock them down with a stone which they throw by hand, pointing at the Bird with the fore finger of the left hand, as it were to take Aim, while the Stone is prepared in Right, and if the Birds are sitting they seldom fail to bring it down but cannot bring one of the Wing—and when a party go into the Mountains on any of the aforesaid occasions their first Care is to send a party in Search of Provisions (as they never Carry any with them) while Others erect huts for their lodgings made of reeds and Covered with the leaves of the *Ti* and others procure fire & fuel—as they seldom take the trouble to Make an Oven they roast their roots & Plantains and dress their fish or Birds in Peices of Green Bamboos. the provisions, being put into the Bamboo and stoped up with leaves, is laid on the fire, and kept turning round like a spit till the Contents are sufficiently dressd, the Moisture inside keeping the bamboo Wet it keeps its form tho burnt nearly to peices—In this Manner they live when on these excurtions and tho they have hard labour in hand they turn the work into pleasure, and taking no thought for tomorrow they leave off & return when they think Proper–

As they are very fond of the Tail feathers of the *Tropic* Birds which they esteem for dressing their *Paraes* or Mourning dress,[20] they go two together to Hunt for them and as the birds build in the Face of the highest Cliffs they are at Much trouble to get them. Their Method is this the Bird catchers are provided each with 10 or 12 fathoms of Rope of sufficient strength to bear His own Weight, and having fixd their place of abode near the Clift, where provisions are in the greatest plenty they proceed together to the top of the Cliff where bending their ropes together, they make fast a stick of 18 or 20 inches long by the Middle and lower it over the face of the Cliff having a Stake fixd to Make it fast to on the top, if a Tree is Not Convenient, one hand then stays by the rope to haul up or lower down, as the other shall order who goes down & seating himself on the Cross stick, swings from hole to hole in search of the Birds, holding on by the points of the stones which project or the shrubbs which grow among the fisures of the Cliff—when he catches a Bird, he hauls out the Tail feathers which he secures in a Bamboo which he carrys for the purpose, and lets the Bird fly—having examined all the holes within his reach or is tired in the search he goes up and either shifts the rope to another part or attends it for his partner who takes a spell–

This tho it may appear Dangerous to us is no more to them then Amusement, and seldom attended with any Accident tho they hang some hours in this manner, sometimes 20, 30 or 40 fathoms from the top & often four times that from the Bottom and, perhaps do not get a single feather in a whole days search,–

The Shining Black feathers of the Men of War Birds[21] they also hold in high Esteem for which reason they always watch their Coming as they Seldom Visit this Island except when the Westerly Winds and thick Weather prevail—they afford diversion for Numbers as they are only to be caught at the Beach, or When it happens to fall Calm when they perch on the Cocoa Nut trees, and are Caugh by a snare fixd to the end of a long stick with which a man goes up and puts the Noose over the Birds Neck while it is asleep which is in a few Minutes after it lights, and letting the stick go, it brings the Bird to the ground—While they keep on the Wing they entice them down by a Fish into which they thrust a piece of *Purau* to float it, and throw it into the Water keeping it within reach of their Wands, of which each Man has one of 14 or 16 feet long, as soon as the Birds observe the Fish they instantly make towards it, sometimes 8 or 10 together, and the Men stand by and knock them down as they attempt to seize the fish, which they all attempt to do if they do not receive a Blow before they get near enough, these Birds always seize their prey in their Claws which are long, and sharp, and Webbd only to the first Joint—they are Inhabitants of the low Uninhabited Islands in the Neighbourhood of the Society Islands, and never come from home but in thick weather, their Feathers are held in Such Esteem that the Natives will give a hog of 100 Weight for one of them for Making their War, & Heiva dresses &c tho they never eat the bird—during our time we shot several which were deemd grand presents, but We thought the Powder of More Value and therefore made but little Waste of it for that use and seldom took that expencive diversion—the Cock Birds are the Most Valuable and the Back feathers are those they prize highest for their Beautiful shining Black–

The Dress of Both Sexes is Nearly the same except that the Weomens lower garments are something longer then the Mens and being put on in a kind of Neat Negligence together with the Cleaness of their Clothes sets them off to great advantage and as they Wash regularly three times a day, they are free from any disagreeable smell, and a stranger suffers nothing but Heat in the Midst of a thousand of them, their Clothing when put on has some resemblance of that described to be the Dress of the Natives of *Peru* & *Chili*[22] from whence tis possible that it Might Originaley have Come as the present Natives of these Islands are known to drive about those seas to the Distance of some hundreds of Leagues and might in all probability have been at first driven from the Continent to these Islands, first to these Near the Continent and afterwards to the more leeward ones–

It Consists of Square Pieces, and the Mens dress is first a long narrow piece Calld *Maro* which passes between the thighs and round the Waist, one end hanging down near the Knees before and the other being tuckd in behind hangs down in the same manner, serving for Breeches, and is Made either of Cloth or Matting, for Dry & Wet Weather—the Oblong Piece of two Yards long and One to half a one Wide, in the Center of which is a Slit to let the Head pass through & hangs down before and behind—this is also of Cloth or Matting and is Calld *Tiputa*—A square piece doubled so as to pass once & a half, round the Middle over the ends of the *Tiputa,* which is tuckd in on one Hip, and depends on low as the knees, but when worn by Weomen, to the Midleg or Ancle, this is Calld *Pareu*[23] and round the waist they wear a Sash or Girdle, made of Braided hair & wrought into Network calld *Tamau*—all these are Common to both Sexes, except the Maro which the Weomen never wear but when they are fishing or at wrestling, when they are in danger of having their Pareu hauld off—in lieu of the *Maro* they Wear a Shorter *Pareu* by way of an inside petticoat and a large pice of Cloth by way of a Cloak consisting of several fathoms folded up in a square—Over their eyes they wear a kind of shade like the fore part of a bonnet made of Cocoa Nut leaves, which they weave in a few Minutes & Change several times in a day, as they never Carry one of them over sacred Ground, for these shades which they call *Taumata* (the same name they Give our hats) they prefer the Yellow leaves to the Green and are proud to get one of that kind, tho perhaps they must tear it in pieces in half an hour after they have made it, and look for another—these and Garlands of Flowers are the only things they ever Wear on their Heads, except at Heivas, and then none can wear any thing on their heads, but the performers, who wear a kind of Turban; evry other person must be uncovered in presence of a Chief—in War or Mourning the Men may wear Turbans and Other head dresses, made of Wickerwork Covered & decorated with Feathers and Breastplates of the same work Ornamented with dogs hair Pearl shells Sharks teeth & Red & Black feathers Garlands of Feathers &c—The Heiva Dress shall be described in its place—they have also Garlands for Mourning Made of the fibers of the Cocoa Nut Curiously platted in which they fix the Finger Nails of their departed

Figure 25. *Tamau,* braided human hair, Tahiti [Z 31062]. Reproduced with permission of University of Cambridge Museum of Archaeology and Anthropology

friends, with bits of Pearl shells, cut into many forms and of these they are particularly Careful–

The children of both Sexes go Naked till they are 5 or 6 Years old and at about 13 or 14 the Males Cut their foreskin, not from any religious Custom but from a Motive of Cleanlyness, it being only split on the upper part with a sharks tooth and after the Blood is stopt by putting ashes on the wound it is sufferd to get well as it may & nothing more being applyd is sometimes a Month or more before it gets well tho their Flesh in general heals quick—this, like the *Tattowing*[24] or puncturing their hips &c is at their own option, but a person who is deficient of either is reproachd and told of it in Public and it is as bad to want these Marks as it would be among us, not to be Christened or to go Naked tho some want both—They have their *Tattowing* begun about the same age, and both these Offices are performed by a particular set of men who make it a Trade and subsist partly by it, always getting well paid for their Work–

The Instruments used for the Tattowing are made of Hogs tusks fixed to a handle in form of a hoe the Instruments being of different sizes having from 3 to 36 teeth about one eight of an inch long these they strike in with a little Paddle made for the Purpose when they Tattow or Puncture the skin they dip the teeth of the Instrument into a Mixture of Soot (prepared from the Candle Nut) & Water which being Struck in to the skin leaves the Mark of a Black or Blueish Collour. With this the Hips of Both sexes are Markd with four or five arched lines on each side, the Upermost taking the whole sweep of the Hip from the Hip bone to the Middle of the Back, where the two lines Meet on one, which is drawn right a Cross from one hip bone to the other and on this all the other lines begin and end, under this Center line are generally four or five more, sweeping downwards, but Most Weomen have that part blackd all over with the *Tattowing*—but evry one pleases their own fancy in the Number of lines or the Fashion of them, some making only one broad one while others have 5 or 6 small ones ornamented with stars & sprigs &c–

They also mark their feet legs thighs arms &c but the Weomen never mark higher then their Ancle, and few mark their Arms, having only some fancy Spots on their hands it being accounted foolishness to have any other Marks except those on the Posteriors feet & hands but in men it is taken no notice of–

The tools used for the first time on a Chief, or the heir of a large family must be destroyd as soon as they are done with, and deposited in the *Marae* and when all the *Amo'as* (except those of Marriage or friendship) is performd they receive a small spot on inside of each Arm Just above the bend of the Elbow which signifies that they are free to eat and drink of their parents food & that Contrary their parents may eat of theirs, this Mark they Never receive till these rites are performed, nor is it always done, at the time of the last being performd–

The Tattowing is performd at the pleasure of the partys who have it done and will not suffer the performer to leave off while they can bear a stroke tho they make such lamentation while they endure the pain, that a stranger would suppose it was doing against their will and that they were forced to suffer it contrary to their Inclination. The young females are more remarkable for bearing it then the Males tho they cannot suffer more then one side to be done at a time and the other may remain perhaps for a Twelve-month after before it is finishd, till which time they never Conceive themselves Company for Weomen being only Counted as Children till they have their *Tattowing* done—While the Girls are having it done they are always attended by some of their female relations who hold them while they struggle with the Pain and keep their Cloaths from being kikd off and should they from their tears draw pity on themselves, and the person who holds them should perswade them to leave of they are often in such a passion as to strike even their Mother if she should happen to be performing that office which she must not return—on pain of Death—they often suffer so much to be done at once (through their Pride it being a disgrace to give out till one side is finishd) as throws them into a fever–

They have several Exercises among which Wrestling and throwing the Javlin are the Most Common—they are very expert wrestlers both Men & Weomen but never Box, tho this diversion is Common at *Ra'iatea* and the other Islands—When they Assemble to Wrestle as they do at all publick Feasts, a ring is made, into which the Wrestlers being come walk round, Clapping with the Right Hand on the Bend of the left Arm which is bent, so as to bring the Hand to the Breast, making a loud din If any has a Mind to except the Challenge He returns it with a Clap and puts Himself in a posture to receive His Opponnent and they Close immidiately, if either finds the other too strong for him he signifies it, and they part, if Not one Must fall, and the Weomen of the Victors Party Strike up a dance & song the Victor Clapping round the ring till another takes him up while the Vanquishd retiresPeacably, thinking Nothing of His disgrace—they generally Wrestle one district against another and the Weomen always wrestle first, but are more vicious then the Men and Cannot bear to be worsted, at this Sport *'Itia* and her Sister are always first, and often come off with Victory and 'Itia always directs the Ceremony & fixes the Number of falls that must be Wrestled, and which ever side attains the Number first are declared Victorious and the Wrestling being finnishd Dancing takes place among the Weomen and the Men go to throw the Javlin–

Their Javlins are from 8 to 16 feet long being made of Wands of Purau with the Bark stripd off, and pointed with the *Fara* or Palm tree, with these they Heave at a Mark at 30 or 40 Yards distance with Great exactness & Count their Game by the Uppermost Javlin which has held in the Mark which is mostly part of the Plantain Stock their Method of throwing is under handed, poising the Javlin on the fore finger of the left hand while they send it home with the Right—or the Contrary if left Handed the Weomen also play at this Game but never for any Wager the District in which they Play always providing a Feast

Another Diversion is with Bows Made of *Purau* and Arrows of Bamboo pointed with *Toa* with these they shoot for Distance, or up the side of a hill without any Mark, after this Game they have also a Feast made as before—The Weomen shoot as well as the Men but by themselves and those who follow it must have Clothing sacred to the Game which must not be worn at any other time—for which reason it is left Chiefly for those of rank who can pay the proper attention to it these Bows are for Diversion only–

They practice the quarter staff from their youth and are well versed in the Use of it, and defend themselves amazing well it being no honor to receive a wound in War except from a spear and even them they hide as much as possible

They also Practice the Sling and will throw a stone with some exactness and great force, the sling is made of Cocoanut fibers platted having a broad part wove in the Center to contain the stone (which is Mostly of the size of a hens egg) and a loop at one end, to put over their wrist to keep it from flying away when they let go the other end, when they throw a stone they keep the Sling a Cross their Shoulders and with their thumb keep the stone in its place when by a quick Motion let go the stone Jumping at the same time off their feet and grasping the right wrist in the left hand swing the stone three times round their head before they discharge it when it flys with such force as to break the Bark of a Tree at 200 Yards distance keeping in a Horizontal direction nearly the whole way

Heiva is the General Name of Diversion whether Music Dance Song &c—The Dance Calld *Hura* is performed by two, four, Six, or More Young Weomen neatly dressd and any Convenient Number of Men, with one who is promptor or director having Drums & flutes playing through the whole performance, the Weomen beating regular time with Various Motions of the Hands as well as feet, this dance is generally performd on Matts spread for the Purpose and at Night it is always under Cover of an Open house or Shed build for the purpose with torch and other lights

The Dress of the Weomen in these Dances is elegant and their figure Graceful it Consists of a *Turban* of *Tamau* or Platted hair of several Hundred fathoms long,[25] decorated with Sharks Teeth, Pearls & flowers, their arms and shoulders are bare and a kind of Vest of White or Colloured Cloth covers their Breasts, over each of which a large rose of Black Feathers is fixd, and on their Back are several pieces of Cloth in regular folds painted with a red border and so fixed as to represent Wings, on each side from the Hip to the Shoulder, and from the Waist depends a kind of Petticoat which reaches the feet, this has also a red Border and a Stripe of the same Collour with another of Yellow each about an inch broad about ten inches from the Bottom, from the Waist also depends several Tassels of Black feathers which reach the Knees, and two or three red or Black feathers on each fore finger–

When the Weomen retire to take breath their place is supplyd by the Music and singers which is no way disagreeable when understood being soft and pleasing—at other times a set of Actors supplys their place, the principal part which the perform is Satyr, which is often directed at their Chiefs, and they never fail to expose such Charracters as draw their attention and tho they treat thier Chiefs with great freedom they incur no displeasure so long as they keep to the truth—by this Method they rebuke them for their faults in Publick, having first diverted them to draw their attention—this is done in a kind of Pantomime at which they are so good that any person who knows the Man they mean to represent may easily perceive who they are making the subject of their sport, Nor was it so badly done before we became acquainted with them as to prevent evry spectator from observing that one of their Plays at Which our Commander was present was entirely a representation of Himself and of which He was a Most distinguished Charracter—This was performed at the request of Mate or Tu and several of the Officers and Crew of the Bounty Were Present–

The Houses where they hold these Plays or Dances are in Common no other then a Shed Open at the Front and both ends, the Back part being screend in with Cocoa Nut leaves wove into a kind of Matting for the Purpose, the Back part generally forms one part of a Square which is raild in with a low railing the Whole Square being laid with Grass, and the part they perform on laid with Matts—without the railing which is not more then a Foot High sit or stand the Audience—they sometimes may act at the Houses of the Chief when they leave all the Dresses as a Present Many of them Contain from 20 to 30 fathoms of Cloth from one to four wide—with the Matting Cloth & Feathers–

The *Hura* is the Dance performd by the relations of Warriors Slain in Battle when they make friends with the Man who Killd Him or them—as these Dresses are very Expencive to those At whose Expence they are found, they seldom have More then Four and Oftener two then any other Number tho they may have 20 if they can afford it

Another Dance is the *Ponara* which is performed almost evry evening in evry district through the Island. To this Dance the Weomen of evry age and discription resort to dance young & old, Rich and Poor mix promiscusly, but no Men Join with them—when they attend the *Ponara* they are always Neat, and dressd in their best, their Heads decorated with Garlands of sweet scented Flowers, having fixd on the Ground they devide themselves in two partys and separate at 30 or 40 Yards from each other, when one of the Best players having provided a small green Bread fruit for a Ball with which she runs out about half way between the two kicks the Ball with as Much force as she is able, striking it with the upper part of the foot near the instep, if she sends the Ball through the other part or past them so as none can stop it till it stops itself then the Opposite or Her party strike up a Song & Dance beating time to it with hands & feet with much exactness and regularity—after they have finnishd their dance, which lasts about 5 or 6 Minutes, the Other Party kick the Ball which if it Passes they who kick it Dance, but if it is stopt by them who Danced first then they dance again. Meantime the Others Stand still—after they have Playd at this for some Hours they Kick the Ball to one side, and both Partys strike up together, when each to draw the Spectators to their exibition, produce two or three Young Wantons, who stripping of their lower Garments Cover them selves with a loose piece of Cloth and at particular parts of the Song they throw Open their Cloth and at particular parts of the song they throw open their Cloth [repetition in original—Eds.] and dance with their fore part Naked to the Company making many lewd gestures—however these are not merely the effects of Wantoness but Custom, and those who perform thus in Publick are Shy and Bashful in private, and seldom suffer any freedom to be taken by the Men on that account

The Single Young Men have also dances wherein they shew many indecent Gestures which would be reproachable among themselves at any other time, but at the dance, it being deemd shameful for either Sex to expose themselves Naked even to each other, and they are more remarkable for hiding their Nakedness in Bathing then many Europeans, always supplying the place of Cloaths with leaves at going in and coming out of the Water and the Weomen Never uncover their Breasts at any other time–

Besides these Amusements they have several other and are very fond of Cock fighting which is Mostly their Morning diversion—they never trim the Cocks nor use any Spurs, but their natural ones, while the Cocks are fighting the owners are praying for the Success of their Cocks an as soon as they appear fatigued by the Heat they part them till they are recovered, and then put them together again they never fight for any wager but Merely for sport, and sometimes 200 Cocks are brought to the Pit one Part of the District fighting their Cocks against the Other and a Feast is provided by the part who send the Challenge let whoever wins or loose—In the evenings they Play the Flute and sing till bed time—sometimes they accompany their Music with drums—their Flutes are made of Bamboo having only three holes Consequently have but few Notes, which however they Vary and tune to each other and their sound is soft and Not inharmonious, they blow the instrument with one Nostril, stopping the other with one thumb, and with the second finger of the same hand stop the second hole, the third being near the lower end is stopd or Opened by the fore finger of the Other hand–

Their Drums are Hollow Cellinderical peices of Wood Covered with a Sharks Skin on which they beat with their fingers, and they are loud and Clear, they generally have two for base & Tennor, the one about 4 feet high & 10 or 12 inches over and the other of the same diameter but only 18 or 20 inches high—They have also large Base Drums in their *Maraes* which with Conch Shells are used by the Priests on Solem religious Ceremonies—these Drums are constantly beating when any thing ails the Chief–

When the Westerly Winds prevail they have a heavy surf Constantly running to a prodigious height on the Shore & this Affords Excellent diversion, and the part they Choose for their Sport is where the Surf breaks with Most Violence—when they go to this diversion they get peices of Board of any length with which they swim out to the back of the surf, when they Watch the rise of a surf somtimes a Mile from the shore, & laying their Breast on the board, keeping themselves poised on the Surf so as to come in on the top of it, with amazing rapidity watching the time that it breaks, when they turn with great Activity and diving under the surge swim out again, towing their plank with them—at this diversion both Sexes are Excellent, and some are so expert as to stand on their board till the Surf breaks—the Children also take their sport in the smaller surfs and

Figure 26. *Pahu,* drum, Tahiti [D 1914.26]. Reproduced with permission of University of Cambridge Museum of Archaeology and Anthropology

as Most learn to swim as soon as walk few or no accidents happen from Drowning[26]

They resort to his sport in great Numbers and keep at it for several Hours, and as they often encounter each other in their passage out, and in, they require the greatest Skill in swimming to keep from running foul of each other—which they somtimes cannot avoid in which case both are Violently dashd on shore where they are thrown neck & heels and often fine very Coarse landing which however they take little Notice of and recovering themselves regain their boards & return to their sport

The Chiefs are in general best at this as well as all other Diversions, nor are their Weomen behind hand at it *'Itia* is one of the Best among the Society Islands & able to hold it with the Best of the Men Swimmers.

This Diversion took place during the time the Bounty lay in *Matavai* Bay when the Surf from the Dolphin Bank ran so high as to break over her, and we were forced to secure the Hatches expecting the Ship to go on shore evry Minute–

After they have been at this sport they always wash in the Fresh Water, as they always do when they have been out in their Canoes or have been wet with salt water

They have also a diversion in Canoes which they steer on the top of the Surf with Great dexterity, and can either turn them out before it breakes or land safe tho it Break ever so high–

Their Natural aversion to filth which they detest and their Unparralled Cleanliness of Body and Cloaths, not only renders their persons agreeable to Strangers and themselves but keeps them free from many disorders which we have—Nor do they Give Way to Sickness till death stops their Career—Young and Old Constantly bathe in running water three times a day, some Oftener, and when they become too old to Walk far, fix their habitation near a stream to enjoy that Convenience—they always wash their hands & mouth before and after Meals, and when they are not at some diversion either go to sleep, in the Heat of the day or employ themselves trimming their Hair Beards &c a black Cocoa Nut Shell serves for a looking Glass when filld with water, fish scales for Tweesers, with which they pick their beards into form and the hairs from the legs arms armpits and other parts of the Body which are apt to gather filth from Sweat & Dust a sharks tooth answers evry purpose of Scisars, for trimming their hair, which they keep always in neat order. Both sexes have their ears bored, in which they wear flowers, or hand their Pearls on which they set much value, they mostly wear three in a bunch hung two or three inches from the ear, seldom having both Ears decorated in the same Manner. Cocoa Nut Oil is used for Pomatum,[27] and their Combs are made of Bamboo their Cloaths are always Neat and they take a Pride in Shining at Publick assemblys–

Their Disorders as beforesaid are few and for any inward Complaint they have no remedy except it is applyd by Chance tho they always administer Some Medicine with their prayers—but in surgerey they are excellent and make surprizing Cures—We have been Eye witness to some—one of which was from a Musquet ball which a Man received in his Breast, and passd through the Shoulder blade, another with his arm broke by a ball, a third having a Ball through his thigh, & a fourth received one through His Thigh while stooping, which passd under his ribbs and out by the Collar bone; with several others Wounded with Stones, all of which were perfectly cured within two Months—among those wounded with Stones was one who had all his Upper Jaw stove in and 6 or 7 teeth knockt out, several splinters of the bone were extracted and the Juice of herbs with Clean water was the only remedy ever we saw used, they cannot bear their wounds bound up and are Constantly Washing them to keep them from smelling for this reason should they get a leg broke it is certain Death as they Cannot be kept from the Water tho they know the Consequence always flying to the water as soon as the smell becomes disagreeable, and often grate sandal wood on the part to take away the Smell, for Splints they use bamboo, and often repair broken Arms whether gotten by War or Accident

Their Chief Disorders are Madness or Insanity—Agues Coughs & Colds, Swelld legs & Arms,[28] Swellings under their Ears like the Evil, Ruptures & some few others–

The Insanity is only temporary, and perhaps may proceed from too great a flow of Blood & spirits, and a Want of Exercise, as it generally commenced when the Bread begins to be ripe—at which Season others are troubled with Boils on their legs and thighs, this being the Wet Season and the Sun over head when they are More Confined to their houses by the rain, this generally leaves them when the Sun returns to the Northward, and it is Not Common for a Man or Woman to have it return, tho during its stay with them they are very Mischevious and go quite Naked, with some it stays longer then others, and they have it in different degrees from a heavy dull Melancholy to raving Mad, they never bind them but let them run and some travel all round the Island Naked, in the time of their Madness and none interupts them unless they do some Mischief as they suppose them posessd with some evil spirit, this is Common to Weomen as well as Men, who are not restrained but sufferd to take their own Course till the spirit leaves them[29] when they return home and wear their Cloaths as usual.

The Ague is a Common disorder for which as well as Madness they have No Cure and this Carrys them off, as does that terrible disease the

Venereal for which Death is their only remedy and such was the fate of those who Contracted it from the Europeans, for as soon as any one is known to have it, no person will toutch them nor theirs Nor will they bathe near them in the river, their food is also carried to them, they not being suffered to touch any but what is for themselves—their Companions forsake them and they languish out the remainder of their days in a Miserable Manner tho they want no food, yet they Pine at seeing themselves Neglected and soon die–

They know that this disorder was brought by the Europeans, but are not Certain whether by the Spaniards or French for which reason they Blame both, nor do we escape blameless sin all points, for they Charge us with Several other disorders with which they say they were unacquainted before they knew us and particularly with bringing Fleas among them which they say were brought by the Cats—however it is possible that they may be Natives of their own Country as it is Clear that Most of their disorders are, the Ague being the effects of the sudden heats and Colds which they often experience as they always Jump into the River when they sweat to Cool themselves, and often sleep in Heavy dews—

Their Coughs & Colds are often Gotten in the Same Manner and their Hot bath into which Weomen go after Childbearing is Sufficient to Carry off those of the best Constitution—this is Made by screening in part of a House, or erecting a hut or Tent of Cloth and Mats, into which they bring a quantity of Hot Stones and spread grass & herbs over them, the person intending to bathe then goes in with a shell of water, the place is shut close & the Water being sprinkled on the Grass & Stones, makes a Steam In this they stay as long as they are Able, when Throwing a Cloth loosely round them they Come out, and run directly to the River into which they Plunge head formost, this bath is also used by both sexes merely for the Sake of making themselves thoroughly clean when their skin appears too rough or greasy to be cleand in the River—this We have Seen often Repeated by both Sexes, without any immediate good or bad Consequence

The Swelld legs and Arms are a disorder perhaps peculiar to themselves, these swellings often breake out in Small Ulcers, but never deminish, they seldom effect above the Knees or Elbow, being Confined to the Arm & Leg which swells to a prodigious size—the Swellings under the Ears are like the Kings evil, making large scars, for neither of these have they any remedy but Clean washing never suffering their Head to be bound up which often occasions large wounds in their Necks and, altho we often Convinced them that binding up their wounds would be the Means of a Speedy Cure yet as they must either stay at home, or remove their bandage evry time they pass over sacred Ground, they could never be perswaded to do it–

Ruptures are Very Common, frequently Swelling to a Prodigious size, these are perhaps occasioned by too great an exertion of Strength when Wrestling, which however we were not able to perswade them to beleive, nor is it possible to perswade them that disorders proceed from such things as sleeping on damp ground or in heavy dews &c—as they beleive that all their diseases are immediately sent from the Deity as a punnishment for some fault, consequently that it is impossible to prevent or escape it–

They have few Cripples tho they have several Blind, and Dumb. Most of the deformity found amongst them are from Accident—their limbs in general are straight & it is very rare to see a Bow legd or knock kneed person—their Children are free from the ricketts, and the Mother takes much pains to form the features & keep the limbs in their proper Places while they are young, and if a Child is not very Deformd they will bring it into shape before the bones are set,—If the Child has any of these faults, the Mother is blamed, and any Stranger will tell Her that she does not understand Nursing her Children–

They Have also a kind of leprosy which Changes the Body to a Dead Wite in some parts, while the natural Collour is heightened to Black, this Change of Collour extends to the Hair on the head & body some of which is as white as snow, while the rest is Jet Black, which gives them a very odd appearance, some are Changed all over but this does not effect their Health or Strength[30]–

These are the principal of their disorders and it appears to me that they live to a Good old age and are Vigourous & healthy. Several are Now on the Island who were alive at the time the African Gally was lost (the Ship before spoken of) on *Tapuhoe* an Island to the NE of *Tahiti,*[31] and Many Mentioned by Captains Wallis & Cook are yet but hale harty men—and Many who appear to be near 100 Years old are Sturdy Men–

The Weomen in this Climate as in other warm ones are sooner ripe then in the Colder Northern & Southern Countrys and generally Marry at 13 or 14 Years but those of rank often reach 16 or 18 Years, by which time in this Country they are Weomen Grown they also appear to fade sooner, Nevertheless handsom features may often be traced under Grey hairs, and it is somthing remarkable that many who were once faded revive and hold their Beauty with all the Sprightlyness of Youth at 50, While others who have broken their Constitution in their Youth by their disolute Manner of living, are perfectly withered at 30–

When any person dies the relations flock to the House in numbers making much lamentation and the Weomen Cut their heads with sharks teeth, both sexes cut their hair off different parts of their heads, sometimes Cutting all but a lock over one Ear, sometimes over both & the rest Close cut or shaven, the Weomen often Cut themselves on these occasions till they bring on a fever, and I have known a Woman Cut herself for the loss of a Child, till a delirium was brought on which ended in the total loss of her reason–

For the loss of a relation they Cut a square place bare on the fore part of their head which they keep bare for 6 Moons or longer, according to the love they bear the deceased; but for a favourite Child they wear it so for two or 3 Years and all the hair they Cut off is either thrown into the Sacred Ground or Carried to the Marae–

If any Person dies of a Disorder they are Buried in their own Ground and a Priest always puts a Plantain tree into the Grave with them and some of the relations put them in the Grave, praying them to keep their disorder in the Grave with them and not afflict any person, with. when their Soul is Sent on that Business, they also bury or burn evry thing belonging to them, or that has been used by them while in their Sickness, house and furniture to prevent the disorder from spreading or Communicting to others—these are the only people that have any funeral Prayers—those who die without disease are either laid on a beir, or embalmd their Method of embalming is by taking the Bowells out and Stuffing the Body with Cloth and grated Sandal wood anointing the skin with Cocoa Nut oil scented with the Same wood, the Body is laid on a Beir in a house by itself & Covered with Cloth which the relations present as they Come to the Place which they all do if they are in the Island, the body is often dressd in the same Manner as it used to do while alive, the Head Ornamented with Flowers, the house is fenced in and hung round with Cloth finely scented, and the beir is ornamented with Garlands of Palm Nuts which having an agreeable Smell keep off any foul one—The Tears Shed on these Occasions are saved on pieces of Cloth, together with the Blood from their heads, and thrown within the rails of the Sacred house, all which they suppose gives satisfaction to the departed soul, who hovering about the Body while it remains without Moldering—Others are hung up on a Beir under a thatchd Covering Covered and dressd with Cloth, they are also ornamented with Palm Nuts, Cocoa Nut leaves platted in a Curious Manner, and raild in with reeds which the Man that is appointed to take Care of the Body keeps in repair, and he is obliged to have a Man to feed him as he must not toutch any sort of food for one Month, after he has toutchd a dead body or any of the things which belong to it—they also offer Provisions &c near the Corps not for it but the Deity who presides over it–

The body is Calld *Tupapa'u,* the Beir *Fata* and the House wherein it is Containd *Fare Tupapa'u*—those who are embalmed are Calld *Tupapa'u Miri*—They are kept each on their own land and Not Carryd to the *Marae,* where none are interrd, but those Killd in War, or for Sacrafice or the Children of Chiefs, who have been Strangled at their birth

When Chiefs or People of rank die their bodys are Embalmed and they are Carried round the Island to evy part where they have any Posessions, in each of which the *Taiaia* or Weeping Ceremony, is renewd; and after a Journey of 6 or 8 Months returns to their own estate where they are kept till the Body decays when the bones are intered. Some who have a great Veneration for the deceased wrap up the Scull and Hang it up in their house in token of their love, and in this Manner is the Sculls of several kept—these bodys while they are whole are liable to be taken in War and the Man who takes one of them gets the Name, and honors as if He had killd a Warrior, and should the body of a Chief be Carried off in this Manner before an other was Named the District would fall to the Conqueror as if he had killd him, for this reason they are always removed, having each a Steady Man to Carry them away into the Mountains if they should be in War, in this Manner Captn. Cooks picture is also removed lest it should be taken—While the Body remains they keep the Beir well supplyd with Cloth & new is always substituted in lieu of that which is decayd and the Cloth is in general good and neatly painted

Besides the Weeping and Cutting their Heads they have another Mourning Ceremony wherin they wear the *Parae* or Mourning Dress described by Captn. Cook[32] this is Mostly worn by two or three of the

Figure 27. “A Toopapow, with the Corpse on it—Island of Otahytey,” George Tobin, 1792 [Call no. PXA 563 no. 31]. Reproduced with permission of the Mitchell Library, State Library of NSW

Nearest Male relations each of which are Armd with a Weapon Calld (Paeho) edged with a row of sharks teeth for three feet or four of its length, the Upper part forming a blade like that of a Gardners knife, they are attended by forty or fifty Young Men & Weomen who disguise themselves by blacking their bodys and faces with Charcoal, and spotting them with pipe Clay, these seldom wear any other Cloths but a *Maro* and each is armd with a Spear or Club, and parade about the district like Madmen, and will bear Cut or even kill any person who offers to stand in their way—therefore when any one sees them Coming they fly to the *Marae,* it being the only place where they Can be safe, or Get refuge from the rage of the Mourners, who persue all that they see, the *Marae* alone they must enter, and while this Ceremony lasts, which is sometimes 3 weeks or a month, they pay no respect to persons nor are the Chiefs safe from their fury, unless they take sanctuary in the *Marae,* the Weomen and Children are forced to quit the place as they Cannot take refuge in the *Marae*–

Should any person be stubborn or foolish enough to stop one of the Mourners or Not get out of their way and they should be killd no law can be obtaind nor any blamed but himself as the Mourners are look'd on as lunaticks, driven Mad through Grief for the Death of their relations, therefore none attempt to obstruct them but fly at their approach, this Ceremony is also Calld *Taiaia* or Mourning, the Performers are Calld *Neneva* Madmen *Heiva taiaia*—Mourning Spirits, Gost, or Spectres–

These are the whole of their Mourning rites and are of longer or shorter duration according to the Circumstances of the Family, who have lost their relation, they are more particularly observed for Children then Grown persons–

Among their Societys (of which they have several, evry profession or Calling being a distinct Society and all of the same profession are made Welcome by the rest all through these Islands) is one in particular distinguish'd by the Name of *Arioi* which Name signifies a restless or unsettled Chief—this Society is composed of a Set of Young Men of Wild Amorous & Volatile dispositions who from their Infancy devote the youthful part of their lives to Roving, Pleasure & Debauchery: they are continually going from one Island to another and from one District to another in Companys of four or five Hundred together upon Partys of Pleasure, and as Nearly all the Chiefs are of this Society they ever Meet with the best entertainment from them all in their respective districts.[33] So greatly are they indeed respected throughout all the Islands, that if any of the Members take a liking to the Cloaths which they see any person wearing they are never refused them or any thing else they may chuse to Demand, and are always sure to carry off the finest weomen in the Country—The Old Members of this Society are distinguished by having a black Oval tattow'd tunder their left Breast, one on the right side of the back below the shoulder, their Legs & thighs entirely blackd from the Ancle to the short ribs and their arms from the finger ends to the Shoulder—They are always well dressd, with the best Cloth that can be made, their hair Scented and Adorn'd with Various kinds of odoriferous flowers, the Younger Members, and indeed all in general being fond of variety, seldom remain any length of time with one Woman but care [*sic*] Constantly Changing and if any of their Wives prove Pregnant, they go away and leave them immediately on the first discovery that they may not be obstructed in their future persuit and enjoyment of Pleasure by the domestic cares of a Wife and Child, and as it is deemed reproachful for a Child not to know who his Father is (which would be almost impossible in that Society) when they are Pregnant with a Child of which they know not the true Father, to prevent its being treated with Indignity in its passage through Life (and as it could have no inheritance without a Father) it is no sooner born then some other strangles the little innocent and burys it, these *Arioi* ladies of Pleasure easily agree to this as they think that Nursing Children spoils their Beauty in the prime of Youth and debars them from the Happiness of having so many Suitors as before–

If an *Arioi* preserves any of His Children (which they seldom do till they advance in Years and the Fire of their Youthful Passions is a little quench'd) they are not treated with so much respect as when Batchelors and are then denominated (*Arioi Fanaunau* or a Childbearing *Arioi*) and are not entertaind at the feasts till the Batchelors, are served tho they are always lookd on as part of the Society and treated as such they are Never Calld upon in War and May pass through the Countrys at war without Molestation, and be well received, tho part of them belongs to the enemys District.

If any Person wishes to have his son or Daughter instituted into the Society he procures an *Arioi* to be His Son or Daughters Friend and Adopts him for His Son by performing the *Amo'a* (before described) towards Him and His Son or Daughter at the *Marae* and the Child is acknowledged an *Arioi* immediately the Ceremony is over, and May Continue to follow their Methods while He or she thinks Proper

There are many People who are not of this Society that kill their Children for this Reason—If a Man takes a Wife of inferior rank to himself and has a Child by her it is strangled immediately it is born to prevent its bringing disgrace on the Blood of His Family and tho he wishd to preserve its life himself his relations would oblige him to kill it or declare himself no longer of their Family—and it is the same if the Wife be superior in rank to the Husband both of which frequently happens If the Child should chance to cry out in Coming into the World, or should the Mother Chance to see it before it is killd Nature takes place of Custom and the Child is Saved

Such was the Case with the present *Temari'i* the only Child which *Purea* Saved, being delivered by herself she saved the Child tho she had killd several others, both Her and *Amo* being of the *Arioi* society, for which reason he left Her but they afterwards became friends & the Boy was acknowledged their Heir–

And here it May not be improper to remark that the Idea formd of this Society and of the Inhabitants of this Island is general by former Voyagers could not possible extend much further then their own Oppinion, None having remaind a sufficient length of time to know the Manner in which they live and as their whole system, was overturned by the arrival of a ship, their Manners were then as much altered from their Common Course, as those of our own Country are at a Fair, which might as well be given for a specimen of the Method of living in England—and such was always their situation as soon as a ship Arrived their whole thought being turnd towards their Visitors, & all Method tryd to win their Friendship. Meantime they were forced to living in a different way of life that they might the better please their New Friends

Their general Notion of delicacy is undoubtedly different from Ours, perhaps from their want of refinement without which many of our own Countrymen would be as bad if not worse then them, many of whom would not keep within bounds but for fear of the law

A woman is not ashamed to shew her limbs at a dance, or when bathing, if they are perfect; if they are not, she will avoid being seen, as much as possible, and tho the Men and Weomen frequently bathe together they are more remarkable for their decency then levity at such a time

They have no Walls to their houses nor do they require any, Notwithstanding which they cannot be charged with holding Carnal Conversation in Publick, and like privacy in such cases as much as we do nor did I see any thing of the kind during our stay in the Islands, tho they are not remarkable for their vertue, Yet this is not the General Charracter and the large Familys of some shew that there are some of that stamp

Their Actions might possibly be for the sake of Gain brought to a stile of what we call indecency, but where are the Countrys that do not produce Weomen of the Same discription—Iron is to them More Valuable then Gold to us, for the possession of which some of our own Country weomen would not stick at acts of indency nor even horrid Crimes which these People would tremble to think of. Nay, they Challenge us with the Verry

Crime, and say we are ashamed of Nothing, using these things which we knew they were fond of to perswade them to commit such acts as their innocence had taught them to be ashamed of. If they can purchase Iron at the expence of their Beauty, or are able to get it by theft, they will. Neither of which Methods I hold to be a Crime in them they know its Value and think no price to great for it

Gold is preferd in Other Countrys and some as fine Weomen as any in Europe are said to prefer it to Virtue yet we upbraid these untaught and uncontrould people with such actions as we ourselves help them to Commit.[34]

They lay no restraint on their Children because they are the Head of the Family and therefore do as they please, having no law nor Custom to prevent them they have a Number of amusements which would not suit the Idea of Europeans, which however are dropd as they Grow up—when they become ashamed of these Childish sports but are not Compelld unless they think proper themselves—and as there are always sufficient in all Countrys to promote evil practices they who do not like them, can only reform themselves, having no power over others for which reason they are sufferd to proceed in their own way

Those who Make a Trade of Beauty know how to value it, and when they come on board, bring with them their Pimps or Procurers under the denomination of relations to receive and secure the Price and these ladys are as well quelified to Act their part as any of their profession in other Countrys and are no way bashful in making their Demands—but if a Man Makes a friend that Friend can never have any Connection with any female of the Family except His friends Wife, evry other becoming His relations which they hold an abomination to have any Conexion with, nor can they be perswaded to alter that Custom on any Consideration detesting as much as we do to have their own relations as wives

The Weomen of rank are Most remarkable for their licentious practices and Many of them have a Number of Favourites, in which they pride themselves, tho many of the lower Class are what may honestly be Calld Virtuous, never admitting a Second to share in their Favours

The Famous Queen *Purea* being herself an *Arioi,* it is not to be wondered at, that evry licentious practice was carried on by her followers and Attendants, her Court being filld with such as preferd the Rites of Venus to those of Mars and as she saw that they were also more agreeable to her

Visitors (the general Case with Sailors after a long Voyage) they were no doubt practised and carried to the utmost verge of their lattitude, it being in all Countrys the Case that those in power always lead the fashions, let them be good or evil

However the ladys who act these parts are not to be taken as a standard for the Whole no more then the Nymphs of the Thames or Syrens of Spithead are to be taken as Samples of our own fair Country Weomen

Their Ceremonies have also been misunderstood by Former Voyagers—The Flys being Numerous they are forced to use fly flaps and when they have none, they use branches of the first tree,[35] and with these they are ever ready to supply evry stranger, especially if any Food is at hand, as they cannot bear to see a Fly toutch what they Eat, and have a number of Hands always employd to drive them away with these branches

The other branches used in Ceremonies are the *Rauava* and are Commissions borne by substitutes for Chiefs and evry person bearing one of them is treated in the same Manner as the Chief would be if he were present, these Commissions, or Emblems of truth, are Never Assumed by any unless on such occasions as they would suffer death for such fraud, the Plantain as before mentioned being the only Emblem of Peace—When any person is sent with such a Commission he gives a leaf to each of the party to whom he is sent, on the receipt of which, and being informd who sent him, his word is never doubted–

Besides the different Classes & Societys already discribed they have a Set of Men Calld *Mahu* these Men are in some respects like the Eunuchs in India but are Not Casterated they Never Cohabit with weomen but live as they do they pick their Beards out & dress as weomen, dance and sing with them and are as effeminate in their Voice they are generally excellent hands at Making and painting of Cloth Making Matts and evry other Womans employment they are esteemd Valuable friends in that way and it is said tho I never saw an instance of it, that they Converse with Men as familiar as weomen do—this however I do not aver as a fact as I never found any who did not detest the thought[36]

The Manners and Customs of the other Islands are as Near the same as those of Different Countrys in the Same Kingdom, and their produce nearly the Same & the Inhabitants of all the Society Isles are one and the same people—*Tahiti* is by Much the largest and most powerful when the Strength of the Island is united and is therefore acknowledged Mistress

Paramount of the whole, they all distinguish their Language Customs &c by the Name of *Tahiti* as well at home as when they are at *Tahiti,* and there but few Men of Property who do not visit Tahiti once in their lifetime and many visit it frequently–

It must be acknowledged that Captain Cook when he first thought of stocking these Islands with Cattle Poultry and the Fruits & Roots of Europe intended it for the Good of Mankind, but these people knew not the Value of them, and for want of Europeans to take Care of them they were soon distroyd, the Curiosity of the Natives to see such Strange Animals made each wish to have one by which means they were seperated and their Increase prevented, the Poultry soon became extinct—the Sheep who did not as in Other Warm Climes lose their Wool, died for want of Sheering—the Black Cattle alone thriving tho kept Mostly separate, the Seeds & Plants were destroyd by being removed as soon as they made their Appearance evry one Wishing to posess some part of the Curiositys which they esteemd the whole and would part with the best Cow for a Good Axe, setting No Value on them for food tho they Killd several and eat part of them in the Wars but having No Method of taking of the Hides they Cleand them as hogs but could not fancy they were good therefore took No pains to save a Breed

The Rams & the Goats they could Not abide from their disagreeable Smell and Many of the Goats were banishd to the Mountains as their Flesh was not a Compensation for the Mischief they did to the Cloth plantations, those they keep now are always tyed if they are near one of these Plantations and at best are not esteemd equal to a Dog—this Method of treating them prevents the Island from being over run with them which it soon would if they were suffered to range at large

Notwithstanding their having lost all these Valuable Curiositys they still remember Captn Cook for bringing them and take More Care of his Picture then all the rest they Made frequent enquiry after him & Sr. Josh. Banks both of whom will never be forgotten at *Tahiti*—they were exceeding sorry when they heard of Captn. Cooks death and Wishd that His Son might come and take possession of His Fathers land, He being acknowledged Chief of *Matavai* and will be as long as his Picture lasts[37] They were also very inquisitive about all their friends and were happy when we entertaind them with an Account of their Welfare–

Their Language is Soft and Melodious, abounding in vowels they have only seventeen letters yet they can express any thing with ease, tho for want of the others which Compose our Alphabet they never could pronounce any English word which Contains them

They Count their time by Years of 12 Months which they have Names for and Calculat it by the Suns passing & repassing over their heads, they Call the Month *Marama* or Moon tho they do not always begin or end with the Moon—they have Names for evry day of the Moons age and can tell Her age to a Certainty at first Sight without the Assistance of Figures

As they never keep an account of their time they can easily reconcile any mistake in their reckoning at the end of the year when the Sun is over their heads—they devide the day and Night into 12 equal parts and can tell their time exactly by the Sun in the Day time and the stars at Night—they have also Names for evry Wind and are excellent Judges of a Change and can tell whether the Season will be uncommonly dry or Wet before it commences, They have No Method of Measuring distance but by the length of time it requires to pass it, but can Measure any depth of water with exactness by the Fathom, Yard or Span all of which they Name alike with the addition of longer or shorter

They are able hands at Conversing by signs and perfectly Masters of the Language of the Eyes at both of which I have seen a Dumb man so well learnt that he might be sent to the distance of 60 Miles with a Message and return with his answer as well as if he could hear & speak–

They are for ever Changing their Names from Making New friends and Many other Accidents, and tho they do not loose their former ones, it would be difficult for a Stranger to know who they were talking of or what about or be able to find an old acquaintance by his Name—as No word must be used which Contains any of the Syllables of the Chiefs Name while he is alive—They Never compare any kind of Food to a Mans head, for which reason the Heads of Animals have a different Name nor can they think of eating any thing that has toutched a mans head and Nothing Can Offend them More than laying a hand on their heads, Brown, who was left here by Captn Cox, was thought worse then a Cannibal for Carrying Provisions on His head of which none ever partook with him—tho they were always ready to excuse him saying he knew no better which In fact was Nearly the Case but it was his sole study to be Contrary to them in evry thing and he took more pains that way then in Conforming to their Ways which made him disagreeable to them all–

Such is the best account that I have been able to Collect of these Islands and their Inhabitants who are without doubt the Happiest on the Face of the Globe, and shall now proceed to give such a Vocabulary of their language as we were able to obtain during our Stay among these Islands.[38]

THE END

Appendix I: Morrison's Polynesian Words and Terms

Standard	Morrison	English	Notes
amoʻa	*amoa*	–	Series of rites aimed at the removal of restrictions relating to the personal *tapu* of chiefly individuals (especially following the birth of a high-ranking child)
ariʻi	*earee*	district chief	–
ariʻi rahi	*earee ra hi*	principal chief	–
ariʻi nui	*earee nooe*	principal chief	–
Arioi	*areeuoy*	–	High-ranking and mobile sect associated with the worship of ʻOro. *Arioi* performed in both a ritual and a dramatic capacity in return for the hospitality of districts; their practices of tattooing and infanticide (a means of preserving the nobility of their rank) became notorious among early visitors, with reactions ranging from mild distaste to horror.
arioi fanaunau	*arreuoy fwhanownow*	–	*Arioi* who (in contravention of infanticide rules) kept their offspring
atua	*eatooa*	god	
atua fanau po (roa)	*eatooa fwhanow po (roa)*	–	Gods born of, or brought forth from, *te po (roa),* lit. "the (long) dark night"
atua raʻa	*eatoe raa*	–	God (sacred or *tapu*)
fare atua	*effarre attooa or farre eatooa*	god house	Container in which *tapu* objects (god images, feathers) were stored when not in ritual use
fare tupapaʻu	*farre toopapow*	–	Sheltered platform on which a chiefly corpse was laid for the duration of mortuary rites (including preparation of the body for embalming)

Appendix I *(continued)*

Standard	Morrison	English	Notes
fata	*fwhatta*	–	Altar or bier on which (*a*) sacrificial food was placed when offered in ritual to *atua* within the *marae* precinct or (*b*) on which the body of a chiefly corpse was laid out for mortuary rites
fenua	*venooa*	land	
heiva	*heiva or heva*	–	Gathering of people for ritual or social purposes
hoa	*hoa*	friend	
huhu	*hoohoo*	–	*Huhu* beetle (*Prionoplus reticularis*)
hura	*hewra or heovra*	–	Dance (gestural, rhythmic) or performance
ihi ari'i	*eehee aree*	–	Offering of first fruits to *atua* (gods) and/or the presiding district chief(s)
ma'a ra'a	*maa raa*	–	Sacred, *tapu* food; restricted foods included delicacies such as turtle, which was prohibited except for priests or chiefs/*ari'i* during ritual practice.
mahi	*mahee*	–	A sour paste made from fermented breadfruit
mahu	*mahoo*	–	Member of a chiefly entourage, young male attendant (often lover) to the chief; now refers to the transgender identity of a man who adopts women's roles and styles
manahune	*mannahownee or mannohowne*	–	Lower-ranking individual or laborer
manuia	*mannowa, manoa*	–	Greeting (lit. "Welcome, good health")
marae	*morai*	*marae*	A restricted space for gathering to effect ritual practice/interaction with *atua*
marama	*marrama*	moon or month	
maro	*marro*	sash, girdle, or belt	A barkcloth or woven sinnet sash or belt worn by men
maro e atua	*marro eatooa*	–	Sash or girdle (lit. "of the gods"), e.g., *tapa* wrappings placed strategically around trees from which hogs were hung as a means of marking boundaries in a challenge to war

Appendix I *(continued)*

Standard	Morrison	English	Notes
maro 'ura	*marro ooora*	feather sash	A sash or belt formed of rare and valuable feathers (principally red, but also yellow and black) that were incorporated into a woven foundation. Associated with the 'Oro cult, the *maro 'ura* was the most significant component of ritual regalia associated with the investiture of the *ari'i rahi,* or principal chief.
mataeina	*mattaeyna*	–	Landholding tenants within a district
metua	*medooa*	parent or relation	Respectful way of addressing an elder
monoi	*monnoe*	monoi oil	Scented oil used to rub on the skin and on the hair to render it glossy and attractive
neneva	*naynevva*	–	Group or band of *Arioi* who accompanied a chief mourner through districts during the extended period of mourning for a prominent chief
noa	*noa*	–	Ordinary, everyday; not bounded by restrictions associated with *tapu*
opio	*opeeo*	baked breadfruit	Also the large *'umu* (earth oven or pit) itself in which large quantities of bread-fruit were placed, covered with leaves, hot stones, and earth and left to bake for 3–4 days
'opu nui	*oboo nooe*	–	Ritual practitioners, *marae* attendants; commonly translated as "big bellies" due to their perceived access to ready supplies of offerings for their own consumption. The association with a distended stomach, however (deemed to be the seat of knowledge), more likely referred to their highly developed mental capacities and extensive retention of esoteric knowledge, expertise, and traditions.
paeho	*paaeho*	–	Long weapon edged with a row of sharks' teeth
parae	*parais, pari*	–	Cap or headpiece with tropic bird tail feathers. Morrison refers to *parae*

Appendix I ***(continued)***

Standard	Morrison	English	Notes
			generically as "Mourning dress" (Chap. 7), yet technically this was a single (albeit significant) component of the entire assemblage used by *Arioi* during ritual events such as those following the death of a prominent chief.
pareu	*parew*	–	Length of cloth worn by women (down to the calf or ankle)
patu	*patdoo*	–	Subdivision of a district
piha ra'a	*pehha rea*	–	Sacred or *tapu* box, a chest in which god images and accoutrements associated with ritual use (*tapa* wrappings, red feathers) were kept
popoi	*popoe*	–	Pudding made of baked breadfruit
popoi fe'i	*popoe fayee*	–	Baked breadfruit pudding prepared with mountain plantain, or *fe'i*
ra'a	*raa*	sacred, *tapu*	–
ra'atira	*ratirra*	–	Lesser or district chief
rahui	*raahooe*	restriction	–
tahu'a	*tahowwa*	–	Priest or ritual expert who officiated over ritual procedures on *marae*
tahu'a marae	*tahowwa morai*	–	Priest or ritual expert renowned in particular for his skill of reciting lengthy chants, or *'upu,* in complex, esoteric language (see also *taura e atua*)
taiaia	*tyehua, tyehaa*	–	Expression of communal grief during a period of mourning. Women in particular engaged in keening and wailing while they lacerated their heads with shark-toothed implements until they drew blood, which mingled with their tears. Morrison referred to it as the "Weeping Ceremony" (Chap. 7), while Davies' dictionary records the definition: "to weep for the *aia,* or lost land, food &c." (1851: p. 224).
tamau	*tamow*	–	Sash of finely braided strands of hair

Appendix I *(continued)*

Standard	Morrison	English	Notes
Tane or *e atua nui, e atua mana*	Taane or Eatooa Nooe, Eatooa Munna	–	Tane, the first or principal god, creator god
tatau	tattow	tattoo	To mark the skin, or tattoo
taura e atua	*tawra tooa*	–	Priest or ritual expert whose focus was divine inspiration: these priests were deemed to be directly linked, in fact physically bound to a god during ritual procedure when they were consulted on the outcomes of unknown events (such as war or sickness)
ʻoromatua	*oromattowtooa*	–	Spirit of a deceased person; skull or relic of a deceased relative
tapa	cloth	barkcloth	Made by beating sodden strips of fibrous bark into sheets to make a soft yet thick, textured fabric; prepared from the beaten inner bark of the paper mulberry, bread-fruit, etc.
taumata	*tow matta*	–	A shade for the eyes worn on the head (commonly made of woven coconut leaves)
taumi	*tawmee*	–	Breastplate worn by men of rank incorporating feathers, sharks' teeth, and dog hair on a wickerwork frame with sinnet bindings
te po	*te po*	–	The realm associated with darkness and night where deceased relatives, ancestors, and gods are deemed to reside. In contrast, *te ao* is the realm of light inhabited by light, life, and the living.
teuteu	*tewtew*	–	Servant, attendant on a chief
tiʻi	*tee*	–	Image of carved wood or stone; used as boundary markers
tiʻipa huamanu	*Teepahooa-mannoo*	–	A feather god or ancestor. Like most early visitors to Tahiti, Morrison attempted to cite specific names and attributes of the gods in the Tahitian pantheon. In fact *tiʻipa huamanu* was likely a generic term

Appendix I *(continued)*

Standard	Morrison	English	Notes
			for an ancestor or god of great antiquity linked genealogically to the time of the creation of the cosmos; the term is formed from *ti'i,* the name of the first man created + *pa,* a term of respect and reverence for a chief or person of higher rank and status. *Huamanu* also refers to a cluster or bunch of red feathers—an essential component of god images, indeed of all ritual activity, as these were believed to activate the channel with *te po,* the vital and charged domain in which ancestors and *atua* resided.
tiputa	*teeboota*	–	*Tapa* or barkcloth poncho (with a central opening through which the head was passed)
to'ofa	*towha*	–	Chief next in rank to *ari'i*
tupapa'u miri	*toopapaow mere*	–	Embalmed ("rubbed," "massaged") corpse
tuparu	*tooparroo*	–	Sweet custard-like pudding made of breadfruit (or taro), grated coconut, and ripe bananas
taiero	*tyeyro*	–	Fermented sauce made of grated coconut and shrimps in salt water; used to accompany meat and fish
tutae	*tewty*	excrement, feces	Morrison notes the double entendre of the term *teuteu,* or servant: "called Tewtew in General but those who wait on Weomen are Calld *Tewty* by way of derision" (Chap. 6).
utu	*oodoo, ootdoo*	–	Presentation or gift made to visitors. Offerings established a framework for future exchange relations and reciprocity between parties. Its efficacy was determined by a number of essential component parts, which included young plantain trees and/or red feathers, and pigs or fowl, accompanied by cloth and foodstuffs.
vahi	*bahooe*	–	Subdivision of land

Appendix II: Morrison's People

Note: Morrison's usual spellings are in parentheses; not every variant is given.

Amo (Oammo)
Formally known as Tevahitua-i-Patea, Amo was the principal titleholder of Papara and traced his descent from the senior line of the Teva clan. His father, Tuitera'i, had been the paramount leader of the Teva-i-tai people, while his mother was from a chiefly lineage in the northern district of Ha'apape. A high-ranking *Arioi,* he had strong political ambitions for the son Temari'i (or Teri'irere), whom he fathered with the high-ranking chieftainess Purea.

Ari'ipaea (Arrepaeea)
Born circa 1758, Ari'ipaea was the second son of Teu and Tetupaia and the younger brother of Mate (Tu or Pomare I). A celebrated warrior, he was also known as Teari'ifa'atau (or "Tarevatoo" during Cook's time). Ari'ipaea married Teri'itua (known to the English as Ino Metua), a high-ranking *Arioi* of Hitia'a and daughter of Aromaitera'i.

Ari'ipaea Vahine (Areepaeea Waheine)
The second daughter of Teu and Tetupaia, Terereatua Vau'o-vahine (Tirrayraydooa or Tarreredooa) of Ha'apaiano'o was the elder sister of Pomare I (Tu Vaira'atoa or Mate) and the highest ranking woman in Tahiti. A leading *Arioi,* she had no children. She also bore the title Ari'ipaea Vahine and Fa'ataua (Fatowwa), in keeping with their younger brother Ari'ipaea, who was also addressed as Teari'ifa'atou. Resident for an extended period in Ra'iatea, Ari'ipaea Vahine returned to Pare with a naval fleet in 1791 during Morrison's residency in Tahiti.

Hitihiti (Heeteheete)
A high-ranking Society islander, originally from the island of Borabora with familial ties to the renowned ari'i warrior Puni, Hitihiti joined the *Resolution* under Captain Cook between September 1773 and June 1774 and visited Tonga,

New Zealand, Rapa Nui, and the Marquesas, among other places, where he played a key role in brokering negotiations with islanders. One of several islanders to stow away on the *Bounty* when it left Tahiti, Hitihiti proved useful to Christian during their brief sojourn in Tubuai, defending the mutineers' interests with a musket given him by Christian when relationships with locals became strained and descended into violence.

Hitirere (Heterere)
A Tubuaian chief, Hitirere exercised dominion over the northern district of the island, To'erauetoru, now called Mata'ura. Morrison also notes that Christian and his party were met by a chief Hitirere when they put in to land in the district of Nahitorono along the southern coast of Tubuai, but does not make it clear whether this is the same Hitirere.

'Itia (Eddeah)
'Itia was the first wife of Mate (also Tu or Pomare I), a high-ranking Pare-'Arue woman whose full title was Tetuanuireia-i-te-Ra'iatea-i-Nu'urua. As trusted adviser and counselor to her husband Tu, she came to be one of the most politically powerful individuals in the Society Islands throughout the final decade of the eighteenth century and into the early 1800s. 'Itia had a brother Metuaro and sister Teano, who married into the Pomare and Vehiatua dynasties respectively.

Mahine (Maheine)
Mahine was the chief of the district surrounding Opunohu in Mo'orea and the uncle of Metuaro. A shrewd political strategist, he was constantly engaged in the orchestration of alliances that aimed at countering Tu Vaira'atoa's (or Mate's) consolidation of power. Despite his nephew Metuaro's legitimate claim to the chieftanship of Mo'orea, Mahine engineered the rise to power of his own protégé, Teri'iamoeatua, in order to establish there a political base of his own. Mahine's manipulation of events saw him finally seize power, forcing Metuaro to flee Mo'orea and seek refuge (along with his sisters 'Itia and Teano) with his brother-in-law Tu.

Ma'i (Omai, O'Mai)
Originally from the island of Ra'iatea, Ma'i was living in exile on Huahine when he requested passage on the *Adventure* under Captain Tobias Furneaux. Arriving in England on 14 July 1774, Ma'i was greeted in person by the Earl of Sandwich, at the time the first Lord of the Admiralty and one of Cook's most important

patrons. Fêted by London society, in the company of Joseph Banks he toured cities and country estates where he was introduced to the foremost figures of science, art, literature, and politics, including King George III and Sir Joshua Reynolds (who famously painted his portrait). Returning to Huahine in 1777 on Cook's third voyage, Ma'i lived in relative isolation among the finery and gifts he had brought back with him from London (which included pistols, a suit of armor, a pair of horses, and a monkey) before dying from a fever within two and a half years.

Maititi (Mydiddy)
Royal servant or *teuteu* to the Pomares, the shrewd Maititi proved himself adept at pitting the crew of the *Bounty* against each other and played a pivotal role in the violent quarrel that had led to the deaths of both Churchill and Thompson. Having supported Churchill in executing his plot to steal Thompson's muskets, Maititi nevertheless harbored resentment from a beating he had received at Churchill's hands and therefore had few qualms about informing Thompson of Churchill's underhanded behavior—an act that led directly to Thompson's decision to shoot Churchill. When Pataea later avenged Churchill's death by killing Thompson with repeated blows to his head, Maititi was once again present, this time securing Thompson's arms while the house was plundered. He later accompanied Bligh on the *Providence* voyage, dying in London in 1793.

Mate (Matte)
Pomare I, (also known as Tu or Tu Vaira'atoa or Tina), was the preeminent Pare-'Arue chief of Cook's time, having used the advantages and influence afforded him by European visitors to Matavai Bay, which was under his jurisdiction. Born c. 1750, he was the first son of Teu (principal chief of 'Arue) and Tetupaia, a chiefly woman of Ra'iatean descent who traced her lineage from the Tamatoa title. He died in 1803, within a year of his father.

Metuaro (Mottooarro)
Known formally as Teri'i-tapu-nui and referred to as Mahau by Vancouver during his 1791–1792 visit, Metuaro was the son of Vavea. Metuaro was challenged in his claim to inherit the chieftainship of Mo'orea by his own uncle Mahine, who strategized to maneuver his own candidate, Teri'iamoeatua, into the position. The marriage of Tu Vaira'atoa to Metuaro's sister 'Itia (and his own marriage to Tu's youngest sister, Vai'io in turn) strengthened their allegiances to such an extent that it threatened Mahine's own claims to the leadership of Mo'orea and he remained bitterly opposed to these matches.

Paitia (Pyeteea, Pyreteea)
A chief of the northern district of Matavai, Paitia is the bearded figure who appears stripped to the waist and crouching in the left-hand foreground of Robert Smirke's celebrated painting "The Cession of Matavai to Captain James Wilson." This was commissioned by the directors of the London Missionary Society in 1798 to commemorate the occasion and is now in the Council for World Mission, School of Oriental and African Studies, London.

Pataea (or Pataia, Pataya) (Patirre)
The islander Pataea avenged the violent death of Churchill at the hands of Thompson by leading a party to murder the latter. Having buried his body, Pataea took the skull to the *marae* at Tautira, where Morrison saw it and confirmed that it was Thompson's, as he recognized a scar on the forehead. The sudden death of Vehiatua had acted as a catalyst for the dispute that escalated between Churchill and Thompson in Taiarapu. Quick to capitalize on his status as the chief's *taio,* Churchill had attempted to set himself up as sovereign of Taiarapu, sparking jealousies in his fellow *Bounty* crew member Thompson who, exasperated, resolved to shoot him. Pataea insisted that their subsequent murder of Thompson was not motivated by the dispute over stolen muskets but to exact *utu,* or revenge, for Churchill's death.

Poeno
A chief of Matavai and, significantly, bound into a *taio* relationship with Morrison. Poeno and his wife (with whom Millward was bound in *taio* friendship) invited the two to take up residence with them. Morrison and his supporters built a shed on Poeno's land (near Point Venus) where they set about building the ocean-going vessel in which they planned to leave Tahiti and return to England. In 1791, Poeno was keeper of the Webber portrait of Cook that had been executed for Pomare I.

Pohuetea (Pohooataya) or **Potatau**
Pohuetea, or Potatau, was the stately chief of Puna'auia, aged between sixty and seventy years in Morrison's estimation and married to Purutihara. A formidable *ari'i,* Pohuetea had allied himself in December 1768 with Vehiatua to contest Amo and Purea's attempts to install their son Teri'irere as paramount chief. Leading the Puna'auia warriors alongside Tutaha's army from Pare-'Arue, their combined efforts against the people of Papara forced Amo and Purea to take refuge in the mountains along with Tupaia and their son Teri'irere, where they remained in exile and accepted defeat.

Purea (Pbooraya)
Formally known as Te Vahine-a'i-roto-atua-i-Ahurai (and called Oberea by Captain Cook), Purea was a high-ranking titleholder born into the Fa'a'a district. Her elder brother was Te Pau of Ahurai and their younger brother, Teihotu (married to Vave'a). An influential *Arioi* in her own right, Purea had ambitious plans for the son she bore to Amo, Teri'irere, for whom the pair consolidated their titles and resources in order to construct the complex Mahaiatea *marae.* A politically active woman, she was much involved with European visitors to Tahiti. The defeat of her Paparan forces during the conflict with Taiarapu in 1768 curbed the political ambitions she entertained for her son and herself.

Ta'aroamaeva (Taroameiva, Taroamira)
Ta'aroamaeva, the youngest son of the elderly Tubuaian chief Tahuhuatama of the Natieva district, entered into a *taio* bond friendship with Fletcher Christian. On the mutineers' departure from Tubuai, Ta'aroamaeva insisted that he and two companions accompany Christian and the crew aboard the *Bounty,* claiming that he would most certainly be killed if Christian left him on Tubuai.

Ta'aroatehoa (Taroatihoa or Taroatehoa)
Ta'aroatehoa was the eldest son of the Tubuaian chief Tahuhuatama, who exercised control over the north easterly district of Natieva, directly to the east of rival chief Tamatoa. Ta'aroatehoa accepted red feathers from Christian in exchange for a site within his jurisdiction for the mutineers' construction of Fort George.

Tahuhuatama (Tahoohooatumma)
Tahuhuatama was an older chief of Tubuai who had exercised control over the northeastern district of Natieva and was now succeeded by his son Ta'aroatehoa. Tahuhuatama was accompanied by his children during a ceremonial gift presentation to Fletcher Christian and crew members during their stay on Tubuai, which was reciprocated the following day when the Tubuaians were entertained with a Tahitian *heiva.* Morrison mentions his sons Ta'aroatehoa and Ta'aroamaeva, and one of his daughters, 'Aiata, "the young woman who had Come on board at our first anchoring" (see Chap. 2).

Taipo (Tyepo)
Taipo was the father of Vehiatua's nephew (a young boy of about four years old during the time of Morrison's residency), who had been appointed to Vehiatua's name and titles following their refusal to acknowledge the legitimacy of the

young Tu's claim to paramount chiefdom. Taipo assumed the position of regent in Taiarapu during his son's minority.

Tamatoa

The Tubuaian chief Tamatoa, of Ra'iatean descent, was the son of Hitirere and exercised dominion over the district known as To'erauetoru (now Mata'ura) on the northern coast of Tubuai. Christian entered into a *taio* relationship with Tamatoa (the first of several during his brief sojourn on the island) and was received at Tamatoa's *marae* Tonoha'e by allied district chiefs and the principal heads of families. Tamatoa claimed descent from the principal chiefly lineage of Ra'iatea; according to Morrison, he was the great-great-grandson of Tamatoa, the renowned chief of Ra'iatea who had been blown off course during a fishing expedition (see Chap. 2).

Teano

The sister of 'Itia and Metuaro, Teano became the wife of Vehiatua, the preeminent chief and titleholder of Taiarapu on the isthmus of Tahiti.

Temari'i (Tommaree)

The high-ranking son of Amo and Purea, Temari'i was born circa 1763, the sole heir of the Teva-i-uta clan. Known also as Teri'irere (or Teridiri by Cook), he was the preeminent chief of Papara during Morrison's residence in Tahiti and was described by the latter as "a Handsom[e] well made man of about 27 or 28 years old and about 6 feet high." His parents had great political ambitions for him (see above, Amo, Purea), but their strategy was contested and eventually eclipsed by the rise of the young Tu, who became Pomare II.

Tenania (Tennanea)

A chief of Huahine, Tenania was the brother of Teri'itaria, the paramount leader of Huahine. Following the death of her husband Pomare I, 'Itia married Tenania, convincing the Huahine chief that it would be politically expedient to join forces with the Boraboran chief Tapoa in support of her son Pomare II's cause. As a friend and ally of Ma'i, Morrison mentions that Tenania received the muskets Ma'i had brought back with him from England when he distributed the spoils of his voyage prior to his death in Huahine.

Teri'itahi (Tereetahi)

Also known as Toimata, Teri'itahi was the eldest sister of Tu Vaira'atoa (or Pomare I) and was married to Amo and Purea's son Teri'irere. She was also known under the title Te Ari'i-na-vaho-roa, which linked her to the cult of 'Oro.

Teri'itaria (Tayreetarieea)
Teri'itaria was principal chief and titleholder of Huahine and the brother of Tenania. As he was still young during the visits of Cook to the Society Islands, his uncle Ori and mother, Teha'apapa, had served as regents. Henry's genealogy indicates that his mother Teha'apapa was the only child of her parents, which made her the highest-ranking titleholder of Huahine (Henry 1928:257).

Teu or Hapai (Tew or Whappai)
The eldest son of forebears Ta'aroa Manahune and Tetua-e-huri of Taiarapu, Teu was the preeminent titleholder of the 'Arue clan—although his younger brother Tutaha actively exercised political power until Teu produced an heir and son in Tu (also Mate, Pomare I) with his first wife Tetupaia. Teu (or Hapai) died circa 1802, just one year before his own son.

Ti'itorea (Teetorea)
An *Arioi* and titleholder of Mo'orea, Ti'itoria became the consort of Purahi following the demise of her husband Vehiatua I, adopting the role of adviser and counselor to the two sons she had produced from that union—Vehiatua II and Vehiatua III. The politically ambitious and high-ranking Purahi (also known as Te Vahine Moeatua) was the firstborn child of Amo's elder sister, Tetua Unurau, and therefore considered herself senior to Amo.

Tinarau (Tinnarow)
Tinarau exercised chiefly dominion over the extreme easterly district of Tubuai known as Paorani and was married to the sister of Tahuhuatama, principal chief of the northeasterly district of Natieva. Christian's decision to construct Fort George in the district of Natieva strained relations with his former *taio* Tamatoa, so the rival chief formed an alliance with Tinarau against the mutineers and both chiefs forbade their people any contact with the crew of the *Bounty.* Volatile relations deteriorated further when Christian ransacked Tinarau's house, burning it to the ground and seizing weapons and household gods; in the final violent clash that ensued Tinarau's own brother was shot dead by Christian himself.

(Te) To'ofa (Towha, Tetowha Tetowho, T'towha and Te'towha)
Born circa 1768, the tall and imposing To'ofa descended from the chiefly clan based in Paea, one of two groups essentially unified as Te Oropa'a of Atehuru. To'ofa was the son of and successor to the venerable chief To'ofa of Paea, commander of the naval fleet that had gathered in April 1774 during Cook's return visit to Tahiti to contest Mahine's manipulations regarding the succession to the chieftaincy of Mo'orea.

Tu or Tu-nui-e-a'a-i-te-atua (Too, Toonooeaiteatooa, or Toonooeayeteatooa)
Also known as Pomare II and born circa 1782, the young high chief of the northern district of Pare-'Arue was the son of Tu Vaira'atoa (or Pomare I) and 'Itia, though the legitimacy of his parentage was disputed. Expertly manipulating his claims to title by steadily accumulating the god images and *maro 'ura* (or feather girdles) that reinforced his political and chiefly status, Pomare II consolidated his position to assume the highest-ranking title and was recognized as the *ari'i maro 'ura,* or paramount chief of the island.

Tupairu (Toobyroo)
Tupairu was the brother of Poeno, the Tahitian chief of the district in which Matavai Bay was located. He forged a *taio* relationship with Joseph Coleman, armorer on the *Bounty,* and was one of several islanders to stow away on the *Bounty* as it sailed from Matavai Bay.

Tutaha (Tootahah)
Tutaha was the younger brother of Teu (or Hapai). An important political leader in the Pare-'Arue district, Tutaha exercised active political control over the district until his brother Teu's son (Tu, Pomare I) was born, when this role evolved into an advisory capacity. Despite the fact that he had supported Vehiatua in rejecting Teri'irere's attempts to claim legitimate chiefly status, Tutaha opposed attempts to install Vehiatua's son as *ari'i rahi* or principal chief of the island, considering that his great-nephew had the stronger claim. Tutaha (also known as Ha'amanemane) was *taio* to Cook during his first voyage to Tahiti in 1769. He died in March 1773 when Tu Vairato'a (Pomare I) took over active authority of Pare-'Arue district.

Vaetua (Wyetooa)
Born circa 1763, Vaetua was the younger brother of Tu Vaira'atoa or Pomare I. A prominent *Arioi* and warrior who entered into *taio* relationship with Hayward of the *Bounty,* he was also known as Paiti and Te Tupua'i-e-te-ra'i.

Vehiatua (Vayheeadoa, Vayheeodooa, Vaydeeadooa)
Formally known as Vehiatua-i-te-mata'i, Vehiatua was the paramount chief of Taiarapu and leader of the Seaward Teva, who were rivals of the Pomare clan. Vehiatua contested Teri'irere's claim to Mo'orea with ambitions for his own son Teri'iamoeatua, whom he had fathered with Purahi (Te Vahine Moeatua), Amo's niece—that is, the firstborn child of Amo's elder sister, Tetua Unurau. On his death, this title passed to his *taio,* the *Bounty* mutineer Churchill, and then to Pomare I's younger son.

Appendix III: Morrison's Place-names

A. Society Islands

Morrison	Standard
Affwhaheetdee (or Affwhateetee)	Afa'ahiti
Attahooroo	Atehuru
Borabora	Borabora
Eymayo (or Eimeo, Morea)	Mo'orea
Fwhapyeano (or Fwhassyeano)	Ha'apaiano'o (or Papeno'o)
Heedeea	Hitia'a
Huaheine (or Hooaheine)	Huahine
Mataavye	Matavai
Matowwye	Mataoae
Mayteea (or Myetoo, Myetea)	Me'etia
Oparre	Pare
Ora Fwhanna	Orohena
Orapaa	Te Oropa'a
Paparra	Papara
Poonoohoo	Opunohu
Ryeatea	Ra'iatea
Tabonna, Taboona	Ta'apuna
Tahaa	Taha'a
Taheite	Tahiti
Taheite Nooe	Tahiti Nui
Taheite Eete	Tahiti Iti
Tetooroa (or Tetooraa, Tettooroa)	Tetiaroa
Towtirra (or Oheitepeha in Cook's time)	Tautira
Teeahhoroa (or Tiahharoa)	Te Aharoa
Tedevvaeuta	Teva-i-uta
Teparre	Tepare

A. Society Islands *(continued)*

Morrison	Standard
Tettaha	Tetaha (now Fa'a'a)
Teearey	Tiarei
Tiepirreonoo (or Tippirreonoo, Tipperroonoo)	Te Porionu'u
Tyarrabboo (or Terooaboo)	Taiarapu
Tye taboo	Taitapu
Vyeerre (or Vyerre)	Vaiari or Papeari
Vye Heereea	Vaihiria
Vyeooreede (or Vyeooreedee)	Vaiuriti
Vyeooroo	Vaiuru (now Vairao)
Vyeowtaya (or Vyeowtea)	Vaiaotea
Yunnowheea (or Yunnowheaa)	Puna'auia

B. Neighboring Island Groups

Morrison	Standard
Annamooka	Nomuka, Ha'apai group (Tongan archipelago)
Kao	Kao, Ha'apai group (Tongan archipelago)
Poenammoo	Te Wai Pounamu (South Island, New Zealand)
Savage Island	Niue
Tappoohoe	Tapuhoe (Tuamotus)
Toobouai	Tubuai (Austral Islands)
Toofoa	Tofua (Tongan archipelago)
Wytootaekee	Aitutaki (Cook Islands)

Appendix IV: Morrison's Plants

Standard	Morrison	Species/genus	English/notes
aito (or *toa*)	*eyto* (or toa)	*Casuarina equisetifolia*	Ironwood; a hardwood used to fashion clubs, spears, and arrowheads. Bark used to dye cloth, lines, and nets
'amae	*amai*	*Thespesia populnea*	Known also as *miro, toromiro,* this was planted close to marae and the leaves used for ritual and ceremonial purposes, including sacrifice and head binding (see also *rauava*).
'ape	*'yappe*	*Arum costatum*	Plant with starchy, edible root
'aute	*yowte*	*Broussonetia papyrifera*	Paper mulberry tree; cultivated in large plantations to yield bark for manufacture of the finest white *tapa*
'ava	*yava*	*Piper methysticum*	Kava; refers to the plant itself and to the narcotic drink made by pounding the root and blending it with water
fara	*fwharra*	*Pandanus tectorius*	Leaves used to thatch houses, weave mats, or make into sails; fragrant blooms used to scent oil and cloth
fe'i	*fayee*	*Musa troglodytarum*	Mountain plantain or banana used for cooking
'ie'ie	*leie*	*Freycinetia arborea*	Densely branched climber that attaches itself to a host tree using aerial roots. Used extensively in basketry and as a foundation or frame for complex ritual artifacts such as headdresses and gorgets.
nono	*nonno*	*Morinda citrifolia*	Sour fruit seldom eaten, though the bark of its root was used to make yellow dye for cloth; juice now marketed and sold as a superfood in healthstores
pia	*peea*	*Tacca leontopetaloides*	Species of arrowroot
purau	*poorow*	*Hibiscus tiliaceus*	Yellow flowering bush or tree; wood used for building canoes and making paddles

Appendix IV ***(continued)***

Standard	Morrison	Species/genus	English/notes
rauava	*rowavva*	–	Leaves of the *miro* plant or *'amae* tree (*Thespia populnea*); used in rituals, e.g., to bind the head (see *amo'a*) or as a substitute for a chief in his absence
roa	*roaa*	*Urtica argenta*	Bark fibers twisted into strands to make cord and used for fishing nets
tamanu	*tamannoo*	*Calophyllum inophyllum*	Large, spreading tree whose wood is used for making the larger canoes as well as stools, dishes, and bowls; nut used to scent cloth
taro	*tarro*	*Colocasia esculenta*	Taro; staple root vegetable
ti	*tee*	*Cordyline fructicosa*	Plant with large and sweet root (stalk can be as long as 6 ft). Widely planted throughout Polynesia, the plant had strong ritual associations (*umu ti*). Note that Davies classifies it as *Dracoena terminalis* (Davies 1851).
toa	*toa*	refer to *aito* above	
tou	*tow*	*Cordia subcordata*	Species of flowering tree in the borage family, Boraginaceae, with soft, durable and easily worked wood; the leaves were also used in preparation of dye for *tapa*
tutui	*toodooe*	*Aleurites moluccana*	Candlenut; used as lights—the kernels burn well due to their high oil content
'umara	*oomarra*	*Ipomoea batatas*	Sweet potato
uru	*ooroo*	*Artocarpus incisa*	Breadfruit
vi	*vee*	*Spondias dulcis*	Pomme Cythère or Tahitian apple

Notes

Preface

1. The most significant recent scholarly intervention in this debate is Greg Dening's historiographically groundbreaking *Mr. Bligh's Bad Language: Passion, Power and Theatre on the* Bounty (Cambridge: Cambridge University Press, 1992).

2. Rutter, "Introduction" to his edition of James Morrison, *The Journal of James Morrison, Boatswain's Mate of the* Bounty, *describing the mutiny and subsequent misfortunes of the mutineers, together with an account of the island of Tahiti* (London: The Golden Cockerel Press, 1935), 8–9.

3. In his introduction to the Golden Cockerel edition of Morrison's *Account,* Owen Rutter noted that the then Principal Librarian of the New South Wales Public Library suggested Lady Belcher's as a potential hand here, but cites correspondence with the Admiralty librarian to support his contention that Heywood was the sole editor of the manuscript. Rutter, "Introduction," 6.

Introduction

1. Banks was appointed one of the naturalists on Cook's first voyage to Tahiti and had since 1778 been president of the Royal Society, a position he held until his death in 1820.

2. For recent scholarly engagement with European economic, political, and rhetorical investment in the breadfruit, see Vanessa Smith, "Give Us Our Daily Breadfruit: Bread Substitution in the Pacific in the Eighteenth Century," *Studies in Eighteenth-Century Culture* 35 (2006): 53–75; Elizabeth De Loughrey, "Globalizing the Routes of Breadfruit and Other Bounties," *Journal of Colonialism and Colonial History* 8, no. 3 (Winter 2007), 10.1353/cch.2008.0003; and Jennifer Newell, *Trading Nature* (Honolulu: University of Hawai'i Press, 2010), 141–170.

3. It was also probably at this stage unknown to Christian. H. E. Maude carefully traced the *Bounty*'s journey after leaving Tahiti, via Rarotonga, Tongatabu, the Southern Lau group of Fiji, and to Pitcairn, arguing that, while Christian would have had a clear idea of the generic island he wished to find (uninhabited, unvisited, and without a harbor for shipping), it would only have been after the search had taken him as far west as Fiji that he might have turned to the

copy of Hawkesworth's voyages known to be among the books in Bligh's cabin and located Carteret's description of his 1767 discovery of Pitcairn's island: "it appeared like a great rock rising out of the sea: it was not more than five miles in circumference, and seemed to be uninhabited. . . . I would have landed upon it, but the surf, which at this season broke upon it with great violence, rendered it impossible"; John Hawkesworth, *An Account of the Voyages Undertaken by the Order of His Present Majesty for Making Discoveries in the Southern Hemisphere, and successively performed by Commodore Byron, Captain Carteret, Captain Wallis, and Captain Cook, In the* Dolphin, *the* Swallow, *and the* Endeavour*: Drawn up from the Journals which were kept by the several Commanders, And from the Papers of Joseph Banks, Esq.,* 3 vols. (Dublin: Leathley, 1773), 1:561; H. E. Maude *Of Islands and Men* (Melbourne and London: Oxford University Press, 1968), 32; Vanessa Smith, "Pitcairn's Guilty Stock: The Island as Breeding Ground," in Rod Edmond and Vanessa Smith, eds., *Islands in History and Representation* (London: Routledge, 2003), 116–132. Because the latitude of the island was incorrectly recorded in Hawkesworth, the *Bounty* spent a further two months cruising in the vicinity before locating the island.

4. Maude, *Of Islands and Men,* 2; Greg Dening, *Mr Bligh's Bad Language: Passion, Power and Theatre on the* Bounty (Cambridge: Cambridge University Press, 1992), 74.

5. Belcher, Lady Diana Joliffe, *The Mutineers of the* Bounty *and Their Descendants in Pitcairn and Norfolk Islands* (New York: Harper and Brothers, 1870), 145.

6. Edward Edwards and George Hamilton, *Voyage of H.M.S.* Pandora, *despatched to arrest the mutineers of the* Bounty *in the south seas, 1790–1791: being the narratives of Captain Edward Edwards, R.N. the commander and George Hamilton, the surgeon,* ed. Basil Thomson (London: Francis Edwards, 1915), 33.

7. Owen Rutter, "Introduction" to his edition of James Morrison, *The Journal of James Morrison, Boatswain's Mate of the* Bounty, *describing the mutiny and subsequent misfortunes of the mutineers, together with an account of the island of Tahiti* (London: The Golden Cockerel Press, 1935), 6.

8. Morrison in Owen Rutter, ed., *The Court-Martial of the* "Bounty" *Mutineers* (Edinburgh and London: William Hodge, 1931), 166.

9. Douglas Oliver, *Return to Tahiti: Bligh's Second Breadfruit Voyage* (Melbourne : Melbourne University Press, 1988), 75.

10. George Mackaness, ed., *Fresh Light on Bligh, being Some Unpublished Correspondence of Captain William Bligh, R.N., and Lieutenant Francis Godolphin Bond, R.N., with Lieutenant Bond's Manuscript Notes made on the Voyage of H.M.S. 'Providence', 1791–1795* (Sydney: D. S. Ford, 1953), 71, 69.

11. Rolf E. Du Reitz, *Fresh Light on John Fryer of the* "Bounty" (Uppsala: Dahlia Books, c. 1981), 4.

12. John Fryer, *The voyage of the* Bounty*'s launch as related in William Bligh's despatch to the Admiralty and the journal of John Fryer,* ed. Owen Rutter (London: Golden Cockerel Press 1934), 63; for Bligh's launch journal, see John Bach, ed., *The Bligh Notebook: 'Rough Account—Lieutenant Wm Bligh's voyage in the* Bounty*'s Launch from the ship to Tofua & from thence to Timor' 28 April to 14 June 1789 With a draft list of the* BOUNTY *mutineers* (Sydney: Allen and Unwin, 1987).

13. James Wilson, *A Missionary Voyage to the Southern Pacific Ocean, performed in the years 1796, 1797, 1798, in the Ship Duff, commanded by Captain James Wilson* (London: Published for the benefit of the society, printed by S. Gosnell for T. Chapman, 1799; reprinted, with introduction by Irmgard Moschner, New York: Frederick A. Praeger, n.d. [c.1979]), 13–14, xcvii.

14. William Bligh, *A Narrative of the Mutiny, on board his Britannic Majesty's ship* Bounty*: and the subsequent voyage of part of the crew, in the ship's boat, from Tofoa, one of the Friendly Islands, to Timor, a Dutch Settlement in the East-Indies* [1790] (Philadelphia: Printed in Franklin Court, 1977), 9.

15. Owen Rutter, ed., *The Court-Martial of the* "Bounty" *Mutineers* (Edinburgh and London: William Hodge, 1931), 8–9.

16. William Bligh, *A Voyage to the South Sea, undertaken by command of his majesty, for the purpose of conveying the bread-fruit tree to the West Indies, in his majesty's ship the* Bounty, *commanded by Lieutenant William Bligh* (London: George Nicol, 1792; facs. ed. Melbourne: Hutchinson, 1979), 67.

17. Oliver, *Return to Tahiti,* 125.

18. For the Spanish sources, see Bolton Glanvill Corney, trans. and ed., *The Quest and Occupation of Tahiti by the Emissaries of Spain during the years 1772–1776* (London: Hakluyt Society, 1919). William Mariner and a series of other texts are anthologized and discussed in Jonathan Lamb, Vanessa Smith, and Nicholas Thomas, eds., *Exploration and Exchange: A South Seas Anthology, 1680–1900* (Chicago: University of Chicago Press, 2000). The book commonly referred to as "Mariner's Tonga" is John Martin, *An Account of the Natives of the Tonga Islands* (London: Murray, 1818).

19. William Bligh "An Answer to certain Assertions contained in the Appendix to a Pamphlet entitled Minutes of the Proceedings on the Court Martial held at Portsmouth, 12 August 1792, on Ten Persons charged with Mutiny on Board his Majesty's Ship the *Bounty*" (London: G. Nicol, 1794), in William Bligh and Others, *A Book of the* 'Bounty', (London: J. M. Dent and Sons, 1938), 277, 275.

Chapter 1 The Voyage and the Mutiny

1. I.e., to sail before the wind.
2. Drip-stones: a technique for distilling water.
3. I.e., pumpkins.

4. "The people" conventionally referred to ordinary seamen, i.e., those other than officers and supernumeraries. For the complexity of shipboard hierarchies in the period, see N. A. M. Rodger, *The Wooden World* (London: Collins, 1986).

5. Grog: a mix of spirit, such as rum, and water; routinely issued to seamen in the period.

6. Banyan day: a day on which vegetable rations only were provided (the name deriving from the vegetarian nature of some south Asian diets).

7. Bligh, like Cook before him, was purser as well as captain of his ship. Pursers distributed provisions and accounted for expenditures to the Navy Victualling Board. For a detailed discussion of the contradictions involved, and the suspicions aroused, in combining these two roles, see Greg Dening, *Mr Bligh's Bad Language* (New York: Cambridge University Press, 1992), 22–23.

8. This contradicts Bligh's account in his log, where for 9 February 1788 he writes, "This afternoon those who had never crossed the line before underwent the usual ceremony except ducking, which I never would allow for of all the customs it is the most brutal and inhuman." The practice he refers to was ducking from the yardarm, an initiation required of those who had not previously crossed the equator. Instead, the 27 novices of Bligh's crew were tarred and shaved with a piece of iron hoop and required to pay a forfeit in rum.

9. The notoriously difficult and hazardous passage around Cape Horn was famously related by Anson; see George Anson, *A Voyage round the World in the years MDCCXL, I, II, III, IV,* ed. Glyndwr Williams (London: Oxford University Press, 1974 [orig. 1748]), especially chapter 8.

10. Bargoo: oatmeal gruel, a staple of seamen.

11. The specific point underscores the larger issue of the contentious and bad management of provisions. See our Introduction for the centrality of this in Morrison's account of the underlying causes of the mutiny.

12. See again Anson, *A Voyage round the World,* chap. 8.

13. An isolated island in the southern Indian Ocean, approximately halfway between southern Africa and Australia.

14. Adventure Bay, on Bruny Island off the southeast coast of Tasmania, had been previously visited by Bligh in late January 1777, during Cook's third voyage. See J. C. Beaglehole, ed., *The Journals of Captain James Cook* (Cambridge: Hakluyt Society, 1955–1967), 3:50ff., for this visit. The limited contacts Morrison describes are consistent with the cautious engagement of the Tasmanians during that first visit.

15. An indifference or resistance to gifts had previously been noted among Indigenous Australians during Cook's first voyage, for example, and was associated implicitly by Europeans with a lack of curiosity and civility.

16. Advocates of slavery in the period argued that so-called negroes constituted a species distinct from that of other humans; it was claimed that they had "wool" rather than hair; hence the interest here in the nature of indigenous Australian hair, as Tasmanians' skin color led them to be classed with "negroes." For a recent essay concerned in part with racial assessments of Tasmanians by visiting Europeans in the late eighteenth century, see Bronwen Douglas, "The Lure of Texts and the Discipline of Praxis," *Humanities Research* 14 (2007): 11–30.

17. Almost certainly a "hump-backed" man "not less distinguishable by his wit and humour" who was met by Cook on January 29 (refer to Beaglehole, *Journals of Captain James Cook,* 3:54) and is represented in John Webber's drawing of "An Interview between Captain Cook and the natives" (Ministry of Defence, London); reproduced on page 298 in Nicholas Thomas, *Discoveries* (London: Penguin, 2003).

18. This assessment was typical of the period; foraging populations were sometimes evaluated more positively in hot regions, where their apparently simple technologies appeared to be consistent with the exigencies of a warm climate, but were more generally considered miserable and debased in temperate regions. Tierra del Fuegians were similarly denigrated.

19. Bligh's particularly difficult relationship with the Carpenter, William Purcell, was to persist during the launch voyage following the mutiny. The Master, John Fryer, recollects in his own retrospective journal of the voyage an eruption of violence between the pair when the launch made landfall at Sunday Island off the northeast coast of Australia. The argument over an allowance of oysters replayed many of the themes of the build-up to the mutiny. See Fryer, in Owen Rutter, ed., *The voyage of the* Bounty*'s launch* (London: Golden Cockerel Press, 1934), 71.

20. A group of rocky islets south of New Zealand, around 47°44' S, 179°09' E.

21. Me'etia: the easternmost of the Society Islands, 110 km east of Tahiti. It appears to have been politically subordinate to the chiefs of Tahiti's Taiarapu peninsula (Tahiti Iti) and, as Morrison explains, to have been involved in regular trade with both Tahiti and atolls in the Tuamotu archipelago. The first Europeans encountered by the people were the participants in Wallis's voyage, who passed by in June 1767.

22. The precise significance of this is unclear, but *tapa* (barkcloth) was often ritually offered.

23. Bligh's prohibition on sailors bartering for curiosities (shells and birds, but more notably "artificial" curiosities, i.e., indigenous artifacts) drew, like much of his management of the voyage and the encounter, from Cook voyage precedents. On a number of occasions Cook was irritated by his men's passionate interest in

acquiring local specimens; this sometimes led to prices for pigs and other foods rising sharply; he therefore typically banned, or tried to ban, trafficking in objects until such time as he considered the needs for supplies had been met. For a discussion of Bligh's prohibition notice and its relationship to Cook's precedent, see Vanessa Smith, *Intimate Strangers* (Cambridge: Cambridge University Press, 2010), 239–240.

24. The sandy point at the eastern end of Matavai Bay, so named by the British as the site of the observation of the transit of Venus during the *Endeavour*'s visit to Tahiti. Though, as Bligh found, the anchorage was exposed to heavy seas under some conditions, this had become established as the British port of call on the island since Wallis's visit.

25. Thomas Huggan, the ship's surgeon, died of the effects of long-term alcohol abuse. His drunkenness and personal squalor had scandalized and enraged Bligh during the voyage to Tahiti.

26. "Friends" here refers not to casual friendships but to exclusive bond friendships known to European visitors as *taio* relationships. (Morrison describes the ceremonies surrounding such friendship formation in detail in the later part of his account.) Such friendships involved an exchange of names, which identified the parties concerned with one another and entailed a whole series of further exchanges, primarily of goods and services. They also served frequently in the early contact period as a way of negotiating sexual exchanges. A detailed account of the bond and its complex politics can be found in Smith, *Intimate Strangers,* chap. 2.

27. Bittacle: earlier form of "binnacle"— that is, a box on the deck near the helm where the compass is placed.

28. The bank on which the *Dolphin* had struck during the visit of 1767.

29. This name is pronounced Ma-tay, not as the English "mate."

30. Joseph Coleman sailed on both the *Resolution* and the *Discovery* during Cook's third voyage. David Nelson was officially servant to the astronomer William Bayly of the *Discovery,* but had been a Kew gardener and was actually sent out to collect plants for Joseph Banks.

31. The reference to "friends" here is ambiguous: it may be Morrison's euphemistic way of describing sexual relationships, or he may equally be referring again to the *taio* bond.

32. One of the subsidiary aims of Cook's third voyage was to provide the islands of Polynesia with breeding pairs of various domestic animals; see Thomas, *Discoveries,* 344–347.

33. The correct spelling of the name of this local or district chief is uncertain. He must have been of some consequence, otherwise it is unlikely that he would have been given charge of Cook's portrait, but his relationship to other promi-

nent chiefs is not known. He remained a significant figure for at least a few years and is mentioned by Vancouver, among other navigators. He was still in possession of Cook's portrait at the time of his January 1792 visit. George Vancouver, *A Voyage of Discovery to the North Pacific Ocean,* ed. W. Kaye Lamb (London: Hakluyt Society, 1984), 1:399.

34. In September 1777, the high chief Tu, after being drawn himself by John Webber, requested a portrait of Cook in return. He was given one, which was framed, glazed, and presented in a box and which he guarded carefully. The picture was evidently incorporated into his ritual regalia, it was presented and displayed in various contexts—even, as Morrison subsequently describes, set up to receive offerings on *marae* (sacred gathering spaces). It was also shown to a number of visiting captains and, as on this occasion, brought aboard vessels for a period during their stay, as if to incorporate them in the historic relation that had linked the Pomares with Cook and the British. There is no evidence about the size or style of the painting, but Webber produced at least two smaller head-and-shoulders portraits (in the National Portrait Gallery, London, and the Kelton Foundation, Los Angeles), and the work may well have resembled them; see Rüdiger Joppien and Bernard Smith, *The Art of Captain Cook's Voyages* (New Haven, CT: Yale University Press, 1985–1987), 3:649. Here it is stated that the work was last sighted by Vancouver in January 1792 (see previous note), but London Missionary Society sources make it clear that it existed at the time of their arrival in March 1797, if not later; William Wilson, *A Missionary Voyage to the southern Pacific Ocean performed in the years 1796, 1797, 1798* (London: T. Chapman, 1799), 60). It was no doubt destroyed in the period of war that followed.

35. Ma'i, generally known as Omai, was the famous Ra'iatean who joined Cook's second voyage consort, the *Adventure,* and visited England in 1774–1776. He was the first Polynesian to visit England and was much celebrated, painted, and discussed. His voyage seems to have been regarded as a way of securing weapons and authority in order to pursue war with Ra'iatea's enemies in Bora Bora. After returning to Tahiti he established himself at Huahine, but was unable successfully to capitalize on his status as traveller and collector of British prestige objects. The *Bounty* later sought news of him at Huahine, where his death was confirmed. For assessments of Ma'i's legacy, see *Cook and Omai: The Cult of the South Seas* (Canberra: National Library of Australia, 2001).

36. Bligh refers to the leading figures of the Pare-'Arue dynasty, who loomed large in Tahitian politics through the period of early contact with Europeans, and indeed through the first decades of French colonial administration. The Tu referred to at the start of the paragraph, husband of 'Itia, was recognized as a leading chief by Cook; once he was succeeded by his son, he was known (and

referred to by Bligh) as Tina, and he is now conventionally referred to as Pomare I and his son as Pomare II, though both had other names at different stages of their lives. Europeans were perplexed by the Tahitian (and Society Island) practice whereby a high chief was theoretically succeeded by his infant son. This was an aspect of a broader regime of sanctity: since infants and children were closer to the other world than their elders, they were understood to be more *tapu,* and hence outranked their parents. There was, however, a complex set of rites associated with gaining maturity, and others associated with accession to titles. See, among other discussions, Alfred Gell, *Wrapping in Images: Tattooing in Polynesia* (Oxford: Oxford University Press, 1993), 124ff.

37. Society Islanders of high rank were commonly carried in this fashion.

38. By this time Tahitians had seen the effects of guns of various kinds on many occasions, and it appears unlikely that people would be truly "amazed," though it is possible some were, presumably those who had not personally witnessed the use of firearms before.

39. Tetaha is the district immediately west of Pare-ʻArue, known today as Faʻaʻa.

40. Moana was identified by Bligh as "a" chief of Matavai, as opposed to Poeno, who was termed "the" chief of Matavai; Douglas L. Oliver, *Ancient Tahitian Society* (Honolulu: University of Hawaiʻi Press, 1974), 1:156. Ariʻipaea was the brother of Tina (Pomare I). Hitihiti originally hailed from Bora Bora. He had joined the *Resolution*'s crew at Raʻiatea in August 1773, visiting Tonga, New Zealand, the Antarctic, and the Marquesas, but unlike Maʻi decided to remain in Tahiti rather than travel to Britain. There Tu (Pomare I) made him an aide and he married into the Pomare family.

41. It was later understood that this had been a deliberate attempt to scuttle the ship.

42. The brevity of Morrison's reference to the actual project of collecting the breadfruit, so obsessively detailed in Bligh's log, is notable.

43. In this more self-consciously "literary" passage, Morrison is keen to suggest that mutiny was the last thing on the crew members' minds as they departed Tahiti. Such assertions would be designed to militate against Bligh's claim that the mutiny was premeditated, and that connections formed in Tahiti were a significant cause of it.

44. This fleeting visit marked the first European contact with the people of Aitutaki in the southern Cook Islands.

45. I.e., Niue, briefly visited during Cook's second voyage.

46. This recalls experiences of contact during Cook's third voyage, when there was much dispute between Cook and other officers as to how best to deal with the intrepid and incessant appropriation of property by Tongans, who appeared

frequently to be stealing "on commission" for persons of higher rank immune from punishment.

47. The Tongans' oceangoing canoes, which sailed regularly around the archipelago and to Fiji, Samoa, and Niue among other places, were probably the largest and most impressive indigenous vessels sighted by European mariners in the Pacific in the late eighteenth century. Cook, among others, had expressed his admiration for these canoes' capacity for "distant navigation."

48. This observation is certainly indebted to the publication from Anson's voyage; see his *A Voyage round the World,* 306.

49. Considerable numbers of Tongan fishhooks of the kind described were obtained by early collectors. There were various kinds of Tongan barkcloth indeed including types that were varnished and resistant to rain.

50. These ceramics were not made in Tonga but traded from Fiji; this was an aspect of the exchange system that linked the Tongan, Fijian, and Samoan archipelagoes.

51. It is correct that fingers were deliberately amputated in commemoration of deceased relatives. On Tongan tattooing, see Gell, *Wrapping in Images* (Oxford: Clarendon Press, 1993).

52. None of the other accounts corroborates this particular punishment of the chiefs, which would have been an extraordinary breach of respect on Bligh's part.

53. Self-mutilation was a common expression of grief, often manifest in mourning, which caused consternation to European observers; see Vanessa Smith, "Performance Anxieties: Grief and Theatre in European Writing on Tahiti," *Eighteenth-Century Studies* 41, no. 2 (Winter 2008): 149–164. It was not commonly practiced by men.

54. This appears to be a further instance of the type of contention that arose between commander and ordinary seamen concerning the appropriate approach to conflicts with Islanders that marked Cook's third voyage. It is unclear from Morrison's account whether the view was that Bligh should have punished the chiefs more vigorously for their potential complicity in the theft or let the matter drop.

55. The voyage text referred to by Morrison is James Cook and James King, *A voyage to the Pacific Ocean . . . for making Discoveries in the North Hemisphere* (London: W. & A. Strahan for G. Nicol; T. Cadell, 1784).

56. In the Tongan archipelago of Ha'apai.

57. The passage between the northern tip of Australia, Cape York, and Thursday Island in Torres Strait.

58. As Thomas Ellison was to explain at the mutineers' trial: "the meaning of the word is, 'Sillance'"; Owen Rutter, *The Court-Martial of the* Bounty *Mutineers*

(Edinburgh: Hodge, 1931), 175. The fact that Christian expressed insubordination in Tahitian may have been either an attempt at obfuscation or an explicit statement of his allegiance to a new language and way of life.

59. In the dispersed Austral Islands group. This had been sighted by Cook in August 1777 en route to Tahiti during his third voyage. Christian was evidently already thinking of an appropriately remote and obscure place of refuge.

60. It is not clear how many breadfruit plants were disposed of at this point. John Adams later claimed that breadfruit trees remained on board until the *Bounty* arrived at Pitcairn, and were only disposed of once it was found there were established breadfruit plantations on the island. When John Williams visited Rarotonga in 1823, he heard reports of an earlier visit by a vessel they described as "a floating island; that there were two large *taro* plantations, with sugar-cane, bread-fruit, and other trees"; John Williams, *Missionary Enterprises in the South-Sea Islands* (London: John Snow, 1838), 201–202. Williams concludes that the island was visited by the mutineers, "and that the two plantations, bread-fruit trees, etc., were the large boxes which were fitted up throughout the vessel for these exotics."

Chapter 2 The Occupation of Tubuai

1. J. C. Beaglehole, ed., *The Journals of Captain James Cook* (Cambridge: Hakluyt Society, 1955–1967), 3:185: "there was a good anchorage without the reef and a break or opening in it."

2. Tubuai-Rurutu was in fact closely cognate with Tahitian but not identical; see Niko Besnier, "Polynesian Languages," in William Bright, ed., *International Encyclopedia of Linguistics* (New York: Oxford University Press, 1992), 245–251.

3. Morrison is explicit about there being no hogs on Tubuai. Indeed, this lack of ready livestock was the major motivation for the mutineers' return to Tahiti: "Mr. Christian having formd a resolution of settling on this Island, determined to return again as soon as he could procure sufficient stock of Hogs Goats & Poultry of which we Saw None on the Island."

4. The Islanders' response here recalls that of the Tahitians in the course of first contact with Wallis in 1767. If, broadly speaking, Polynesians were open to contact with outsiders and interested in the scope for exchange and alliance, they were nevertheless initially often cautious or hostile, treating visitors as potential invaders until more friendly intentions were plausibly demonstrated.

5. In fact, sinnet cords were an intrinsic component of formal ritual. Bound during the steady recital of chants, they facilitated interaction with gods. The binding of sinnet cords in this scenario likely served as a spiritual safeguard for the Islanders as they approached the unknown quantity of the *Bounty.*

6. Bloody Bay is located in the district of Mata'ura on the northern shore of Tubuai.

7. This most likely resulted from deliberate evasion on the part of the Islanders.

8. Christian had no doubt read John Hawkesworth's account of the voyages of Byron, Wallis, Carteret, and Cook, and imagined that the people of Tubuai could be subdued on the model, as it were, of Wallis's assault on the Tahitians.

9. Mutiny was, of course, a capital offence.

10. This story was obviously prompted by the First Fleet settlement at Port Jackson; the ships had left England in May 1787.

11. I.e., the island in the southern Cooks called at during the *Bounty*'s cruise westward toward Tonga.

12. The extreme reaction of the Tubuaians may have owed more to astonishment than terror given the sheer quantities of hogs that Christian and his crew were landing, which was a clear indication of the potential of the newcomers. If Tubuai had few stocks of their own, we know that on neighboring Rurutu the sacrifice of hogs was certainly a principal feature of ritual (hence its repeated incorporation into significant ritual objects such as whale ivory and bone necklaces and ear ornaments, see Figs. 6 and 7).

13. Morrison's versions of the names of Tubuai individuals have been changed to standard orthography (see Preface), but whereas these are well established for Tahiti, this can only be done more conjecturally for Tubuai, as Morrison appears to be the only extant source for these particular people.

14. We are grateful to Mark Eddowes for establishing that the *marae* likely visited by Christian for this ceremony of welcome and name exchange with Tamatoa would have been *marae* Tonoha'e in Mata'ura (Mark Eddowes, pers. comm., 21 Feb. 2008).

15. During Cook's second voyage, the mariners had learned that Tahitians, Marquesans, and others valued red feathers above virtually all other goods they could offer in trade. Feathers generally were associated with divinity and incorporated into sacred objects of various kinds; red was a *tapu* (taboo) color, and red feathers were especially scarce and sacred. On Cook's third voyage, and on subsequent voyages, it had therefore become common practice to include feathers from England with other goods (nails, mirrors, fabric, etc.) intended for trade with Pacific Islanders.

16. The use of plantain leaves as emblems of peace is well attested in accounts from Tahiti.

17. The fort was constructed on a site in the district of Taahuaia. The English conchologist Hugh Cuming mentions investigating the site during his brief visit to Tubuai in 1828: "The fort built by Fletcher Christian during his short stay on the North part of the Island is overgrown with trees. [. . .] had I not been advised

where to look for it by John Adams when at Pitcairns Island I should not have been able to find it." Hugh Cuming, "Journal of a Voyage from Valparaíso to the Society and Adjacent Islands Performed in the Schooner *Discoverer,* Samuel Grimwood, Master in the year 1827 and 1828," Mitchell Library, State Library of New South Wales, Sydney, CY 194 (A1336); 119–129, 128.

18. There are no relevant subsequent accounts of Tubuai mortuary rites with which to compare this, but the account of ritual grief, cutting, etc., is consistent with practice elsewhere in Polynesia. Mark Eddowes confirms that the *marae* associated with Tahuhuatama and this district is *marae* Pe'etau in Taahuaia (Mark Eddowes, pers. comm., 21 Feb. 2008).

19. The difference in form between European axes and Polynesian adzes probably meant that the technical efficiency of the former was not immediately evident. When Tahitians and others adopted iron axes they typically rehafted them into adze form (with the blade at right angles to the axis of the haft).

20. This presumably refers to the same type of varnishing of *tapa* as was common, for example, in Tonga.

21. No Tubuai god or ancestor figures survive. Complex and dynamic interactions between the islands have made it difficult to plot the precise provenance of much Austral Islands material culture, and Tubuai in particular is very sparsely represented in ethnographic museum collections, its art and material culture poorly described. The class of object most reminiscent of that described by Morrison are the finely carved flywhisks with Janus figures that also incorporate pearl shell, hair, feathers, etc. (Fig. 11). Christian's action on this occasion would indeed have been effective, as god images were appropriated and contested in the course of local warfare. For a recent analysis of complex ritual assemblages produced in the Austral islands, see Maia Jessop [Nuku], "Unwrapping Gods: Encounters with Gods and Missionaries in Tahiti and the Austral Islands, 1797–1830," doctoral thesis, University of East Anglia, 2007.

22. Note that Morrison's original orthography for this woman, the daughter of the Tubuai chief, is Wyakka.

23. Tahitian mourning costumes were extraordinary assemblages made up of intricate woven shell panels, *tapa,* feathers, pearl shell, and various other elements. They had been highly sought after by European visitors from the time of Cook's first visit to Tahiti; see Smith, *Intimate Strangers,* 172–175. Earlier evidence suggests that these costumes were made and used exclusively in mortuary rites, and while it seems somewhat contradictory to read here of their use in entertainment, recent scholarship argues for a much broader understanding of *Arioi* ritual in which entertainment and performance were of course a vital component; Anne Salmond, *Aphrodite's Island: The European Discovery of Tahiti* (Auckland: Viking, 2009), 28–30. Morrison may also have been referring more

specifically to the upper component, the *parae* or mask, which featured large pearl discs fringed dramatically with a spray of red-tipped tropic bird tail feathers.

24. Unsound, shaky.

25. This aspect of Tahitian warfare was not commonly noted, but during his tour with Banks around the island of Tahiti in June–July 1769, Cook did see a set of men's jawbones, very likely trophies of war; Beaglehole, *Journals*, 1:110.

26. I.e., the Bullhead (*Cottus gobio*), but this is a freshwater fish, unlike whatever small coastal species Morrison refers to here.

27. This is probably a reasonable estimate of the population at the time. Estimates from the 1840s range from 300 to 900. Census figures from the second half of the nineteenth century range from approximately 400 to approximately 500; Robert T. Aitken, *Ethnology of Tubuai* (Honolulu: Bishop Museum Press, 1930), 4. It would be consistent with the better documented depopulation trajectories from elsewhere in eastern Polynesia for a population of some 3,000 to be reduced by 75–80% as a result of epidemics, sexually transmitted disease, etc., over the 1780–1850 period.

28. Turmeric: widely used not as a condiment but as a dye of fabric and in self-decoration in Oceania.

29. I.e., pandanus.

30. A posy of flowers.

31. Infanticide was widely practiced in the Society Islands, partly in order to limit the transmission of high rank. Morrison's reference to the people of Tubuai not knowing "Societys" must mean that there was no counterpart to the Tahitian *Arioi* society that he observed or understood existed there; he makes the association because *Arioi* practiced infanticide more or less routinely.

32. Morrison's bold assertion is not grounded in any evidence and is highly unlikely.

33. It is probable that the larger pearl shell discs were traded down to Tubuai from the Tuamotu archipelago and/or Tahiti. Morrison says as much in his "Account of the island of Tahiti and the Customs of the Islanders" when he writes: "the Iron work left at Tahiti is distributed among all the Islands they are acquainted with; in return for which get Pearls, Pearl shells &c.—Some of the Islands they sail to are at the Distance of more than 100 Leagues."

34. Paper mulberry (*Broussonetia papyrifera,* a.k.a. *Morus papyrifera*) was the tree most widely used for making *tapa* across the Pacific, though others such as breadfruit and *ficus* species were also used.

35. In Tahiti by contrast, men's and women's houses were typically separate; however, the practice here of dividing the house has parallels elsewhere in Oceania.

36. Again, these *tapu* restrictions are consistent with those of the Society

Islands, the Marquesas, and elsewhere in eastern Polynesia. Morrison does not make it clear whether women of high rank were exempted, though this may well have been the case.

37. This description makes Tubuai canoes closer to those of Maori than those of the Society Islands, though the basic forms are cognate.

38. I.e., a Nurse shark (*Ginglymostoma cirratum*), though whether this particular species is specifically intended is unclear.

39. The bark fibres of roa (*Urtica Argenta*) were twisted into strands to make cord and lines for fishing nets (see also Appendix IV).

40. This bold statement may derive from Morrison's simply not having seen large oceangoing vessels during his time in Tubuai or from an assumption on his part that the vessels he did see could not manage the vast distances involved in interisland voyaging. Again, while Morrison seems keen to insist on the relative isolation of Tubuai, declaring "nor do they know any thing of [the] Societys," there is no reason to believe that Tubuaian navigational skills would depart markedly from those of the rest of Polynesia.

41. This is an overstatement, though it may well have been the case that agricultural labor was only conspicuously dedicated to taro: other trees and plants such as coconuts, yams, bananas, ʻava, and gourds, were certainly planted and to some extent tended, even if, to a European visitor, they appeared to grow spontaneously.

42. As was noted earlier, this artifact type, described precisely here, is the only sculptural form from Tubuai even moderately well represented in collections. See Thomas, *Oceanic Art* (London: Thames and Hudson, 1995), fig. 126; and Steven Hooper, *Pacific Encounters: Art and Divinity in Polynesia 1760–1860* (London: British Museum Press, 2006), 206–208.

43. It would be more accurate to say that these *marae* differed specifically from the Tahitian type, which typically featured stepped-stone structures; the *marae* of Huahine. among those of other parts of the Society Islands, were made up of flat pavements with upraised stones representing deified ancestors at one (seaward) end, similar to what is described here.

44. *Ti* (*Cordyline fruticosa*) was widely planted throughout Polynesia and had ritual associations.

45. Illness was to be sure, typically understood as the result either of some transgression of *tapu,* wrongdoing, or of sorcery, but the Tubuaian willingness to accommodate the Europeans when they returned may well have been motivated by other considerations, such as a sense that they could make useful allies in local disputes.

46. This observation seems similarly speculative.

47. Mark Eddowes confirms that the Tamatoa, Tahuhuterani, and Tehuhu-

hatama chiefly lines remain to this day in Tubuai and notes that the Hitirere line seems to have been eclipsed at some point during the nineteenth century (Mark Eddowes, pers. comm., 21 Feb. 2008).

48. No doubt forms of rank and status were broadly congruent. The paucity of complementary information makes it more or less impossible to judge whether Morrison might have been correct in considering Tubuai priests more consequential than their Tahitian counterparts.

49. Here Morrison repeats the broad environmentalism characteristic of major strands of thought about human variety in the eighteenth century, influenced particularly by Montesquieu's *Esprit des loix* (1748). Among voyagers who had applied these ideas to the Pacific, Johann Reinhold Forster was most notable, though Morrison is unlikely to have read his scholarly treatise, *Observations made during a voyage round the world* (1778). Morrison's sense that the peoples of the more bountiful tropics might be more indolent and less robust than those of harsher climates is, however, more or less consistent with Forster's more theorized discussion. For a discussion of further hierarchies of labor and indolence within Polynesia as represented in accounts from Cook's voyages, see Harriet Guest, *Empire, Barbarism, and Civilisation: Captain Cook, William Hodges, and the Return to the Pacific* (Cambridge: Cambridge University Press, 2007), 91–123.

50. The question of whether the Pacific Islands were settled from Asia or America has intermittently been controversial, though by this time those who knew insular Southeast Asia either from direct observation or literature recognized cultural and linguistic affinities and hypothesized correctly, as subsequent archaeological and linguistic work has demonstrated, that the islands of Oceania were settled from there. For the most recent overview, see Patrick Vinton Kirch, *On the Road of the Winds: An Archaeological History of the Pacific Islands before European Contact* (Berkeley: University of California Press, 2002). Morrison was however correct to note, as Cook and others had before him, that the languages of the Pacific Islanders he had encountered were closely related.

51. Canoes were commonly driven off course or away from home ports by storm; there are many similar accounts of people reaching islands at a considerable distance, such as those in the Australs or Cooks, alive, and resettling among communities there.

52. Genealogical links between the Austral Islands and Ra'iatea are recorded in the *puta tupuna* of leading Rurutuan family Te Uruari'i, formerly known as Te Manu-ura and noted by Alan F. Seabrook in his unpublished manuscript "Rurutuan Culture" (Honolulu: Bernice P. Bishop Museum, 1938), 17–19. This line of chiefs navigated southwards from Ra'iatea (or Avai'i, as it was then called) to settle in Ra'ivavae, and over the course of generations moved westwards to

Tubuai and from there to Rurutu, planting stones and establishing *marae* with similar names on each island (ibid., 23).

53. This island cannot be obviously identified; the term "Hiva," however, was common in island names of the Marquesas (Nuku Hiva, Hiva Oa, etc.).

54. Though the precise nature of what happened in this case is unclear, Polynesian chiefs commonly were immigrants who somehow managed to usurp local titles. On the broader theme, see Marshall Sahlins, *Islands of History* (Chicago: University of Chicago Press, 1985), chap. 3.

55. Although there is archaeological evidence for cannibalism from parts of eastern Polynesia, and the practice was referred to mythically or attributed by people to the supposedly savage inhabitants of other islands, it was not practiced by people of these archipelagoes at the time of contact with Europeans.

Chapter 3 Return to Tahiti

1. Poeno had also made a *taio* bond with Bligh. Both he and his wife figure in Bligh's logbook as having registered great distress on Bligh's behalf when the *Bounty* was menaced by a storm in Matavai Bay; William Bligh, *The log of the* Bounty: *being Lieutenant William Bligh's log of the proceedings of His Majesty's armed vessel* Bounty *in a voyage to the South Seas, to take the breadfruit from the Society Islands to the West Indies,* ed. Owen Rutter (London: Golden Cockerel Press, 1937), 1:416. Although *taio* bonds seem to have been most often forged between individuals of the same sex, a number were initiated between Europeans and high-ranking women—most famously that between Samual Wallis and Purea during the *Dolphin*'s visit to Tahiti and that between George Tobin and 'Itia during Bligh's second breadfruit expedition. For a detailed discussion of the gender politics of the *taio* relationship, see Vanessa Smith, *Intimate Strangers: Friendship, Exchange, and Pacific Encounters* (Cambridge: Cambridge University Press, 2010), 93–99.

2. The resemblances between friendship and marriage bonds, both in terms of entailments and rituals of initiation, are commented on by Morrison in the *Account* (see Introduction). The capacity of the mutineers' existing *taio* relationships to provide sustenance and shelter, connection and community status, would have doubtless weighed in their internal debates as to whether to remain in Tahiti or seek a more secure destination for settlement.

3. As Oliver notes, this was unusual in the sense that the Taiarapu people were generally hostile to the Pare-'Arue chiefs; he suggests that since Vehiatua was dying, Mate may have been attempting to engineer his son's accession to the Taiarapu titles. Douglas L. Oliver, *Ancient Tahitian Society* (Honolulu: University of Hawai'i Press, 1974), 3:1259.

4. Referred to in Chapter 2.

5. For Cox's fur-trading voyage, see George Mortimer, *Observations and Remarks made during a voyage to the Islands of Teneriffe, Amsterdam, Maria's Islands near Van Diemen's Land; Otaheite, Sandwich Islands . . . in the Brig Mercury* (London: Cadell, Robson and Sewell, 1791). The picture of Cook's death shown to the Islanders must have been a copy of the engraving after John Webber's famous painting, published in 1784 and reprinted in abridged popular editions of the voyages during the 1780s.

6. It was in fact a conventional ritual requirement to strip one's upper body when in the presence of a person of high rank, at least under ceremonial circumstances.

7. This improvisation no doubt typified much modification of Polynesian ritual that occurred over these early decades of contact: practices were compromised and adapted to incorporate the incomprehension, or in this instance lack of cooperation, of Europeans while sustaining the spirit of deference appropriate to the occasion.

8. These variously civil and uncivil dealings and solicitations on the part of rival chiefs of Taiarapu, Papara, and Atehuru reflect their efforts to lure the mutineers into their entourages. The mariners were among the first beachcombers, and their value to locals was as yet undetermined. Though no longer associated with a ship, they still had some stocks of trade goods, and benefited from the prestige associated with Cook, Bligh, and other navigators.

9. I.e., Muslim.

10. We are unable to confirm these details of Brown's biography, though there is nothing implausible, or even atypical for the period, in this checkered maritime career.

11. The "books" are presumably histories of voyages or navigational guides that might have been useful in an escape attempt, though officers often also took literary and other works along on voyages.

12. Thomas Haselden's *Seaman's Daily Assistant* was a navigational guide reprinted regularly by the London maritime publishers Mount and Page from 1761 onward.

13. "The case or cover containing feathers, flocks, or the like, forming a mattress or pillow" (*OED*).

14. No doubt this and the observation made previously regarding Sunday prayers were included in his account to plead Morrison's good character, and indeed his effort to exemplify a civilized Christian life in Tahiti as opposed to a lapsing into the native way of life.

15. The well-known flowering bush or tree *Hibiscus tiliaceus;* see Appendix IV.

16. The term *heiva* was well understood by mariners from the time of Cook's

voyages and used loosely in their accounts to embrace a wide range of performances, entertainments, and rites.

17. Though there is extensive evidence for Cook having been highly regarded by Tahitians, this is an exceptional account in specifically describing his incorporation into Tahitian ritual as the recipient of sacrifice. The question of Cook's worship, apotheosis, or deification has been contentious in the Hawaiian context; see Gananath Obeyesekere, *The Apotheosis of Captain Cook: European Mythmaking in the Pacific* (Princeton, NJ: Princeton University Press, 1992), and Marshall Sahlins, *How "Natives" Think, About Captain Cook for Example* (Chicago: University of Chicago Press, 1995). If Morrison could not have been mistaken about what he observed, and very likely understood correctly what he had heard, the motivation for the practice here may be clearer and less controversial: Cook was closely associated with the Pare-'Arue chiefs and with Pomare I (here called Mate) in particular; his representation as a chief was above all an appropriation that served primarily to aggrandize those seen as his local allies.

18. This unwrapping or divestment of *tapa* (and here mats) was formalized; it typically marked the culmination of ceremonies of this kind. See Serge Tcherkezoff, "On Cloth, Gifts, and Nudity: Regarding Some European Misunderstandings during Early Encounters in Polynesia," in Chloe Colchester, ed., *Clothing the Pacific* (Oxford: Berg, 2003), 51–75.

19. At least one Polynesian man had been punished for theft in this manner during Cook's third voyage, though in Tonga rather than Tahiti.

20. It would not in fact be surprising if by this time the mutineers, or at least those of them with any linguistic facility, were well advanced in their grasp of Tahitian. During the first sojourn, communication would have been facilitated by the prior knowledge of those who had participated in Cook's voyages, such as Bligh himself, and mutineers may have had access to word lists from previous voyages. They themselves had gained exposure during the breadfruit-collecting stay, and had also benefited from some three months spent among speakers of a closely related language on Tubuai.

21. This was very likely an *Arioi* group. Morrison discusses the society in detail in Chapter 7.

22. This solicitation certainly reflected the long-standing political antagonism between two major groups, the Teva-i-tai (sometimes referred to as the "Seaward Tevas") of Tahiti Iti, the eastern peninsula, and the Teva-i-Uta (the "Landward Tevas"), around the south and west of the main part of the island. The Vaitepiha valley and district, led at this time by the chief, Vehiatua, were preeminent within the former group; he no doubt wished to bring some of the mutineers to his party.

23. This paragraph is written on the verso of the previous page.

24. The best commentary upon these events is Oliver, *Ancient Tahitian Society,* vol. 3, chap. 28. A series of conflicts and machinations tended to strengthen the position of the Pomares over the period, though in no final or conclusive fashion.

25. "Inspired priest" refers to a *taura* or shaman, not the "official priest" or *tahu'a,* who had probably inherited his position and was identified with a specific *marae* where he conducted rites. *Taura* were inspired individuals who might prophesy, but could be loose cannons relative to the interests of chiefs and the established order.

26. Maititi was one of four Tahitians who joined the Spanish captain Domingo de Boenechea, who had spent six weeks at Tahiti Iti in late 1773. Of the four, two died; the survivors, Maititi and Pautu, were repatriated in November 1774. On the same voyage Boenechea established Catholic fathers, who failed to establish any rapport with the Tahitians; when a supply ship arrived twelve months later, they insisted upon being taken on board and returned to Peru. See Bolton Glanvill Corney, *The Quest and Occupation of Tahiti by the Emissaries of Spain* (London: Hakluyt Society, 1913–1919).

27. Over this period Pomare II made a series of challenges to his father's authority, which in due course led to the substantial consolidation of his own power yet created enduring contention that was not decisively resolved until 1815, by which time he had converted to Christianity. See C. W. Newbury, *The History of the Tahitian Mission 1799–1830* (Cambridge: Hakluyt Society, 1961). The editor's introduction provides a useful overview of events of the 1790s and early nineteenth century.

28. I.e., a killick, a type of anchor.

29. By claiming that the vessel had been named after Cook's Royal Navy sloop, Morrison seeks to legitimate his claim that the boat-building project was one of innocent men trying to make their way home, rather than mutineers seeking to evade capture. Bligh had served as sailing master on the *Resolution* on Cook's third voyage.

30. The "maro of the god." *Maro* have been referred to as feather girdles or sashes. They were fabric and feather assemblages, crucial in Tahitian politics as repositories of power and sanctity, but more specifically important as bearers of legitimate chiefly paramountcy. The *maro 'ura* (red sash) was of particular significance for its associations with the 'Oro cult, and it was possession of this *maro* that exemplified the ascendancy of the Pomares during the late decades of the eighteenth century. The *maro* referred to here cannot have been one of these high chiefly *maro,* but a lesser form of more local significance.

31. These conflicts are traced in Oliver, *Ancient Tahitian Society,* chap. 28.

32. "Each would have his man": i.e., each of the warriors would have a corpse to offer up at the *marae.*

33. I.e., the vanguard.

34. Taputapuatea is the famous *marae* complex central to the 'Oro cult on the island of Ra'iatea. What is referred to here is what is known as a "portable" or "moveable" *marae,* a feathered woven god image that would have been transported inside a carved wooden house, though this *fare atua,* or god house, would itself normally have been kept within *marae* precincts. Mate (Pomare I) had lost control of these crucial exemplifications of sovereignty to the Atehuru people and sought the assistance of the mutineers in his attempt to retrieve them. Like Cook before him and the missionaries after him, Morrison writes as though the Pomares were legitimate sovereigns periodically challenged or displaced by rebels or usurpers such as, in this case, the Atehuru. This was false. All of these chiefly parties, and the districts they represented, were vying for power, although the misconception was, needless to say, one in which both Pomares were willing to collude.

35. This is not the place for an extended analysis of Tahitian warfare, but it is important to note, first, that it clearly possessed a strong performative dimension—warriors appeared en masse, in great finery, and made challenges—and, second, that the basic nature of Tahitian fighting was undergoing a change from sea-based engagements between canoe fleets to land-based skirmishes that were often more destructive, not least to opponents' food crops, which were typically ravaged by the victors.

Chapter 4 From Tahiti to England

1. The name may be generic, referring to his age and status, as "pa" was an honorific, a term of respect for a chief or person of higher rank.

2. The decisive victory of the Porionu'u and Paparans, secured with the support of the mutineers, represented a key moment in the consolidation of the power of Pomare II and was here marked by the surrendering of key sacred objects: the *maro* that incorporated Wallis's pennant and the god house ("ark") that would have contained the 'Oro image. These were key emblems and foundations of "pre-eminent rank status," and their appropriation enabled Pomare II to conduct sacrifices within his own territory. See Douglas L. Oliver, *Ancient Tahitian Society* (Honolulu: University of Hawai'i Press, 1974), 3:1265–1266.

3. The intention seems to have been to undertake a short trial voyage to the Tetiaroa atolls, where a small population specialized in fishing for trade with the main island.

4. In this respect, Bligh was following Cook in understanding the introduction of breeding pairs of useful species to the islands as a highly important expres-

sion of British benevolence; cf. Jennifer Newell, *Trading Nature: Tahitians, Europeans, and Ecological Exchange* (Honolulu: University of Hawai'i Press, 2010).

5. Here as elsewhere Morrison uses "landed men" to gloss the Tahitian *ra'atira;* anthropologists and historians have followed him and other early European observers in seeing the independent ownership of property as the defining characteristic of this middle stratum between the common people and the aristocrats, though it is likely that their rights to land were embedded, as they were to some degree virtually everywhere in Polynesia, in several layers of practical-use rights and in higher-level sovereignty associated with ritual precedence. The details of these conceptions and their practical effect are not fully apparent from the historical sources, which are clearly distorted by European assumptions about forms of tenure and property in land.

6. November to around March is not only the wet but also the cyclone season in the South Pacific.

7. The preceding passage is of considerable significance for being the only detailed report of the life and fate of Ma'i (Omai), who travelled to England with Captain Furneaux in the *Adventure,* Cook's consort during his second voyage, after his return to the Society Islands. Ma'i's primary motivation for travelling appears to have been to secure the support of Britain in local conflicts. His attendant's suggestion that opponents were always in awe of him, and that his military efforts were effective, is not generally supported. He was in fact of relatively low social status and was unable to capitalize upon his foreign experiences and travels. The precise nature of the illness that killed him, *hotate,* is not known. The Maori who resided with him, Te Weherua and Koa, had joined the *Resolution* at Queen Charlotte Sound in February 1777 and had elected to remain in the Society Islands rather than continue the voyage. Among works that discuss his life and the Society Islands context are E. H. McCormick, *Omai: Pacific Envoy* (Auckland: Auckland and Oxford University Presses, 1977), and Anne Salmond, *Aphrodite's Island: The European Discovery of Tahiti* (Auckland: Viking, 2009).

8. This investiture followed the military victory in which the mutineers had played a critical part. It is important to note that while Pomare II's precedence was secured in principle, tension, uncertainty, and outright conflict would mark Tahitian politics for many subsequent years.

9. These were routine entertainments at festive occasions and were depicted by several of the Cook voyage artists.

10. This exemplifies both the sense in which *tapu* worked as contagious sacredness—objects associated with people of particularly high rank and sanctity were dangerous to others—and the manner in which Europeans were frequently exempted, or partially exempted, from this regime. Tahitians appear to have been

ready to "bracket off" dealings with foreigners from the cosmological principles that underpinned their own social interactions.

11. Here the flag obtained from the *Mercury* was treated in a manner analogous to the indigenous flags (*reva*) that accompanied chiefly processions and ritual circuits of the land: these were occasions for the testing and affirmation of sovereignty. The most informative account of the use and significance of these flags in pre-European contact Tahiti can be found in Oliver, *Ancient Tahiti,* 185–186:

> On the same day that the marae ceremonies were performed [marking the birth of a chiefly child], messengers called *arere* or *ti'ati'a-vea,* were despatched in opposite directions to officially announce the birth and well-being of the child. Each messenger bore above his head a flag, generally torn off from red marae cloth, called *reva hahae* (flags torn), in honor of which when they were leaving a human sacrifice . . . was offered and buried at the national marae.
>
> . . The flag was set up on the assembly ground of each district of the kingdom as the messenger passed, and there the people were summoned. . . . When the news was well received by the people they allowed the flag to stand until taken by the messenger but when the news was displeasing, the flag was torn down by order of the chief and gentry, the pole to which it was attached was broken, and the messenger was returned to his master with a challenge to settle the matter in war—a circumstance that sometimes happened in newly conquered possessions, when people still hoped to recover their liberty.

Given that fabrics were seen as vehicles for sanctity within Polynesia, there was considerable congruence between the European flag as a symbol of political sovereignty and Tahitian interests in sacred fabric expressions of high status and political preeminence. There are references to Pomare II's flag in accounts from Vancouver's visit of December 1791–January 1792.

12. The paramount importance of the *maro* in Tahitian politics has been discussed by most scholars of the islands' politics over this period; for a recent account, see Salmond, *Aphrodite's Island,* 26. This passage is interesting for the suggestion that a feathered woven headdress or sunshade was also a vital element of the regalia. No Tahitian example appears to have survived, but counterparts from the Austral Islands can be found in a number of collections; see Steven Hooper, *Pacific Encounters: Art and Divinity in Polynesia, 1760–1860* (London: British Museum Press, 2006), 215.

13. Though Cook, too, witnessed human sacrifice during his final visit to Tahiti, this is one of the few eyewitness accounts of rites of this type, described by many later ethnographers only on the basis of recollections or secondhand reports. Some sense of the cosmological context is provided by Teuira Henry,

Ancient Tahiti (Honolulu: Bishop Museum, 1928), especially 196ff.; for a synthesis of information, see Oliver, *Ancient Tahitian Society,* 1:90–92. In the Hawaiian context, Valerio Valeri's major study, *Kingship and Sacrifice* (Chicago: University of Chicago Press, 1985), offers an extended analysis informed by the classic French anthropological studies.

14. For commentary on these political contests and developments, see Oliver, *Ancient Tahitian Society,* vol. 3, chap. 28; and Anne Salmond, *Bligh: William Bligh in the South Seas* (Berkeley: University of California Press, 2011), chaps. 13 and 14.

15. This attests again to the appropriation of the flag within the local ritual economy and to the diversity of Tahitian feather garments and accoutrements—all expressive of sanctity and political authority. These took various forms, though the precise nature of the "cloak" and "garland" referred to here is unclear. *Metua* refers generally to parents or progenitors and in this context is presumably a term of deference, implying that the addressee is generationally senior, not specifically that he is an "uncle."

16. As Morrison soon realized, this was the *Pandora,* which had been sent in pursuit of the mutineers, sailing from Portsmouth in November 1790.

17. For the account of the mutineers' capture from the naval perspective, see Edward Edwards and George Hamilton, *Voyage of H.M.S.* Pandora, *despatched to arrest the mutineers of the* Bounty *in the south seas, 1790–1791: being the narratives of Captain Edward Edwards, R.N. the commander and George Hamilton, the surgeon,* ed. Basil Thomson (London: Francis Edwards, 1915), especially 30–37 and 102–107.

18. Dutch gin.

19. Morrison goes on to explain the practice whereby women cut their foreheads with sharks' teeth or shells in token of grief. This was one of the most commented upon of Tahitian rituals, noted for its combination, to European eyes, of gruesomeness and nonchalance. For a discussion of the ways in which female cutting rites caused European observers to reflect on the relationship between surface and deep sentiment, see Vanessa Smith, "Performance Anxieties: Grief and Theatre in European Writing on Tahiti," *Eighteenth-Century Studies* 41 (2008): 149–164.

20. The *Pandora*'s travels from this point until the departure from Nomuka on 2 August were in fruitless quest of the *Bounty* and its crew of remaining mutineers. Harry Maude reconstructs the likely trajectory of the *Bounty*'s voyage to Pitcairn in the first chapter of his foundational work of Pacific scholarship, *Of Islands and Men* (London: Oxford University Press, 1968), entitled "In Search of a Home." Maude's reconstruction depends heavily on two published accounts by a Tahitian woman Tihuteatuaonoa, known as "Jenny," one of nineteen women,

a female child, and six men—three from Tahiti, two from Tubuai, and one from Ra'iatea—who were abducted by the *Bounty.* See Teehuteatuaonoa (Jenny) (1819) [Narrative I], *Sydney Gazette,* 17 July, and Teehuteatuaonoa (Jenny) (1829) [Narrative II], *United States Service Journal,* 589–593.

21. Compare "Captain Edwards' reports," in Edwards and Hamilton, *Voyage of H.M.S. Pandora,* ed. Basil Thomson (London: Francis Edwards, 1915), 38–39.

22. Compare "Captain Edwards' reports," in Edwards and Hamilton, *Voyage of H.M.S. Pandora,* 43: "the tender joined us that night and informed me that she had found a yard on the island marked 'Bounty's Driver Yard' and other circumstances that indicated that the *Bounty* was, or had been there."

23. The footnotes to the 1915 edition refer to this as Savaii in the Samoa Islands; Edwards and Hamilton, *Voyage of H.M.S. Pandora,* 49.

24. Compare "Captain Edwards' reports," in Edwards and Hamilton, *Voyage of H.M.S. Pandora,* 52–53.

25. 2 August in Edwards.

26. Edwards's account of the wreck is at Edwards and Hamilton, *Voyage of H.M.S. Pandora,* 72–75, and is notable for the fact that it makes no mention whatsoever of the prisoners. The notes to the 1915 edition cite an account ascribed to Second Lieutenant Robert Corner that substantiates Morrison's, but further claims that all four of the prisoners who died were still manacled. The source of the account is not given, however, and the same level of detail is not to be found in Corner's testimony at the trial of the mutineers; Owen Rutter, ed., *The Court-Martial of the* "Bounty" *Mutineers* (Edinburgh and London: William Hodge, 1931), 134–135.

27. Meaning unclear: possibly "transferred to a beaker [or other container]?"

28. Bali Strait, a 2.4-kilometer strait between the islands of Bali and Java.

29. The *Gorgon,* under the command of John Parker, had arrived in Port Jackson on 21 September 1791 with the third fleet, bringing much needed provisions to the starving colony. The ship departed Port Jackson on 18 December 1791. As well as the surviving prisoners of the *Pandora,* at the Cape of Good Hope the *Gorgon* took on board the contingent of escaped convicts that included Mary Bryant and her husband, William. Their remarkable open-boat voyage of 66 days from Port Jackson to Kupang is comparable to Bligh's open-boat voyage following the mutiny.

Chapter 5 The Tahitian World

1. The modern determination of Point Venus's location is latitude 17° 28' 12" S., longitude 149° 29' 48" W.

2. The first of Morrison's figures, for the circumference of Tahiti Nui, is close to the mark: the correct distance is around 120 km (74.6 miles); he underesti-

mates the circumference of Tahiti Iti, which is approximately 65 km, or just over 40 miles.

3. Orohena, at 2,441 meters, is the highest mountain in Tahiti.

4. These and the broader geographic description that follows are broadly accurate. For further information, see Douglas L. Oliver, *Ancient Tahitian Society* (Honolulu: University of Hawai'i Press, 1974), vol. 1, chap. 2; and, for a recent discussion embracing environment and archaeology in Polynesia generally, Patrick Vinton Kirch, *On the Road of the Winds: An Archaeological History of the Pacific Islands before European Contact* (Berkeley: University of California Press, 2000).

5. Here it is clear that Morrison had, at some point, read Hawkesworth's account of the voyages of Wallis, Byron, Carteret, and Cook in the *Endeavour.* In June 1769, Cook and his companions were favorably impressed with dog prepared in an earth oven; see John Hawkesworth, *An account of the voyages undertaken by the order of his present Majesty for making discoveries in the southern hemisphere* (Dublin: Leathley, 1773), 2:170–171. However, the comparison with English lamb is Morrison's, not Hawkesworth's, and neither this passage nor others where Morrison makes observations analogous to those in the voyage sources suggest either that he had Hawkesworth, or any other work, before him as he wrote, or that any earlier published text was fresh in his mind.

6. Of these animals, rats, pigs, dogs, and chickens were introduced by the early Polynesian settlers, but by 1790 the local varieties may have been altered by breeds brought there by Cook and other visitors. Goats and cats were introduced, as were cattle, at first less successfully.

7. For identifications of these species, where we are able to provide them, see Appendix IV. Morrison's observations on the useful Tahitian flora are generally accurate and consistent with more detailed and more scientific later studies. For a short survey, see J. Barrau, *Useful Plants of Tahiti* (Paris: Société des Océanistes, 1971).

8. I.e., *tapa* beaters.

9. "Pandanus" is in fact the Linnean name for the genus; its name derives from Malay rather than from any south Asian language; and it was in the East Indies rather than any part of India that this widely used plant is likely to have been first encountered by Europeans.

10. Jalap: a cathartic medication derived from plants of the Ipomoea genus, introduced into Europe from Mexico.

11. I.e., a gill, five fluid ounces or approximately 142 ml.

12. The three voyages of the Spanish to Tahiti between 1772 and 1776, under the command of Domingo de Boenechea and Lángara y Huarte. They are summarized in O. H. K. Spate, *Paradise Lost and Found* (Canberra: Australian

National University Press, 1988), 122–126; Bolton Glanvill Corney, trans. and ed., *The Quest and Occupation of Tahiti by the Emissaries of Spain during the Years 1772–1776* (London: Hakluyt Society, 1913–1919).

13. Some of these are well-known species; in other cases Morrison is transferring names in common use in England to approximate Pacific equivalents, which we are unable to identify specifically. For a broad guide, see Raymond Bagnis, Philippe Mazellier, Jack Bennett, and Erwin Christian, *Poissons de Polynésie* (Pape'ete: Les Éditions du Pacifique, 1972).

14. The inhabitants of the atolls of Tetiaroa were primarily engaged in fishing for trade with Tahiti, and some appear to have been dependents of chiefly families to whom they supplied fish.

15. This is accurate in the sense that there were no markets in Tahiti, nor was there systematic barter; though in addition to major presentations of goods such as cloth, there were no doubt more casual give-and-take arrangements at the local level. The manner in which quantities of barkcloth and other major products such as canoes could be commissioned, is described in Chapter 7.

16. The information provided here by Morrison is more detailed than that in any other early source. For general accounts of *tapa* (barkcloth) in the Pacific, see Nicholas Thomas, *Oceanic Art* (London: Thames and Hudson, 1995), Roger Neich and Mick Pendergrast, *Pacific Tapa* (Auckland: David Bateman, 1997).

17. The barkcloth collected from Tahiti during Cook's voyages was decorated only by staining and by the printing of circular motifs made with the ends of cut sections of bamboo. By the time of the *Bounty*'s visit, however, a fashion for using the leaves of plants as stencils had emerged, possibly stimulated by fabrics featuring botanical motifs possessed or traded by the voyagers. See Peter Brunt et al., *Art in Oceania: A History* (London: Thames and Hudson, 2012). This must be among the earliest references to this innovation.

18. A large woven pandanus sail from Tahiti is extant in the collections of the British Museum (Oc1999,Q.139) See Tara Hiquily, Jenny Newell, Monique Pullan, Nicole Rode, and Arianna Bernucci, *Sailing through History: Conserving and Researching a Rare Tahitian Canoe Sail* (London: British Museum Technical Research Bulletin, 2009).

Chapter 6 Tahitian Society, History, and Culture

1. Modern scholarship would broadly agree with this division of Tahitian districts or peoples and their political alignments. It perforce agrees because Morrison is the single most important early source for these divisions and allegiances, though on most points his account is consistent with both the more limited information presented in the various Cook voyage sources and the missionary

accounts of the social relationships from the late 1790s on. However, there is a basic distortion that most European commentators reproduced: the imputation that Pomare I and II were legitimate rulers of the island as a whole, against whom some districts "rebelled." To the contrary, the Pomares sought and eventually secured an unprecedented degree of preeminence; they were attempting to create a new kind of polity, not reestablishing an accepted order that had been challenged.

2. This account of Tahitian social strata has been generally accepted by modern scholars such as Douglas Oliver (*Ancient Tahitian Society* [Honolulu: University of Hawai'i Press, 1974])—again because Morrison offered the earliest detailed account. It is broadly accurate, in that most evidence suggests that the statuses referred to were related in more or less the way Morrison describes, but his European feudal comparisons are obviously only approximate and relative. Political affiliations and relationships of dominance and dependency were flexible, opportunistic, and based on a range of links, through both men and women, to a greater extent than is often acknowledged.

3. This striking feature of Society Islands rank and succession perplexed many observers and commentators but was a logical consequence of a notion of *tapu*—namely, that a child had newly emerged from the other world and therefore carried sacredness to a greater degree, or with greater intensity, than any mature person.

4. While a range of eighteenth-century commentators took Tahitians to be more polished or refined than most indigenous peoples of Oceania, this suggestion that they were devoid of any "tincture" of "barbarity" is unusually categorical. On the broader theme of European adjudications of Pacific peoples in the period, see the introductory essays to Johann Reinhold Forster, *Observations Made during a Voyage round the World,* N. Thomas, H. Guest, and M. Dettelbach, eds. (Honolulu: University of Hawai'i Press, 1996); and Harriet Guest, *Empire, Barbarism, and Civilisation: Captain Cook, William Hodges, and the Return to the Pacific* (Cambridge: Cambridge University Press, 2007).

5. This classicism was a major theme of Pacific travel commentary and visual art of the period; see Bernard Smith, *European Vision and the South Pacific,* 2nd ed. (London: Yale University Press, 1985).

6. This estimate is considerably below those made during Cook's voyages. See, for example, Forster, *Observations Made during a Voyage round the World,* 148–150, which gave 141,750 for Tahiti and Mo'orea; Cook himself proposed over 200,000. These figures, like those for the contact-period populations of other Pacific islands, have been highly controversial: historical demographers have generally argued for lower numbers, while archaeologists have typically considered higher figures appropriate. For a recent set of studies, see Patrick Vinton

Kirch and Jean-Louis Rallu, eds., *The Growth and Collapse of Pacific Island Societies* (Honolulu: University of Hawai'i Press, 2007).

7. It is important to understand that Morrison is referring not to a customary approach to warfare but to strategies that were undergoing fundamental change: "the character of Tahitian warfare had altered since the last great naval battle of 1771: manoeuvres in large fleets of canoes off the coast had given place to deadly skirmishes by land and widespread devastation of property"; C. W. Newbury, "Introduction," in C. W. Newbury, ed., *The History of the Tahitian Mission, 1799–1830, Written by John Davies* (Cambridge: Hakluyt Society, 1961), xli–xlii.

8. These seven or so paragraphs dealing with Tahitian religious beliefs are, from the perspective of the historical anthropologist or scholar of indigenous religion, the most problematic in Morrison's text and in fact amount to virtually the only section of his account in which his understanding of indigenous culture has to be considered badly scrambled. The reasons are twofold and obvious: first is that beliefs of this nature are harder than anything else for an outsider, even a linguistically competent one, to understand properly; and second, that he took for granted underlying affinities with Christian (and, as he understood them, classical) beliefs. Morrison's construction of a quasi Trinity is gratuitous, and on other points there is a mixture of observations that are in all likelihood sound (the soul being understood as travelling during a dream, for example) and others that are dubious (each person having a particular "Guardian Angel"). That said, it is not easy to reconstruct Society Islands religion in an authoritative manner. It is well understood that these beliefs were not static but were undergoing change prior to European contact. For the early contact period, the primary sources are fragmented and complex; looming large among them are the papers of LMS missionaries such as J. M. Orsmond, which are rich but reflect inquiries made when beliefs were changing further, were being challenged, or had indeed been repudiated. Orsmond's papers form the basis of Teuira Henry's highly important but historiographically problematic *Ancient Tahiti* (Honolulu: Bishop Museum, 1928). More recent studies include Alain Babadzan, *Les Dépouilles des dieux. Essai sur la religion tahitienne à l'époque de la découverte* (Paris: Éditions de la Maison des Sciences de l'Homme, 1993), and Alfred Gell, *Wrapping in Images: Tattooing in Polynesia* (Oxford: Clarendon Press, 1993), chapter 3 of which deals with cosmology and *tatau* in the Society Islands.

9. Morrison gives "fwhatoe," possibly an approximation of "oeahou," which Davies translates as "a young comer; a young person just come to age"; John Davies, *Tahitian and English dictionary . . .* (Tahiti: LMS Press, 1851), 158.

10. This term has historic senses referring to special times of emancipation,

indulgence, or repentance; Morrison somewhat confusingly applies it to the prohibition on the use of certain resources rather than to the feast that follows the lifting of the prohibition.

Chapter 7 Arts, Rites, and Customs

1. As Morrison observes, *marae* were the principal built structures of the Tahitian environment. They loomed large in terms of sheer visibility, as they did in their ritual and sociopolitical importance, and from the earliest observations Europeans recognized their importance. They were systematically studied from the early twentieth century onward by Bishop Museum researchers; see, for example, Kenneth P. Emory, *Stone Remains in the Society Islands* (Honolulu: Bishop Museum, 1933). An interesting recent study, which incorporates a literature review, is Jennifer G. Kahn, "A Spatio-temporal Analysis of ʻOro Cult *Marae* in the Opuʻnohu Valley, Moʻorea, Society Islands," *Archaeology in Oceania* 45 (2010): 103–110.

2. For a recent discussion of customary architecture, see Catherine Orliac, *Fare Tahiti: Habitat traditionnel de Polynésie* (Marseille: Parenthèses, 2000).

3. What is being referred to here is unclear. To our knowledge, the Tahitian material culture repertoire included no sort of large storage chest; but neither does it seem especially likely that chests would have been given away in trade by mariners.

4. Sharkskin, not fish skin, was used as sandpaper in carpentry.

5. This comparison with Australian implements presumably was prompted by Morrison's observations of Tasmanian technology in the course of the voyage out.

6. I.e., gunwale.

7. This is significant in that it implies that Tahitians seldom sailed to islands *more than* "100 leagues" away. This distance is equivalent to 300 U.S. nautical miles, or about 555 kilometers. Parts of the Tuamotu archipelago are well within this range, but the Marquesas, which are some 1,500 km north and east of Tahiti, are well beyond it. The growing interest in Polynesian voyaging over recent decades has led to assumptions that long-distance two-way voyaging between such archipelagos was common in the late pre-contact period. Though a great deal of interisland sailing took place, particularly within island groups, Morrison does not substantiate the claim that regular, longer-distance expeditions took place.

8. Tapuhoe, a small atoll in the Tuamotu archipelago close to the neighboring, larger island of Takapoto, which is generally taken to be the island off which *De Africaansche Galey* wrecked (see n. 9).

9. *De Africaansche Galey* was wrecked on the windward side of Takapoto

in May 1722. See Andrew Sharp, ed., *The Journal of Jacob Roggeveen* (Oxford: Oxford University Press, 1970), 120–124; and Hank Driessen, "Outriggerless Canoes and Glorious Beings: Pre-contact Prophesies in the Society Islands," *Journal of Pacific History* 17 (1982): 17, n. 83.

10. There is a substantial and important literature around traditional navigation in Polynesia, which since the 1970s has been revived through voyages such as those of the Hawaiian voyaging society canoe, the *Hokule'a.* See Ben Finney et al., *Voyage of Rediscovery: A Cultural Odyssey through Polynesia* (Berkeley: University of California Press, 1994), and Finney, "Traditional Navigation and Nautical Cartography in Oceania," in G. Malcolm Lewis and David Woodward, eds., *The History of Cartography,* vol. 3, part 2: *Cartography in Traditional African, American, Arctic, Australian and Pacific Societies* (Chicago: University of Chicago Press, 1998), 443–492.

11. While no large Tahitian canoe is extant either in the islands or in any museum collection, smaller dugouts with simple outriggers, often around 12–15 feet in length and without sails, are still used for subsistence fishing in many parts of the Society Islands and may be seen, for example, on the beach around Point Venus. Though the techniques employed in their construction have obviously been modernized, they are basically not different in their nautical architecture to the smaller ordinary boats of their owners' eighteenth-century ancestors. For an early twentieth-century review, see E. S. C. Handy, *Houses, Boats and Fishing in the Society Islands* (Honolulu: Bishop Museum, 1932).

12. I.e., fastened with a rope or string.

13. This gives a useful indication of how labor was mobilized through relationships and reciprocity toward major projects such as the building of canoes.

14. This account of the selection and procurement of victims, and the conduct of human sacrifice, is fully consistent with but more detailed than other accounts such as Cook's eyewitness report from the beginning of September 1777: see J. C. Beaglehole, *The Journals of Captain James Cook on His Voyages of Discovery* (Cambridge: Hakluyt Society, 1955–1967), 3:198–205; or Bligh's, from the voyage of the *Providence:* see the journal entry for 12 July 1792 in Douglas L. Oliver, *Return to Tahiti: Bligh's Second Breadfruit Voyage* (Melbourne: Melbourne University Press, 1988), 230–232.

15. These paragraphs outline restrictions associated with *tapu,* contagious sacredness. The Polynesian category was introduced into European languages as "taboo," and variants have loomed large in anthropological theories as well as through Sigmund Freud's discussion in his book *Totem and Taboo* (many editions, but originally published in German in 1913). This history of ideas is beyond the scope of this edition, but it is important to understand that the Polynesian cosmologies that stimulated the theoretical "problem" were misrecognized

in various ways. In the 1980s, work by F. Allan Hanson, Hank Driessen, and Nicholas Thomas argued for an understanding related to the need to control the empowering but dangerous sacred power that emanated from other worlds. For an overview, see Caroline Ralston, "Introduction," in "Sanctity and Power: Gender in Polynesian History" (special issue), *Journal of Pacific History* 22 (1987): 115–122. This line of argument was taken further by Alfred Gell in the context of tattooing; see chapter 3 in his *Wrapping in Images: Tattooing in Polynesia* (Oxford: Clarendon Press, 1993).

16. Though Gananath Obeyesekere's arguments concerning cannibalism in the Pacific as colonialist fantasy are overstated and problematic, he is certainly right to see "cannibal talk" as a space of cross-cultural rhetoric involving fearful and hostile identifications of others as cannibals, certainly made by Islanders with respect to Europeans as well as vice versa. See Obeyesekere, *Cannibal Talk: The Man-Eating Myth and Human Sacrifice in the South Seas* (Berkeley: University of California Press, 2005).

17. *Sic;* probably a contraction of "tint and colour."

18. The event is referred to in J. C. Beaglehole, ed., *The* Endeavour *Journal of Joseph Banks 1768–1771* (Sydney: Public Library of New South Wales / Angus and Robertson, 1962), 1:345: "No one except the people employed by them [the 'old women' engaged in the preparation of *mahi*] is allowed to come even into that part of the house where it is; I myself spoild a large heap of it only by inadverten[t]ly touching some leaves that lay upon it as I walkd by the outside of the house where it was." This is the basis of a passage in John Hawkesworth (*An Account of the Voyages . . .* [Dublin: Leathley, 1773], 2:221–222), which would of course have been Morrison's source, rather than Banks' manuscript. The rendering of the incident suggests that this was indeed most likely a case of recollection rather than access to the book: Banks' trespass was not in fact prompted by curiosity. The text states that as a result of the mishap, he got to see the pit in which the paste was prepared, which would not otherwise have been visible to him.

19. First-fruits rites were important across much of Polynesia. For a magisterial ethnographic description, albeit one dealing with a Polynesian outlier culture very different to that of Tahiti, see Raymond Firth, *The Work of the Gods in Tikopia* (London: Athlone, 1967).

20. Morrison makes the high valuation of feathers sound like a mere matter of fashion or fancy, but their profound significance stemmed rather from their associations with divinity, which were potent and pervasive. For an overview, see Nicholas Thomas, *Oceanic Art* (London: Thames and Hudson, 1995), chap. 7.

21. That is, frigate birds, Fregatidae, common in the Pacific.

22. This refers to the poncho or *tiputa,* an upper-body garment made and worn in the Society Islands and apparently parts of the Cook Islands prior to con-

tact and to missionary influence. The form was later adopted as an expression of Christian identity in Samoa, Niue, and elsewhere. Morrison's suggestion that the garment form was actually borrowed from South America is not inconceivable, given that the sweet potato was introduced into the Pacific from the continent, most probably by Islanders making voyages to and back from the South American coast, rather than (and despite Thor Heyerdahl's strenuous but discredited claims) through native American voyaging into the Pacific. But an independent Tahitian innovation is equally plausible: a shirt made out of a rectangle with a hole in the middle of it is hardly so specific an artifact type as to be explained necessarily or most parsimoniously by emulation.

23. This term refers to the sarong-style printed cotton fabrics that are now ubiquitous in Society Islands life and have their equivalents elsewhere in the Pacific (e.g., Samoan lavalava).

24. For background, and a range of perspectives upon this major topic, see Gell, *Wrapping in Images;* and Nicholas Thomas, Anna Cole, and Bronwen Douglas, eds., *Tattoo: Bodies, Art and Exchange in the Pacific and Europe* (London: Reaktion, 2005).

25. This important form is discussed by Anne d'Alleva, "Captivation, Representation, and the Limits of Cognition: Interpreting Metaphor and Metonymy in Tahitian Tamau," in Christopher Pinney and Nicholas Thomas, eds., *Beyond Aesthetics: Art and the Technologies of Enchantment* (Oxford: Berg, 2001).

26. Surfing was a routine recreation in Polynesia and was first described by participants in Cook's voyages. Only in the Hawaiian archipelago, however, does it appear that dedicated surfboards were customarily made: as Morrison implies, Tahitians improvised boards that had been cut for other purposes. See Ben R. Finney and James D. Houston, *Surfing: A History of the Ancient Hawaiian Sport* (Rohnett Park, CA: Pomegranate Art Books, 1997).

27. I.e., pomade, an ointment for the hair or scalp.

28. Referring presumably to elephantiasis, a form of filariasis, an infectious parasitic disease formerly common in tropical regions.

29. I.e., as is or was common elsewhere in the world, certain expressions of madness were associated with spirit possession.

30. Albinism has long been relatively common in the Pacific—a village or community of 300 to 400 people would often contain an albino.

31. A young child at the time of the *Galey*'s wreck would have been about seventy-five years old during Morrison's time on Tahiti.

32. See the account of this arresting rite, which captivated Banks and in which he participated, in Hawkesworth, *An Account of the Voyages . . .* , 2:162–164.

33. The constitution of and rationale for the existence of the *'Arioi* society has long perplexed analysts of Tahitian society but over recent decades has been

well documented—for example, in Douglas L. Oliver, *Ancient Tahitian Society* (Honolulu: University of Hawai'i Press, 1974), 2:913–964—and deftly analyzed by Gell, *Wrapping in Images,* 146ff.

34. Observations along these lines—excusing apparent Polynesian promiscuity on the grounds of the extreme desirability of trade goods, the suggestion that a minority of women were involved, and that visitors to England would be struck (as indeed they were) by the proliferation of prostitutes in certain quarters—quickly became commonplace in voyage narratives of the period; see, e.g., NicholasThomas and Oliver Berghof, eds., George Forster, *A Voyage Round the World* (Honolulu: University of Hawai'i Press, 2000), 1:184–185. However, it is likely that, even if these propositions were commonly aired among ships' officers, their expression here is Morrison's own: there is no evidence that he read Forster; and Hawkesworth, whom he certainly had read, to the contrary claimed that Tahitians exemplified an absolute and unprecedented licentiousness: "there is a scale in dissolute sensuality, which these people have ascended, wholly unknown to every other nation whose manners have been recorded from the beginning of the world to the present hour, and which no imagination could possibly conceive" (*An Account of the Voyages . . .* , 2:231).

35. I.e., the first tree they come across. Morrison's point here appears to be that, whereas green branches had been presumed by previous voyagers to be emblems of peace, they were in fact just improvised fly flaps.

36. On the larger topic of "third sex" roles in the Pacific, see Niko Besnier, "Polynesian Gender Liminality through Time and Space," in Gilbert Herdt, ed., *Third Sex, Third Gender: Beyond Sexual Dimorphism in Culture and History* (New York: Zone Books, 1994), 285–328.

37. For the Cook portrait given to Pomare I and held by various other chiefs, see Chapter 1.

38. This vocabulary appears never to have reached the State Library of New South Wales and has not been cited by any modern scholar.

Select Bibliography

The Original Text

Morrison, James. 1792. "Journal on HMS *Bounty* and at Tahiti, 9 Sept. 1787–1791." Sydney: State Library of NSW; A1221.

Previous Editions

Maxton, Donald A., ed. 2010. *After the* Bounty: *A Sailor's Account of the Mutiny and Life in the South Seas.* Washington, DC: Potomac Books.

Rutter, Owen, ed. 1935. *The Journal of James Morrison, Boatswain's Mate on the* Bounty, *describing the Mutiny & subsequent misfortunes of the mutineers together with an account of the Island of Tahiti.* London: Golden Cockerel Press.

Unpublished works

Cuming, Hugh. 1827–1828. "Journal of a Voyage from Valparaíso to the Society and Adjacent Islands Perform'd in the Schooner *Discoverer,* Samuel Grimwood, Master, in the years 1827 and 1828." Sydney: Mitchell Library / State Library of NSW; A1336.

Jessop [Nuku], Maia. 2007. "Unwrapping Gods: Encounters with Gods and Missionaries in Tahiti and the Austral Islands 1797–1830." Doctoral thesis, University of East Anglia.

Seabrook, Alan F. 1938. "Rurutuan Culture." Unpublished manuscript. Honolulu: Bernice P. Bishop Museum.

Other works

Aitken, Robert T. 1930. *Ethnology of Tubuai.* Honolulu: Bernice P. Bishop Museum.

Babadzan, Alain. 1993. *Les Dépouilles des dieux. Essai sur la religion tahitienne à l'époque de la découverte.* Paris: Éditions de la Maison des Sciences de l'Homme.

Bach, John, ed. 1987. *The Bligh Notebook: Rough Account—Lieutenant Wm Bligh's voyage in the* Bounty*'s Launch from the ship to Tofua & from thence to Timor,*

28 April to 14 June 1789 with a draft list of the Bounty *mutineers.* Facs. ed. 2 vols. Sydney: Allen and Unwin / National Library of Australia.

Bagnis, Raymond, Philippe Mazellier, Jack Bennett, and Erwin Christian. 1972. *Poissons de Polynésie.* Pape'ete: Les Éditions du Pacifique.

Barrau, J. 1971. *Useful Plants of Tahiti.* Paris: Société des Océanistes.

Beaglehole, J. C., ed. 1955–1967. *The Journals of Captain James Cook on His Voyages of Discovery.* Cambridge: Hakluyt Society.

———, ed. 1962. *The* Endeavour *Journal of Joseph Banks 1768–1771.* Sydney: Public Library of New South Wales / Angus and Robertson.

Besnier, Niko. 1992. "Polynesian Languages," in William Bright, ed., *International Encyclopedia of Linguistics.* New York: Oxford University Press.

———. 1994. "Polynesian Gender Liminality through Time and Space," in Gilbert Herdt, ed., *Third Sex, Third Gender: Beyond Sexual Dimorphism in Culture and History,* 285–328. New York: Zone Books.

Bligh, William. 1790. *A Narrative of the Mutiny on board His Majesty's Ship the* Bounty *and subsequent voyage of part of the crew in the ship's boat, from Tofoa, one of the Friendly Islands, to Timor, a Dutch settlement in the East-Indies.* Philadelphia: Printed in Franklin Court, 1977.

———. 1792. *A Voyage to the South Seas . . . for the purpose of conveying the Breadfruit Tree to the West Indies in His Majesty's Ship the* Bounty. London: G. Nicol.

———. 1794. *An Answer to certain Assertions contained in the Appendix to a Pamphlet entitled Minutes of the Proceedings on the Court Martial held at Portsmouth, 12 August 1792, on Ten Persons charged with Mutiny on Board his Majesty's Ship the* Bounty. London: G. Nicol.

Brunt, Peter, et al. 2012. *Art in Oceania: A History.* London: Thames and Hudson.

Cook, James, and James King. 1784. *A Voyage to the Pacific Ocean undertaken, by the Command of his Majesty, for making Discoveries in the Northern Hemisphere . . . performed under the direction of Captains Cook, Clerke, and Gore in his Majesty's Ships the* Resolution *and* Discovery *in the years 1776, 1777, 1778, 1779 and 1780* in three volumes, vols. I and II written by Captain James Cook, F.R.S., volume III by Captain James King, L.L.D. and F.R.S. London: W. and A. Strahan for G. Nicol . . . and T. Cadell.

Corney, Bolton Glanvill, trans. and ed. 1913–1919. *The Quest and Occupation of Tahiti by the Emissaries of Spain during the Years 1772–1776.* London: Hakluyt Society.

d'Alleva, Anne. 2001. "Captivation, Representation, and the Limits of Cognition: Interpreting Metaphor and Metonymy in Tahitian Tamau," in Christopher Pinney and Nicholas Thomas, eds., *Beyond Aesthetics: Art and the Technologies of Enchantment,* 79–96. Oxford: Berg.

Davies, John. 1851. *A Tahitian and English dictionary with introductory remarks on the Polynesian language, and a short grammar of the Tahitian dialect: with an Appendix containing a list of foreign words used in the Tahitian Bible, in commerce, etc., with the sources from whence they have been derived.* LMS Press, Tahiti.

de Loughrey, Elizabeth. 2007. "Globalizing the Routes of Breadfruit and Other Bounties," *Journal of Colonialism and Colonial History* 8: 3.

Dening, Greg. 1992. *Mr. Bligh's Bad Language: Passion, Power and Theatre on the* Bounty. Cambridge: Cambridge University Press.

Douglas, Bronwen. 2007. "The Lure of Texts and the Discipline of Praxis," *Humanities Research* 14: 11–30.

Driessen, Hank. 1982. "Outriggerless Canoes and Glorious Beings: Pre-contact Prophesies in the Society Islands," *Journal of Pacific History* 17: 3–28.

Du Reitz, Rolf E. 1981. *Fresh Light on John Fryer of the* Bounty. Uppsala: Dahlia Books.

Edmond, Rod. 1992. *Representing the South Pacific: Colonial Discourse from Cook to Gauguin.* Cambridge: Cambridge University Press.

Ellis, William. 1829. *Polynesian Researches.* London: Fisher, Son and Jackson.

Emory, Kenneth P. 1933. *Stone Remains in the Society Islands.* Honolulu: Bishop Museum Press.

Finney, Ben. 1998. "Nautical Cartography and Traditional Navigation in Oceania," in G. Malcolm Lewis and David Woodward, eds., *The History of Cartography,* vol. 3, part 2: *Cartography in Traditional African, American, Arctic, Australian, and Pacific Societies.* Chicago: University of Chicago Press.

Finney, Ben, et al. 1994. *Voyage of Rediscovery: A Cultural Odyssey through Polynesia.* Berkeley: University of California Press.

Finney, Ben R., and James D. Houston. 1997. *Surfing: A History of the Ancient Hawaiian Sport.* Rohnett Park, CA: Pomegranate Art Books.

Firth, Raymond. 1967. *The Work of the Gods in Tikopia.* London: Athlone.

Gell, Alfred. 1993. *Wrapping in Images: Tattooing in Polynesia.* Oxford: Clarendon Press.

Guest, Harriet. 2007. *Empire, Barbarism, and Civilisation: Captain Cook, William Hodges, and the Return to the Pacific.* Cambridge: Cambridge University Press.

Handy, E. S. C. 1932. *Houses, Boats and Fishing in the Society Islands.* Honolulu: Bishop Museum.

Haselden, Thomas. 1761. *The Seaman's Daily Assistant, being a short, easy and plain method of keeping a journal at sea . . . .* London: Mount and Page.

Hawkesworth, John. 1773. *An Account of the Voyages undertaken by the order of His Present Majesty for making discoveries in the Southern Hemisphere and succes-*

sively performed by Commodore Byron, Captain Carteret, Captain Wallis, and Captain Cook, in the Dolphin, *the* Swallow, *and the* Endeavour*: Drawn up from the Journals which were kept by the several Commanders, and from the papers of Joseph Banks, Esq.* 3 vols. Dublin: Leathley.

Henry, Teuira. 1928. *Ancient Tahiti.* Honolulu: Bishop Museum.

Hiquily, Tara, Jenny Newell, Monique Pullan, Nicole Rode, and Arianna Bernucci. 2009. *Sailing through History: Conserving and Researching a Rare Tahitian Canoe Sail.* London: British Museum Technical Research Bulletin.

Hooper, Steven. 2006. *Pacific Encounters: Art and Divinity in Polynesia, 1760–1860.* London: British Museum Press.

Joppien, Rüdiger, and Bernard Smith. 1985–1987. *The Art of Captain Cook's Voyages.* New Haven, CT: Yale University Press.

Kahn, Jennifer G. 2010. "A Spatio-temporal Analysis of ʻOro Cult Marae in the Opuʻnohu Valley, Moʻorea, Society Islands," *Archaeology in Oceania* 45: 103–110.

Kirch, Patrick Vinton. 2000. *On the Road of the Winds: An Archaeological History of the Pacific Islands before European Contact.* Berkeley: University of California Press.

Kirch, Patrick Vinton, and Jean-Louis Rallu, eds. 2007. *The Growth and Collapse of Pacific Island Societies.* Honolulu: University of Hawaiʻi Press.

Lamb, Jonathan, Vanessa Smith, and Nicholas Thomas, eds. 2000. *Exploration and Exchange: A South Seas Anthology, 1680–1900.* Chicago: University of Chicago Press.

Lamb, W. Kaye, ed. 1984. *A Voyage of Discovery to the North Pacific Ocean and Round the World, 1791–1795,* by George Vancouver (orig. 1798). London: Hakluyt Society.

Mackaness, George, ed. 1938. *A Book of the* Bounty, by William Bligh and others. *Accounts of the Voyage and Mutiny of HMS* Bounty, *from the Writings of W. Bligh and the Minutes of the Court Martial of the Mutineers Compiled by Stephen Barney.* London: J. M. Dent and Sons.

———, ed. 1953. *Fresh Light on Bligh, being Some Unpublished Correspondence of Captain William Bligh, R.N., and Lieutenant Francis Godolphin Bond, R.N., with Lieutenant Bond's Manuscript Notes made on the Voyage of H.M.S.* Providence, *1791–1795.* Sydney: D. S. Ford.

Martin, John. 1818. *An Account of the Natives of the Tonga Islands.* London: Murray.

Maude, H. E. 1958. "In Search of a Home: From the Mutiny to Pitcairn Island (1789–1790)," *Journal of the Polynesian Society* 67/2: 104–131.

———. 1968. *Of Islands and Men: Studies in Pacific History.* Melbourne and London: Oxford University Press.

McCormick, E. H. 1977. *Omai: Pacific Envoy.* Auckland: Auckland and Oxford University Presses.

Mortimer, George. 1791. *Observations and Remarks made during a Voyage to the Islands of Teneriffe, Amsterdam, Maria's Islands near Van Diemen's Land; Otaheite, Sandwich Islands; Owhyhee . . . in the Brig* Mercury *commanded by John Henry Cox Esq.* London: T. Cadell, J. Robson and J. Sewell.

Neich, Roger, and Mick Pendergrast. 1997. *Pacific Tapa.* Auckland: David Bateman.

Newbury, C. W., ed. 1961. *The History of the Tahitian Mission, 1799–1830, Written by John Davies.* Cambridge: Hakluyt Society.

Newell, Jennifer. 2010. *Trading Nature: Tahitians, Europeans, and Ecological Exchange.* Honolulu: University of Hawai'i Press.

[NLA]. 2001. *Cook and Omai: Cult of the South Seas.* Canberra: National Library of Australia and Humanities Research Centre.

Obeyesekere, Gananath. 1992. *The Apotheosis of Captain Cook: European Mythmaking in the Pacific.* Princeton, NJ: Princeton University Press.

———. 2005. *Cannibal Talk: The Man-Eating Myth and Human Sacrifice in the South Seas.* Berkeley: University of California Press.

Oliver, Douglas L. 1974. *Ancient Tahitian Society.* Honolulu: University of Hawai'i Press.

———. 1988. *Return to Tahiti: Bligh's Second Breadfruit Voyage,* Melbourne: Melbourne University Press.

Orliac, Catherine. 2000. *Fare Tahiti: Habitat traditionnel de Polynésie.* Marseille: Parenthèses.

Ralston, Caroline. 1987. "Introduction," in "Sanctity and Power: Gender in Polynesian History," special issue, *Journal of Pacific History* 22, nos. 3–4.

Rodger, N. A. M. 1986. *The Wooden World.* London: Collins.

Rutter, Owen. 1931. *The Court-martial of the* Bounty *Mutineers.* Edinburgh and London: William Hodge.

———, ed. 1934. *The voyage of the* Bounty's *launch as related in William Bligh's despatch to the Admiralty and the journal of John Fryer.* London: Golden Cockerel Press.

———, ed. 1937. *The log of the* Bounty: *being Lieutenant William Bligh's log of the proceedings of His Majesty's armed vessel* Bounty *in a voyage to the South Seas, to take the breadfruit from the Society Islands to the West Indies.* 2 vols. London: Golden Cockerel Press.

Sahlins, Marshall. 1985. *Islands of History.* Chicago: University of Chicago Press.

Salmond, Anne. 2009. *Aphrodite's Island: The European Discovery of Tahiti.* Auckland: Viking.

———. 2011. *Bligh: William Bligh in the South Seas.* Berkeley: University of California Press.

Sharp, Andrew, ed. 1970. *The Journal of Jacob Roggeveen.* Oxford: Oxford University Press.

Smith, Bernard. 1985. *European Vision and the South Pacific.* 2nd ed. London: Yale University Press.

Smith, Vanessa. 2003. "Pitcairn's Guilty Stock: The Island as Breeding Ground," in Rod Edmond and Vanessa Smith, eds., *Islands in History and Representation,* 116–132. London: Routledge.

———. 2006. "Give Us Our Daily Breadfruit: Bread Substitution in the Pacific in the Eighteenth Century," *Studies in Eighteenth-Century Culture* 35: 53–75.

———. 2008. "Performance Anxieties: Grief and Theatre in European Writing on Tahiti." *Eighteenth-Century Studies* 41, no. 2 (Winter): 149–164.

———. 2010. *Intimate Strangers: Friendship, Exchange, and Pacific Encounters.* Cambridge: Cambridge University Press.

Spate, O. H. K. 1988. *Paradise Lost and Found.* Canberra: Australian National University Press.

Tcherkezoff, Serge. 2003. "On Cloth, Gifts, and Nudity: Regarding Some European Misunderstandings during Early Encounters in Polynesia," in Chloe Colchester, ed., *Clothing the Pacific.* Oxford: Berg.

Teehuteatuaonoa (Jenny). 1819. Narrative I. *Sydney Gazette,* 17 July 1819.

———. 1829. Narrative II. *United States Service Journal:* 589–593.

Thomas, Nicholas. 1995. *Oceanic Art.* London: Thames and Hudson.

———. 2003. *Discoveries: The Voyages of Captain Cook.* London: Penguin.

———. 2010. *Islanders: The Age of Empire in the Pacific.* London: Yale University Press.

Thomas, Nicholas, and Oliver Berghof, eds. 2000. *A Voyage Round the World,* by George Forster (orig. 1777). Honolulu: University of Hawai'i Press.

Thomas, Nicholas, Anna Cole, and Bronwen Douglas, eds. 2005. *Tattoo: Bodies, Art and Exchange in the Pacific and Europe.* London: Reaktion.

Thomas, Nicholas, Harriet Guest, and Michael Dettelbach, eds. 1996. *Observations Made during a Voyage Round the World,* by Johann Reinhold Forster (orig. 1778). Honolulu: University of Hawai'i Press.

Thomson, Basil, ed. 1915. *Voyage of HMS* Pandora, *despatched to arrest the mutineers of the* Bounty *in the south seas, 1790–91: being the narratives of Captain Edward Edwards, R.N. the commander and George Hamilton, the surgeon.* London: Francis Edwards.

Valeri, Valerio. 1985. *Kingship and Sacrifice.* Chicago: University of Chicago Press.

Williams, Glyndwr, ed. 1974. *A Voyage Round the World in the Years MDCCXL,*

I, II, III, IV by George Anson; compiled by Richard Walter and Benjamin Robins (orig. 1748). London: Oxford University Press.

Williams, John. 1838. *A Narrative of Missionary Enterprises in the South Sea Islands.* London: John Snow.

Wilson, James. 1799. *A Missionary Voyage to the Southern Pacific Ocean Performed in the years 1796, 1797, 1798 in the Ship* Duff *commanded by Captain James Wilson.* London: T. Chapman.

Index

Page numbers in **boldface** type refer to illustrations.

Adventure Bay, Bruny Island, Tasmania, 290n. 14; birds, 33; inhabitants, 33–34; introducing plants, 33; soils, 33
adzes and axes, 298n. 19; European, 35, 45, 59, 63, 66, 68, 95, 99, 136–137, 265; Tahiti, 68, 160, 164, 182, 222, 239; Tubuai, 68, 80
agriculture / arboculture: Nomuka, 48; Tahiti, 157, 159–170, 225; Tubuai, 60, 76, 81, 300n. 41
Aitutaki, Cook Islands, 61, 139, 284, 294n. 44
animals: Nomuka, 48; "Rockey Island," 32; Tahiti, 160, 170; Tubuai, 67, 79. *See also* fauna
appearance of people: Australian Aborigines, 145; Nomuka, 46; Tahiti, 188–190, 238; Tubuai, 57, 76
Armorer (Armourer) [on the *Bounty*]. *See* Coleman, Jos[ep]h
artifacts. *See* adzes and axes; barkcloth; carvings; conch shell trumpet; curiosities; drums; feathers; fishing and implements; furnishings; headdresses; mats; ornaments; weapons
Austral Islands, 64, 65, 82, 83, 298n. 21, 301n. 52, 308n. 12. *See also* Ra'ivavae; Rurutu; Tubuai
Australia (New Holland), 144; escaped convicts, 148, 150; Sydney, 17, 148
Australian Aborigines, 145, 222. *See also* Tasmanians
'ava (kava): Tahiti, 168–169, 170, 184, 218–219, 234, 285; Tubuai, 63, 67, 68, 69, 81, 93

barkcloth, 312n. 16; beater, 164, **167**, 181; coloring, 76, 77–78, 164, 165, 179–181, 299n. 28; glazing of, 68, 77; manufacture, 178–181; Nomuka, 46, 295n. 49; printed with plant motifs, 180, 312n. 17; ritually offered, 63, 100, 291n. 22; scented, 77, 164, 167, 168, 180, 181; Tahiti, 68, 92, 100, 118, 119, 124, 132, 164–166, 168, 178–181, 200, 273, 304n. 18, 312n. 17; Tahitian offered to Tubuaians, 63, 68; Tonga, 92; Tongan and Tubuaian offered to Tahitians, 92; trees used, 77, 165, 166, 178–181, 299n. 34; Tubuai, 68, 76, 77–78
Barrow, Sir John, xv
barter: Aitutaki, 44; Nomuka, 45, 47; regulated by Bligh's instruction, 11, 291n. 23; regulated by Cook's instruction, 291n. 23; Tahiti, 35, 36
Batavia, 95, 126, 148, 149–150, 225
beachcombers, xvi, 18, 303n. 8, 351. *See also* Brown, John; Mariner, William
Belcher, Lady Diana, xv, xvii, 4
birds: Adventure Bay, Australia, 33; "Rockey Island," 32; Tahiti, 170, 241–243; Tubuai, 76
Bligh, William, Lieut.: accounts of the mutiny by, 4–5, 7; attitude to

alternative accounts, 6–8, 11, 21–22; attitude to Tahitians' entanglement with mutineers, 9; on Cook's third voyage, 10, 305n. 29; draws from Cook's experience, 10, 291n. 23, 304n. 20, 306n. 4; instructions re. interaction with islanders, 10–11, 35; interactions with Tahitians, 9–11, 38–39, 43, 295n. 52, 54; library on board the *Bounty,* 287n. 3; logbook, 302n. 1; on Morrison, 21–22; and mutiny, 3, 49–52, 294n. 43; open boat voyage, 291n. 19, 310n. 29; and popular imagination, 1; purser on the *Bounty,* 10, 290n. 7; second breadfruit voyage, 5–6, 302n. 1, 316n. 14; at Tahiti, 35–43; Tahitians' attitude to, 62, 91–92; *taio* relationship on Tahiti, 302n. 1; treatment of his crew, 7, 10, 290n. 8; voyage on the *Bounty,* 25–35, 43–52. *See also* mutiny on the *Bounty*

Boatswain [on the *Bounty*]. *See* Cole, W[illia]m

Borabora, Society Islands, 128, 275, 280, 283, 293n. 35, 294n. 40

Bounty Isles, New Zealand, 34, 291n. 20

Bounty, HMS: attempted desertion, 40–41; Bligh's instructions re. interaction with Tahitians, 10–11, 35; cockroach invasion, Tahiti, 40; cramped conditions on, 1, 3; crew's confrontation with Bligh, 27–28, 34, 35, 48–49; dogs left behind by the *Bounty,* 110; fraternity between officers and men, 3; line crossing, 28, 290n. 8; list of mutineers and those who departed with Bligh, 53–53; provisions provided by Tahitians, 35–38, 43; provisions rationed, 26–29, 34; purpose of visit to Tahiti, xiii, 1; scurvy, 34; sojourn on Tahiti, 1, 35–43; visit to Nomuka, 44–48; voyage from England to Tahiti, 1, 25–35. *See also* mutiny on the *Bounty*

Bounty's crew and Tahitians: barter, 35; friendship between, 37, 38; gift exchange, 43; *heiva* performance for, 249; interaction using hand signs, 13, 38; local knowledge, 10–13; portrait of Cook, 43; sexual encounters, 13, 38; Tahitians manipulate Bligh's rationing, 11–12, 37; Tahitians support their *taios* in conflict with Bligh, 91–92; weapon given to Mate, 43. *See also* Tahitians and European visitors

breadfruit, **2**, 287n. 2; Bligh's instructions to the crew about, 10–11; and *Bounty*'s mission, xiii, 1, 294n. 42; breadfruit gum / pitch, 110–111; cultivation for transporting, 1, 36, 38, 43; disposing of breadfruit plants after mutiny, 54, 296n. 60; as part of South Pacific stereotype, 10; transporting to West Indies, 5–6. *See also* food and cooking; trees and plants

Britain: Deptford, 25; Portsmouth, 4, 25, 152, 289n. 19, 309n. 16; Spithead, 25, 27, 152

Brown, John, beachcomber, 14, 91, 94–95, 96, 100, 102–103, 106–108, 114, 115, 117, 134–137, 233, 266, 303n 10,

Brown, William, Botan[is]t's Assistant, 54, 66, 88

Bryant, Mary and William, escaped convicts from Australia, 148, 151, 310n. 29

burials: Tahiti, 132, 257–258; Tubuai, 79

Burkitt (Burket, Burkett), T[homa]s, 2nd Gunner, 4, 49, 52, 54, 73–74, 88, 89, 91, 94, 95, 105, 107, 108, 109, 115, 117, 119, 121, 129, 130, 131, 134, 135, 138, 142, 143, 144

Byrn, Mich[ae]l, Able Seaman, 4, 54, 67, 88, 89, 91, 95, 105, 111, 114, 126, 127, 131, 133, 134, 137, 139, 144

cannibalism and allegations of, 87, 233, 302n. 55, 317n. 16
canoes: Aitutaki, 44; Ladrones, 46; Maori, 300n. 37; Nomuka, 45–46; Savai'i (Chatham Island), 140; Society Islands, 300n. 37; Tahiti, 15, 89, 98, 164–165, 183, 191, 194, 217, 222–224, **224**, 226–230 316n. 11; Tonga, 295n. 47; Tubuai, 80, 300n. 40
Cape Horn, 1, 26, 28, 30
Cape of Good Hope, 1, 28, 31, 33, 152
Caribbean islands. *See* West Indies
Carpenter [on the *Bounty*]. *See* Purcell, W[illia]m
Carpenter's Mates [on the *Bounty*], 50
carvings: Austral Islands, **83**, 298n. 21; Nomuka, 46; Tahiti, **197**, 200, 214, 220, 222, 226, 273, 306n. 34; Tubuai, 69, 78–79, 80, 81, 298n. 21
cats: aboard ship, 144; introduced to Tahiti, 160, 255, 311n. 5; left on Tubuai, 67, 75; taken from Tahiti to Tubuai, 62, 67, 75
Chatham Island. *See* Savai'i (Catham Island), Samoa
chiefs: Nomuka, 45, 47; Polynesia, 302n. 54; Tahiti, 14, 20, 38, 39, 40, 61, 99, 109, 131, 169, 185–189, 232, 240–241, 252–253, 258, 306n. 1; taken as hostages, 47–48, 295n. 52, 54; Tubuai, 57, 63, 74, 80, 85, 87, 300–301n. 47. *See also* Tahitian and Society Islanders, individuals; Tubuaians
child's sanctity: Tahiti, 39, 186, 206, 208–209, 294n. 36. 313n. 3; Tubuai, 79
children: Tahiti, 166, 207–209, 245, 251–252, 256, 261, 263, 294n. 36; Tubuai, 76–77
Christian, Fletcher, Lieutenant: attempts to settle Tubuai, 56–60, 62–75, 276, 279, 296n. 3, 297n. 12, 14, 17, 298n. 21; conflicts with Bligh, 45, 48–49; departure from Tahiti, 90–91; knowledge of voyagers' accounts, 287n. 3, 297n. 8; and mutiny, 3, 6, 49–55; and popular imagination, 1; redistributes duties and effects after the mutiny, 53, 54, 60; searches for island to settle on, 89–90, 287n. 3, 296n 59; suspicious of plot against him, 54–55; in Tahiti, 36, 41, 60–62, 88–91; Tahitians' attitude to, 61, 62, 88–89; *taio* relationship with Mate, 5–6; *taio* relationship with Tubuai chiefs, 63, 64, 70, 75, 279, 280, 281; tattoos, 21–22; trial of, 295n. 58; during voyage on the *Bounty*, 26. *See also* mutiny on the *Bounty*
Churchill, Cha[rle]s, Master at Arms, 14, 29, 40–41, 49–50, 52, 53, 55, 60–61, 88, 91, 93, 95, 96, 102–109, 277, 278, 282
circumcision, 245
Clerk [on the *Bounty*]. *See* Samuel, John [Jno.]
clothing, 317n. 22, 318n. 23; Nomuka, 46; Tahiti, 168, 243–245, 248–249, 272, 273, 274, 317n. 22; Tubuai, 77
Cole, W[illia]m, Boatswain, 49–50, 52, 53
Coleman, Jos[ep]h, Armorer, 4, 36, 38, 50, 52, 53, 54–55, 61, 66, 70, 86, 88, 91, 101, 104–105, 110, 111, 113, 114, 115, 117, 124–125, 126, 133, 137, 139, 141, 143, 144, 148, 149, 152, 282, 292n 30
conch shell trumpet, 56–57, 63, 83, 193, 251
conflicts and warfare: Tahiti, 74, 86,

106, 114–120, 128, 191–195, 200, 214, 293n. 34, 299n. 25, 306n. 35, 306n. 2, 314n. 7; Tubuai, 81–83; with Europeans at Nomuka, 44–45; with Europeans at Tubuai, 56–57, 59, 68, 69–70, 72–75, 276, 281
Cook Islands, 301n. 51. *See also* Aitutaki; Palmerston; Rarotonga
Cook, James: accounts of the Pacific, 20; Bligh hides his death from Tahitians, 10, 61, 91; Captain Cox informs Tahitians of his death, 91, 303n. 5; Christian misinforms Tahitians about meeting, 61; fame as navigator, 1; first voyage, 290n. 15, 299n. 25; 311n. 5; instructions re. interacting with islanders, 10; introduction of domestic animals in Polynesia, 39, 265, 292n. 32, 306n. 4, 311n. 6; introduction of plants in Polynesia, 163, 166, 265; islanders' attitude to, 99–100, 119, 127, 128, 189, 192, 265, 293n. 34, 304n. 17; knowledge of voyagers' accounts, 16, 19; and Ma'i (Omai), 127–128, 276–277, 293n. 35, 307n. 7; observation of the transit of Venus, 17, 292n. 24; portraits and Tahitians, 39, 43, 91, 99–100, 258, 265, 278, 292n. 33, 293n. 34, 303n. 5, 305n. 17; prohibition of barter for curiosities, 291n. 23; as purser on board his ship, 290n. 7; second voyage, 294n. 45, 297n. 15; *taio* relationships on Tahiti, 282; third voyage, 10, 290n. 14, 292n. 32, 294n. 46, 295n. 54, 297n. 15, 304n. 19; 305n. 29; visits to Tahiti, 1, 16–17, 38, 39, 118, 127–128, 163, 189, 192, 275–276, 281, 282, 291n. 17; 293n. 34, 298n. 23, 308n. 13
Cooper [on the *Bounty*]. *See* Heidbrandt, Hen[r]y
curiosities: acquired at Nomuka, 46–47; Bligh's prohibition of barter for, 11, 35, 291n. 23; collected in the cabin after the mutiny, 54; Cook's prohibition of barter for, 291n. 23; Tahitians attitude to introduced domestic animals and plants as, 124, 128, 163, 166, 168, 265

dances: Society Islands, 76; Tahiti, 129, 217, 247, 249–250; Tonga, 76; Tubuai, 70, 76. See also *heiva*
Davies, John, 17, 272, 286, 314n. 9
diseases: Tahiti, 166, 169, 253–255, 318nn. 28–30; Tubuai, 84, 300n. 45; venereal, 254–255
dogs: aboard ship, 57; as food, 160, 311n. 5; hair in ornaments, 244, 273; killed for sacrifice, 204; left on Tahiti by the *Bounty,* 110; Tahitians attitude to, 106, 265; taken from Tahiti to Tubuai, 62; Tubuaians surprised at, 57
domestic animals, European, 292n. 32, 311n. 6; Aitutaki, 44; Huahine, 128; Mo'orea, 39, 124, 306n. 4; Tahiti, 39, 124, 160, 166, 192, 265; Tubuai, 57, 59–60, 63, 297n. 12
drums, 83, 100, 118, 248, 251, **252**
Dutch West Indian Company, 225
dwellings, 299n. 35; Tahiti, 158, 164–168, 188, 220–222, 231, 299n. 35; Tasmanians, 33; Tubuai, 78–79

East Indies, 48, 161, 163, 168, 311n. 9
Ellison, Tho[ma]s, Able Seaman, 4, 54, 66–67, 88, 91, 95–96, 102, 105, 111, 114, 126, 131, 133, 135, 136, 139, 144, 146–147, 295n. 58
Elphinstone, W[illia]m, Master's Mate 48, 53
encounter with islanders: Aitutaki, 44; Australia, 145; Bligh's instructions re. interaction with, 10–11; Nomuka, 44–45; Me'etia, 35; Tahiti, 35, 296n.

4; Tasmania, 33–34; Tubuai, 56–60, 63, 84
Endeavour Straits, Australia, 3, 49
entertainments, 129, 217, 247–251. *See also* dances; *heiva;* music; sports
European travel writing 16–19; conventions of, 19
exchange of goods and services, 178, 183–184, 312n. 15. *See also* barter; inter-island voyaging and connections

family and marriage: Tahiti, 206–207, 209–210, 218, 256, 261; Tubuai, 77
fauna: introduced by Polynesian settlers, 160, 311n. 6. *See also* animals; birds; cats; dogs; domestic animals, European
feasts, ceremonial, 84, 121, 130, 132, 183, 184, 193, 199, 202, 204–205, 208, 209, 210, 212–213, 217–219, 229–230, 231, 240–241
feathers: birds hunted for, 242–243; as fishing lure, 174; flywhisks, **82**, **83**, 298n. 21; headdresses, 82, 92, 118, 131, 133, 244, 271, 298n. 23, 308n. 12; as ornamentation, 82, 130, 131, 132, 133, 203, 227, 244, 249, 271–272, 273, 298n. 23, 309n. 15; red feathers, 62, 63, 66, 68, 69, 92, 93, 131, 132, 200, 212, 230, 241, 244, 249, 271, 274, 279, 297n. 15; sacred, 69, 131, 200, 203, 230, 269, 272, 273–274, 298n. 21, 306n. 34, 317n. 20; in sash (*maro 'ura*), 131, 271, 282, 305n. 30; Tahiti, *passim;* Tubuai, 62, 63, 68, 69; used for trade or as gifts, 62, 63, 92, 93, 212, 274, 279, 297n. 15
Fiji, 287n. 3, 295n. 47, 295n. 50, 331
firearms: Bligh's prohibition to use, 11, 45; brought to Tahiti with mutineers, 89; Tahitians knowledge of, 294n. 38; used to entertain Tahitians, 39–40, 100, 103, 130
fish: Tahiti, 171–178, 232, 312n. 13; Tubuai, 76
fishing and implements: Nomuka, 46; Tahiti, 165, 166, 168, 169, 171–178, **175**, 182, 218, 225, 312n. 14; Tetiaroa, 306n. 3; Tonga, 295n. 49; Tubuai, 80, 300n. 39
food and cooking, 225–226, 231–241; animal food, 160; breadfruit, 79, 161–162, 228, 232, 233–236, 238–241, 270, 271, 272, 274, 286; coconuts, 35, 48, 79, 116, 162, 163, 225, 228, 233–237, 241, 274; dogs, 160, 311n. 5; earth oven, 237, 271; fire obtaining, 236–237; fish, 34, 76, 79, 171, 232–233; fruits, 161–164; goats, 160; hogs, 160, 237–238; *mahi,* 62, 79, 162, 169–170, 234, 238, 239–241, 270, 317n. 18; plantain, 79, 163, 170, 178–179, 180, 235–237, 241, 247, 272, 285; *popoi,* 234–239, 272; restrictions, 79–80, 129, 206, 208, 216–219, 231–232, 270; taro, 76, 79, 81, 160–161, 170, 184, 233, 235, 236, 238, 274, 286, 300n. 41; vegetable food, 160–161, 168–170. *See also* Tahitian and Society Islanders: *ihi ari'i* (first fruit rites); yams
Friendly Islands. *See* Tonga
Fryer, John [Jno.], Ship's Master, 7–8, 12, 27, 35, 37, 38, 41, 45, 49–50, 53, 288n. 11, 289n. 12, 291n. 19
furnishings: Tahiti, 162, 164, 182, 220–221, **221**, Tubuai, 79

gifts, ceremonial: Aitutaki, 44; originating from Pacific islands, 92–93; Tahiti, 178, 185, 204, 210, 275; Tubuai, 63, 67, 68, 69, 279
god / ancestral images: Tahiti, 117, 121, 195, 200, **201**, 269, 272, 273, 306n. 2, 306n. 34; Tubuai, 69, 79, 89, 92, 93, 298n. 21

government. *See* social structure
Great Barrier Reef, Australia, 3
greetings, 211
Gunner [on the *Bounty*]. *See* Peckover, W[illia]m

hair and hairstyles: Nomuka, 46; Tahiti, 190, **245**, 257; Tasmanians, 34, 291n. 16; Tubuai, 57, 76–77
Hall, Tho[ma]s, Cook, 29, 54
Hallet, John [Jno.], Midshipman, 49, 52, 53, 95
Hawkesworth, John, 19, 287n. 3, 297n. 8, 311n. 5
Hayward, Tho[ma]s, Midshipman, 40–41, 49, 52, 53, 91, 95, 134–138, 140, 144, 150–151, 282
headdresses, 118, 131, 271–272, 308n. 12
health and hygiene, 189, 243, 245, 253
Heidbrandt (Heildbrandt), Hen[r]y, Cooper, 26, 42, 54, 67, 88, 91, 95, 98, 104, 105, 110, 111, 113, 133, 135, 142–143
heiva (dances and performances), 39, 70, 99–100, 244, 248–249, 303n. 16
Heywood, Peter, Midshipman, xvii, 4, 8, 36, 51, 53, 70, 88, 91, 102–103, 133, 137, 143, 287n. 3
hogs: absent on Tubuai, 57, 60, 296n. 3; acquisition in Nomuka, 45; acquisition in Tahiti, 12, 35, 61, 62; Bligh's appropriation of, 12, 37; of different islands compared, 48, 140, 160; as food, 160, 206, 232, 237–238; as gifts, 93, 97, 110, 119, 124, 207, 212, 241; hidden by Tahitians from Bligh, 61; introduced on Tubuai, 63; meat salted by mutineers, 113; as remuneration, 110–111, 183, 214, 229; in rituals, 115, 129, 132–133, 204–205, 208, 210, 218–219, 229, 230, 270, 297n. 12; in Rurutu, 297n. 12; Tahitians manipulate Bligh's rationing, 11–12; 35, 37; temporary restriction to use (*rahui*), 216–218; value of, 243; women restrictions to eat, 232
Huggan, Tho[ma]s, Ship's Surgeon, 30, 35, 36–37, 292n. 25
human sacrifices, 308n. 13; Hawai'i, 308n. 13; Tahiti, 128, 132–133, 187, 193, 195, 199–201, 202, 204, 206, 230–231, 258, 285, 308n. 11, 308n. 13, 316n. 14, 317n. 16; Tubuai, 84
human variety: Tasmanian skin color, 34; theories of, 85, 291n. 16, 301n. 49. *See also* hair and hairstyles: Tasmanians
hunting, 241–243

infanticide: Society Islands, 76, 299n. 31; Tahiti, 192, 258, 261–262, 269; Tubuai, 77
inter-island voyaging and connections, 80, 86–87, 223–226, 243–244, 265, 299n. 33, 300n. 40, 301n. 51; 301n. 52, 315n. 7, 317n. 22. *See also* navigation skills
iron and ironware: as "currency," 47; demand for, 61, 62, 124; distributed by trade routes, 223–224; first iron imported to Tahiti, 225; indifference of Nomuka islanders to, 68; made by armorer for trade, 36, 61, 66; presents of, 92; on Tahiti, 178, 222; value of, 174, 176, 182, 262–263. *See also* adzes and axes

Kao, Tonga, 44, 284

L'Estrange, A. G. K., xv
Labogue, Law[ren]ce, Sail Maker, 53
labor mobilization, in Tahiti, 100–111, 112, 179, 183, 201–202, 229, 316n. 13
Lamb, Rob[er]t, Butcher, 51, 52, 54
land ownership, Tahiti, 187, 214–216, 307n. 5

languages: related in South Pacific, 86, 301n. 50; Tubuai, 85, 296n. 2. *See also* Tahitian language
Ledward, Tho[ma]s, Surgeon's Mate, 53
Lieutenant [on the *Bounty*]. *See* Christian, Fletcher
Linkletter, Peter, Quartermaster, 30, 53

Ma'i (Omai), 39, 43, 127–128, 276–277, 280, 293n. 35, 294n. 40, 307n. 7; Maori, 127–128, 300n. 37, 307n. 7
marae: 293n. 34, 300n. 43; Tahiti, 108, 109, 114, 116, 117, 120, 121, **122**, 129–131, 191, 195, **199**, 199–205, 220, 230–231, 246, 251, 257, 258–261, **259**, 270, 271, 272, 278, 279, 280, 285, 293n. 34, 300n. 43, 305n. 25, 306n. 32, 306n. 34, 308n. 11, 315n. 1; Tubuai, 63, 84, 280, 297n. 14, 298n. 18, 300n. 43. *See also* Tahitians and Society Islanders: family *marae*
Mariner, William, beachcomber, 18, 289n. 18
Marquesas Islands, 276, 294n. 40, 297n. 15, 299n. 36; 302n. 53, 315n. 7, 331
Martin, Isaac, Able Seaman, 51, 52, 53, 88
Master [on the *Bounty*]. *See* Fryer, John [Jno.]
mats, 181; as clothing, 46, 77, 244; as coverings, 100, 113, 230, 248, 249; manufacture of, 165, 167, 168, 264, 285; Nomuka, 46, 47; as partitions, 249, 255; as sails, 46, 108–109, 114–116, 226, 228; scarcity, 114, 123–124, 126; for sleeping on, 79, 220; Tahiti, *passim;* as trade items or gifts, 47, 63, 92, 100, 178, 183, 195, 224, 304n. 18; Tubuai, 77, 81; washing mats, 164
McCoy, W[illia]m, Able Seaman, 47, 52, 53, 61, 66, 88
McIntosh, Tho[ma]s, Carpenter's Mate, 4, 50, 53, 88, 91, 95–99, 105, 106, 114, 125, 131, 133, 135, 138, 139, 141, 144, 146–149, 152
Me'etia, Society Islands, 35, 88, 224, 283, 291n. 21
Mills, John [Jno.], Gunner's Mate, 53, 88
Millward, John [Jno.], Able Seamen, 4, 22, 40–41, 49–50, 53, 88, 90, 91, 93, 95, 103, 105, 119, 121–122, 125, 131, 133, 135, 138, 144, 278
Missionaries: Congregation of the Sacred Hearts of Jesus and Mary, 15–16; Ellis, William, 17, 20; Greatheed, Samuel, 8; London Missionary Society, 8–9, 16, 278, 293n. 34, 314n. 8; Rodríguez, Máximo, missionary, xv, 18; Spanish, xv, 18, 305n. 26; Williams, John, 296n. 60
Morrison, James: attitude to proposed settlement on Tubuai, 60; builds a vessel to flee Tahiti, 95–99, 101, 103–107, 110–112, 305n. 27; composes "Journal," 4, 153, 311n. 5; defense at court martial, 5; describes mutiny, 49–55; as an empirical ethnographer, 19; gives up upon arrival of *Pandora,* xiii, 3, 134–137; knowledge of Cook's accounts, 48, 56, 157, 192, 199, 220, 258, 311n. 5; during the mutiny, 3, 49–51; pardoned after trial, 5, 8; as participant observer, 9; physical description of, 21–22; plans to flee from Tubuai to Tahiti, 70–71; plans to resist mutineers, 49–50, 54; return voyage to Britain, 139–152; service in the British Navy, 1; shipwrecked on the *Pandora,* 3, 141–144; social and cultural background, 19; stay at Tahiti, 3, 35–43, 61–62, 87–139; stay at Tubuai, 56–60, 62–87; suggestion that mutiny was not premeditated,

294n. 43; tattoo, 21–22; tried for mutiny, 4, 152–153; writing utensils stolen and returned, 127

Morrison, James' "Journal" and "Account," xiii, xv, 8; as an artifact of the *Bounty* mutiny, 5; compared with other writers, 16–22; comparison between Tahiti and Europe, 170; composition of the initial text, 4–5, 7, 18; correlations between them, 13–15; critique of European notion of "savages," 194; current edition of, xvi-xvii; editorial decisions applied to spelling, xvii, 297n. 1; as ethnohistorical source, 16–20; first edition, xv-xvi; on government and social hierarchy, 20, 313n. 2; manuscript, xvii; on religious beliefs, 20, 314n. 8; sample of manuscript, **xiv**; Tahitian words used, 269–274; unknown to later writers, 20; vocabulary collected, 8–9, 267, 319n. 38; on voyagers' misconceptions, 262, 264; writing skills, 18–19

mortuary rites and mourning dress: Tahiti, 70, 182, 206, 242, 244–245, 257–260, 269, 271–272, 274, 298n. 23; Tubuai, 67, 79, 298n. 18. *See also* burials

music and musical instruments: Tahiti, 100, 118, 193, 251, **252**; Tubuai, 83. *See also* drums

Muspratt (Musprat), Will[ia]m, Captain's Steward, 4, 40, 49, 53, 88, 91, 105–106, 114, 117, 119, 123, 134, 135, 138, 142–143, 144

Mutineers and Tahitians: acquiring tattoos, 21–22; advice on warfare methods, 115, 116; alleged mistreatment of women, 101, 124–125; assist Tahitians in power struggle, 114–120, 306n. 2; conflicts between, 61, 100, 101–103, 105–106, 125, 277, 278; death of Churchill and Thompson, 14, 107–109; demonstrate weapons at request, 100, 103, 130; employ traditional exchange structures, 110–111; exchange of gifts, 92–93; hide the truth about the mutiny, 60–62; launch newly built boat, 112; learn Tahitian language, 101; liaisons with women, 9, 124, 138, 292n. 26, 292n. 30; livestock acquisition, 62; observe British customs, 95, 97–98, 303n. 14; offer alcohol to the chiefs, 61, 93; response to ceremonies, 92. *See also* Tahitians and mutineers: *taio* relationship

mutiny on the *Bounty:* 3, 48–55; accounts of, 4–8; attempt to settle at Tubuai, 56–60; boiling salt, 113; *Bounty*'s movements after the mutiny, xiii, 3, 53–75, 88–91; building a vessel to flee Tahiti, 95–99, 101, 103–107, 110–112; disposing of breadfruit plants after mutiny, 54, 296n. 60; making cider, 111; mutineers' conflicts, 107–108; mutineers' settling on Tahiti, 88–139; *Pandora* arrives to Tahiti, 134–137, 309n. 16; and popular imagination, 1; redistribution of duties and property, 53, 54, 60, 88–89; return to Tahiti, 60–62; salting meat, 113; second visit to Tubuai, 62–76; stocking newly built boat with provisions and equipment, 113–114, 122; tensions between Christian and the crew, 66; treatment of the captured mutineers on the *Pandora,* 137–143; treatment of the captured mutineers on the voyage to England, 139–152; trial of the mutineers, 4–5, 152–153. See also *Bounty,* HMS; Mutineers and Tahitians; Tahitians and mutineers

mutual assistance, in Tahiti, 238, 239–240

nakedness, Tahiti, 245, 250, 262, 304n. 18; Tubuai, 76
name exchange: Tahiti, 92–93, 194, 195, 207, 210, 266; Tubuai, 63, 64
navigation skills, 225, 316n. 10
Nelson, David, Botanist, 33–34, 35, 36, 38, 43, 52, 54, 292n. 30
New Holland. *See* Australia
New Zealand, 294n. 40, 331; Queen Charlotte Sound, New Zealand, 307n. 7
Niue (Savage Island), 44, 294n. 45, 295n. 47, 317n. 22
Nomuka, Tonga, 46–48, 140–141, 309n. 20
Norman, Char[le]s, Carpenter's Mate, 4, 52, 53, 88, 89, 91, 95, 97, 98, 99, 104–105, 107–108, 110, 111, 121, 122, 124, 125, 131, 133, 135–137, 139, 140, 144, 148, 149, 152
Norton, John [Jno.], Quartermaster, 3, 53

oil: anointing, 183, 190, 205, 253; bamboo as container for, 115, 166, 183, as gifts and commodity, 110, 115, 178, 183, 224, 225, 229; production of, 162, 182–183; sandal wood used for scenting, 241, 257; scented, 110, 167, 168, 257, 271, 285; used to color cloth, 76
Omai. *See* Ma'i
ornaments: Austral Islands, **64**, **65**; Rurutu Island, 297n. 12; Tahiti, 92, 165–166, 190, 203, **205**, 244, 248–250, 253, 257–258, 273; Tubuai, 57, 76, 77, **78**; 81–82
'Oro cult, 269, 271, 280, 305n. 30, 306n. 2, 306n. 34, 315n. 1. *See also* Tahitian and Society Islanders: *maro 'ura*

Palmerston, Cook Islands, 139
Pandora, HMS, and its crew, 15; arrival to Tahiti, xiii, 3, 134–139, 309nn. 16–17; Bowling, M[aste]r's Mate, 143; Corner (Cornor), Robert, 2nd Lieutenant, 136–137, 140, 141, 144, 310n. 26; cruising in search of mutineers, 139–141; Edwards, Edward, Captain, xiii, 3, 15, 136, 140–146, 149, 151, 152, 310nn. 21–26; Hambleton, Surgeon, 139–140; Hodges, Joseph, Armorer's Mate, 142; Larkan, 1st Lieutenant, 139, 143, 144, 145, 148–149, 150, 152; Moulter, William, Boatswain's Mate, 143; Richards (Rickards), Master's Mate, 137; Sevill, Midshipman, 137, 139; travel from Batavia to Britain, 151–152; travel to Timor, 145–147; treatment of mutineers aboard, 137–147; wrecked on reef, 3, 4, 9, 141–145, 310n. 26
parae (pearlshell mask), **71**, 271–272, 298n. 23
Peckover, W[illia]m, Gunner, 35–36, 42, 49, 52, 53
peoples, character of: Tahitians, 189–190, 313n. 4; Tubuaians, 77
Pitcairn, 296n. 60; Christian's search for, 287n. 3; mutineers' settlement comes to light in Europe, xiii
plantain, used in rituals: Tahiti, 84, 92, 112, 129, 132, 204, 208, 212, 215, 217, 219, 241, 257, 264, 274, 297n. 16; Tubuai, 63, 67
Polynesia: early contact history, xvi, 16; social and cultural change, xvi, 16, 314n. 7; social structures compared with European, 20–21
population estimates, 299n. 27; depopulation, 299n. 27; Tubuai, 76, 299n. 27
Port Jackson. *See* Australia, Sydney
pottery: Nomuka, 46; 295n. 50; Tahiti, absence of, 231
priests: Tahiti, 106, 111, 119, 121,

129–130, 131–132, 193, 197–205, 207–208, 210, 212, 218, 229, 240–241, 271, 305n. 25; Tubuai, 84, 85, 301n. 48
promiscuity and adultery, Tahiti, 207, 260–261, 263–264, 319n. 34
property rights, Tahiti, 206–207. *See also* land ownership
punishments, Tahiti, 183, 230–231
Purcell, W[illia]m, Carpenter, 25, 32, 34, 36, 37, 43, 49–50, 52, 53, 291n. 19

Quintrell, Matt[he]w, Able Seaman, 49, 52, 54, 66, 88

Ra'iatea, Society Islands, 3, 44, 87, 114, 127, 128–129, 139, 191, 228, 247, 275, 276, 277, 280, 283, 293n. 35, 294n. 40, 301n. 52, 306n. 34, 310n. 20; islanders accompanying mutineers, 3, 309n. 20
Ra'ivavae, Austral Islands, 301n. 52
Rarotonga, Cook Islands, 287n. 3, 296n. 60
reception of visitors, Tahiti, 184, 211–213, 218, 221, 233
religion and beliefs: compared with European, 195–198, 314n. 8; Society Islands, 314n. 8; Tahiti, 20, 132, 185–186, 195–199, 236, 256, 269, 273, 314n. 8; Tubuai, 84–84
Reynolds, Joshua (artist), 277
rituals and ceremonies: Tahiti, 92–93, 129, 131–132, 187–188, 199–205, 207–211, 216–219, 240–241, 257–260, 303n. 6, 307n.10; Tubuai, 63, 76, 296n. 5
Rockey (*sic*) Island, 32
ropes and cords: Nomuka, 45; Tahiti, 111, 113, 164, 182; Tubuai, 59, 296n. 5
Rotterdam Island. *See* Nomuka
Rurutu, Austral Islands, 87, 296n. 2, 297n. 12, 301n. 52
Rutter, Owen: publication of Morrison's "Journal," xv; 4

Samarang, Java, 149
Samoa, 295n. 47, 50, 139, 310n. 23, 318nn. 22–23, 331. *See also* Savai'i
Samuel, John [Jno.], Clerk, 26–27, 49, 53
sanctity, Tahiti, 187–188, 208–209, 246, 294n. 36
Savage Island. *See* Niue
Savai'i (Chatham Island), Samoa, 139, 310n. 23; canoes, 140; language, 140; theft, 140
self-mutilation: Nomuka, 46, 47; *taiaia* in Tahiti, 138, 206, 210, 211, 215, 257, 272, 309n. 19; Tubuai, 67, 298n. 18
servants: Tahiti, 112, 128, 169, 187, 189, 198, 208, 217, 219, 221, 230, 231, 232, 239, 273, 274, 277; Tubuai, 79
sexual relations, Tahiti, 263–264. *See also* family and marriage
Simpson, Geo[rge], Quartermaster, 53
Skinner, Rich[ar]d, Master's Servant, 30, 54, 74, 88, 91, 117, 133, 137, 142, 143
Smirke, Robert (artist), 278
Smith, Alex[ande]r, Able Seaman, 50, 52, 54, 69, 88
Smith, John [Jno.], Captain's Cook, 53
social structure, 307n. 5; Tahiti, 20, 128, 185–187, 209, 214, 307n. 5, 313n. 2; Tubuai, 85
Society Islands, 10, 16, 21, 44, 48, 70, 76–77, 79, 81, 83–86, 153, 158, 186, 243, 253, 264, 275, 276, 281, 283–284, 294nn. 36–37, 299n. 31, 299n. 36, 300n. 37, 300n. 43, 307n. 7, 313n. 3, 314n. 8, 316n. 11, 317n. 22, 318n. 23. *See also* Borabora; Me'etia; Taha'a; Tahiti; Tetiaroa
songs: Tahiti, 112, 179, 247, 248, 250; Tubuai, 57

South America, 86, 108, 301n. 50, 317n. 22; Chili, 243; Lima, 108, 171; Patagonia, 28; Peru, 108, 243, 305n. 26; Tierra del Fuegians, 291n. 16
South Pacific: contact history of, xvi; cosmology of, xvi; environmental exchanges in, xvi; exchange systems in, 295n. 50; literary culture in, xvi; settling of, 85–86; 243–244, 301n. 50, 317n. 22; social and cultural change, xvi; stereotypes of, 10, 190, 313n. 5. *See also* inter-island voyaging and connections
Southeast Asia, 301n. 50
sports: Hawai'i, 318n. 26; Tahiti, 247–248, 251–253, 318n. 26
St. Helena Island, 5, 152
St. Paul Island, 33
St. Vincent Island, 5
State Library of New South Wales: images from its pictorial collections, 2, 36, 90, 122, 199, 224; Morrison's manuscript at, xv, xvii, xix
Staten Land, 29
Stuart (Stewart), Geo[rge], Midshipman, 22, 51–52, 53, 56, 70, 88, 91, 113, 133, 137, 142, 143
Sumner, John [Jno.], Able Seaman, 53, 66, 88, 91, 95, 105, 115, 117, 134–135, 138, 143
Sunday Island, Australia, 291n. 19
Surgeon [on the *Bounty*]. *See* Huggan, Tho[ma]s

Taha'a, Society Islands, 44, 87, 128, 139, 283
Tahiti, geographical locations: Afa'ahiti, 130, 185, 283; Ahurai, 279; Atehuru, 86, 93, 96, 102, 103, 106, 114–115, 116, 117–119, 121, 131, 134, 136, 185, 191, 200, 281, 283, 303n. 8, 306n. 34; Fa'a'a district, 279, 284, 294n. 39; Ha'apaiano'o (Papeno'o), 86, 160, 185, 275, 283; Ha'apape, 275; Hitia'a, 86, 102, 121, 131, 185, 275, 283; Huahine, 17, 43, 87, 127, 128, 139, 228, 276, 277, 280, 281, 283, 293n. 35, 300n. 43; Mahaiatea, 279; Mataoae, 185, 283; Matavai, 9, 14, 35, **36**, 39–41, 42, 60, 86, 88, **90**, 91, 93–96, 99–100, 102–104, 107, 109–110, 115–117, 121, 123, 126, 129, 131, 133–134, 136, 157–158, 176, 185, 193, **199**, 253, 265, 277, 278, 282, 283, 292n. 24, 294n. 40, 302n. 1; Mo'orea Island (Eimeo), 39, 43, 103, 106, 110, 123–126, 127, 129, 131–132, 159, 191–193, 228, 231, 276, 277, 281, 282, 283, 313n. 6, 315n. 1; Opunohu, Mo'orea, 123, 276, 283; Orohena, 157, 283, 311n. 3; Paea, 281; Papara, 93, 102, 105–107, 114, 115–119, 121, 129, 131, 134, 136–137, 185, 191, 199, 275, 278, 279, 280, 283, 303n. 8, 306n. 2; Pare, 9, 38, 40, 86, 91–93, 96, 100, 101, 103–105, 114, 116–119, 121, 126, 129, 131, 133, 158, 185, 191, 200, 209, 210, 275; Pare-'Arue, 276, 277, 278, 282, 283, 294n. 39; Point Venus, 35, 37, 41, 93, 101, 111, 112, 157, 158, 159, 225, 278, 292n. 24, 310n. 1, 316n. 11; Puna'auia, 86, 185, 278, 284; Ta'apuna, 86, 118, 123, 126, 134, 283; Tahiti Iti, 157, 185, 191, 283, 291n. 21, 304n. 22, 305n. 26, 310–311n. 2; Tahiti Nui, 121, 157, 185, 189, 191, 283, 310–311n. 2; Taiarapu, 14, 86, 91, 93, 94, 96, 101, 102–110, 128, 130–131, 133, 157, 159, 189, 190, 192, 224, 278, 279, 280, 281, 282, 284, 291n. 21, 302n. 3, 303n. 8; Taitapu, 134, 136, 284
Tautira, 104, 107, 108–109, 130, 185, 278, 283; Te Aharoa, 86, 185, 283; Te Oropa'a, 86, 283; Te Porionu'u, 86,

118, 131, 185, 284, 306n. 2; Tepare, 185, 283; Tetaha (Fa'a'a), 41, 96, 105, 114–115, 116, 117, 121, 123, 185, 284, 294n. 39; Teva-i-uta, 185, 283; Tiarei, 86, 185, 284; Vaiaotea, 104, 107, 108, 185, 284; Vaiari or Papeari, Mo'orea, 103, 110, 123, 124, 125–126, 130, 185, 284; Vaihiria, 180, 284; Vaitepiha, xv, 18, 304n. 22; Vaiuriti, 102, 180–181, 185, 284; Vaiuru (Vairao), 185, 284

Tahiti, geography: animals, 160, 170; birds, 170, 241–243; climate, 37–38, 97, 123, 126, 127, 158–159; coastline, 158–159; districts, 185, 312–313n. 1 (*see also* Tahiti, geographical locations); fish, 171–178, 232, 312n. 13 (*see also* fishing and implements); geographical description, 158–160; geology, 160; insects, 40, 111, 170–171; map, **186**; pests, 170–171, 221, 233, 253, 264; population estimates, 190–191, 313–314n. 6; soils, 159–160

Tahitian and Society Islanders: *amo'a* and *oeahou* ceremonies, 207–209, 261, 269, 285, 314n. 9; *ari'i* (district chief), 14, 39, 185–187, 188–189, 214, 269, 270, 278; *Arioi* society, 101, 180–181, 213, 217, 260–262, 272, 299n. 31; 304n. 21, 318n. 33; chiefly succession, 39, 189, 294n. 36, 313n. 3; conversion to Christianity, 305n. 27; cosmology, 197–198, 273, 316n. 15 (*see also* religion and beliefs); *fare atua* (god house, movable *marae*), 117, 121, 131, 200, 269, 306n. 34, 2; family *marae*, 207–208, 218, 220 (see also *marae*); *ihi ari'i* (first fruit rites), 240–241, 270, 317n. 19; *mahu*, 264, 270, 319n. 36; *manahune or mata'eina'a* (lower-ranking individual or laborer), 128, 187, 214, 240, 270; *maro* (sash or belt), 165, 168, 179, 244, 259, 270; *maro e atua* (boundary marking), 115, 270; *maro 'ura* (feather sash), 117, 119, 128–129, 131–132, 133, 186, 187, 191, 200, 231, 271, 282, 305n. 30, 306n. 2, 308n. 12; 'Oro cult, 269, 271, 280, 305n. 30, 306n. 2, 306n. 34, 315n. 1; persons of high rank carried on shoulders, 39, 92, 133, 294n. 37; political districts, 185–186; power struggle, 105, 106, 110, 114, 120, 185, 187, 191, 200, 305n. 24, 31, 306n. 34, 306n. 2, 312n. 1; *ra'a* (sacred, *tapu*), 187, 218, 219, 272; *ra'atira* (lesser or district chief), 187, 212, 214, 216, 217, 218, 229, 230, 238, 240–241, 272, 307n. 5; *rahui* (restriction), 187, 216–218, 233, 272, 314n. 10; removal of clothing, 92–93, 99–100, 187–188, 200, 205, 214, 250, 256, 278, 304n. 18, 303n. 6; *reva,* ceremonial flags, 129–130, 185, 187, 218, 231, 308n. 11 (*see also* Tahitians and European visitors: British flag incorporated into rituals); sacredness of the young king, 39, 92, 129, 133, 313n. 3; *tahu'a* (ritual expert) or *tahu'a marae,* 202–203, 272, 305n. 25; *taura e atua,* 106, 193, 202–204, 273, 305n. 25; *to'ofa* (chief next in rank to *ari'i*), 186, 214–215, 216, 217, 229, 240–241

Tahitian and Society Islanders, individuals: Amo, 121, 186, 191, 262, 275, 278, 280, 281, 282; Ari'ipaea (Teari'ifa'atau), 41; 91, 92, 93, 114, 115, 116, 119, 123, 124, 126, 136, 275, 294n. 40; Ari'ipaea Vahine (Fa'ataua), 114, 115, 127, 129, 191, 275; Aromaitera'i, 275; Hitihiti (Borabora), 41, 62, 73, 93, 106, 117–118, 134, 139, 275–276, 294n. 40; 'Itia, 39, 43, 101, 128–129, 189, 191, 192, 247, 253, 275, 276, 277,

280, 282, 293n. 36; 302n. 1;Mahine, 106–107, 191–193, 276, 277, 281; Maititi, 108, 109, 277, 305n. 26; Matahiapo, 116; Mate (Pomare I, Tu Vaira'atoa, Tina) 1, 5–6, 38, 39, 40, 41, 42, 43, 87, 91, 93, 94, 95, 97, 104, 105, 106, 107, 108–109, 110, 113, 117, 130, 185, 189, 191–193, 194, 200, 249, 275, 276, 277, 280, 281, 282, 293n. 34, 293n. 36; 294n. 40, 302n. 3, 304n. 17, 306n. 34, 313n. 1, 319n. 37; Metuaro, 103, 106–107, 110, 121, 123–124, 125, 126, 131–132, 191–192, 275, 276, 277, 280; Moana, 41; 193, 294n. 40; Moananui, 103, 130; Ori (Huahine), 281; Paitia, 115, 116, 278; Pare-'Arue family, 276, 277, 281, 293n. 36, 302n. 3, 304n. 17; Pataea, 109, 276, 278; Pautu, 305n. 26; Poeno, 39, 43, 90, 93, 94, 95, 96, 97, 98, 99, 100, 104, 105, 109, 110, 112, 115, 116, 121, 123, 130, 136, 278, 282, 294n. 40, 302n. 1; Pohuetea (Potatau), 118, 119–120, 123, 134, 136, 191, 192, 278; Pomare family, 1, 276, 293n. 34, 294n. 40, 305n. 24, 305n. 30, 306n. 34, 313n. 1; Puni, 275; Purahi, 281, 282; Purea (Oberea), 87, 102, 103, 186, 191–192, 262, 263, 275, 278, 279, 280, 302n. 1; Purutihara, 278; Ta'aroa Manahune, 281; Taipo, 110, 279–280; Te Pau, 279; Teano, 101, 128, 191, 276, 280; Teha'apapa, 281; Teihotu, 279; Temari'i (Teri'irere, Teridiri), 93, 102, 105, 107, 115, 117, 121, 129–131, 133–136, 186, 191–192, 200, 262, 275, 278, 279, 280, 282; Tenania, (Huahine), 128, 280, 281; Terereatua, 123, 192; Teri'iamoeatua, 106, 135–136, 193, 276, 277, 282; Teri'itahi, 192, 280; Teri'itaria (Huahine), 128, 280, 281; Teri'itua, 275; Tetua Unurau, 281, 282; Tetua-e-huri, 281; Tetupaia, 275, 277, 281; Teu (Hapai), 112, 116, 192, 275, 277, 281, 282; Teva clan, 275; Teva-i-tai ("Seaward Tevas"), group 275, 282, 304n. 22; Teva-i-uta ("Landward Tevas"), 185–186, 280, 304n. 22; Ti'itorea (Mo'orea), 107, 281; Tihuteatuaonoa (Jenny), 309n. 20; To'ofa (Te To'ofa), 93, 102, 117, 119, 121–122, 191, 192, 200, 281; Tu (Pomare II, Tu-nui-e-a'a-i-te-atua), 39, 89, 91, 92–93, 101, 103, 110, 114, 115, 117, 119, 120, 121, 129, 130–133, 185–186, 189, 192, 231, 279–280, 282, 294n. 36, 305n. 27, 306n. 2, 307n. 8, 308n. 11, 313n. 1; Tuitera'i, 275; Tupaia, 278; Tupairu, 86, 282; Tutaha, 130, 193, 278, 281, 282; Vaetua, 91, 193, 282; Vai'io, 277; Vave'a, 277, 279; Vehiatua family, 276, 281; Vehiatua, 14, 91, 93, 101, 102–105, 107, 108–110, 191, 278, 279, 280, 281, 282, 302n. 3, 304n. 22. *See also* Ma'i (Omai)

Tahitian language, 265–266; known by *Bounty* expedition members, 49, 57, 61, 295–296n. 58, 304n. 20; known by Cook's expeditions members, 16–17; learnt by missionaries, 17; learnt by mutineers, 101, 304n. 20; prohibited during detention on the *Pandora,* 137; sign language, 266; vocabulary collected, 8–9, 153, 267, 319n. 38

Tahitians and European visitors: Bligh's contacts with, 9; Bligh's second visit to, 5; Bligh's visit on the *Bounty,* 33–43; *Bounty* mutineers stay at, 3; 88–139; *Bounty* revisits after abandoning Tubuai, xiii, 3, 88–91; *Bounty's* arrival after mutiny, xiii, 60–61; British flag incorporated into rituals, 130,

133, 308n. 11, 309n. 15; change between 1790 and 1810, 18; change in traditional techniques as the result of visits, 312n. 17; Cook's portrait incorporated into rituals, 99–100, 258, 265, 293n. 34, 304n. 17; Cook's visits to, 16, 39; desire for iron, 262–263; diseases introduced, 18, 255; domestic animals introduced, 39, 124, 160, 166, 192, 265, 311n. 6; hiding hogs from Bligh, 61; historiography of, 16, 305n. 27; missionaries accounts of, 17–18, 306n. 34, 312n. 1, 314n. 8; missionaries at, xv, 17, 18, 305n. 26; pests introduced, 171, 255, 311–312n. 12; plants introduced, 166, 168; and popular imagination, 1; sexual encounters, 263–264; study history of, xvi; voyagers' accounts of, 16–17, 262, 264, 312–313n. 1

Tahitians and mutineers: accompany mutineers, 3, 62, 282, 309–310n. 20; assist with work, 110–111; attitude to Christian, 62; attitude to, 126, 133, 137, 139; boat launch ritual, 112; desire for iron, 61–62; gifts to mutineers, 93, 100, 103, 110, 124, 128; incorporate mutineers into Tahitian ceremonial protocol, 92–93; interested in boat building, 98, 101, 111–112; interested in British customs and religion, 97–98; involve mutineers in power struggle, 105, 106, 110, 114, 116, 128, 130, 133, 305n. 24, 306n. 34, 307n. 8; master Tubuai language, 63; name exchange, 92–93; provide land for mutineers, 93, 133; provide ropes and mats, 109, 113, 115, 123–124; seek mutineers' protection, 231; Society Islanders' visits to mutineers, 127; supply provisions to, 101, 115; *taio* relationship, 9, 89, 90, 91, 92–93, 108, 129, 278, 282, 292n. 26, 302n. 2; theft from mutineers, 100–101, 127; at Tubuai with mutineers, 66, 67, 68, 70, 72–74, 276, 279

taio relationship, 302nn. 1–2; with Bligh, 302n. 1; with Cook, 282; with mutineers, 5–6, 9, 63, 64, 70, 75, 89, 90, 91, 92–93, 108, 129, 278, 279, 280, 281, 282, 292n. 26, 302n. 2; Tahiti, 13–14, 91–92, 108, 188, 194, 195, 206, 208, 210–211, 216, 263, 292nn. 26, 31; Tubuai, 63, 279, 280; by women 302n. 1

Takapoto, Tuamotu, 315n. 8, 9

tapa. See barkcloth

tapu, 294n. 36, 297n. 15, 299–300n. 36, 316–317n. 15; Tahiti, 129, 133, 187–188, 206, 207–209, 231–232, 246, 266, 270, 271, 307n.10, 313n. 3, 316n. 15; *tapu* vs "taboo," 316n. 15; Tubuai, 79–80, 299n. 36

Tapuhoe, Tuamotu, 224–215, 256, 315n. 8

Tasmanians, 33–34, 290nn. 14–15, 291n. 16, 291n. 18, 315n. 5

tattooing / *tatau,* 316n. 15; Nomuka, 46; Society Islands, 314n. 8; Tahiti, 17, 245–247, 260, 269; Tonga 295n. 51; Tubuai, 77, 299n. 32

Tenerife, 25, 33

Tetiaroa, Society Islands, 41, 94, 111, 114, 123, 126, 176, 225, 283, 306n. 3, 312n. 14

theft: experienced by Cook, 294n. 46, 304n. 18; Nomuka, 140; punishment of thief, 42, 100, 127, 304n. 18; Savai'i (Chatham Island), 140; Tahiti 40, 42, 100, 102, 103–104, 105, 127, 214, 230–231; Tonga, 304n. 18; Tubuai, 57, 68

Thompson, Matt[he]w, Able Seaman, 14, 52, 54, 88, 91, 95, 101–105, 107–109, 130, 277, 278

time and space measurements, Tahiti, 265

Timor, 3, 7, 141, 145, 147–148; Kupang, 3, 5, 7, 21, 310n. 29
Tinkler, Rob[er]t, Midshipman, 52, 53
Tobin, George (artist), 2, 36, 90, 122, 224, 302n. 1
Tofoa (Tofua) Island, Tonga, 44, 53; and mutiny, xiii, 3; volcano observed, 48
Tonga, 10, 18, 54, 76, 85, 92, 139, 140, 289n. 18, 294n. 40, 294n. 46, 295nn. 47, 49, 50, 51, 56, 298n. 20, 304n. 19, 331; Tongatapu, 20, 287n. 3. *See also* Kao; Nomuka; Tofoa
tools: Australian Aborigines, 222; Tahiti, 160, 164, 181, 182, 222, **234**, **235**, 237, 239, 315n. 4; Tubuai, 80. *See also* adzes and axes
tree and plant products usage: Tahiti, 161–183, 247, 311n. 7; Tubuai, 76, 77–78, 79, 81. *See also* barkcloth; food and cooking; mats; oil
tree ownership, Tahiti: 159, 233
trees and plants, 33, 98, 111, 134, 157, 159–170, 178–183, 285–286, 303n. 15, 311n. 7; breadfruit tree, 93, 96, 104, 110–111, 118, 121, 157, 159–162, 170, 174, 179, 204, 211, 228, 250, 273, 299n. 34; candlenut tree, 165, 228, 246; coconut, 157, 159, 162, 180, 181, 182–183, 194, 205, 220, 222, 225, 229, 241, 243, 244, 248, 249, 253, 257, 258, 273 (*see also* oil); *fara* (pandanus), 76, 78, 134, 159, 166–167, 247, 285, 311n. 9, 312n. 18; Morrison's description of, 19. *See also* 'ava; breadfruit; food and cooking; plantain, used in rituals; yams
Tuamotu archipelago, 291n. 21, 299n. 33
Tubuai, Austral group, 75, 139, 296n. 59; accounts of, xvi, 15–16; Bloody Bay, 59, 62, 84; fish, 76, 79, 80; Fort George, 67–68, 279, 297n. 17; map of, 58; mutineers' attempt to settle at, xiii, 3, 53, 56–60, 62–75; Nahitorono, 276; Natieva district, 279, 281; Paorani, 281; pests, 79; plants and trees, 75–76; population estimate, 76, 299n. 27; Taahuaia district, 297n. 17, 298n. 18; To'erauetoru (Mata'ura), 276, 280, 297n. 6, 297n. 14
Tubuaians: accompanying mutineers, 3, 75, 88, 279, 309n. 20; 'Aiata, 70, 279; gifts received from mutineers, 57, 59, 63, 64; Hitirere, 68, 85, 276, 280, 300n. 47; ritual gifts to mutineers, 63, 67, 68, 69, 279; Ta'aroamaeva, 73, 75, 88, 279; Ta'aroatehoa, 64–67, 70, 73, 85, 279; Tahuhuatama, 70, 73, 85, 279, 281, 298n. 18; Tamatoa, junior, 63, 64, 85, 87, 277, 279, 280, 281, 297n. 14, 30n. 47; Tamatoa, senior, 86–87, 280; Tinarau, 63–65, 68, 69–70, 73, 75, 85, 281; using musket balls as pendants, 63; women and mutineers, 69; 70, 71–72; women visit the ship, 57, 59

Valentine, Ja[me]s, Able Seaman, 34
Vessels: *Adventure,* 128, 276, 293n. 35, 307n. 7; *De Africaansche Galey,* 224–225, 315nn. 8–9; *Assistant,* 5; *British Queen of London,* 28; *Discovery,* 292n. 30; *Dolphin,* 10, 16, 292n. 28, 302n. 1; *Dublin,* 31; *Duff,* 9; *Duke,* 4, 5, 152; *Endeavour,* 16–17, 292n. 24, 311n. 5; *Gorgon,* 152, 310n. 29; Gardner, Lieutenant, 152; *Mercury,* 14, 94, 95, 308n. 11; *Neptune,* 148; Parker, Captain, 152; *Providence,* 5, 6, 277; *Rembang,* 148; *Resolution,* 275–276, 292n. 30; 294n. 40, 305n. 29, 307n. 7; *Termagant,* 1; *Vreedenbergh,* 151. See also *Bounty; Pandora*
Voyagers: Anson, George, 28, 30, 290n. 9; 295n. 48; Banks, Joseph, Sir, 1,

7, 17, 127, 239, 265, 277, 287n. 1, 292n. 30, 299n. 25, 317n. 18, 318n. 32; Bayly, William (on *Discovery*), 292n. 30; Boenechea, Domingo, 18, 171, 305n. 26, 311n. 12; Bond, Francis Godolphin (on *Providence*), 6, 8; Burney, James, 7; Byron, John, 165, 297n. 8, 311n. 5; Carteret, Philip, 287n. 3, 297n. 8, 311n. 5; Clarke, William (on *Dolphin*), 10; Cox, James Henry, 91, 94, 101, 130, 131, 233, 266, 303n. 5; Cuming, Hugh, 15, 297–298n. 17; Dalrymple, Alexander, 19; Dumont d'Urville, Jules, 20; Forster, George, 17, 19; Forster, Johann Reinhold, 17, 19, 20, 301n. 49, 313n. 4, 313n. 6, 319n. 34; Furneaux, Tobias, 276, 307n. 7; Robertson, George (on *Dolphin*), 10; Roggeveen, Jacob, 224–225, 256, 315n. 8, 9; Spanish voyages, 171, 305n. 26, 311n. 12; Tasman, Abel, 44–45; Vancouver, George, 277, 292n. 33, 293n. 34, 308n. 11; Wallis, Samuel, 16, 18, 191, 256, 291n. 21, 292n. 24, 296n. 4, 297n. 8, 302n. 1, 306n. 2, 311n. 5; Wilson, James, 9, 278. *See also* Bligh, William; Cook, James

weapons: Nomuka, 46; Tahiti, 164, 193–194, 247–248, 271; Tasmania, 33; Tubuai, 56, 69, 73, 75, 81–83. *See also* firearms

Webber, John (artist), 291n. 17, 278, 293n. 34, 303n. 5

West Indies, xiii, 1, 48, 163, 168, 171; Jamaica, 5

Williams, John [Jno.], Able Seaman, 26, 52, 53, 88

women: accommodation, 220–221; appearance, 46, 76, 77, 188, 190, 257; *ari'i*, 188–189; and *arioi* society, 260; barkcloth manufacture, 179, 180–181; clothing, 243–244, 248–249; feasts, 219; fishing, 173–174; food restrictions, 171, 188, 208, 231–232; maturity, 209, 256–257; Nomuka, 46, 47; restrictions, 79, 209, 231–232, 299n. 36; rituals, 63, 70, 188, 198–199, 203–204; segregation from men, 79, 231–233, 299n. 35; sports, 247–248, 251–253; Tahiti, 79, 171, 173–174, 179–181, 188–189, 190, 198–199, 203–204, 208–209, 220–221, 231–234, 243–244, 246–249, 251–253, 256–257, 260, 299n. 35, 299n. 36, 302n. 1; and *taio* relationship, 302n. 1; Tasmania, 33; tattooing, 246–247; Tubuai, 57, 59, 63, 69; 70–72, 76, 77, 79; use of 'ava, 234. *See also* dances; family and marriage; *heiva;* mortuary rites and mourning dress; promiscuity and adultery; self-mutilation

Wreck Island, Australia, 143–145

yams: as food aboard ships, 43–44, 45, 47, 49, 141, Nomuka, 48; planted by mutineers, 66; Tahiti, 160–161; Tubuai, 76, 79, 300n. 41

Young, Edward, Midshipman, 53, 88

About the Editors

Vanessa Smith teaches at the University of Sydney, where she is Associate Professor in the Department of English, and publishes across the disciplines of literary studies, history, and anthropology. She began visiting the Pacific islands in 1994 while researching the early impact of print culture in Samoa and Tonga. More recently she has focused on Tahiti and the Hawaiian and Marquesas Islands while exploring the politics of friendship in contacts between Oceanians and Europeans. Her interest in the *Bounty* stories has morphed from a focus on beachcomber narrative, via an excursus on breadfruit, to an exploration of the colonialist politics of the Pitcairn island settlement, and analysis of the shifting allegiances manifest in the mutiny and the mutineers' trial. Her most recent book is *Intimate Strangers: Friendship, Exchange and Pacific Encounters* (2010).

Nicholas Thomas first visited the Pacific islands in 1984 to research his PhD thesis on the Marquesas Islands. He later worked in Fiji and New Zealand, and has written widely on art, voyages, colonial encounters, and contemporary culture in the Pacific. He is the Director of the Museum of Archaeology and Anthropology at the University of Cambridge, and a Fellow of Trinity College. He is author, coauthor, or editor of more than thirty books, including *Entangled Objects* (1991), *Oceanic Art* (1995), *Discoveries: The Voyages of Captain Cook* (2003), and collaborations with Pacific artists, such as *Hiapo* (with John Pule, 2005), and *Rauru* (with Mark Adams, Lyonel Grant, and James Schuster, 2009). *Islanders: The Pacific in the Age of Empire* (2010) was awarded the Wolfson History Prize.